Fair Value Measurements

Fair Value Measurements

Practical Guidance and Implementation

MARK L. ZYLA

WILEY

John Wiley & Sons, Inc.

ISBN-13 978-0-470-50024-8

Printed in the United States of America.

10   9   8   7   6   5   4   3   2   1

To my wife, Jo Ann, and my son, Jack.
You make this all possible...

Contents

Preface

F air Value Measurements is one the more controversial statements introduced by the Financial Accounting Standards Board (FASB) in decades. *Fair Value Measurements* is a by-product of a very fundamental change in the measurement of assets and liabilities for financial reporting purposes. No longer are financial statements prepared primarily on historical cost-based information. Accounting standards for financial reporting, particularly for business combinations, require the measurement of certain assets and liabilities at their current, fair value. Fair value measurement often requires the financial statement preparer to use judgment in the measurement of both assets and liabilities, contributing to the controversy about the use of fair value as a standard of measurement.

The use of fair value measurements is generally referred to as fair value accounting. Despite the controversy, *Fair Value Measurements* (FASB ASC 820 or SFAS 157, as originally issued) doesn't create any new accounting. Fair value measurement has been part of financial reporting standards for some time, although its use has expanded greatly in recent years. *Fair Value Measurements* was issued to clarify the concepts relating to fair value in financial reporting.

There are many reasons for this fundamental change in accounting toward fair value measurement. Investors are clamoring for more relevant information in order to make investment decisions. Investors question the usefulness of historical cost-based accounting and reporting in an age where all types of information is shared by billions of people almost instantaneously. Currently, most financial statement measurements provided by traditional accounting methods provide information to investors that is months old in the best case. In many cases, the asset measurements are recorded several years prior to the financial statement date. Investors question whether there should be a better measurement model for financial reporting.

Additionally, fair value accounting has become more prevalent because of changes in the economy over the last twenty five or thirty years. The economies of the United States and many other countries worldwide have undergone a fundamental change where the primary driving factors of a corporation's value are based upon its intangible assets rather than its fixed assets, such as manufacturing plants, other real property, and equipment. The market valuations of Microsoft, Oracle, and Google, for example, greatly exceed reported asset values that appear on their respective balance sheets. Much of the market's perception about the equity value of these companies is attributed to their intangible assets, such as technology, trade names, and customer relationships, which are typically not recorded as assets on their balance sheets. Traditional financial statements generally provide no indication that these companies' intangible assets even exist, with the exception of intangible assets recognized through business combinations. In contrast, a more reliable indication of the current fair value of these intangible assets can be derived from the financial markets based on the trading price of the companies' underlying shares of stock.

Economic globalization over the last thirty years or so has spotlighted differences in worldwide accounting standards. As the global economy expanded, cross-border acquisitions became more common. Yet the acquiring and acquired entities often reported financial results using completely different sets of accounting standards with different measurement systems creating accounting issues relating to comparability and assimilation. The FASB and the International Accounting Standards Board (IASB) recognized these issues and called for one set of uniform accounting standards worldwide in 2002. These Boards plan to create convergence between the two most widely used standards, U.S Generally Accepted Accounting Principles (GAAP) and the International Financial Reporting System (IFRS). IFRS is a principles-based system of accounting with an underlying philosophy that calls for the current fair value measurement of assets and liabilities in more circumstances than is required by U.S. GAAP. Convergence of GAAP into IFRS will further increase the use of current or fair values as a measurement standard in financial reporting.

The accounting profession itself recognizes the shortcomings of its traditional, historical, cost-based system of measurement. The heads of the largest international accounting firms have publicly stated that the profession needs to rectify current shortcomings and provide an alternative that will provide more relevant and timely information to users of financial statements. Two of the more significant shortcomings recognized by members of the profession who lead international accounting firms are the lack of relevancy provided by historical, cost-based financial statements and the lack of information about the value of internally generated intangible assets. Fair value accounting is a step toward correcting these shortcomings. The heads of these international firms fully support the convergence of U.S. GAAP and IFRS.

Another controversy surrounding *Fair Value Measurements* is the statement's role in the credit crisis that began in mid-2008. When the credit crisis began, Fair Value Measurement had been partially implemented as a basis for measuring certain financial assets and liabilities. Many financial institutions and investment banks had also elected to measure certain financial assets and liabilities at their respective fair values under another accounting statement, the *Fair Value Option*. At the time of the election, fair value was relatively easily measured since most financial instruments were actively traded in secondary markets. However, with the arrival of the credit crisis, the trading activity in these markets was severely curtailed, almost overnight. The proper fair value measurement of these formerly actively traded instruments became an issue since there was no longer an active market for the instruments on which one could pin a valuation. A controversy resulted when the following question was raised, "Where does one go for an indication of value when the market for these instruments is distressed and no longer considered active?" The debate intensified as the pertinent issue became "Does an inactive market mean that the fair value of the underlying asset is severely distressed as well?" As bankers and the owners of millions of businesses will agree, the answer is a resounding no.

The proximity of *Fair Value Measurements'* full implementation date to the beginning of the credit crisis further heightened the controversy surrounding the statement. Fair value accounting, or mark-to-market accounting as it is commonly referred to, was blamed for causing or at least contributing to the credit crisis. The accounting concept became a political issue in the 2008 presidential campaign and it was the subject of several congressional hearings. However, an SEC report to congress found no connection between the credit crisis and fair value measurements. As discussed in the appendix to Chapter One (Appendix 1A), the credit crisis issues were largely resolved through additional FASB staff clarifications about *Fair Value Measurements*.

Fair Value Measurements introduces a new dynamic in financial reporting. *Fair Value Measurements* inherently increases the need for judgment in the preparation of financial statements. Under traditional historical, cost-based accounting, the basis for measurement was typically based on the amount paid to purchase an asset or the amount received in exchange for incurring a liability. While historical cost accounting has its own challenges and limitations, the measurement of fair value can sometimes be easily determinable from an acquisition price. In other circumstances, fair value accounting requires the measurement of complex assets and liabilities for which there is no transaction price. In these situations, the measurement of the fair value is often beyond the expertise of management. Management often retains the services of an outside valuation specialist to assist with the measurement of fair value. The valuation specialist provides guidance to management and provides an opinion about the fair value measurement of specifically identified assets and liabilities. Management then uses the outside specialists' guidance to measure the fair value of the specified assets and liabilities for financial reporting purposes. The valuation specialist's report can be used as audit evidence to support the fair value measurement. The auditor's internal valuation specialist, working as part of the audit team, tests the outside specialists report for reasonableness.

Fair Value Measurement has recently been fully implemented and incorporated into required accounting standards. Both the accounting profession and the valuation profession are working toward refining best practices for the measurement of fair value. The purpose of this book is to provide a summary of implementation guidance and best practices to date. Valuation theory is constantly evolving, which creates divergence in practice. Where there is a divergence in current practices, I have attempted to present both positions. This book should be useful not only to valuation specialists, but to preparers of financial statements, auditors, and academics to understand the development of fair value measurements.

Critics have cited the difficulties associated with measuring fair value. Valuation does require a certain amount of judgment. However, this judgment is no less than the judgment required by an investor when deciding upon a price to pay for any form of investment. The trade-off is between the subjectivity of fair value measurements based in part on the preparer's judgment and the relevance of current fair values to financial reporting compared to the relevance of historical cost accounting. Clearly, there are some challenges. Hopefully this book will help with those challenges.

MARK L. ZYLA
Atlanta, Georgia
September 2009

Acknowledgments

First and foremost, a very special thank you to Lynn Pierson for her assistance with this book. Without her help, the book would not have been completed with nearly the quality and depth of guidance. Also thank you to Zondra Lay, Gina Miller, Mary Jo Duffy, and Barbara Brown for their assistance in research and preparation of many of the exhibits. I also want to express my heartfelt thanks to Charles Phillips and our other colleagues at Acuitas, Inc. for their patience and support for this project.

Also thank you to Bill Kennedy of Anders Minkler & Deihl LLP, Julie DeLong of Navigant Consulting, Teresa Thamer of Brenau University, Brian Steen of Dixon Hughes LLP, Brent Solomon and Tara Marino of Reznick Group, Mark Edwards of Grant Thornton LLP, Michael Blake of Habif Arogetti & Wynn LLP, John Lin of McKesson Corporation, Adrian Loud of Bennett Thrasher LLP, Tracy Haas of Roake Capital, Harold Martin, Peter Thacker, and Brian Burns of Kieter, Stephens, Hurst, Gary & Shreaves, P.C., Bernard Pump of Deloitte LLP, Jim Dondero of Huron Consulting Group, Ellen Larson of FTI, Steve Hyden of the Financial Valuation Group, and David Dufendach of Grant Thornton LLP. Their comments and suggestions on various aspects of fair value measurements were invaluable in assisting me in developing the book. Any errors, however, are my own.

About the Author

Mark L. Zyla CPA/ABV, CFA, ASA is a Managing Director of Acuitas, Inc., an Atlanta, Georgia–based valuation and litigation consultancy firm. Zyla has provided valuation consulting for more than twenty five years for various types of entities for the purposes of mergers and acquisitions, financial reporting, tax planning, and corporate recapitalizations, as well as valuing various types of intellectual property and other intangible assets for many purposes.

Zyla received a BBA in finance from the University of Texas at Austin and an MBA with a concentration in finance from Georgia State University. Zyla also completed the Mergers and Acquisitions Program at the Aresty Institute of the Wharton School of the University of Pennsylvania and the Valuation Program at the Graduate School of Business at Harvard University. He is a Certified Public Accountant, Accredited in Business Valuation (CPA/ABV), Certified in Financial Forensics (CFF) by the AICPA, a Chartered Financial Analyst (CFA), and an Accredited Senior Appraiser with the American Society of Appraisers (ASA) certified in Business Valuation.

Zyla is a member of the American Society of Appraisers (ASA), the American Institute of Certified Public Accountants (AICPA), CFA Institute, and the CFA Society of Atlanta. Zyla is a former member of the Business Valuations Committee of the AICPA, and a former Chairman of the ABV Examination Committee of the AICPA. He is also a former member of the Business Valuation Standards Subcommittee of the ASA. He was named as Vice Chairman of the Appraisal Foundation's first Business Valuation Best Practices Working Group and to the AICPA's Fair Value Resource Panel, working as a member of the AICPA's Impairment Practice Aid Task Force. He was the first chairman of the AICPA's Fair Value Measurements conference. He is also a member of the Atlanta Venture Forum, a professional organization of the venture capital community. He is one of the authors of the *International Glossary of Business Valuation Terms*, which has been adopted by the major valuation organizations.

Zyla is also the co-author of the AICPA courses *Fair Value Accounting: A Critical New Skill for All CPA* and *Accounting for Goodwill and Intangible*

Assets published by the AICPA. He is also co-author of *Fair Value Measurements: Valuation Principles and Auditing Techniques* published by Tax Management, Inc., a division of the Bureau of National Affairs.

Zyla regularly teaches valuation topics for the AICPA. He has taught for the Federal Judicial Center and is on the faculty of the National Judicial College, teaching valuation concepts to judges.

CHAPTER 1

Fair Value Accounting

Welcome to the new world of accounting! Where once financial statement preparation involved primarily the use of historical cost information, accounting now involves the use of judgment as to the current value of assets and liabilities. Fair value—or as it is sometimes referred to, mark-to-market accounting—has become the preeminent issue in financial reporting today. The concepts introduced by fair value accounting change the way financial information is presented. An increasing amount of information in financial reporting is presented at current or market values on the reporting date rather than historical costs, which has been the bedrock of traditional accounting.

Advocates of fair value accounting believe that this presentation best represents the financial position of the entity and provides more relevant information to the users of the financial information. Detractors of fair value accounting point to its complexity and inherent use of judgment. Either way, fair value accounting is becoming more prominent in financial statement presentation and will continue to be the fundamental basis for accounting in the future.

Introduction

Fair value has been a standard of measurement in financial reporting for decades. The Financial Accounting Standards Board (FASB) has issued more than three dozen statements that use the term *fair value* as the measurement of value. Most prominent among these pronouncements is the recently issued revised FASB ASC 805, *Business Combinations* (SFAS No. 141(R)),[1] which incorporates fair value as the fundamental standard of measurement in accounting for business combinations. Fair value is also the standard of measurement used in subsequent testing for impairment of the acquired assets under FASB ASC 350, *Goodwill and Other Intangible Assets* (SFAS 142) and SFAS 144, *Testing for Impairment of Long Lived Assets*. The concept of fair value is interesting because each of these statements about the measurement of fair value is the value to the market as of the measurement date, not necessarily the value to the preparer of the financial statement. As such, measuring fair value for participants in those markets requires some judgment.

The FASB issued FASB ASC 820, *Fair Value Measurements and Disclosures* (Statement of Financial Accounting Standard (SFAS) No. 157), to clarify the concepts related to its measurement. According to the FASB, the purpose of the statement is to define fair value, establish a framework for measuring fair value, and expand disclosure about fair value measurements.[2] *Fair Value Measurements* does not introduce any new accounting per se. *Fair Value Measurements* was issued by the FASB to provide one uniform statement under which the concept of fair value in all financial reporting is more fully explained.

FASB ASC 820, *Fair Value Measurements and Disclosures* (SFAS No. 157), was not initially universally accepted without some controversy. The day before its scheduled implementation, the FASB delayed the full implementation date of the statement in response to concerns by certain preparers of financial statements. The statement was revised to become effective for just financial assets and liabilities for the first year. The statement became fully effective for all items, both financial and nonfinancial for fiscal years beginning after November 15, 2008. The reason provided by the FASB for the partial implementation was "to allow the Board and constituents additional time to consider the effect of various implementation issues that have arisen, or that may arise, from the application of Statement 157."[3] Even the partial implementation did not allay all of the controversy. Some critics of fair value accounting claimed that the credit crisis that began in 2008 was at the very least exacerbated by the statement's implementation by financial institutions.

History of Fair Value in Financial Reporting

Even though it has become more prominent recently, fair value has been a standard of measurement in financial reporting for some time, particularly in measuring certain financial assets and liabilities. One of the first prominent accounting statements to use fair value as the standard of measurement in financial reporting is APB (Accounting Principles Board) 18, which was issued in the early 1970s. APB 18 introduced the equity method of accounting in financial statement reporting for investments. APB 18 described the financial statement treatment and measurement of investments losses considered other than temporary as requiring recognition if the investment's fair value declined below its carrying value. APB 29, *Accounting for Nonmonetary*

Transactions, introduced in early 1973, actually outlined ways to measure fair value in those types of transactions. Financial Accounting Standard 15 (FAS 15) in the late 1970s defined fair value as a willing buyer and willing seller and described market value and discounted cash flows in accounting in troubled situations. Fair value measurements were introduced in pension accounting in a couple of statements in the 1980s. In 1991 FAS 107, *Disclosures about Fair Value in Financial Instruments,* required the disclosure of fair value in financial instruments. FAS 115, *Accounting for Certain Investments in Debt and Equity Securities,* was introduced in 1999. FAS 115 requires fair value as the standard of measurement for many types of debt and equity securities. In 2000, the FASB introduced FAS 133, *Accounting for Derivative Instruments and Hedging Activities,* which required fair value as the measurement for derivative securities. SFAS 159, *The Fair Value Option for Financial Assets and Financial Liabilities—Including an Amendment of FASB Statement No. 115,* which allowed certain entities to elect to measure selected assets and liabilities at fair value, was implemented by the FASB in 2007. Although many accounting pronouncements refer to fair value and have been a part of financial reporting for a long time, the concept of what exactly is meant by fair value became most prominent in financial reporting in accounting measurements in business combinations.

During the technology boom in the late 1990s—brought on by the initial commercialization of the Internet—FASB began a project to update the Accounting Principles Board's Opinion No. 16, *Business Combinations* (APB 16). APB 16 was the accounting standard at that time for acquisitions and other business combinations. The FASB observed during the 1990s that many mergers and acquisitions were transactions where most of the economic value was created by the technology and other intangible assets of the acquired company. However, under the accounting at the time (APB 16) much of the value of the transaction showed up on the balance sheet as goodwill. The FASB's project was the result of the conclusion that APB 16 did not fairly represent the economic substance of those business combinations. The project concluded that the value of intangible assets in business combinations had dramatically increased, particularly when compared to the value of tangible assets. Yet these results were not being fairly presented on the resulting financial statements.

The board determined that under the old APB 16, companies had too much leeway in reporting the value of intangible assets in acquisitions, and financial statements were not fairly representing the allocation of the acquisition price to the acquired assets. Under the old accounting rules, most of the value in allocation of purchase price was being recorded as goodwill, which could then be amortized for up to 40 years.

On June 29, 2001, the FASB issued SFAS 141, *Business Combinations,* the original FASB standard on business combinations, which has since been superseded by FASB ASC 805, *Business Combinations* (SFAS 141(R)). *Business Combinations* placed stricter requirements on the acquirer to recognize acquired intangible assets in the financial statements. Paragraph 39 in SFAS 141 requires that "An intangible asset shall be recognized as an asset apart from goodwill if it arises from contractual or other legal rights or, if not contractual, only if it is capable of being sold, transferred, licensed, rented or exchanged. An assembled and trained workforce, however, is not valued separately from goodwill."[4] Under SFAS 141, only purchase accounting was allowed. The pooling of an interests accounting method for acquisitions where one entity combines with another at book value, if the acquisition met certain criteria, was no longer allowed. The FASB believed that the purchase method of accounting provided a better representation of the true economics of the underlying transaction than the pooling method that presented the combined transaction on a pure historical cost basis.

As part of the convergence of U.S. Generally Accepted Accounting Principles (GAAP) with international accounting standards, the FASB revised SFAS 141 for fiscal years beginning after December 15, 2008. Under FASB ASC 805, *Business Combinations* (SFAS No. 141(R)), purchase accounting is replaced by the Acquisition Method. Under the Acquisition Method the fair value of acquired assets are no longer determined by an allocation of the purchase price. The fair value of those assets acquired in the business combination is independent of the price that was paid in the transaction.

FASB ASC 805, *Business Combinations* (SFAS 141(R)), still requires that the acquirer recognize the identifiable intangible assets acquired in a business combination separately from goodwill. SFAS 141 introduced a comprehensive list of intangible assets, and lists the criteria for recognition of intangible assets acquired, which was extended in FASB ASC 805, *Business Combinations*. An intangible asset is considered identifiable in a business combination if it meets either the separability criterion or the contractual-legal criterion. An intangible asset meets the separability criterion if it meets one of two criteria:

> *(1) Is separable, that is, capable of being separated or divided from the entity and sold, transferred, licensed, rented, or exchanged, either individually or together with a related contract, identifiable asset, or liability, regardless of whether the entity intends to do so*
> *(2) Arises from contractual or other legal rights, regardless of whether those rights are transferable or separable from the entity or from other rights and obligations*[5]

In the initial 1999 exposure draft of SFAS 141, the FASB proposed that goodwill be identified in the business combination and amortized over its remaining life. However, in response to numerous comments to the initial exposure draft suggesting that the useful life of goodwill would be difficult to determine thus difficult amortize, the FASB changed its mind and introduced an alternative to the amortization of goodwill. So, goodwill was not amortized under SFAS 141. Instead, goodwill received an alternative accounting treatment: It must be tested annually for impairment.

To reinforce the impairment testing alternative, the FASB also issued FASB ASC 350, *Goodwill and Other Intangible Assets* (SFAS 142), in 2001. FASB ASC 350 (SFAS 142) provides guidance on determining whether goodwill recorded after the acquisition becomes impaired. FASB ASC 350 (SFAS 142) was introduced by the FASB as the result of comments by various respondents to the initial exposure draft of *Business Combinations*. Under FASB ASC 350 (SFAS 142), goodwill that is recorded as the result of a business combination is tested annually for impairment under a two-step test. The first step is to estimate the fair value of the appropriate reporting unit by comparing the fair value to its carrying value (book value). If the fair value is *greater* than book value, then goodwill is not impaired. If the fair value is *less* than the carrying value, then the goodwill may be impaired and a second step is required.

The second step is to estimate the fair values of all of the assets of the reporting unit as of the testing date. This step is similar to the allocation of purchase price under *Business Combinations*. The new goodwill is then compared to the current carrying value of the goodwill. If the fair value of the new goodwill is less than the fair value of the current goodwill, the difference is the amount of impairment and must be written off. As such, fair value is the standard of measurement in both tests under FASB ASC 350, *Goodwill and Other Intangible Assets*.

FASB ASC 805, *Business Combinations*, and FASB ASC 350, *Goodwill and Other Intangible Assets*, are the two statements where fair value measurements of assets other than financial instruments are most often seen in practice. Since these statements were introduced, both the accounting profession and the valuation profession have begun projects to determine the "best practices" in fair value measurements. Many of these projects are still in process.

Why the Trend toward Fair Value Accounting?

Fair value has been a standard of measurement in financial reporting for some time, but recently the trend has been toward an increased use of fair value accounting. There are a number of factors that are influencing the trend from traditional rules-based accounting under U.S. Generally Accepted Accounting Principles (GAAP) to more principles-based measurements, which include more fair value measurements in financial reporting. U.S. GAAP has been more historical cost-based in its measurements than other accounting standards, which are more principles-based and have more of an emphasis on fair value accounting. However, certain trends are causing this emphasis in U.S. GAAP to change.

The first trend is the change in the general economic environment that impacted the relevance of accounting measurements in certain transactions. Over the last 25 years, the overall enterprise value of many entities is composed of more intellectual property and other intangible assets that have not been effectively measured under tradition GAAP. In addition, the entire global economy has become much more intertwined. Where once only the Fortune 1,000 or so were able to conduct business internationally, the advent of the Internet has allowed any size company to establish an international presence.

The globalization of the economy is an important factor in the trend toward more fair value measurements in accounting. Globalization has increased the need for standardization in accounting across national boundaries. The FASB and the International Accounting Standards Board (IASB) have begun a project to "converge" U.S. GAAP into international accounting standards. IASB accounting standards are considered principle-based, which requires more fair value measurements. As the accounting standards converge, U.S. GAAP will require more fair value accounting measures.

The Changing Economic

The economy in the United States has undergone tremendous changes over the last 25 years. One significant change in the economic environment was brought on by the commercialization of the Internet, which resulted in what some call the "information revolution." The result was that a significant portion of the U.S. economy shifted from the "bricks and mortar"–based businesses to ones that were more information-based. Commercialization of the Internet has led to substantial advances in information technology that have had a profound impact on the U.S. and global economies.

Exhibit 1.1 demonstrates the increase in the percentage of the market capitalization of the S&P 500 attributable to intangible assets as compiled by the investment banking firm Ocean Tomo. Intangible assets only comprised 17 percent of the market capitalization of the S&P 500 in 1975. By 2008 this percentage had increased to 75 percent.

The change in the economic environment from the commercialization of the Internet and the globalization of the economy has created some challenges for the accounting profession. The relevance of financial statements became a concern of the FASB, as an increasing percentage of many companies' values are generated by intangible assets. The increasing transnational nature of business has created a need for consistent accounting standards across national boundaries as well.

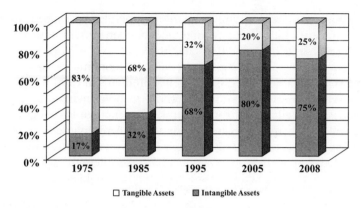

EXHIBIT 1.1 Components of S&P 500 Market Value
Source: Ocean Tomo.

The FASB and the IASB recognize that the users of financial statements would benefit from consistent standards. As a result, both organizations have jointly created a framework to bring U.S. accounting standards in line with international standards. The Securities and Exchange Commission in the U.S., which has been given the authority of setting standards by the U.S. Congress, has strongly signaled that it supports the convergence of U.S. GAAP into international standards.

The FASB and IASB Convergence Project

One issue that the FASB has heard from users of financial statements is that they are concerned about the differences in financial reporting in different countries. With the increase in the global economy and increasingly transnational businesses, investor and other users of financial statements require one standard set of financial information. "The FASB is committed to working toward the goal of producing high-quality reporting standards worldwide to support healthy global capital markets."[6] To address this concern, the FASB and the IASB have "acknowledged their commitment to the development of high-quality, compatible accounting standards that could be used for both domestic and cross-border financial reporting."[7]

In September 2002 at a meeting in Norwalk, Connecticut, the FASB and IASB agreed to "use their best efforts to a) make their existing financial reporting standards fully compatible as soon as is practicable and b) to coordinate their work program to ensure that once achieved, compatibility is maintained."[8] The project has become known as the Convergence Project.

In February 2006, the FASB and the IASB issued what has become known as a Memorandum of Understanding (MoU). The MoU was based on three joint principles:

1. Convergence of accounting standards can best be achieved through the development of high-quality, common standards over time.
2. Trying to eliminate the differences between two standards that are in need of significant improvement is not the best use of the FASB's and the IASB's resources—instead a new common standard should be developed that improves the financial information reported to investors.
3. Serving the needs of investors means that the boards should seek convergence by replacing standards in need of improvement with jointly developed new standards.[9]

A goal set by the International Accounting Standards Committee Foundation (IASCF) is one of *harmonization*. Harmonization will be achieved when companies around the world follow one set of international accounting standards. In a step toward convergence, the FASB and the ISAB have agreed to a timeline for harmonization of GAAP into IFRS, the international standards. Part of the timeline includes issuance of joint standards on an ongoing basis. The revised statement, FASB ASC 805, *Business Combinations* (SFAS No. 141(R)), is the first statement that was jointly issued by both bodies.

The Future of the Accounting Profession

One group advancing fair value accounting is the accounting profession itself. The changes in the global economic environment have created challenges for the accounting profession. The Global Public Policy Symposium is a series of conferences that has an "objective . . . to provide an international forum for the exchange of views on how we can collaborate in maintaining healthy global capital markets and contribute to improvements in the quality, reliability, and accessibility of financial and other information that stakeholders need."[10] The symposiums are sponsored by the six largest accounting and auditing firms: BDO International, Ernst & Young, Grant Thornton International, KPMG International, Deloitte, and PricewaterhouseCoopers. At one of the initial symposia, the CEOs of these international accounting firms issued a white paper, "Global Capital Markets and the Global Economy: A Vision from the CEOs of the International Audit Networks." The intent of the paper was to provide and "stimulate a robust dialogue about how global financial reporting and public company auditing procedures could better serve capital markets around the world."[11] The paper concluded that the accounting profession "has undergone a fundamental change from being largely self-regulated to regulated around the globe." That change will require that "all stakeholders look to the future and consider how investors' needs will change in a rapidly evolving global market."[12]

After the issuance of the initial white paper, the symposia conducted a series of roundtable discussions in various financial centers around the world. The discussions were held on a not-for-attribution basis in order to promote open discussion. In January 2008, a fourth symposium was held and another white paper was issued, titled "Global Dialogue with Capital Market Stakeholders: A Report from the CEOs of the International Audit Networks," summarizing the results from the roundtables. The discussions were organized into four categories in the white paper:

1. Global convergence: the need for consistency in financial reporting
2. Audit quality: the need for continuous improvement and greater consistency
3. Prevention and detection: a two-pronged approach to fraud
4. The future of business reporting[13]

One of the most discussed topics at the roundtables was the global convergence of accounting standards. The report concluded that there is a "near-universal support" for one set of high-quality international accounting standards. However, the report noted that there is not a consensus about what the single set of standards should be or how it should be established. Nonetheless, the users of global capital markets agree that a goal of the accounting profession should be one set of common standards.

While agreeing on the need for one set of common accounting standards across international boundaries, the participants also had other concerns related to these standards. The participants expressed a strong preference for principles-based rather than rules-based standards. The view was that rules-based standards created a level of complexity that was not necessary for proper financial reporting.

Another theme resulting from the roundtable discussions was the concern that there is not currently sufficient education and training in place to support the convergence to one set of standards. There was an acknowledgment that the convergence of standards would require a tremendous amount of training at every level for preparers and auditors. Participants also noted that there will have to be a significant change in technology, particularly software that is currently used in financial reporting.

A final issue related to one set of auditing standards was that the participants recognized that small and medium-sized businesses have unique needs and may have more difficulty transitioning to international standards (IFRS). In order for convergence to be effective, the process has to include consideration of the needs of these businesses.

SEC Recent Releases

The U.S. Congress has given authority for establishing accounting standards to the Securities and Exchange Commission (SEC). The SEC has delegated the authority for standard setting to the FASB. Even so, the SEC has still maintains active influence over the setting of standards through its oversight of public company registrants. Therefore, the SEC has tremendous influence in the trend toward increased usage of fair value accounting.

As an example of this influence, the SEC has issued two concept releases that provide additional incentive for international companies reporting in the United States to report using international accounting standards.

In July 2007, the SEC voted unanimously to eliminate reconciliation requirement for foreign issuers and issued Concept Release No. 33-8818, "Acceptance from Foreign Private Issuers of Financial Statements Prepared in Accordance with International Financial Reporting Standards without Reconciliation to U.S. GAAP." Likewise, on November 29, 2007, the EU Commissioner called on European regulators to eliminate the reconciliation requirement for U.S. GAAP issuers.

After a public comment period, the SEC issued a final ruling allowing foreign issuers of financial statements prepared under IFRS to file with the SEC without reconciliation to U.S. GAAP. Implementation required amendments to various regulations under the Securities Act and the Securities Exchange Act, which became effective March 4, 2008.[14]

The impact of this release is that in effect there is a dual reporting system in the United States. Foreign registrants can report under IFRS while domestic companies are required to report under U.S. GAAP.

In response to concerns by U.S.-based registrants, in August 2007, the SEC issued Concept Release No. 33-8831, "Concept Release on Allowing U.S. Issuers to Prepare Financial Statements in Accordance with International Financial Reporting Standards." This release explored allowing U.S.-based registrants to choose between current U.S GAAP and International Accounting Standards. Supporting this release, the American Institute of Certified Public Accountants (AICPA) issued a comment letter that recommended the SEC to allow U.S. firms to report using IFRS. Although never finalized, the initial concept release evolved into another concept release that was issued in November of 2008, entitled "Roadmap for the Potential Use of Financial Statements Prepared in Accordance with International Financial Reporting Standards by U.S. Issuers," Concept Release No. 33-8982.[15] Through this release, the SEC is demonstrating its support for the FASB and IASB's Convergence Project for the convergence of U.S. accounting standards with international accounting standards. The Roadmap identifies several milestones that, if achieved, would require U.S. issuers to use IFRS by 2014. The SEC recently extended the comment period for the Roadmap.[16]

The impact on financial reporting of these releases is that the SEC is furthering the emphasis on fair value accounting in U.S. financial reporting of publicly traded entities. However, SEC Chairman Mary Shapiro has given some indications that she may slow the convergence process.

SFAS 157, *Fair Value Measurements*

The FASB introduced FASB ASC 820, *Fair Value Measurements and Disclosures* (SFAS 157), to provide additional guidance and to provide additional information on issues related to the measurement of fair value. FASB ASC 820, *Fair Value Measurements*, technically does not create any new accounting, but rather provides preparers of financial statements additional information on how the FASB intends fair value be measured in any instance it is required in financial reporting. There are certain exceptions related to share-based payment transactions. One common share-based payment is discussed in SFAS 123 (R). The fair value measurement described in SFAS 123 (R) is generally considered consistent with the fair value definition under *Fair Value Measurements and Disclosures;* however, the FASB considers these transactions fair value–based measurements, not fair value measurements because they are transactions with employees that are consistent with the exit value under the definition of fair value.[17] Some of the more important highlights of FASB ASC 820, *Fair Value Measurements and Disclosures*, introduced or expanded upon in the statement are:

Revised definition of fair value
Discussed the issue of price in the measurement
Defined market participants
Expanded on the concept of principal market or most advantageous market
Introduced the concept of defensive value
Described valuation technique
Introduced the fair value hierarchy
Expanded required disclosures

When first issued, FASB ASC 820, *Fair Value Measurements* (SFAS 157), was to be effective on fiscal years beginning after November 15, 2007. However, on November 14, 2007, the day before the statement was to become fully implemented, the FASB delayed implementation of part of the statement.[18] The reason for the partial implementation and partial delay was that preparers of statements felt they did not fully understand the implications of implementation of the statement. So the FASB agreed to a partial implementation. Therefore, FASB ASC 820, *Fair Value Measurements* (SFAS

157), was partially implemented for financial assets and liabilities, as well as for any other assets and liabilities that are carried at fair value on a recurring basis in financial statements. Examples of assets and liabilities carried at fair value on a recurring basis provided by the FASB include derivatives, loan-servicing assets and liabilities, and some loans and debt linked to business combinations.

The board provided a one-year deferral for the implementation of FASB ASC 820, *Fair Value Measurements* (SFAS 157), for nonfinancial assets and liabilities. These nonfinancial assets and liabilities are related to goodwill, business combinations, and discontinued operations, as well as to some nonfinancial intangible assets. The statement is now fully implemented for fiscal years beginning after November 15, 2008. Although the FASB agreed to adopt the one-year delay, it had encouraged the earlier adoption of FASB ASC 820, *Fair Value Measurements* (SFAS 157), for nonfinancial assets and liabilities.

Background of Fair Value Measurements

Prior to the implementation of FASB ASC 820, *Fair Value Measurements* (SFAS 157), the application of fair value measurements in financial reporting varied among three dozen or more of the pronouncements that required a fair value measurement. These statements referred to different accounting concepts, so over time inconsistencies developed in applying fair value measurements under different statements. After the introduction of SFAS 141 and 142, one of the most common applications of fair value measurements was in business combinations and the subsequent testing of goodwill and other long-lived assets. These statements required the fair value measurements of assets that were not readily measureable by the market place. Preparers of financial statements were concerned about measuring fair value in the absence of quoted market prices. FASB ASC 820, *Fair Value Measurements* (SFAS 157), establishes a framework for applying fair value measurements. The FASB believes that the implementation of FASB ASC 820, *Fair Value Measurements* (SFAS 157), will provide improvements to financial reporting as a result of increased consistency, reliability, and comparability.

Concepts Introduced by SFAS 157

FASB ASC 820, *Fair Value Measurements* (SFAS 157), introduces several new concepts to clarify the measurement of fair value in financial reporting. These concepts include a new standard definition of fair value, which is used throughout financial reporting. The definition of fair value implies that the measurement is an exit price, meaning that the measurement is not necessarily what was paid for the asset or interest, but what it could be sold for in the marketplace. As such, the statement introduces the concept of principal market or most advantageous market to measure fair value as to where the asset or interest in the business could be sold. Also the statement expands on the market participant concept that was introduced in the original version of SFAS 141, *Business Combinations.* The statement further describes that fair value measurement is based on the asset or interest's "highest and best use." Finally, the statement introduces the concept of defensive value that measures fair value of an asset that the acquirer may not ever directly use in the business operations.

Definition of Fair Value

SFAS 157 provides one standard definition of fair value, which is required to be used throughout financial reporting. Fair value is defined in SFAS 157 as:

> *the price that would be received to sell an asset or paid to transfer a liability in an orderly transaction between market participants at the measurement date.*[19]

This definition of fair value has introduced some interesting concepts that impact the measurement. Since fair value is the price to sell an asset, it is considered an exit price rather than an entry price. Exit price is what one could sell the asset for, not necessarily what one paid for the asset. This definition "presumes the absence of compulsion"[20] and that buyers and sellers are independent and knowledgeable, which is similar to the standard definition of fair market value for tax matters. Since fair value is a price that an asset could be sold to a market participant, the statement further describes how fair value measurement is for a transaction assumed to occur in what is described as a principal market. A principal market is "the market in which the reporting entity would sell the asset or transfer the liability with the greatest volume and level of activity for the asset or liability."[21] If a principal market as described earlier does not exist, then fair value is measured by a sale to a market participant in the most advantageous market.[22] The statement describes the most advantageous market as one in "which the reporting entity would sell the asset or transfer the liability with the price that maximizes the amount that would be received for the asset or minimizes the amount that would be paid to transfer the liability."[23]

A fair value measurement under FASB ASC 820, *Fair Value Measurements* (SFAS 157), is for a particular asset or liability. The definition of fair value primarily relates to individual assets and liabilities. The reason provided by the FASB is that assets and liabilities are a primary subject of accounting measurement.[24] A common example of this concept is in business combinations where the assets and liabilities of the acquired entity are measured at individual fair values as of the date of the change of control in the acquisition. The definition of fair value is also applied to interests that are considered part of invested capital of the enterprise. Invested capital is commonly considered to be the shareholder's equity plus interest-bearing debt. Invested capital is how the enterprise is financed over the long term. An example of fair value measurement of this type of interest is the reporting unit described in SFAS 142, which is used for the testing of goodwill for impairment.

The statement notes that the measurement of fair value should consider attributes that are specific to that asset or liability. However, there are two alternatives in considering the specific attributes of the asset or liability. The first alternative is that the asset or liability may be recognized on a stand-alone basis. An example may be a building or unique technology. The second alternative is that the measurement may consider the attributes of a group of assets and/or liabilities. An example would be customer relationships that are valued along with technology used in the production of goods sold to those customers. Another example of a group would be an entire reporting unit.

Whether the asset or liability is measured on a stand-alone basis or as part of a group depends on what is sometimes described as its unit of account. The unit of account determines what is being measured by referring to the level at which the asset or liability is aggregated.[25]

One issue addressed by the statement is how to measure fair value when the business enterprise holds a significant position in another company. Suppose that in a business combination the acquired corporation owns marketable securities, which includes 5 percent of another corporation's publicly traded common stock. If the shares were sold at one time, the introduction of these shares to the market would likely depress the per share price because of the change in the level of trading volume. Financial theory suggests that the value of the shares would decrease. However, paragraph 27 of FASB ASC 820, *Fair Value Measurements* (SFAS 157), states that the "quoted price shall not be adjusted because of the size of the position relative to trading volume."[26] Thus, fair value measurements should not consider a "blockage factor." The FASB sometimes refers to the issue as the *aggregation problem* or as *specifying the unit of account*.[27]

Breaking Down the Definition of Fair Value

In applying the definition of fair value to the measurement of individual assets and liabilities, it is important to understand certain concepts that are part of the definition. These specific concepts within the definition of fair value have meaning that impacts how fair value is measured. The specific concepts of price, principal market, and/or most advantageous market, and market participant are discussed in the next sections.

PRICE FASB ASC 820, *Fair Value Measurements* (SFAS 157), describes the concept of price in the definition of fair value:

> *A fair value measurement assumes that the asset or liability is exchanged in an orderly transaction between market participants who wish to sell the asset or transfer the liability at the measurement date. An orderly transaction is one in which there has been exposure to the market for a period prior to the measurement date to allow for the usual and customary marketing activities involved in transactions for such assets or liabilities. An orderly transaction is not a forced transaction, such as a forced liquidation or a distress sale. From the perspective of a market participant that holds the asset or owes the liability, the transaction to sell the asset or transfer the liability is a hypothetical transaction at the measurement date. Therefore, the objective of a fair value measurement is to determine the price needed to sell the asset or that must be paid to transfer the liability at the measurement date (an exit price).*[28]

Fair value measurement as described earlier is an exit price. An exit price is what the assets could be sold for or what must be paid to transfer liabilities to any market participant. Therefore, *fair value is not necessarily the value to the acquiring entity.* Nor is it necessarily, although it could be, the price that the acquiring entity actually paid for the asset. The same is true with liabilities. Fair value may not be the obligation for the liability of the specific entity itself.

The concept of "price" in the definition of fair value is an exit price. Fair value measurements may not necessarily be based on historical prices or even on expected future prices. Fair value is the price as of the date of measurement that the asset could be sold or the liability transferred to a market participant.

The concept of exit value in the definition of fair value also assumes that both the buyer and the seller are independent and that both have all the relevant information to make a prudent decision about buying and selling the asset or transferring the liability. The concept also assumes that the buyer and the seller are presumed to be independent, with equal knowledge, that the parties are unrelated, and that no party has a price advantage with respect to the transaction. The concept of exit price also assumes that the buyer and seller are willing, not compelled, to either buy or sell.[29]

The concepts are similar to the definition of fair market value as promulgated in tax reporting under Revenue Ruling 59-60, which refers to:

> ... *the price at which property would change hands between a willing buyer and a willing seller when the former is not under any compulsion to buy and latter is not under any compulsion to sell and both parties having reasonable knowledge of relevant facts.*

The FASB actually considered using this definition of fair market value as the definition of fair value in financial reporting, but noted the extensive tax case law relating to this definition and did not want to inadvertently introduce that case law into financial reporting. Even so, while similar, the definition of fair value introduced by FASB ASC 820, *Fair Value Measurements* (SFAS 157), has the additional concept of principal or most advantageous market and the concept of market participants, which creates some differences in the two definitions.

PRINCIPAL OR MOST ADVANTAGEOUS MARKET   A natural question in thinking about the definition of fair value introduced by FASB ASC 820, *Fair Value Measurements* (SFAS 157), is that if fair value is an exit price to a market participant, what market should be considered? The FASB introduces two concepts to answer that particular question. First, the principal market is defined as the market that has the most volume or most activity for that particular asset or for the transfer of that particular liability. If there is no principal market then the market would be where a prudent investor would obtain the highest price for the assets or best benefit for transferring the liability. FASB ASC 820, *Fair Value Measurements* (SFAS 157), refers to these concepts as:

> *A fair value measurement assumes that the transaction to sell the asset or transfer the liability occurs in the principal market for the asset or liability or, in the absence of a principal market, the most advantageous market for the asset or liability. The* principal market *is the market in which the reporting entity would sell the asset or transfer the liability with the greatest volume and level of activity for the asset or liability.*
>
> *The* most advantageous market *is the market in which the reporting entity would sell the asset or transfer the liability at a price that maximizes the amount that would be received for the asset, or minimizes the amount that would be paid to transfer the liability, considering transaction costs in the respective market(s).*
>
> *In either case, the principal or most advantageous market and, thus, market participants should be considered from the perspective of the reporting entity. This perspective allows for differences between and among*

entities with different activities. If there is a principal market for the asset or liability, the fair value measurement must represent the price in that market whether that price is directly observable or otherwise determined using a valuation technique. This is true even if the price in a different market is potentially more advantageous at the measurement date.[30]

However, FASB ASC 820, *Fair Value Measurements* (SFAS 157), also says that the price in the principal or most advantageous market used to estimate the fair value measurement of the asset or liability should *not* contain any transaction costs for that particular asset or liability. Transaction costs are the direct costs that would be incurred to sell the asset or transfer the liability in the principal or most advantageous market for the asset or liability. The FASB decision to not include transactions cost is based on the idea that transaction costs are not a part of the asset or liability. Transaction costs are typically unique to a specific transaction and may differ depending on the transaction not the asset or liability. However, fair value measurement may include the costs of transportation of the asset or liability to or from its principal or most advantageous market. FASB ASC 820, *Fair Value Measurements* (SFAS 157), notes that "the price in the principal or most advantageous market used to measure the fair value of the asset or liability must be adjusted for any costs that would be incurred to transport the asset or liability to or from its principal or most advantageous market."[31] As an example, in estimating the fair value of a piece of machinery that is used in a production line one would consider the costs that would be incurred to transport the piece of equipment to the plant of the reporting entity. However, fair value would not include the cost of a machinery and equipment broker that may have been used to acquire the equipment.

Under the acquisition method, the fair value of assets acquired and liabilities assumed are measured on the balance sheet at each of its respective fair values as of the date of change in control in a business combination. As discussed earlier, fair value is not necessarily the price for which the asset was acquired or the liability assumed, but is an exit price for which the asset can be sold or the liability transferred to a market participant. Market participants operate in either the principal market or in absence of a principal market, the most advantageous market.

MARKET PARTICIPANTS   FASB ASC 820, *Fair Value Measurements* (SFAS 157), clarifies that "the transaction to sell the asset or transfer the liability is a hypothetical transaction ... considered from the perspective of a market participant that holds the asset or owns the liability."[32] Market participants are willing and able to transact in the most advantageous market. Fair value is defined as an exit price that is based on a concept of a market participant's, not necessarily entity-specific, assumptions. The FASB defines market participants as buyers and sellers in the principal or most advantageous market for the asset or liability who are:

- Independent of the reporting entity—that is, they are not related parties
- Knowledgeable, having a reasonable understanding about the asset or liability and the transaction based on all available information, including information that might be obtained through due diligence efforts that are usual and customary
- Able to transact for the asset or liability
- Willing to transact for the asset or liability—that is, they are motivated but not forced or otherwise compelled to do so[33]

The fair value measurement of an asset or liability is based on the assumptions that market participants would use in pricing the asset or liability, not the owner of the asset or the party responsible for the liability. As a practical measure, management does not have to identify specific market participants in measuring fair value. However, in measuring fair value, the reporting entity should identify characteristics of market participants considering factors specific to (a) the asset or liability, (b) the principal or most advantageous market for the asset or liability, and (c) market participants with whom the reporting entity would transact in that market.[34] Market participants would likely include other potential buyers that also initially bid for the assets when estimating fair value in a business combination.

ENTRY PRICE VERSUS EXIT PRICE   Under the definition of fair value as presented in FASB ASC 820, *Fair Value Measurements* (SFAS 157), fair value is again defined as ". . . the price that would be received to sell an asset or paid to transfer a liability in an orderly transaction between market participants at the measurement date." Under this definition, fair value might not necessarily be the price that the asset was acquired. Fair value is the price that the asset could be sold to a market participant. This concept is referred to as an exit price. An exit price differs from an entry price, which is the price paid to acquire the asset or the price received to assume the liability. There are some important distinctions between entry prices and exit prices. Sometimes a business may pay more for an asset because it can utilize that asset in a way other businesses cannot. For example, a business may acquire some proprietary technology that it can use in conjunction with its own technology to develop a new product line. The acquired proprietary technology may be worth more to the acquirer in that circumstance and the acquisition price may reflect its potential use by the acquirer. Entities may not necessarily be able to sell assets at the prices paid to acquire them. Similarly, entities may not necessarily have the ability to transfer liabilities at the prices received to assume them.[35]

In many cases, the transaction price will equal the exit price and, therefore, represent the fair value of the asset or liability at initial recognition. In determining whether a transaction price represents the fair value of the asset or liability at initial recognition, the reporting entity must consider factors specific to the transaction and to the asset or liability. For example, a transaction price might not represent the fair value of an asset or liability at initial recognition if any of the following four criteria are met:

1. The transaction is between related parties.
2. The transaction occurs under duress or the seller is forced to accept the price in the transaction. For example, if the seller is experiencing financial difficulty, he might be forced to accept a lower price.
3. The unit of account represented by the transaction price is different from the unit of account for the asset or liability measured at fair value.
4. The market in which the transaction occurs is different from the market in which the reporting entity would sell the asset or transfer the liability; that is, the principal or most advantageous market.[36]

HIGHEST AND BEST USE APPLICATION CRITERIA A fair value measurement as described by FASB ASC 820, *Fair Value Measurements* (SFAS 157), assumes "the highest and best use" of the asset by market participants. Highest and best use considers the use of the asset that is physically possible, legally permissible, and financially feasible. The highest and best use is the use that maximizes the value of the asset, or the group of assets within which the asset would be used by a market participant rather than by the reporting entity. As such, assumptions in the fair value measurements as to the highest and best use of an asset or group of assets are determined by how the asset or group of assets would be used by market participants, even if the intended use of the asset by the reporting entity is different.[37]

As an example, suppose a reporting entity acquires a telecommunications company in a business combination. The telecommunications company had developed some viable technology that is outside its core business. Consequently, the technology had not been implemented in the company's existing services. The acquiring reporting entity also does not have any intention of exploiting the technology. However, if the technology would be exploited by other market participants, the fair value of the technology would be based on its highest and best use. The fair value would be determined as though it would be utilized by other market participants and reported as such on the reporting entity's financial statements.

FASB ASC 820, *Fair Value Measurements* (SFAS 157), introduces the concept of valuation premise when discussing the highest and best use of an asset. The valuation premise can be either highest and best use as part of a group of assets, which is referred to in the statement as "in-use," or its highest and best use can be on a stand-alone basis, which is referred to in the statement as "in-exchange."

FASB ASC 820, *Fair Value Measurements* (SFAS 157), describes in-use and in-exchange as follows:

> *The highest and best use of the asset is* in-use *if the asset would provide maximum value to market participants principally through its use in combination with other assets as a group, as installed or otherwise configured for use. That might be the case for certain nonfinancial assets. If the highest and best use of the asset is in-use, the fair value of the asset must be measured using an in-use valuation premise. When using an in-use valuation premise, the fair value of the asset is determined based on the price that would be received in a current transaction to sell the asset, assuming that the asset would be used with other assets as a group, and assuming that those assets would be available to market participants. Generally, assumptions about the highest and best use of the asset should be consistent for all of the assets of the group within which it would be used.*
>
> *The highest and best use of the asset is* in-exchange *if the asset would provide maximum value to market participants principally on a stand alone basis. That might be the case for a financial asset. If the highest and best use of the asset is in-exchange, the fair value of the asset must be measured using an in-exchange valuation premise. When using an in-exchange valuation premise, the fair value of the asset is determined based on the price that would be received in a current transaction to sell the asset standalone.*
>
> *Because the highest and best use of the asset is determined based on its use by market participants, the fair value measurement considers the assumptions that market participants would use in pricing the asset, whether using an in-use or an in-exchange valuation premise.*[38]

The following examples illustrate the FASB's concepts of highest and best use "in-use" or "in-exchange." Additional examples can also be found in Appendix A of FASB ASC 820, *Fair Value Measurements* (SFAS 157).

EXAMPLE OF HIGHEST AND BEST USE BY A MARKET PARTICIPANT   A strategic buyer of a technology consulting company acquires another similar company in a business combination. Assume that the acquired entity has only three assets: (1) developed technology, (2) a trade name, and (3) customer relationships. The developed technology was created by the acquired entity for its own use in conjunction with providing services to its customers. Under the acquisition method of accounting, the acquiring company measures the fair value of each of the assets individually, taking into consideration the specified unit of account for the assets. The acquiring company assumes that each of the three assets would provide the most value to market participants through its use in combination with the two other assets as a group. In other words, the highest and best use premise is in-use.

In a business combination, the acquiring company assumes that the market in which the assets could be sold is the same market in which it acquired the assets. The exit price under the definition of fair value (the price at which the assets could be sold to a market participant) may be the same as the entry price (the price at which the assets were acquired). However, the acquiring company would have to consider the most likely market participants to which the assets could be sold. The acquiring entity determines that there are two broad groups of potential market participants for these assets: financial buyers and strategic buyers.

The acquiring company performs an analysis to measure the fair value of each of these assets to both broad groups of market participants, strategic buyers and financial buyers. The results of their analysis are presented in Table 1.1.

The acquiring company determines that to a strategic buyer, the fair value of the customer relationships are $1,250, the fair value of the developed technology is $2,000, and the fair value of the trade name is $500. To a financial buyer, the acquiring company determines that the fair value of the customer relationships is $800, the fair value of the developed technology is $1,750, and the fair value of the trade name is $750. The total fair value of the three assets to a strategic buyer is $3,750 but only $3,300 to a financial buyer. What is the fair value of the three assets that the acquiring entity should record on its balance sheet?

First, what would be the likely differences in fair values for each asset between the two groups of market participants? The fair value of the technology and customer relationships may be more to the market participant who is a strategic buyer because any market participant within this group would likely integrate the technology and customer relationships with their own product lines, which would create more value for them in a business combinations than it would for a market participant who is a financial buyer who may not have the opportunity to integrate those assets with

TABLE 1.1 Strategic versus Financial Buyers

Asset	Strategic Buyer	Financial Buyer
Customer relationships	$1,250	$ 800
Developed technology	2,000	1,750
Trade name	500	750
Totals	$3,750	$3,300

others. However, the fair value of the trade name to a market participant who is a strategic buyer may not be as great as it would be for a market participant who is a financial buyer because the strategic buyer may already have an established trade name while a financial buyer may not.

Second, what is premise for the fair value measurement, in-use or in-exchange? The fair value of these particular assets is likely to be enhanced in conjunction with the use of the other two assets. For example, the value of customer relationships on its own would likely not be as great as it is with developed technology and an established trade name. The acquiring company's analysis indicates that the fair value of these three assets is maximized by strategic market participants using an in-use premise of value.

The fair value of the three assets under the acquisition method and recorded on the balance sheet would be:

Customer relationships	$1,250
Developed technology	2,000
Trade name	500

Even though the fair value of the trade name is higher to a financial buyer market participant, the maximum value of these assets would be in-use to a strategic buyer market participant.

ANOTHER EXAMPLE OF HIGHEST AND BEST USE OF IN-USE VERSUS IN-EXCHANGE

A pharmaceutical company acquires another similar smaller pharmaceutical in a business combination. The acquired pharmaceutical company owns the building, which it uses as both its headquarters and a manufacturing plant to produce its product. The building is considered state of the art and was built by a developer so that it could have multiple uses. Similar buildings nearby have recently been developed for commercial use as sites for high-end shopping centers. The acquiring pharmaceutical company determines that the building could easily be converted for use as a retail shopping center.

The highest and best use of the building would be determined by having a real estate appraiser estimate (a) the value of the building in its current use as a manufacturing operation (in-use), and (b) the value of the building as converted to a retail shopping center, considering the costs to convert (in-exchange). The highest and best use of the building is the higher of those values.

DEFENSIVE (OR LOCKED-UP) VALUE
An interesting concept that is recognized by FASB ASC 820, *Fair Value Measurements* (SFAS 157), is one of defensive value. Defensive value is the concept that in some circumstances acquisitions are made to prevent the acquired company and/or its assets from

competing with the acquirer. The value to the acquirer is the competitive enhancement of its own products and resulting cash flow. FASB ASC 820, *Fair Value Measurements*, recognizes that the value from a defensive acquisition should be measured at the fair value, taking into consideration how the acquired asset would be used by marketplace participants. An example of how fair value is measured from a defensive acquisition can also be found in Appendix A of FASB ASC 820, *Fair Value Measurements* (SFAS 157).[39]

In Appendix A, the FASB example describes the acquisition of an in-process research and development (IPR&D) project in a business combination. IPR&D is a technology that is under development, is not currently feasible, and has no alternative use. The acquiring company makes the acquisition for defensive purposes and does not intend to complete the IPR&D project because the acquired project would compete with one of the company's own internal IPR&D projects. Instead, the acquiring company intends to lock up the acquired IPR&D project to keep its competitors from gaining access to the technology. The IPR&D project provides a defensive value to the acquiring company by improving the outlook for the acquiring company's own technology.

The fair value of the acquired IPR&D project is based on the highest and best use of the IPR&D by use of market participants. The FASB describes the process of determining fair value as the highest and best use by marketplace participant as:

> *a) The highest and best use of the IPR&D project would be in-use if market participants would continue to develop the IPR&D project and that use would maximize the value of the group of assets in which the IPR&D project would be used. That might be the case if market participants do not have similar technology (in development or commercialized). The fair value of the IPR&D project, measured using an in-use valuation premise, would be determined based on the price that would be received in a current transaction to sell the IPR&D project, assuming that the IPR&D would be used with its complementary assets as a group and that those complementary assets would be available to market participants.*

> *b) The highest and best use of the IPR&D project also would be in-use if, for competitive reasons, market participants would lock up the IPR&D project and that use would maximize the value of the group of assets in which the IPR&D project would be used (as a locked-up project). That might be the case if market participants have technology in a more advanced stage of development that would compete with the IPR&D project (if completed) and the IPR&D project would be expected to provide defensive value (if locked up). The fair value of the IPR&D project, measured using an in-use valuation premise, would be determined based on the price that would be received in a current transaction to sell the IPR&D*

*project, assuming that the IPR&D would be used (locked up) with its
complementary assets as a group and that those complementary assets
would be available to market participants.*

*c) The highest and best use of the IPR&D project would be in-
exchange if market participants would discontinue the development of
the IPR&D project. That might be the case if the IPR&D project is not
expected to provide a market rate of return (if completed) and would
not otherwise provide defensive value (if locked up). The fair value of
the IPR&D project, measured using an in-exchange valuation premise,
would be determined based on the price that would be received in a
current transaction to sell the IPR&D project standalone (which might
be zero).*[40]

Application of Fair Value to Liabilities

Fair value measurement also applies to liabilities. Fair value of a liability assumes that the liability is transferred to a market participant at the measurement date. Fair value also assumes that the liability continues in existence to
the counterparty. The liability is not assumed to be settled as of the measurement date. Since the liability is assumed not to be settled, the measurement
of its fair value also assumes that the nonperformance risk does not change
before and after its transfer. The statement defines nonperformance risk as
the risk that the obligation will not be fulfilled. Nonperformance risk may
affect the value at which the liability is transferred since the ability to fulfill
the obligation may change. Nonperformance risk may include the reporting
entity's own credit risk among the risk factors. The reporting entity must
consider the effect of its credit risk (credit standing) on the fair value of the
liability in all periods in which the liability is measured at fair value. Liabilities may be obligation to deliver cash, which is referred to as a financial
liability, or the liabilities may be an obligation to deliver goods or services,
which are referred to as nonfinancial liabilities.

A common method to measuring the fair value of a particular liability
is to adjust the discount rate to current market rates when computing the
present value of the future cash flows related to the liability. The adjusted
discount rate would be higher than the implied interest rate of the liability if
nonperformance risk was judged to be greater. The impact on the fair value
of the liability would be to lower the value of the liability to be recorded
on the balance sheet. If nonperformance risk is judged to be lower than the
opposite, impact occurs.

The accounting treatment of this measurement aspect of the fair value
of liabilities seems a bit counterintuitive. As the credit risk of the reporting
entity increases, the fair value of the liability declines. As the credit risk of the
reporting entity decreases, the fair value of the liability increases. However, if

one considers this treatment of fair value measurement from the perspective of the market participant, then it begins to make a bit more sense. If one were counterparty to a liability and that liability is transferred to another entity whose credit risk was greater than the original entity's credit risk, the likelihood of repayment decreases. If the likelihood of repayment decreases, then the value of the liability to the counterparty decreases. A higher credit rating would increase the probability of repayment and increase the value to the counterparty.

An example of a disclosure about the impact of a change in credit risk on the fair value of liabilities can be found in a recent financial report from Merrill Lynch.

> *Merrill Lynch elected the fair value option for certain short-term and long-term borrowings that are risk managed on a fair value basis, including structured notes, and for which hedge accounting under SFAS No. 133 had been difficult to obtain. The changes in the fair value of liabilities for which the fair value option was elected that was attributable to changes in Merrill Lynch credit spreads were estimated gains of $91 million and $2.2 billion for the three and six months ended June 27, 2008, respectively. The changes in the fair value of liabilities for which the fair value option was elected that were attributable to changes in Merrill Lynch credit spreads were not material for the three and six months ended June 29, 2007. Changes in Merrill Lynch specific credit risk is derived by isolating fair value changes due to changes in Merrill Lynch's credit spreads as observed in the secondary cash market.*[41]

As Merrill Lynch disclosed, a change in the credit spread (Merrill Lynch had become riskier) resulted in a gain of $91 million for the six months ended June 27, 2007, and a gain of $2.2 billion for the six months ended June 27, 2008. A couple of observations about this and similar disclosures: First, of course analysts knew that these gains were the result of the deterioration of Merrill Lynch's own financial position, which caused its outstanding financial instruments to becoming more risky; second, the change in credit risk was from observations in the secondary market, thus a market participant assumption.

The FASB recently issued Accounting Standards Update No. 2009–05, *Measuring Liabilities at Fair Value,* which clarifies the measurement of the fair value of liabilities under ASC 820, *Fair Value Measurements and Disclosures.* One issue related to liabilities that concerned preparers of financial statements is how the concept of exit price is impacted when there is a lack of observable markets or observable inputs to measure the fair value in an assumed transfer. In many situations an entity would likely settle the obligation with the counterparty rather than pay for another entity to assume the obligation. In these situations, preparers are concerned that they are asked to assume a transfer that would not occur.

Another issue that the FASB seeks to clarify is how to measure the fair value of a liability when there is a contractual restriction on the liability's transfer. And finally, the FASB addresses whether the prices of debt instruments traded in the market place as assets represent the fair value of the instrument from the issuer's perspective.

Under the proposed Accounting Standards Update, the FASB reiterates that the quoted market price for an identical liability is the best evidence of fair value, and it would represent a Level 1 measurement. The FSP further explains that in absence of a quoted price for an identical liability, fair value would be measured using an approach maximizing the use of relevant observable inputs and minimizing the use of unobservable inputs, and makes use of one of the following approaches:

a. The quoted price of an identical liability when traded as an asset.
b. The quoted prices for similar liabilities or similar liabilities when traded as an asset.
c. Another valuation technique such as the income or market approach based on the amount the entity would receive if the entity were to transfer the liability or enter into an identical liability at the measurement date.

The FSB states that the fair value of liabilities measured using the price of the liability when traded as an asset is also represents a Level 1 measurement. The board recognizes that quoted prices for liabilities traded as assets may require adjustments for factors specific to asset that are not applicable to the liability. Those factors include the condition or location of the asset, the degree of comparability and the level of volume and activity in the market. Adjustments to the quoted price of the asset will cause the fair value measurement to be lower than Level 1.

The FASB also states that the contractual restriction on the transfer of a liability is already included in the transaction price because both creditor and obligor accepted the transfer price will full knowledge of the restriction. Therefore, an adjustment to inputs based on a contractual restriction on the transfer of the liability is not warranted.[42]

Example of Fair Value of Debt

Suppose a term loan was acquired as part of a business combination on June 30, 20X1. The terms of the loan are $1,000,000 in principal due in three years, with 8 percent annual interest payments due on June 30th of each year. If current interest rates are 10 percent as of the date of the business combination, the fair value of the note is calculated as follows:

The interest payment on June 30, 20X2 of $80,000, discounted for one year at 10 percent is $72,727.

The interest payment on June 30, 20X3 of $80,000, discounted for two years at 10 percent is $66,116.

The final payment on June 30, 20X4 of $1,080,000 ($80,000 interest plus $1,000,000 principal), discounted for three years at 10 percent is $811,420.

The fair value on June 30, 20X1, is the sum of the three amounts, or $950,263. The fair value is less than the $1,000,000 principal amount because the obligation has a favorable interest rate compared to market rates. Fair value is measured using the entity's nonperformance risk, regardless of the loan's contractual interest terms.

Valuation Approaches in Fair Value Measurements

FASB ASC 820, *Fair Value Measurements* (SFAS 157), identifies what is referred to in the statement as valuation techniques that are consistent with the market approach, income approach, and the cost approach. Valuation specialists (also as indicated in *Fair Value Measurement*) believe that in some circumstances a single valuation technique is appropriate. In other circumstances, more than one valuation technique will be more appropriate. If more than one valuation technique is used, the reporting entity should evaluate the indications of fair value for reasonableness. The fair value is the indication from the valuation technique that is most reasonable under the circumstances whether it is one of the indications or some weighing of the indications within the range of indications.

FASB ASC 820, *Fair Value Measurements and Disclosures*, highlights the three basic approaches or techniques that are commonly used to measure fair value: (1) the cost approach, (2) the market approach, and (3) the income approach.

COST APPROACH FASB ASC 820, *Fair Value Measurements and Disclosures*, describes the cost approach to valuation as an approach:

> *based on the amount that currently would be required to replace the service capacity of an asset (often referred to as current replacement cost). From the perspective of a market participant (seller), the price that would be received for the asset is determined based on the cost to a market participant (buyer) to acquire or construct a substitute asset*

of comparable utility, adjusted for obsolescence. Obsolescence encompasses physical deterioration, functional (technological) obsolescence, and economic (external) obsolescence and is broader than depreciation for financial reporting purposes (an allocation of historical cost) or tax purposes (based on specified service lives).[43]

The notion behind the cost approach is that the fair value of an asset or even an entire business is estimated by the current replacement cost of the asset or the entire business less any adjustments for obsolescence related to the subject asset or assets that comprise the business. The replacement cost of the asset is what it would cost as of the measurement date to replace the asset or an entire business with an asset or group of assets of comparable utility. The cost approach is often used to estimate the value of specific assets, such as a building or machinery and equipment, or certain intangible assets, such as customer relationships or an assembled workforce. Because of its nature, the cost approach is difficult to apply in estimating the fair value of an entire operating business; however, an example in financial reporting would be the estimate of the fair value of assets acquired in a business combination under FASB ASC 350, *Goodwill and Other Intangible Assets* (SFAS 142).

MARKET APPROACH FASB ASC 820, *Fair Value Measurements and Disclosures*, describes the market approach as one that:

uses prices and other relevant information generated by market transactions involving identical or comparable assets or liabilities (including a business). For example, valuation techniques consistent with the market approach often use market multiples derived from a set of comparables. Multiples might lie in ranges with a different multiple for each comparable. The selection of where within the range the appropriate multiple falls requires judgment, considering factors specific to the measurement (qualitative and quantitative).

Valuation techniques consistent with the market approach also include matrix pricing. Matrix pricing is a mathematical technique used principally to value debt securities without relying exclusively on quoted prices for the specific securities, but rather by relying on the securities' relationship to other benchmark quoted securities.[44]

The market approach estimates fair value by comparing a financial measurement such as cash flow or earnings or some other metric of the entity to a multiple of similar financial measurement or metric of a similar guideline entity whose shares are transacted in the market place. Commonly used financial measurements are multiples of prices to earnings, or the P/E ratio, or multiple of invested capital to earnings before depreciation and amortization (EBITDA). The market approach conceptually is easily understood because the approach estimates fair value through transactions of similar assets or business interests in the market. The difficulty in applying the market approach in measuring fair value, particularly in estimating the fair value of intangible assets, is in identifying guideline assets or business interests similar enough to support a determinative comparison.

INCOME APPROACH   FASB ASC 820, *Fair Value Measurements*, describes the income approach as one using:

> *valuation techniques to convert future amounts (for example, cash flows or earnings) to a single present amount (discounted). The measurement is based on the value indicated by current market expectations about those future amounts. Those valuation techniques include: present value techniques; option-pricing models, such as the Black-Scholes-Merton formula (a closed-form model) and a binomial model (a lattice model), which incorporate present value techniques; and the multiperiod excess earnings method, which is used to measure the fair value of certain intangible assets.*[45]

Methods under the income approach can be equally applied to estimate the fair value of an entire entity or reporting unit or they can be applied to estimate the fair value of a specific asset, particularly an intangible asset. The income approach is generally used to estimate the fair value of a business or an asset of the business such as an intangible asset through the risk-adjusted cash flows that the entity or specific intangible asset is expected to generate for the life of the entity or intangible asset. There are several common methods that can be used to estimate fair value under this approach. One method commonly used under the income approach is the discounted cash flow analysis. The discounted cash flow method estimates fair value through the sum of expected future cash flows that the entity or intangible asset will generate, discounted to the present at a risk-adjusted rate of return commensurate with the risk of actually receiving the cash flows.

A version of the discounted cash flow method can also be used to estimate the fair value of a specific intangible asset by estimating cash flows that can be generated by the entire business and deducting fair returns on all of the other assets that contribute to the generation of the cash flow. This method is sometimes also referred to as the multiperiod excess earnings method. The residual cash flow after deducting returns on all of the other contributory assets is the cash flow generated by the specific intangible asset. The present value of this residual cash flow is then discounted at a rate reflective of the risk of the intangible asset in order to estimate the fair value of the specific intangible asset.

Inputs

FASB ASC 820, *Fair Value Measurements*, provides an additional new term, inputs, to guide preparers in developing assumptions in measuring fair value. Inputs are the assumptions that market participants would use when pricing the individual asset or liability. For example, when estimating the fair value of a debt instrument, a risk-related input would be the yields on similar types of debt as observed in the market place. Another example of an input would be the growth rate in expected cash flows of a reporting unit over a particular forecast period. As with any type of assumption, inputs vary greatly depending on the type of asset or liability.

Inputs can be either observable or unobservable:

- Observable inputs are those that market participants may use in pricing an asset and are derived from information in the market place. The inputs are therefore verifiable by independent market-based information. An example would be the yield on a similar debt instrument.
- Unobservable inputs are those that are unique to the entity itself. They are not observable by independent market-derived data. An example may be the growth in expected cash flows prepared internally by management described earlier.

Observable or unobservable inputs may be used in a fair value measurement. However, the FASB has expressed a strong preference for observable inputs over unobservable inputs whenever available.

Fair Value Hierarchy

The FASB also provided additional guidance as to what they consider the relative reliability of the inputs by providing a Fair Value Hierarchy in FASB ASC 820, *Fair Value Measurements and Disclosures* (SFAS 157). The purpose of the hierarchy is "to increase consistency and comparability in fair value measurements and related disclosures."[46] The fair value hierarchy prioritizes the inputs to valuation techniques used to measure fair value into three broad levels, with Level 1 having the highest priority and Level 3 having the lowest. The three levels within the hierarchy are:

Level 1. Observable inputs that reflect quoted prices (unadjusted) for identical assets or liabilities in active markets

Level 2. Inputs other than quoted prices included in Level 1 that are observable for the asset or liability either directly or indirectly

Level 3. Unobservable inputs (e.g., a reporting entity's own data)[47]

In many situations, more than one input is used to measure fair value. In these circumstances the inputs may fall into different levels within the fair value hierarchy. The level with the fair value hierarchy in which the fair value measurement is classified as a whole is based on the significance of the lowest level of the input of the measurement. The significance of the input to the fair value measurement is based on judgment. The classification of the level within the fair value hierarchy is important not only from a perceived reliability standpoint; it is important because the classification impacts disclosures as to how the fair value was measured.

EXAMPLES OF MEASUREMENTS WITHIN THE FAIR VALUE HIERARCHY Some examples of typical inputs within the fair value hierarchy include:

Level 1
- Price listed on the New York Stock Exchange prices for securities
- List futures contract prices on the Chicago Board of Exchange

Level 2
- A rate on a debt instrument that is tied to a market rate such as LIBOR
- A dealer quote for a security that may not be traded on a public market; however, the dealer is willing and able to transact

Level 3
- Inputs obtained from broker quotes that are indicative such as a quote for certain machinery and equipment
- Valuation models that are based on management assumptions such as cash flow forecasts that cannot be corroborated with observable market data

SFAS 159, *Fair Value Option*

The FASB furthered the goal of eventually allowing the measurement of all financial assets and liabilities at fair value in financial reporting through the issuance of FASB ASC 825-10-25, *The Fair Value Option for Financial Assets and Financial Liabilities—Including an Amendment of FASB Statement No. 115* (SFAS 159). SFAS 159, *Fair Value Option*, expands the fair value measurements of financial instruments, both assets and liabilities, which are consistent with the board's long-term accounting measurement objectives for financial instruments. The *Fair Value Option* permits entities to choose to measure most financial assets and liabilities and certain other items at fair value. The FASB noted in the implementation of SFAS 159 that the objective of the statement is to improve financial reporting "by providing entities with the opportunity to mitigate volatility in reported earnings caused by measuring related assets and liabilities differently without having to apply complex hedge accounting provisions."[48]

The *Fair Value Option* is interesting from a financial accounting standpoint because it may be applied on an instrument-by-instrument basis, rather than to all financial assets or liabilities. The financial instruments covered by the statement are fairly broad, the one major exception is financial instruments that otherwise are accounted for by the equity method. The *Fair Value Option* is an election. Once an election is made to measure an instrument at its fair value under FASB ASC 825-10-25 (SFAS 159), the election is irrevocable (unless a new election date occurs). The fair value election is applied only to entire financial instruments and not to portions of an instrument.

All entities may elect the *Fair Value Option*, although in practice the majority of entities electing the fair value option to date are in the financial services industry, primarily commercial and investment banks. The statement lists examples of items that may be eligible for the fair value option.

- A financial asset and financial liability.
- A firm commitment that involves only financial instruments and would otherwise not be recognized at inception. The statement provides an example of a forward purchase contract for a loan that is not readily convertible to cash.
- A written loan commitment.
- An insurance contract that is to provide goods and/or services but not cash and is typically not classified as a financial instrument. However, the terms of the contract provide rights and obligations to permit the insurer to settle by paying a third party to provide those goods or services.
- A warranty that is not typically considered a financial instrument. But similar to the insurance contract described earlier, the terms permit the warrantor to settle by paying a third party to provide those goods or services.
- Certain financial instruments resulting from the separation of an embedded nonfinancial derivative instrument from a nonfinancial hybrid instrument. The underlying debt may be settled in cash, but the embedded feature may be settled in some other manner.[49]

A business entity electing the *Fair Value Option* under FASB ASC 825-10-25 (SFAS 159) reports unrealized gains and losses on items for which the fair value option has been elected in earnings at each subsequent reporting date.

Conclusion

The objective of financial reporting is to provide information that investors and other stakeholders find useful about a company's net assets and operating performance. Traditionally, accounting in the United States has been based on historical cost. However, financial reporting has been evolving toward fair value measurement that is based on current values rather than historical costs. Fair value has been a focus in measuring financial assets and liabilities in financial reporting for some time now. More recently, fair value has become the standard of measurement in business combination and the subsequent testing for impairment of assets acquired in a business combination. As such, the FASB issued FASB ASC 820, *Fair Value Measurements and Disclosures* (SFAS 157), to clarify the concept of measuring fair value in all of financial reporting.

Fair Value Measurements is not without controversy, however. The use of many fair value measurements requires some judgment within the measurement. The extended use of judgment is a fundamental change for those of us trained in historical cost-based measurements. The judgment aspect also creates a new dynamic between preparer, the entity's outside auditor, and possibly an outside valuation specialist who may actually perform the measurement. *Fair Value Measurements* was issued to provide clearer direction from the FASB for the application of the concept of fair value to financial reporting.

Notes

1. The references to the FASB Statements are presented in the FASB's new codification format. For additional information about codification see www.fasb.org.
2. SFAS 157, *Fair Value Measurements*, paragraph 1.
3. FASB FSP157-2, paragraph 1.
4. SFAS 141, paragraph 39.
5. FASB ASC 805, *Business Combinations* (SFAS 141(R)), paragraph 3k.
6. www.fasb.org/news/nr102902.shtml.
7. FASB-IASB, *Memorandum of Understanding*, "The Norwalk Agreement," www.fasb.org.
8. *Id.*
9. www.fasb.org/intl/MOU_09-11-08.pd.
10. www.globalpublicpolicysymposium.com/.
11. *Id.*

12. "Global Capital Markets and the Global Economy: A Vision from the CEOs of the International Audit Networks," November 2006, www.globalpublicpolicy symposium.com/.
13. "Global Dialogue with Capital Markets Stakeholders: A Report from the CEOs of the International Audit Networks," January 2008, www.globalpublicpolicy symposium.com.
14. Securities and Exchange Commission. Release No. 33-8879, "Acceptance from Foreign Private Issuers of Financial Statements Prepared in Accordance with International Financial Reporting Standards without Reconciliation to U.S. GAAP," www.sec.gov/rules/final/2008/33-8879fr.pdf.
15. Securities and Exchange Commission, Release No. 33-8982, "Roadmap for the Potential Use of Financial Statements Prepared in Accordance with International Financial Reporting Standards by U.S. Issuers," www.sec.gov/rules/proposed/2008/33-8982.pdf.
16. "Regulatory Actions Proposed Rules 2009 First Quarter 33-9905," February 3, 2009, www.sec.gov.
17. SFAS 157, paragraph C8.
18. FSP FAS 157-2, *Effective Date of FASB Statement No. 157*, www.fasb.org/pdf/fsp_fas157-2.pdf. See also, October 1, 2007, letter to the FASB from the Financial Executives International's Committee on Corporate Reporting and Small Public Company Task Force, www.financialexecutives.org/eweb/upload/FEI/FAS%20157%20101107.pdf.
19. SFAS 157, *Fair Value Measurements,* paragraph 5.
20. *Id.*, paragraph 6.
21. *Id.*, paragraph 8.
22. *Id.*, paragraph 10.
23. *Id.*, paragraph 8.
24. *Id.*, footnote 4.
25. *Id.*, paragraph 6.
26. *Id.*, paragraph 27.
27. *Id.*, paragraph 6.
28. *Id.*, paragraph 7.
29. *Id.*, paragraph 10.
30. *Id.*, paragraph 8.
31. *Id.*, paragraph 9.
32. FAS 157, *Fair Value Measurements*, p. 157–2.
33. *Id.*, paragraph 10.
34. *Id.*, paragraph 11.
35. *Id.*, paragraph 16.
36. *Id.*, paragraph 17.
37. *Id.*, paragraph 12.
38. *Id.*, paragraph 13.
39. *Id.*, paragraph A12.
40. *Id.*
41. Merrill Lynch & Company Form 10-Q, for the quarterly period ended June 27, 2008, page 63.

42. Financial Accounting Standards Board, Accounting Standards Update No. 2009–05, *Measuring Liabilities at Fair Value, to Topic 820*, Fair Value Measurements and Disclosures, August 2009, pp. 1–7, www.fasb.org.
43. SFAS 157 *Fair Value Measurements*, paragraph 18c.
44. *Id.*, paragraph 18a.
45. *Id.*, paragraph 18b.
46. *Id.*, paragraph 22.
47. *Id.*
48. SFAS 159, *The Fair Value Option for Financial Assets and Financial Liabilities—Including an Amendment of FASB Statement No. 115, 159-1.*
49. *Id.*, paragraph 7.

Fair Value Accounting and the Current Economic Crisis

B eginning in the latter part of 2006, an increase in the general level of interest rates caused a sharp rise in the delinquency and default rates by subprime rate mortgage borrowers. Subprime mortgage borrowers are borrowers who typically do not meet the standard mortgage underwriting guidelines and are considered to be riskier borrowers. Even though subprime mortgage borrowers have greater risk, subprime mortgages have become an increasingly greater percentage of total outstanding mortgage debt. The Center for Audit Quality indicated that several hundred billion dollars of adjustable-rate subprime mortgage loans were to be repriced over the 15-to-18-month period beginning in October 2007.[1]

In the late 1990s the federal government began to institute policies that encouraged subprime lending as a social policy. Government-sponsored entities such as Fannie Mae and Freddie Mac were asked by the federal government to increase the percentage of their mortgage loan portfolios in these types of mortgages to encourage mortgage lenders to originate more of these types of loans. The subprime loans were then securitized into collateralized debt obligations (CDOs), which due to perceived diversification were supposed to reduce their overall risk of the securities package. Ratings agencies modeled the risk and the CDOs were rated taking into account the supposed diversification and the assumption of a steadily increasing housing market. The securitized subprime CDOs were sold on the secondary markets to various entities such as Fannie Mae and Freddie Mac as well as to many traditional financial institutions and investment banks.

Beginning in late 2006 the general level of interest rates began to rise. Most of the underlying subprime mortgages were based on adjustable rates. As interest rose, many borrowers were unable to make the higher interest payments on their mortgage. As a result, the default rates in subprime mortgages increased dramatically. The rise in interest rates also contributed significantly to a decline in the overall housing market, which compounded the impact of the defaults caused by limited options for sale of the underlying real estate by the defaulter.

As an increasing number of subprime mortgage borrowers began to default, many financial institutions and investment banks holding CDOs based on subprime mortgages began to experience uncertainty about the reliability of cash flows from these investments, which further eroded their perceived value. As the level of defaults increased, rating agencies significantly downgraded these subprime mortgage securities. The downgrades caused other investors and lenders to refrain from investing in CDOs. The lack of a secondary market created a "liquidity crisis," which began to spread throughout the financial markets. The risk of defaults in the underlying mortgages caused the secondary markets for securitized mortgages to freeze, which impacted a wide range of commercial and investment banks that held these securities.

Mark-to-Market Accounting

At the center of this liquidity crisis is an accounting issue. The issue is how the value of these securities should be measured in the financial reporting of the entities that hold the securities. The FASB issued SFAS 159, *The Fair Value Option for Financial Assets and Financial Liabilities—Including an Amendment of FASB Statement No. 115* (FASB ASC 825-10-25). The *Fair Value Option* permits entities to choose to measure most financial assets and liabilities and certain other items at their respective fair values in fiscal years beginning after November 15, 2007. The *Fair Value Option* incorporates the definition of fair value as presented in FASB ASC 820 (SFAS 157), which includes features such as the fair value hierarchy, market participant assumptions, and the preference for observable inputs.

Financial reporting under both U.S. Generally Accepted Accounting Principles (GAAP) and International Financial Reporting Standards (IFRS) provide various options for measuring the value of investments in these debt securities. Depending on the instrument, the value of the securities can be measured in one of three ways:

1. *Fair value.* Realized and unrealized changes in fair value are reported in the income statement.
2. *Available for sale (AFS).* Unrealized changes in fair value are reported as a component of shareholders' equity, and realized gains/losses are reflected in the income statement.
3. *Held to maturity (HTM).* Carried at historical cost with amortization of historical cost and any impairment realized in earnings[2]

There are two accounting questions at the center of the financial crisis. The first question is: What is the fair value of the securitized subprime mortgages that financial institutions and other entities should report on their balance sheet? The second question is: At what level in the fair value hierarchy is the fair value measurement when the market is considered distressed? In order to understand the issue better, let's review some of the concepts in fair value measurements.

Fair Value Measurement Concepts

Under FASB ASC 820 (SFAS 157), fair value is defined as, "the price that would be received to sell an asset or paid to transfer a liability in an orderly transaction between market participants at the measurement date."[3]

A fair value measurement assumes that the asset or liability, including the collateralized subprime debt, can be exchanged in an orderly transaction between market participants who wish to sell the asset or transfer the liability at the measurement date. Fair value measurements consider an orderly transaction as one in which there has been exposure to the market for a period prior to the measurement date to allow for the usual and customary marketing activities involved in transactions for such assets or liabilities. An orderly transaction is not a forced transaction, such as a forced liquidation or a distress sale. By definition, a nonactive market is not an orderly market or one in which there is sufficient exposure to the market for usual and customary marketing activities. Thus, a price indicated in a nonactive or illiquid market would likely not be an indication of fair value.[4]

The Accounting Implications of Fair Value Measurements in Illiquid Markets

The AICPA's Center for Audit Quality (CAQ) has recently issued several white papers on issues related to measuring fair value of certain financial assets in illiquid markets.[5] One of the papers, "Measurements of Fair Value in Illiquid (or Less Liquid) Markets," provides some guidance as to the measurement of fair value in illiquid markets. The objective of the CAQ's paper is to "discuss issues associated with the measurement of fair value under existing generally accepted accounting principles (GAAP) in the context of illiquid market conditions."[6]

First of all, the paper notes that fair value is defined as "the price that would be received to sell an asset in an orderly transaction between market participants at the measurement date," as discussed earlier. The white paper also emphasizes that current accounting requires the use of quoted prices in active markets whenever they are available (Level 1 of the fair value hierarchy). The white paper further discusses the impact of concepts introduced by SFAS 157, such as the fair value hierarchy, the concept of an active market, and the use of valuation models when quoted prices in active markets are not available (Level 3). The white paper concludes that the objective of a fair value measurement is to estimate the price that would be received under existing market conditions. If, in the judgment of the preparer, quoted prices in an active market are not available, then fair value should be estimated through the use of a valuation model. For example, quoted prices may not be available if the market is thin or if there are unusual market circumstances. In those cases, market prices would not be considered to be representative of market participant assumption, and then a Level 3 valuation model may be used. The assumptions used in a valuation model must be consistent with assumptions that market participants would use to price an asset at the measurement date, using the exit price concept.[7]

The white paper reinforces the concepts introduced by SFAS 157, stressing that the fair value hierarchy is still appropriate in illiquid or distressed markets. One supporting concept is that market observations are preferable to unobservable assumptions; however, unobservable assumptions can be used in absence of observable inputs. If the market conditions are such that an active market does not exist for a particular distressed asset or liability, then it may be more appropriate to use a valuation model to estimate fair value. The assumptions in the model should be consistent with the exit price concepts. One exit price assumption might be that the market participant to which the asset would be sold or liability would be transferred would likely hold the asset or liability to maturity, particularly if an active market is not available to any market participant.

Application of Fair Value Accounting in Illiquid Market

In recent testimony before the Senate Banking Committee, Federal Reserve Chairman Ben Bernanke stated that "Accounting rules require banks to value many assets at something close to a very low fire-sale price rather than the hold-to-maturity price."[8] Bernanke's testimony echoed the views of many critics of fair value accounting. Critics believe that the credit crisis was made much greater by the "mark-to-market" or fair value accounting of financial institutions that had invested in the securitized subprime debt. The criticism by many of fair value accounting is based on an apparent difference between the market value of certain securities in distressed markets and the value indicated by holding the securities to maturity. The credit crisis caused the secondary market for many securities to become thinly traded or simply nonexistent. The question then became whether the fair value of these securities would be the depressed price indicated by the market or the value indicated by the securities' expected future cash flows discounted to the present at a risk-adjusted rate of return.

In response to widespread criticism, the SEC Office of the Chief Accountant and FASB Staff released a statement titled "Clarifications on Fair Value Accounting"[9] on September 30, 2008. The statement responded to several questions raised by the credit crisis.

Can management's internal assumptions (e.g., expected cash flows) be used to measure fair value when relevant market evidence does not exist?

Yes. When an active market for a security does not exist, the use of management estimates that incorporate current market participant expectations of future cash flows, and include appropriate risk premiums, is acceptable. FASB ASC 820 (SFAS 157) discusses a range of information and valuation techniques that a reasonable preparer might use to estimate fair value when relevant market data may be unavailable, which may be the case during this period of market uncertainty. This can, in appropriate circumstances, include expected cash flows from an asset.

Further, in some cases using unobservable inputs (Level 3) might be more appropriate than using observable inputs (Level 2); for example, when significant adjustments are required to available observable inputs it may be appropriate to utilize an estimate based primarily on unobservable inputs. The determination of fair value often requires significant judgment. In some cases, multiple inputs from different sources may collectively provide the best evidence of fair value. In these cases expected cash flows would be considered alongside other relevant information. The weighting of the inputs in the fair value estimate will depend on the extent to which they provide information about the value of an asset or liability and are relevant in developing a reasonable estimate.

Are transactions that are determined to be disorderly representative of fair value? When is a distressed (disorderly) sale indicative of fair value?

The results of disorderly transactions are not determinative when measuring fair value. The concept of a fair value measurement assumes an orderly transaction between market participants. An orderly transaction is one that involves market participants that are willing to transact and allows for adequate exposure to the market. Distressed or forced liquidation sales are not orderly transactions, and thus the fact that a transaction is distressed or forced should be considered when weighing the available evidence. Determining whether a particular transaction is forced or disorderly requires judgment.

Can transactions in an inactive market affect fair value measurements?

Yes. A quoted market price in an active market for the identical asset is most representative of fair value and thus is required to be used (generally without adjustment). Transactions in inactive markets may be inputs when measuring fair value, but would likely not be determinative. If they are orderly, transactions should be considered in management's estimate of fair value. However, if prices in an inactive market do not reflect current prices for the same or similar assets, adjustments may be necessary to arrive at fair value.

Many critics of fair value accounting called for its suspension or revision during the economic crisis. However, the Center for Audit Quality reaffirmed its position on the relevance of fair value measurements:

> *The Center for Audit Quality, Council of Institutional Investors and the CFA Institute—representing the nation's public company auditors, institutional investors and chartered financial analysts—are united in opposing any suspension of "mark-to-market" or "fair value" accounting.*
>
> *Suspending fair value accounting during these challenging economic times would deprive investors of critical financial information when it is needed most. Fair value accounting with robust disclosures provides more accurate, timely, and comparable information to investors than amounts that would be reported under other alternative accounting approaches. Investors have a right to know the current value of an investment, even if the investment is falling short of past or future expectations.[10]*

FSP FAS 157-3, *Determining the Fair Value of a Financial Asset When the Market for That Asset Is Not Active*

On October 10, 2008, the FASB issued a FASB Staff Position 157-3, *Determining the Fair Value of a Financial Asset When the Market for That Asset Is Not Active,* which further clarifies assumptions to be used in measuring fair value in circumstances where there may not be a market price. The statement's overview says, "This FASB Staff Position (FSP) clarifies the application of FASB Statement No. 157, *Fair Value Measurements,* in a market that is not active and provides an example to illustrate key considerations in determining the fair value of a financial asset when the market for that financial asset is not active." The important points of the FSP reinforce the concepts of fair value measurements introduced by SFAS 157, which include:

- Fair value measurement represents the price at which a transaction would occur between market participants at the measurement date. (An exit price.) Determining fair value in a dislocated market depends on the facts and circumstances and may require the use of significant judgment about whether individual transactions are forced liquidations or distressed sales.
- The use of the reporting entity's own assumptions about future cash flows and appropriately risk-adjusted discount rates is acceptable when relevant observable inputs are not available.
- Broker (or pricing service) quotes may be an appropriate input when measuring fair value, but are not necessarily determinative if an active market does not exist for the financial assets.[11]

The FSP provides an example of measuring the fair value of an asset in circumstances where there may not be an active market for that particular asset. The example amends FASB ASC 820 (Statement 157) for paragraphs A32A-A32F.

Example 11—Determining the Fair Value of a Financial Asset When the Market for That Asset Is Not Active

Note: The conclusions reached in this example are based on the assumed facts and circumstances presented. Other approaches to determining fair value may be appropriate. Also, this example assumes that the observable transactions considered in determining fair value were not forced liquidations or distressed transactions.

On January 1, 20X8, Entity A invested in an AA-rated tranche of a collateralized debt obligation security. The underlying collateral for the collateralized debt obligation security is unguaranteed nonconforming residential mortgage loans. Prior to June 30, 20X8, Entity A was able to determine the fair value of the collateralized debt obligation security using a market approach valuation technique based on Level 2 inputs that did not require significant adjustment. The Level 2 inputs included:

- Quoted prices in active markets for similar collateralized debt obligation securities with insignificant adjustments for differences between the collateralized debt obligation security that Entity A holds and the similar collateralized debt obligation securities.

- Quoted prices in markets that are not active that represent current trans-actions for the same or similar collateralized debt obligation securities that do not require significant adjustment based on unobservable inputs.

Since June 30, 20X8, the market for collateralized debt obligation secu-rities has become increasingly inactive. The inactivity was evidenced first by a significant widening of the bid-ask spread in the brokered markets in which collateralized debt obligation securities trade and then by a signif-icant decrease in the volume of trades relative to historical levels as well as other relevant factors. At September 30, 20X8 (the measurement date), Entity A determines that the market for its collateralized debt obligation security is not active and that markets for similar collateralized debt obliga-tion securities (such as higher rated tranches within the same collateralized debt obligation security vehicle) also are not active. That determination was made considering that there are few observable transactions for the collateralized debt obligation security or similar collateralized debt obliga-tion securities, the prices for those transactions that have occurred are not current, and the observable prices for those transactions vary substantially either over time or among market makers, thus reducing the potential rel-evance of those observations. Consequently, while Entity A appropriately considers those observable inputs, ultimately, Entity A's collateralized debt obligation security will be classified within Level 3 of the fair value hierarchy because Entity A determines that significant adjustments using unobservable inputs are required to determine fair value at the measurement date.

Entity A determines that an income approach valuation technique (present value technique) that maximizes the use of relevant observable in-puts and minimizes the use of unobservable inputs will be equally or more representative of fair value than the market approach valuation technique used at prior measurement dates, which would now require significant ad-justments. Specifically, Entity A uses the discount rate adjustment technique described in Appendix B of Statement 157 to determine fair value.

Entity A determines that the appropriate discount rate to be used to dis-count the contractual cash flows of its collateralized debt obligation security is 22 percent after considering the following:

- The implied rate of return at the last date on which the market was considered active for the collateralized debt obligation security was 15 percent. Based on an analysis of available observable inputs for mortgage-related debt securities, Entity A determines that market rates of return generally have increased in the marketplace since the last date on which the market was considered active for the collateralized debt obligation security. Entity A estimates that credit spreads have widened by approximately 100 basis points and liquidity risk premiums have increased during that period by approximately 400 basis points. Other risks (for example, interest rate risk) have not changed. Using this information, Entity A estimates that an indication of an appropriate rate of return for the collateralized debt obligation security is 20 percent. In making that determination, Entity A considered all available market information that could be obtained without undue cost and effort. For this collateralized debt obligation security, the available market information used in assessing the risks in the security (including nonperformance risk [for example, default risk and collateral value risk], and liquidity risk) included:

- Quoted prices that are not current for the same or similar collateralized debt obligation securities
- Relevant reports issued by analysts and ratings agencies
- The current level of interest rates and any directional movements in relevant indexes, such as credit risk indexes
- Information about the performance of the underlying mortgage loans, such as delinquency and foreclosure rates, loss experience, and prepayment rates
- Other relevant observable inputs
- Two indicative quotes (that is, nonbinding quotes) for the collateralized debt obligation security from brokers imply a rate of return of 23 percent and 27 percent. The indicative quotes are based on proprietary pricing models utilizing significant unobservable inputs (that is, Level 3 inputs), rather than actual transactions.

Because Entity A has multiple indications of the appropriate rate of return that market participants would consider relevant in estimating fair value, it evaluates and weighs, as appropriate, the respective indications of the appropriate rate of return, considering the reasonableness of the range indicated by the results. Entity A concludes that 22 percent is the point within the range of relevant inputs that is most representative of fair value in the circumstances.

Entity A placed more weight on the 20 percent estimated rate of return (that is, its own estimate) because (a) the indications of an appropriate rate of return provided by the broker quotes were nonbinding quotes based on the brokers' own models using significant unobservable inputs, and (b) Entity A was able to corroborate some of the inputs, such as default rates, with relevant observable market data, which it used to make significant adjustments to the implied rate of return when the market was last considered active.

In accordance with the requirements of Statement 157, Entity A determines that the risk-adjusted discount rate appropriately reflects the reporting entity's estimate of the assumptions that market participants would use to estimate the selling price of the asset at the measurement date. Risks incorporated in the discount rate include nonperformance risk (for example, default risk and collateral value risk) and liquidity risk (that is, the FSP on FAS 157 [FSP FAS 157-3], compensation that a market participant receives for buying an asset that is difficult to sell under current market conditions).[12]

Study on Mark-to-Market Accounting

The Emergency Stabilization Act of 2008 required the Securities and Exchange Commission (SEC) to conduct a study on "mark-to-market" accounting applicable to financial institutions. Section 133 of the Act specifically called for the following:

> STUDY. The Securities and Exchange Commission, in consultation with the Board [of Governors of the Federal Reserve System] and the Secretary [of the Treasury], shall conduct a study on mark-to-market accounting standards as provided in Statement Number 157 of the Financial Accounting Standards Board, as such standards are applicable to financial institutions, including depository institutions. Such a study shall consider at a minimum:
> - The effects of such accounting standards on a financial institution's balance sheet
> - The impacts of such accounting on bank failures in 2008
> - The impact of such standards on the quality of financial information available to investors
> - The process used by the Financial Accounting Standards Board in developing accounting standards
> - The advisability and feasibility of modifications to such standards
> - lternative accounting standards to those provided in such Statement Number 157
>
> REPORT. The Securities and Exchange Commission shall submit to Congress a report of such study before the end of the 90-day period beginning on the date of the enactment of this Act containing the findings and determinations of the Commission, including such administrative and legislative recommendations as the Commission determines appropriate.[13]

Conclusion of the Report

On December 30, 2008, the Securities and Exchange Commission's Office of the Chief Accountant and Division of Corporate Finance delivered a report to Congress recommending against the suspension of fair value accounting standards.

Among key findings, the report notes that investors generally believe fair value accounting increases financial reporting transparency and facilitates better decision making. The report also observes that fair value accounting did not appear to play a meaningful role in the bank failures that occurred in 2008. Rather, the report indicates that bank failures in the United States appeared to be the result of growing probable credit losses, concerns about asset quality, and in certain cases eroding lender and investor confidence.[14]

Other highlights of the report include:

- SFAS No. 157 applications should be improved, but not suspended. Other improvements would include better understanding the impact of fair value through presentation and disclosure improvements.
- Existing fair values and mark-to-market requirements should not be suspended.
- Additional measures should be taken to improve the application of existing fair value requirements, particularly as they relate to Level 2 and Level 3 estimates. Such measures may include additional assistance in the form of guidance, education, and training for issuers and auditors in applying SFAS No. 157.
- The accounting for financial asset impairments should be readdressed. The FASB should reassess current impairment accounting models for financial instruments by narrowing the number of models that currently exist in U.S. GAAP.
- Implement further guidance to foster the use of sound judgment. This is particularly directed to the SEC and the PCAOB as to whether statements of policy related to the application of judgment in making value measures would be appropriate.
- Accounting standards should continue to be established to meet the needs of investors. U.S. GAAP should not be established or modified to serve the needs of others (i.e., regulators) at the expense of investors.
- Additional formal measures to address the operation of existing accounting standards in practice should be established. Specifically mentioned are implementation of the SEC Advisory Committee on Improvements to Financial Reporting (CIFiR)'s recommendation for a Financial Reporting Forum, implementation by the FASB of a post-adoption review process, and establishment of a formal policy for standard-setting in circumstances that necessitate near-immediate response.
- Address the need to simplify the accounting for investments in financial assets by continuing the joint work by the boards (FASB and IASB). The boards should also complete the measurement phase of the conceptual

framework project in order to inform future decision-makers about appropriate measurement attributes in accounting standards.[15]

New FASB Project to Improve Measurement and Disclosure of Fair Value Estimates

The FASB added a new project to its agenda on February 18, 2009, in response to the recommendations contained in the SEC study on mark-to-market accounting and based on input from the FASB's Valuation Resource Group. The project is intended to improve the application guidance used to determine fair values and disclosures for fair value estimates. Specific issues to be addressed include:

- The projects on application guidance will address determining when a market for an asset or a liability is active or inactive; determining when a transaction is distressed; and applying fair value to interests in alternative investments, such as hedge funds and private equity funds.
- The project on improving disclosures about fair value measurements will consider requiring additional disclosures on such matters as sensitivities of measurements to key inputs and transfers of items between the fair value measurement levels.[16]

This project initiative evolved into what the FASB refers to as the Credit Crisis Projects. As this book goes to press, five of the Credit Crisis Projects have been completed, and they are discussed in the following section. The five completed projects are:

FSP FAS 157-4, *Determining Fair Value When the Volume and Level of Activity for the Asset or Liability Have Significantly Decreased and Identifying Transactions That Are Not Orderly*, which is included in Accounting Standards Codification in section 820-10-65-4.

FSP FAS 115-2 and FAS 124-2, *Recognition and Presentation of Other-Than-Temporary Impairments,* which is located at ASC 350-50-1&2

FSP FAS 107-1 and APB 28-1, *Interim Disclosures about Fair Value of Financial Instruments,* which is located at ASC 825-10-65

Accounting Standard Update 2009–05, *Measuring Liabilities at Fair Value,* was originally proposed as FSP FAS 157-c, and then as FSP FAS 157-f. This credit crisis issue has received a significant amount of attention and public comment. ASU 2009–05 is discussed in Chapter 1, in the section entitled Application of Fair Value to Liabilities.

Accounting Standard Update 2009–12, *Investments in Certain Entities That Calculate Net Asset Value per Share (or Its Equivalent),*was originally proposed as FSP FASB 157-g, *Estimating the Fair Value of Investments in Companies That Have Calculated Net Asset Value per Share in Accordance with the AICPA Audit and Accounting Guide, Investment Companies.* ASU 2009–12 is discussed in Chapter 9, "Fair Value Measurements of Private Equity and Other Alternative Investments.

The FASB's pending Credit Crisis Projects, and the status of these projects is summarized as follows:

Improving Disclosures about Fair Value Measurements. Although the Board has not issued an Accounting Standards Update relating to this topic, it has reached some tentative decisions as the result of feedback it received from preparers about the operationality of proposed disclosures. The Board's tentative decisions are covered in Chapter 11, "Disclosures in Fair Value Measurement: in the section entitled "FAS 157—*Improving Disclosures about Fair Value Measurements.*"

A final credit crisis project with relevance to Fair Value Measurement is *Recoveries of Other-Than-Temporary Impairments (Reversals).* The FASB is considering whether to allow an entity to recover, through earnings, a previously recognized other-than-temporary impairment loss on certain financial instruments. The Board is delaying work on this project until decisions are reached on the joint FASB IASB project Financial Instruments: Improvement to Recognition and Measurement.[17]

Additional FASB Staff Positions (FSPs) to Improve Guidance on Fair Value Measurements and Impairments

On March 17, 2009, in response to the recommendations proposed by the Securities and Exchange Commission's study on mark-to-market accounting standards, the FASB issued two proposed staff positions that are intended to provide further guidance on the implementation of fair value measurements, particularly in a distressed market. The first proposed staff position is FSP 157-e, *Determining Whether a Market Is Not Active and a Transaction Is Not Distressed*, addresses the fair value measurement of an asset, which appears not to be distressed, yet the market for that particular asset is not active as of the measurement date. Financial statement preparers were concerned that

FAS 157-3 did not provide enough guidance on how to determine whether a once active market for a financial asset would be considered not active as of the measurement date, and if the market is considered not active, whether a transaction that would normally occur in that market would be considered distressed. There was also a concern that the Statement 157, fair value hierarchy encouraged the use of an observable market transaction even when the transaction might be distressed or the market for that transaction might not be active. Finally, financial statement preparers and users believe that emphasis on using the so-called last transaction price as the sole or primary basis for fair value measurement has resulted in an inappropriate application of fair value measurement to certain financial assets.

The SEC study on mark-to-market accounting suggests that "additional measures should be taken to improve the application and practice related to existing fair value requirements (particularly as they relate to both Level 2 and Level 3 estimates)." This recommendation further notes that "fair value requirements should be improved through development of application and best practices guidance for determining fair value in illiquid or inactive markets."[18]

In an expedited standards setting process, FAS FSP 157-e was issued on April 9, 2009, as FAS FSP 157-4, *Determining Fair Value When the Volume and Level of Activity for the Asset or Liability Have Significantly Decreased and Identifying Transactions That Are Not Orderly*. The guidance provided by this standard is covered in the next section.

The second expedited standard was also proposed on March 17th. FSPs FAS 115-a, FAS 124-a, and EITF 99-20-b, *Recognition and Presentation of Other-Than-Temporary Impairments*, addresses accounting for impairment losses on securities. It was issued on April 9th as FSP FAS 115-2 and FAS 124-2 under the same title. A final Credit Crisis project was also completed and issued on April 9th. FSP FAS 107-1, *Interim Disclosures about Fair Value of Financial Instruments*, is designed to improve the transparency and quality of fair value disclosures and provide them on an interim basis. Both of these new standards are discussed further in the next section.[19]

FSP FAS 157-4, *Determining Fair Value When Volume and Activity Have Significantly Decreased and Identifying Transactions That Are Not Orderly*

When there has been a significant decrease in the volume and level of activity for an asset or liability, the objective of fair value measurement is to determine the price that would be received when selling the asset in an *orderly transaction* between market participants under *current* market conditions. The objective has not changed, even though market conditions may have changed. When weighing indications of fair value from multiple valuation techniques, the reasonableness of the range of values must be considered. The goal is to determine the point within the range of values that is most representative of fair value. The reporting entity's intention to hold the asset or liability is not relevant when estimating fair value, as it is a market-based measurement not an entity-specific measurement. FSP 157-4 applies to Level 2 and Level 3 assets and liabilities.

The first step in applying FSP 157-4 is to determine whether there has been a decrease in the volume and level of activity in relation to a normal market. The following factors, while not all-inclusive, provide an indication as to the relative activity of the market for a particular financial asset:

- Few recent transactions (based on volume and level of activity in the market). Thus, there is not sufficient frequency and volume to provide pricing information on an ongoing basis.
- Price quotations are not based on current information.
- Price quotations vary substantially either over time or among market makers (for example, some brokered markets).
- Indexes that previously were highly correlated with the fair values of the asset are demonstrably uncorrelated with recent fair values.
- A significant increase in implied liquidity risk premiums, yields, or performance indicators (such as delinquency rates or loss severities) for observed transactions or quoted prices when compared with the reporting entity's estimate of expected cash flows.
- A wide bid-ask spread or significant increases in the bid-ask spread.
- A significant decline or absence of a market for new issuances (a primary market) for similar assets or liabilities.
- Little information is released publicly (for example, a principal-to-principal market).

While the above list provides guidance about the characteristics of a market with a significant decrease in volume and activity, the preparer must still evaluate the relevance of the factors. If the preparer concludes the market has experienced a significant decrease in volume and activity, then transactions or quoted prices may not be determinative of fair value, and the prepare goes to step two to determine whether the transaction is orderly, or not. The circumstances that indicate a transaction is *not* orderly are:

a. There was not adequate exposure to the market before the measurement date to allow for usual and customary marketing activities for the transactions involving such asset or liabilities under current market conditions.

b. There was a usual and customary marketing period, but the seller marketed the asset or liability to a single-market participant.
c. The seller is in or near bankruptcy or receivership (distressed), or the seller was required to meet regulatory or legal requirements (forced).
d. The transaction price is an outlier when compared to other recent transactions for the same or similar asset or liability.

When determining whether a transaction is orderly, a reporting entity shall not ignore information that is available without undue cost and effort, but need not undertake all possible efforts.

FAS 157-4 provides the following guidance for using the transaction price depending on whether the transaction is orderly when there is a significant decrease in the volume and activity of a market:

- When the transaction is not orderly, the preparer should place little if any weight on that transaction price when estimating fair value.
- When the transaction is orderly, the preparer shall consider the transaction price when estimating fair value. Adjustments to the transaction price may be appropriate. The amount of weight placed on the transaction price when compared to other indications of fair value from multiple valuation techniques shall depend on the facts and circumstances, including the relative volume in the market and the proximity of the transaction date to the measurement date. Regardless of the valuation technique, the fair value measurement should include an appropriate risk adjustment reflecting a market participant's premium for uncertain cash flows.
- If there is insufficient information to conclude that the transaction is orderly, or not, then the transaction price shall be considered when estimating fair value. However, that transaction price may not be the sole or primary basis for determining fair value.[20]

FSP FAS 115-2, *Recognition of Other-Than-Temporary Impairments*

FASB Staff Position FAS 115-2, FAS 124-2, *Recognition and Presentation of Other-Than-Temporary Impairments*, amends current U.S. GAAP with respect to the recognition of other-than-temporary impairments for debt securities classified as available-for-sale and held-to-maturity. It also provides new guidance for determining when an "other-than-temporary" (permanent) impairment exists for debt securities.

A debt security is considered impaired if its fair value is less than its amortized cost. The impairment is considered other-than-temporary (permanent) if:

- The entity intends to sell the security.
- It is probable that the entity will have to sell the security before recovering its amortized cost basis.
- The entity does not expect to recover the entire amortized cost basis.
- A credit loss exists, which occurs if the present value of cash flows expected to be collected is less than the amortized cost basis.

FSP FAS 115-2 prescribes new treatment for the recognition of other-than-temporary (permanent) impairments. The amount of the impairment recognized in earnings depends on the entity's intent and ability to hold the security and recover its amortized cost basis:

- If the entity intends to sell the security or will be forced to sell the security before recovering its amortized cost basis, the impairment shall be recognized in earnings. The amount of the impairment is equal to the difference between its amortized cost basis and its fair value on the balance sheet date.
- If the entity intends to hold the security and it is probable that the entity will be able to hold the security and recover its amortized cost basis (less current period credit loss), then the impairment should be separated and reported as follows:
  - The amount representing the current period credit loss shall be recognized in earnings.
  - The remainder shall be recognized in other comprehensive income (equity), net of taxes.

The new cost basis would equal the old cost basis less the impairment recognized in earnings. The new cost basis would not be adjusted for subsequent recoveries of fair value.[21]

FSP FAS 107-1, *Interim Disclosures about Fair Value of Financial Instruments*

The purpose of FAS 107-1 is to require disclosures about the fair value of financial instruments in interim and annual financial statements to improve the transparency and quality of information provided to financial statement users. Most users believe that fair value measurement is more relevant for assessing the effect of current economic events on financial instruments. Users believe this disclosure is particularly important given the lack of comparability among different measurement attributes used by entities to report financial instruments.

The amendment to Statement 107 requires disclosure of fair value in annual statements and whenever summarized financial information is issued for interim periods. Entities must report the fair value of financial instruments in either the body of the financial statements or in the footnotes, when it is practicable to estimate that value. The methods and assumptions used to estimate fair value must also be disclosed. The fair value must be presented with the carrying value and the entity must clearly indicate how the carrying value relates to the statement of financial position.[22]

Financial Crisis Advisory Group (FCAG)

In response to the current financial crisis, the FASB and IASB recently formed a Financial Crisis Advisory Group in early 2009. The group is composed of senior business leaders both within and outside the accounting profession with broad experience with international financial markets. The purpose of the group is to advise both boards about standard-setting implications of:

- The global financial crisis
- Potential changes to the global regulatory environment[23]

The mission of the group is to provide recommendations as to how enhancing transparency and reducing complexity in financial reporting can serve the financial markets and restore investor confidence in those markets. The group conducted several advisory meetings during the first half of 2009 to address the following issues:

- Areas in which financial reporting helped identify issues of concern, or may have created unnecessary concerns during the credit crisis
- Areas in which financial reporting standards could have provided more transparency to help anticipate the crisis or respond to the crisis more quickly
- Whether priorities for the IASB and the FASB should be reconsidered in light of the credit crisis
- Potential areas that require future attention of the IASB and the FASB to avoid future market disruption
- The implications of the credit crisis for the interaction between general purpose financial reporting requirements for capital markets and regulatory reporting, particularly for financial institutions
- The relationship between fair value and off-balance-sheet accounting and the current crisis, both during and leading up to the crisis

- The findings and relevance of conclusions of various studies underway, including the U.S. Securities and Exchange Commission study under the Emergency Economic Stabilization Act of 2008
- The need for due process for accounting standard setters and its implications on resolving emergency issues on a timely and inclusive basis
- The independence of accounting standard setters and governmental actions to the global financial crisis[24]

The Group published its recommendations on July 28, 2009. The report is organized into four main principles and contains recommendations to improve the functioning and effectiveness of global standard setting. In his comments about the report, Hans Hoogervorst, the co-chairman of the FCAG, emphasized the importance of broadly accepted accounting standards that are the result of thorough due process. He said, "The report highlights the importance but also the limits of financial reporting. Accounting was not the root cause of the financial crisis, but it has an important roll to play in its resolution."[25]

Conclusion

Fair value measurements as they may apply in an illiquid market may be summarized by reference to the fair value measurement concepts stressed in FSP 157-3. These concepts reinforce those introduced in SFAS 157. The FSP describes how assumptions as to a fair value measurement may apply in situations where there may not be an active market price.

> *A fair value measurement represents the price at which a transaction would occur between market participants at the measurement date. As discussed in Statement 157, in situations in which there is little, if any, market activity for an asset at the measurement date, the fair value measurement objective remains the same, that is, the price that would be received by the holder of the financial asset in an orderly transaction (an exit price notion) that is not a forced liquidation or distressed sale at the measurement date.*
>
> *Even in times of market dislocation, it is not appropriate to conclude that all market activity represents forced liquidations or distressed sales.* However, it is also not appropriate to automatically conclude that any transaction price is determinative of fair value *(emphasis added). Determining fair value in a dislocated market depends on the facts and circumstances and may require the use of significant judgment about whether individual transactions are forced liquidations or distressed sales.*

In determining fair value for a financial asset, the use of a reporting entity's own assumptions about future cash flows and appropriately risk-adjusted discount rates is acceptable when relevant observable inputs are not available. (Emphasis added) *Statement 157 discusses a range of information and valuation techniques that a reporting entity might use to estimate fair value when relevant observable inputs are not available. In some cases an entity may determine that observable inputs (Level 2) require significant adjustment based on unobservable data and thus would be considered a Level 3 fair value measurement. For example, in cases where the volume and level of trading activity in the asset have declined significantly, the available prices vary significantly over time or among market participants, or the prices are not current, the observable inputs might not be relevant and could require significant adjustment. Regardless of the valuation technique used, an entity must include appropriate risk adjustments that market participants would make for nonperformance and liquidity risks.*[26]

The FSP actually strengthens the concepts behind the definition of fair value introduced by SFAS 157. The FSP notes that the fair value hierarchy is applicable to the assumptions in measuring fair value in illiquid markets. However, in illiquid or nonactive markets, Level 1 or Level 2 assumption in the fair value hierarchy may not be available. Whether Level 1 or Level 2 assumptions are available in those circumstances may require some judgment. An example of one such circumstance is in nonactive markets where there is limited information as to a price in the market that would provide an indication of an exit price that a market participant could (or would) sell the asset. In these circumstances, a holder of a specific asset may realize a much greater value by holding the asset to maturity and realizing a return on those assets rather than sell it in an unfavorable market. If these circumstances of an illiquid or nonactive market exist and market participants would hold on to those assets rather than try to sell in a distressed market, then the value indicated by holding the asset is a better indication of fair value measurement. The fair value measurement in those circumstances would be considered a Level 3 measurement in the fair value hierarchy. Fair value would be the present value of those cash flows resulting from holding the asset to maturity discounted at rate of return adjusted for the risk of actually receiving those cash flows given expected market conditions.

Notes

1. "Measurement of Fair Value in Illiquid (or Less Liquid) Markets," CAQ Alert #2007-51, Center for Audit Quality (October 3, 2007), www.aicpa.org.

2. "Fair Value Accounting: Is It Helpful in Illiquid Markets?" FitchRatings Accounting Research Special Report (April 2008), www.fitchratings.com.
3. FASB SFAS 157 (ASC 820), paragraph 5.
4. *Id.*, paragraph 7.
5. "CAQ Issues White Papers on Illiquidity in the Markets," CAQ Alert # 2007-51, Center for Audit Quality (October 3, 2007).
6. "Measurements of Fair Value in Illiquid (or Less Liquid) Markets," Center for Audit Quality (October 3, 2007).
7. "The Accounting Implications of Illiquid Markets," KPMG Defining Issues (October 2007), No. 07-03.
8. Federal Reserve Chairman Ben S. Bernanke's testimony to the Senate Banking Committee on September 23, 2008.
9. "SEC Office of the Chief Accountant and FASB Staff Clarifications on Fair Value Accounting, 2008-234," September 30, 2008.
10. "Joint Statement of the Center for Audit Quality, the Council of Institutional Investors and the CFA Institute Opposing Suspension of Mark-to-Market Accounting," October 1, 2008.
11. FASB FSP 157-3.
12. *Id.*, paragraph 11.
13. www.sec.gov/spotlight/fairvalue/htm.
14. "Congressionally-Mandated Study Says Improve, Do Not Suspend, Fair Value Accounting," www.sec.gov/news/press/2008/2008-307.htm.
15. "Report and Recommendations Pursuant to Section 133 of the Emergency Economic Stabilization Act of 2008: Study on Mark-to-Market Accounting," Office of the Chief Accountant, Division of Corporate Finance, United States Securities and Exchange Commission, December 30, 2008.
16. "FASB Initiates Projects to Improve Measurement and Disclosure of Fair Value Estimates," FASB News Release 2/18/09, www.fasb.org.
17. FASB Projects—Technical Plans and Project Updates, http://www.fasb.org/jsp/FASB/Page/SecctionPage&cid=1176156240004, accessed 10/2/09.
18. "Report and Recommendations Pursuant to Section 133 of the Emergency Economic Stabilization Act of 2008: Study on Mark-to-Market Accounting," SEC (December 30, 2008).
19. FASB Projects.
20. FASB FSP 157-4, *Determining Fair Value When Volume and Activity Have Significantly Decreased and Identifying Transactions That Are Not Orderly.*
21. FASB FSP FAS 115-2, FAS124-2, *Recognition and Presentation of Other-Than-Temporary Impairments.*
22. FASB FSP FAS 107-2, *Interim Disclosures about Fair Value of Financial Instruments.*
23. Financial Crisis Advisory Group (FCAG), *Financial Accounting Standards Board*, www.fasb.org/fcag/index.shtml.
24. *Id.*
25. Finacial Crisis Advisory Group, Press Release dated 28 July 2009, "FCAG publishes wide-ranging review of standard-setting activities following the global financial crisis.", www.fasb.org/fcag.org
26. FASB FSP 157-3, paragraph 9.

Fair Value Measurements in Business Combinations and Subsequent Testing for Impairment

The Financial Accounting Standards Board (FASB) issued statement FASB ASC 805 (SFAS 141(R)), *Business Combinations,* which revises the accounting for business combinations for fiscal years beginning after December 15, 2008. According to the FASB, there are three fundamental objectives in revising the guidance for accounting for business combinations. First, FASB ASC 805, *Business Combinations*, is designed to improve the transparency of financial reporting and provide investors with a more accurate representation of the true costs of mergers and acquisitions through financial statement recognition and measurement of "identifiable assets acquired, liabilities assumed, and any noncontrolling interest in the acquiree."[1] Second, the acquirer recognizes goodwill when the consideration paid exceeds the fair value of acquired assets, which is consistent with past treatment. However, under SFAS 141(R), when there is a bargain purchase price and the fair values of the assets acquired are greater than the consideration given up, then the acquirer recognizes a gain equal to the excess fair value. Negative goodwill is no longer recognized under *Business Combinations*. Third, improved financial statement disclosure requirements will provide sufficient information to enable financial statement users to evaluate the nature and resulting financial effect of the business combination.[2]

The statement also improves the comparability of financial statements internationally. FASB ASC 805 (SFAS No. 141(R)), *Business Combinations*, is a joint effort of the FASB and the International Accounting Standards Board (IASB) and was the first statement issued under the convergence project between the FASB and the IASB. The IASB issued a similar revised statement on accounting for business combinations, IFRS 3, *Business Combinations*.

Accounting for Business Combinations

The accounting standard for business combinations prior to the introduction of SFAS 141, *Business Combinations,* was Accounting Principles Board (APB) No. 16. Under APB 16, two methods of accounting for a business combination were allowed: (1) the purchase method and (2) the pooling method. Strict criteria had to be met in order to use the pooling method; otherwise, the purchase method was required. Under the pooling of interests method, one entity is combined with another by adding its respective book values and its historic operating results. Under the purchase method, one entity acquires another. The acquiring company includes the acquired company's assets in the financial statements at fair value, just as it would any other asset it purchased. Historic operating results are not combined. Post-merger, historic income statements represent the acquiring company's operating results alone.

Because there were two methods permitted under APB 16, accounting for business combinations was inconsistent. The financial reporting of a combination that met the requirements for pooling was materially different than one that was recorded under the purchase method. In addition to the purchase versus pooling inconsistency, the FASB observed that in many business combinations, the acquired company's intangible assets accounted for most of the transaction's economic value. The use of the purchase accounting method under APB 16 resulted in much, or most, of the transaction's value being recorded on the balance sheet as goodwill. Since transactions are made for reasons other than the acquisition of goodwill, the FASB concluded that APB 16 did not fairly represent the economic substance of business combinations.[3]

APB 16 provided too much ambiguity in reporting the fair value of intangible assets in a business combination. Under APB 16, most of the purchase price was being allocated to and recorded as goodwill, which could then be amortized for up to 40 years. In order to correct these financial reporting inconsistencies, the FASB issued SFAS 141, *Business Combinations*, the original FASB standard for business combinations, on June 29, 2001. SFAS 141 introduced two significant changes to accounting for business combinations. First, it eliminated the pooling of interests method and required purchase accounting for all business combinations. The FASB believes that the purchase method of accounting provides a better representation of the true economic substance of the underlying transaction and is therefore more relevant than the pooling method that presents the combined transaction on a purely historical cost basis. Second, the original SFAS 141 placed more stringent requirements for the recognition of acquired intangible assets on the acquiring company's financial statements. Paragraph 39 in SFAS 141 requires that:

An intangible asset shall be recognized as an asset apart from goodwill if it arises from contractual or other legal rights or, if not contractual, only if it is capable of being sold, transferred, licensed, rented or exchanged. An assembled and trained workforce, however, is not valued separately from goodwill.[4]

In spite of improvements to business combination accounting, purchase accounting under SFAS 141 still has some limitations. One significant shortcoming is inconsistency with international accounting standards. The FASB resolved this problem by issuing a revised statement on business combinations as part of the convergence project with the IASB. The FASB and the IASB issued almost identical statements that require the acquiring entity in a business combination to recognize all, and only, those assets acquired and liabilities assumed in the transaction. The revised statement establishes the acquisition date fair value as the measurement objective for all assets acquired and liabilities assumed. The statement also requires disclosure of additional information that investors and other users might need to evaluate and understand the nature and financial effect of the business combination.[5]

Under the FASB's revised statement, FASB ASC 805 (SFAS 141(R)), *Business Combinations*, the accounting for a business combination is no longer considered to be purchase accounting. Instead, the revised statement introduces the "Acquisition Method" of accounting, which has broader application to all transactions where one entity gains control over another. Some of the other more important changes for business combinations under SFAS No. 141(R) are:

- The definition of a business and a business combination is revised.
- The fair value of the business combination will be measured at the fair value of the business acquired. Transaction-related costs will be expensed under FASB ASC 805, *Business Combinations*, rather than capitalized. Also the fair value of any contingent consideration will be recognized as of the date of the acquisition.
- Restructuring costs that the acquirer expects to incur but is not obligated to incur may no longer be treated as though it is a liability assumed at the acquisition date. Instead, SFAS 141(R) requires that restructuring costs be recognized separately from the business combination.
- The measurement date of the business combination is the date that the acquirer achieves control, which may not necessarily be the date that the acquisition closes.

- In-process research and development will be recognized as an asset in a business combination rather than expensed, as was required under previous accounting pronouncements.
- In a business combination with a "bargain purchase price," acquired assets will no longer be recorded at values below their fair values. Instead, the difference between the sum of the fair value of the assets acquired and the fair value of the consideration given will result in the recognition of an acquisition date gain in earnings.
- Partial acquisitions, where the acquirer purchases less than 100 percent of the target company's shares, and step acquisitions, where the acquirer gains control of the target company through a series of noncontrolling acquisitions, receive new treatment. The acquirer must recognize 100 percent of the fair value of acquired assets and liabilities assumed as of the acquisition date. The fair value of the noncontrolling interest must be recognized in shareholders' equity, as a separate line item.
- The measurement period is more strictly defined and the statement places greater emphasis on recording post-acquisition adjustments to acquisition date values, valuation allowances, and contingencies in the income statement.
- The statement changes a number of items that create deferred tax assets and liabilities as a result of purchase accounting. In addition, remeasurement of tax accounts from previous acquisitions due to the settlement of tax contingencies will impact the income statement. As a result of these changes, the tax provision and effective tax rate will require additional consideration.

The Acquisition Method

FASB ASC 805 (SFAS 141(R)), *Business Combinations,* introduces the acquisition method of accounting for business combinations. The statement identifies four required steps to apply the acquisition method:

1. Identify the acquirer.
2. Determine the acquisition date.
3. Recognize and measure the identifiable assets acquired, the liabilities assumed, and any noncontrolling interest in the acquiree.
4. Recognize and measure goodwill or a gain from a bargain purchase.[6]

Identifying the Acquirer

An initial difference between FASB ASC 805 (SFAS 141(R), *Business Combinations,* and its predecessor is that there was no definitive guidance for identifying the acquirer under the previous statement. Identification of the acquirer is important under the revised statement because the acquisition method does not permit "mergers of equals" in a business combination. Under the acquisition method, one entity acquires another. A key concept in the revised statement is that a business combination occurs when one business entity gains control over another business entity. The entity gaining control is considered the acquirer.

Identifying the acquirer may not be as easy as it seems, particularly in a situation where a business combination transpires through the exchange of equity interests. In an exchange of equity transaction, one of the ways to identify the acquirer is to look at the relative voting rights in the combined entity after the combination. Examining relative voting rights is particularly useful when there is no controlling group. The acquirer will be the group with the largest voting interest after the combination. Another way to determine the acquirer is to look at the composition of the combined organization's governing body. The acquirer will be the entity with the ability to elect the largest number of members to the combined entity's board of directors.

The recent merger of Delta Airlines and Northwest Airlines provides a real-life example that will be used throughout the remainder of this chapter to illustrate some of the important concepts in SFAS 141(R).

DELTA: IDENTIFYING THE ACQUIRER   In April 2008, Delta issued a press release that said in part:

> *Delta Air Lines Inc. (NYSE: DAL) and Northwest Airlines Corporation (NYSE: NWA) today announced an agreement in which the two carriers will combine in an all-stock transaction with a combined enterprise value of $17.7 billion, creating America's premier global airline.[7]*

Based on the wording in the first sentence of the press release, it is difficult to determine which airline is the acquirer for business combination accounting purposes. However the press release goes on to say, "The new airline, which will be called Delta," will have a management structure where, "Delta CEO Richard Anderson will be chief executive officer of the combined company. Delta Chairman of the Board Daniel Carp will become chairman of the new Board of Directors and Northwest Chairman Roy Bostock will become vice chairman." The press release further describes the composition of the combined board of directors as being "made up of 13 members, seven of whom will come from Delta's board, including Anderson, and five of whom will come from Northwest's board, including Bostock and Doug Steenland, the current Northwest CEO. One director will come from the Air Line Pilots Association (ALPA).[8]

Since the management of the combined airline will be led by the Delta Chairman and since Delta will have the majority of the representation on the new board of directors, it appears that Delta would be considered the acquirer for business combination accounting purposes, even though the combination is described as a *merger*.

Acquisition Date

One of the important changes introduced by FASB ASC 805 (SFAS 141(R)), *Business Combinations,* is the identification of the business combination's measurement date. Under the revised statement, the acquisition date is the date on which the acquirer obtains control of the acquired company. FASB ASC 805, *Business Combinations,* says that change of control typically is demonstrated when the acquirer transfers the consideration and obtains responsibility for the assets acquired and liabilities assumed. Often, the transfer of consideration and assumption of control occurs on the closing date of the transaction. However, this may not necessarily always be the case. There may be situations when the acquirer obtains effective control prior to the closing date. Under FASB ASC 805, *Business Combinations,* the measurement date is the date of the change of control.

DELTA: CHANGE OF CONTROL   Delta's Form 10-K for 2008 provided information about the combined company's control structure resulting from the October 28, 2008, merger by saying:

> On the Closing Date, Northwest became a wholly-owned subsidiary of Delta ... Pursuant to the Merger Agreement, each share of Northwest common stock outstanding on the Closing Date or issuable under Northwest's Plan of Reorganization was converted into the right to receive 1.25 shares of Delta common stock. We issued, or expect to issue, a total of 339 million shares of Delta common stock for these purposes, or approximately 41% of the sum of the shares of Delta common stock (1) outstanding on the Closing Date (including shares issued to Northwest stockholders in the Merger), (2) issuable in exchange for shares of Northwest common stock reserved for issuance under Northwest's Plan of Reorganization, (3) reserved for issuance under Delta's Plan of Reorganization and (4) issuable to our employees in connection with the Merger.[9]

Recognize and Measure the Identifiable Assets Acquired, the Liabilities Assumed, and Any Noncontrolling Interest in the Acquiree

In a business combination, identifiable assets acquired and liabilities assumed must meet the definition of assets and liabilities in FASB Concepts

Statement No. 6, *Elements of Financial Statements,* as of the date of the change of control. As a result of the business combination, some assets may be recognized that were not previously recognized by the acquired company because they were developed internally and the costs to develop the assets were expensed.

FASB ASC 805 (SFAS 141(R)), *Business Combinations,* extends the identification criteria first introduced by SFAS 141. An intangible asset is considered identifiable in a business combination if it meets either the separability criterion or the contractual-legal criterion. An intangible asset is identifiable if it:

(1) Is separable, that is, capable of being separated or divided from the entity and sold, transferred, licensed, rented, or exchanged, either individually or together with a related contract, identifiable asset, or liability, regardless of whether the entity intends to do so. Or, it
(2) Arises from contractual or other legal rights, regardless of whether those rights are transferable or separable from the entity or from other rights and obligations.[10]

DELTA: FAIR VALUE OF ASSETS AND LIABILITIES Identifiable intangible assets acquired as part of a business combination are recorded at their respective fair value as of the measurement date. Delta's 10-K provides an example of this process.

On the Closing Date, Northwest revalued its assets and liabilities at fair value in accordance with Statement of Financial Accounting Standards (SFAS No. 141), Business Combinations. *These changes in value did not result in gains or losses, but were instead an input to the calculation of goodwill related to the excess of purchase price over the fair value of the tangible and identifiable intangible assets acquired and liabilities assumed from Northwest in the Merger. Additional changes in the fair values of these assets and liabilities from the current estimated values, as well as changes in other assumptions, could significantly impact the reported value of goodwill.*[11]

In accordance with SFAS 141, the purchase price allocation is subject to adjustment for up to one year after the Closing Date when additional information on asset and liability valuations becomes available. We have not finalized our review of certain liabilities recorded in the Merger. Any changes to the initial estimates of the fair value of the assets and liabilities will be recorded as adjustments to those assets and liabilities and residual amounts will be allocated to goodwill.

The excess of the purchase price over the fair values of the tangible and identifiable intangible assets acquired and liabilities assumed

*from Northwest in the Merger was allocated to goodwill. We believe that
the portion of the purchase price attributable to goodwill represents the
benefits expected to be realized from the Merger, as discussed above. This
goodwill is not deductible or amortizable for tax purposes.*[12]

The following table summarizes the identifiable intangible assets acquired as shown in Delta Airlines Form 10-K for the year ending December
31, 2008 (millions):

Indefinite Lived Intangible Assets	Gross Carrying Amount
International Routes and Slots	$2, 140
Sky Team Alliance	380
Domestic Routes and Slots	110
Other	1
Total Indefinite Lived Intangible Assets	$2, 631
Definite Lived Intangible Assets	
Northwest Trade Name	40
Marketing Agreements	27
Domestic Routes and Slots	4
Total Definite Lived Intangible Assets	71
Total Identifiable Intangible Assets	$2, 702

Source: Delta Airlines Form 10-K; www.sec.gov.

Recognize and Measure Goodwill or a Gain from Any Bargain Purchase

Goodwill is recognized under FASB ASC 805, *Business Combinations,* when
the fair value of the consideration transferred exceeds the sum of the fair
value of assets acquired and liabilities assumed. The fair value of the consideration transferred includes any noncontrolling interest and the fair value
of the acquirer's previously held interest, when applicable. If the sum of
the fair value of assets acquired and liabilities assumed is greater than the
fair value of the consideration transferred, then the business combination
is considered a bargain purchase. If it initially appears that the business
combination may result in a bargain purchase, then the statement suggests
that the acquirer reassess whether the assets acquired were correctly identified and the resulting fair value measurement was properly performed. The
purpose of the reconsideration is to ensure that all available information is
appropriately considered, as of the date of the business combination.

DELTA: RECOGNITION AND MEASUREMENT OF GOODWILL   Delta's December 31,
2008, Form 10-K indicates that:

*Goodwill reflects (1) the excess of the reorganization value of the Suc-
cessor over the fair value of tangible and identifiable intangible assets,*

net of liabilities, from the adoption of fresh start reporting, adjusted for impairment, and (2) the excess of purchase price over the fair values of the tangible and identifiable intangible assets acquired and liabilities assumed from Northwest in the Merger.

The following table of data from Delta's Form 10-K provides an example of financial reporting for a change in the carrying amount of goodwill resulting from a business combination:[13]

	Total (in millions)
Balance as of December 31, 2007	$12,104
Impairment Charge	(6,939)
Northwest Merger	4,572
Other	(6)
Balance as of December 31, 2008	$ 9,731

Source: Delta Airlines Form 10-K; www.sec.gov.

Definition of a Business

Under FASB ASC 805 (SFAS 141(R)), *Business Combinations,* a business is more strictly defined as "an integrated set of activities and assets that is capable of being conducted and managed for the purpose of providing a return in the form of dividends, lower costs, or economic benefits directly to investors or other owners, members, or participants."[14] The key provision in the definition that distinguishes it from the prior definition is that a business must be "capable of being conducted" and "managed to provide a return to investors." The FASB provides examples of business functions as those that are managed for lower costs, a capital return, or other economic benefit. The SFAS 141(R) revised definition of a business introduces the concept that a business is a set of activities.

The SFAS 141(R) definition of a business also removes the presumption that a business is a going concern. Under the new standard, goodwill and its underlying presumption that the entity is a going concern do not necessarily have to exist for something to be defined as a business. For example, now more early stage entities will be considered businesses even though there may be no enterprise value. The new, expanded definition of a business will likely increase the number of transactions that will be classified as business combinations. Intangible assets acquired in a transaction that does *not* qualify as a business combination are recognized in accordance with FASB ASC 350, *Intangibles—Goodwill and Other* (SFAS No. 142). Transactions that are not classified as a business combination will not have any residual goodwill.

A business combination is defined under FASB ASC 805, *Business Combinations,* as "a transaction or other event in which an acquirer obtains control of one or more businesses. Transactions sometimes referred to as 'true mergers' or 'mergers of equals' also are business combinations as that term is used in this Statement."[15] By modifying the definitions of a business and a business combination, the types of transactions that qualify as a business combination will increase. Under these expanded definitions, certain types of acquisitions that were previously classified as asset acquisition will now be considered business combinations.

Fair Value of the Business Acquired

The acquisition price under FASB ASC 805, *Business Combinations,* is generally the fair value of the consideration paid for the acquirer's interest in the acquired company. Payments for the acquired entity may include cash and other assets, equity interests, and contingent consideration. All consideration is measured at the fair value on the acquisition date. Under FASB ASC 805, *Business Combinations,* transaction costs are not included as part of the acquisition price as they were under previous accounting.

In many transactions, the terms of the merger agreement are structured to provide additional consideration to the business's former owners if the entity meets specified financial targets after the acquisition. This contingent consideration is beneficial to both parties in the business combination when the parties are unable to fully agree on an acquisition price. If a business combination has contingent consideration (sometimes referred to as an earn-out), it is recorded at fair value as of the acquisition date. The fair value of the contingent consideration, as with all fair value measurements, follows the guidance under FASB ASC 820 (SFAS 157), *Fair Value Measurements and Disclosures.* Under SFAS 157, the fair value is an exit price that would reflect the probability of payment. Any change in the fair value of contingent consideration is recorded in earnings. Previously, any change in value associated with contingent consideration was treated as adjustment to goodwill.

DELTA: FAIR VALUE OF THE MERGER TRANSACTION   Delta's Form 10-K describes the determination of the purchase price to effect its merger with Northwest. The purchase price represents the fair value of the merger transaction.

> *Pursuant to the Merger Agreement, each share of Northwest common stock outstanding on the Closing Date or issuable under Northwest's Plan of Reorganization was converted into the right to receive 1.25 shares of Delta common stock. We issued, or expect to issue, a total of 339 million shares of Delta common stock for these purposes, or*

approximately 41% of the sum of the shares of Delta common stock (1) outstanding on the Closing Date (including shares issued to Northwest stockholders in the Merger), (2) issuable in exchange for shares of Northwest common stock reserved for issuance under Northwest's Plan of Reorganization, (3) reserved for issuance under Delta's Plan of Reorganization and (4) issuable to our employees in connection with the Merger.

We accounted for the Merger in accordance with SFAS 141, whereby the purchase price paid to effect the Merger was allocated to the tangible and identifiable intangible assets acquired and liabilities assumed from Northwest based on their estimated fair values as of the Closing Date. For accounting purposes, the Merger was valued at $3.4 billion. This amount was derived from the 339 million shares of Delta common stock we issued or expect to issue, as discussed above, at a price of $9.60 per share, the average closing price of our common stock on the New York Stock Exchange for the five consecutive trading days that include the two trading days before, the day of and the two trading days after the public announcement of the Merger Agreement on April 14, 2008, and capitalized Merger-related transaction costs. The purchase price also includes the fair value of Delta stock options and other equity awards issued on the Closing Date in exchange for similar securities of Northwest. Northwest stock options and other equity awards vested on the Closing Date and were assumed by Delta and modified to provide for the purchase of Delta common stock. Accordingly, the number of shares and, if applicable, the price per share were adjusted for the 1.25 exchange ratio. Vested stock options held by employees of Northwest are considered part of the purchase price.[16]

Contingent Assets and Liabilities

Under FASB ASC 805 (SFAS 141(R)), *Business Combinations,* assets and liabilities of a contingent nature were to be recorded at their acquisition date fair values. The accounting pronouncement applied to all contractual contingencies and to noncontractual contingencies that were more likely to give rise to an asset or liability. Those noncontractual liabilities that did not meet the more-likely-than-not criterion would be accounted for under FASB Statement No. 5, *Accounting for Contingencies.*

However, in response to concerns raised by preparers, auditors, and members of the legal profession about difficulties in applying the standard, the FASB revised the statement with the issuance of FASB Staff Position FAS 141(R)-1, *Accounting for Assets Acquired and Liabilities Assumed in a Business Combination That Arise from Contingencies.* FASB FSP 141(R)-1 generally applies to acquired assets and liabilities arising from contingencies that would be within the scope of Statement No. 5, except for the fact that the assets and liabilities were acquired or assumed in a business combination.

FASB FSP 141(R)-1 stipulates that an acquisition date asset or liability shall be recognized if the acquisition date fair value can be determined before the end of the measurement period. If the acquisition date fair value cannot be determined before the end of the measurement period, then an asset or liability should be recognized at the acquisition date if both of the following criteria are met.

1. Information available before the end of the measurement period indicates that it is probable that an asset existed or a liability had been incurred at the acquisition date, and
2. The amount of the asset or liability can be reasonably estimated.

If both criteria are not met, the acquirer should not recognize the asset or liability as of the acquisition date.[17]

The provisions of SFAS 141(R) that provide guidance for contingent consideration in a business combination remain unchanged by SFAS FSP 141(R)-1. Contingent consideration is recognized as part of the consideration transferred in exchange for the acquiree. Subsequent changes in fair value resulting from events after the acquisition date are not treated as measurement period adjustments. Changes in the fair value of contingent consideration are recognized in earnings.[18]

In-Process Research and Development (IPR&D)

One interesting change under FASB ASC 805 (SFAS No. 141(R)), *Business Combinations,* is the measurement of In-Process Research and Development (IPR&D) acquired in a business combination. IPR&D is technology that is under development as of the measurement date, that is not currently feasible, and that is without any alternative future use.

Under Generally Accepted Accounting Principles (GAAP), the potential viability of technology under development is considered to be uncertain; therefore, costs of research and development are expensed as incurred. This conservative reasoning was extended to previous accounting for business combinations, which required IPR&D to be written off as of the date of the acquisition.

Now, under FASB ASC 805, *Business Combinations,* the acquirer will be required to recognize the fair value of IPR&D as an identifiable asset apart from goodwill. This revision to GAAP has created accounting inconsistencies in the treatment of IPR&D. Specifically, while IPR&D acquired in a business combination would be recognized as an asset apart from goodwill, subsequent expenditures for research and development would still be expensed. Also, if IPR&D is purchased as an asset apart from a business combination, the cost of the IPR&D would still be expensed.

Additional inconsistencies exist in impairment testing of IPR&D. Acquired IPR&D measured and recorded at fair value in a business combination is considered an indefinite lived intangible asset until the project has been completed or abandoned. Consequently, any test for impairment is based on IPR&D's fair value and is performed in accordance with SFAS 142, *Goodwill and Other Intangibles*. After the acquisition date, any additional costs to further develop the IPR&D are expensed, until there is a determination that the project is developed or is to be abandoned. Once IPR&D is considered to be "developed," then a life is assigned to the now developed technology. The project is amortized over its remaining life. The developed technology would then be tested for impairment under SFAS 144. Inconsistencies relating to the accounting treatment of IPR&D remain to be resolved by the FASB at a future date.

Subsequent Accounting for Goodwill and Other Intangible Assets

As mentioned, FASB ASC 350, *Intangibles—Goodwill and Other* (SFAS No. 142), was introduced by the FASB in response to comments received about the exposure draft introducing SFAS 141. Originally, the FASB intended for the fair value of goodwill to be measured in a business combination and amortized over its remaining life. However, respondents' comments indicated that they were concerned about the difficulty of measuring the fair value of goodwill and determining a remaining life. Financial analysts also indicated that they did not regard goodwill amortization expense as being useful information in analyzing investments. As a result, the FASB introduced a compromise. The requirement for amortization of goodwill was eliminated in the final version of SFAS 141. Instead, any goodwill recorded in a business combination will have to be tested for impairment at least annually, or more frequently, if necessary.

FASB ASC 350 (SFAS No. 142), *Goodwill and Other Intangibles,* describes the financial accounting and reporting for goodwill and other unidentified intangible assets that are acquired individually or with a group of other assets as the result of a business combination. It provides for the subsequent accounting treatment of goodwill and other intangible assets after they have been initially recognized in the financial statements.

The FASB explained that the reason for issuing FASB ASC 350 (SFAS No. 142) was that analysts and other users of financial statements, as well as company managements, recognized that intangible assets are an increasingly important economic resource for many entities and are an increasing proportion of the value of assets acquired in many transactions. As a result, better information about intangible assets was needed in financial reporting for business combinations.[19]

FASB ASC 350 (SFAS No. 142) improves financial reporting by recognizing the fair values of goodwill and other intangibles arising from the transaction and by reflecting the underlying economics of the acquisition more completely and accurately. As a result, the users of the financial information are better able to understand the investments made in those assets and the subsequent performance of those investments. Subsequent disclosures provide users with a better understanding about any changes in expectations for goodwill and intangibles over time, thereby improving their ability to assess future profitability and cash flows.[20]

GUIDANCE FOR IMPAIRMENT TESTING   The guidelines for testing impairments of intangible assets are found in two pronouncements: FASB ASC 350, *Goodwill and Other Intangibles* (SFAS No. 142), and *General Intangibles Other than Goodwill* (SFAS No. 144). FASB ASC 350 (SFAS No. 144) describes impairment testing for long-lived assets, including both intangible assets and tangible assets subject to depreciated or amortized. The impairment of indefinite lived intangible assets, including goodwill, is tested on FASB ASC 350 (SFAS No. 142). When there is indication that an intangible asset or goodwill is impaired, testing should be immediate. When no impairment is indicated, then such assets are to be tested annually at a minimum. Exhibit 2.1 summarizes the requirements for impairment testing.

Under FASB ASC 350 (SFAS No. 144), a long-lived asset that is currently being depreciated or amortized should be tested for impaired if there is a "triggering event" such as:

- A significant decrease in the market value of the asset
- A significant change in the extent or manner in which the asset is used or significant physical change to the asset

EXHIBIT 2.1 Guidance for Impairment Testing

Long-Lived Asset	Frequency of Testing	Guidance for Testing for Impairment
Goodwill	If indicated by a triggering event or at least annually	FASB ASC 350-20 (SFAS No. 142)
Assets with indefinite lives	Annually or if indicated by a triggering event	FASB ASC 350-20 (SFAS No. 142)
Assets subject to amortization or depreciation	If indicated by a triggering event	FASB ASC 350-30 (SFAS No. 144)

- A significant adverse change in legal factors or in the business climate that could affect the value of an asset, or an adverse action or assessment by a regulator
- An accumulation of costs significantly in excess of the amount originally expected to acquire or construct an asset
- A current period operating or cash flow loss combined with a history of operating or cash flow losses or a projection or forecast that demonstrates continuing losses associated with an asset used for the purpose of producing revenue[21]

A long-lived asset that is not being amortized because its remaining life is unknown is also tested for impairment but under the "triggering events" described in FASB ASC 350 (SFAS No. 142). The triggering events under FASB ASC 350 are similar to those listed earlier; however, there are some differences to note in the following list:

- A significant adverse change in legal factors or in the business climate
- Adverse action or assessment by a regulator
- Unanticipated competition
- Loss of key personnel
- Expectation of sale or disposal of a reporting unit or a significant portion of the reporting unit
- Testing under FASB ASC 350 (SFAS No. 144) of a significant asset group in a reporting unit
- Recognition of a goodwill impairment loss in the financial statements of a subsidiary that is a component of a reporting unit[22]

ORDER OF TESTING AND LEVEL OF VALUE   According to FASB ASC 350 (SFAS No. 142), if goodwill and another asset, or goodwill and a group of assets in a reporting unit (defined as an operating unit per FASB ASC 280, *Segment Reporting* (SFAS No. 131), are tested for impairment at the same time, the other asset, or asset group, is to be tested for impairment before goodwill. In other words, the long-lived assets that are being amortized or depreciated as of the test date under SFAS 144 are tested first, then indefinite-lived assets other than goodwill are tested under SFAS 142. After all other assets have been tested (assuming triggering events) then goodwill is tested for impairment under the two-step test described in SFAS 142.

NATURE OF GOODWILL   In order to understand why the FASB requires that goodwill be tested for impairment, it is important to understand the economic attributes of goodwill. *The International Glossary of Business Valuation Terms,* which was developed with input from representatives of the major North American business valuation societies and organizations, describes goodwill as "that intangible asset arising as a result of name, reputation, customer loyalty, location, products, and similar factors not separately identified."[23] Goodwill is a slightly different concept in financial accounting. Goodwill is defined in the FASB's ASC Master Glossary as:

> *the excess of the cost of an acquired entity over the net of the amounts assigned to assets acquired and liabilities assumed. Goodwill is often viewed as a group of assets that contribute value to a business enterprise currently but are non identifiable or separable as of the measurement date. These assets may include perceived value from assets that may exist sometime in the future such as future customers. The amount recognized as goodwill includes acquired intangible assets that do not meet the criteria in FASB ASC 805,* Business Combinations *(SFAS No. 141(R)), for recognition as an asset apart from goodwill.*[24]

In early exposure drafts for *Business Combinations*, the FASB listed six components of goodwill that had been commonly recognized in accounting practices under existing authoritative guidance. The Board's views about the conceptual components of goodwill remain unchanged from early exposure drafts and they appear in the Basis for Conclusion Appendix to FASB ASC 805, *Business Combinations* (SFAS No. 141(R)). The IASB's Business Combinations also recognizes similar, but not identical components of goodwill. The six FASB goodwill components are:

1. The excess of the fair values over the book values of the acquiree's net assets at the date of acquisition.
2. The fair value of other net assets that the acquiree had not previously recognized. They may not have been recognized because they failed to meet the recognition criteria (perhaps because of measurement difficulties), because of a requirement that prohibited their recognition, or because the acquiree concluded that the costs of recognizing them separately were not justified by the benefits.
3. The fair value of the "going-concern" element of the acquiree's existing business. The going-concern element represents the ability of the established business to earn a higher rate of return on an assembled collection of net assets that would be expected if those net assets had to be acquired separately. That value stems from the synergies of the net assets of the business, as well as from other benefits (such as factors related to market imperfections, including the ability to earn monopoly profits and barriers to market entry—either legal or because of transaction costs—by potential competitors).
4. The fair value of the expected synergies and other benefits from combining the acquirer's and the acquiree's net assets and businesses.

5. Overvaluation of the consideration paid by the acquirer stemming from errors in valuing the consideration tendered.
6. Overpayment or underpayment by the acquirer.[25]

   The recognition of goodwill on the balance sheet of an entity acquired in a business combination can result from any or all of the six components previously mentioned. The FASB and IASB provide insight about the nature of goodwill from a conceptual standpoint and agree that the third and forth components are conceptually part of goodwill. The third component relates to the excess value of the acquiree's assembled assets and represents preexisting goodwill at the time of the business combination. The fourth component relates to the excess value created by the synergies of the business combination. The Boards refer to the third and fourth components of goodwill as "core goodwill."

   The Boards indicate that the intent of Statement 141(R) is to reduce the amount of goodwill recognized in the financial statements to the amount of core goodwill. Specifically, component 1 would be reduced or eliminated by recognizing identifiable acquired assets at their fair values rather than their carrying amounts. Component 2 would be reduced or eliminated by identifying and recognizing all acquired intangible assets. And component 5 would be reduced or eliminated by measuring consideration accurately.[26]

Testing for Impairment

Under FASB ASC 350, *Intangibles—Goodwill and Other* (SFAS No. 142), goodwill is no longer amortized for financial statement reporting purposes, but rather is tested at least annually to determine if its carrying value has been impaired. Previous standards provided little guidance about how to determine and measure goodwill impairment. As a result, the accounting for goodwill impairment was not consistent or comparable, and users of financial statements questioned the usefulness of those standards.

   FASB ASC 350 (SFAS No. 142) provides specific guidance for testing goodwill for impairment using a two-step process that begins with defining the reporting unit and measuring its fair value. The first step is a test for potential impairment. If the reporting unit fails the first step, the second step is performed to determine whether an impairment has occurred and to measure the amount of the impairment.

   Under the first step, the fair value of the reporting unit is measured through a discounted cash flow analysis, or other appropriate method. The fair value is compared to the reporting unit's carrying amount, or book value. If the reporting unit's fair value is greater than its carrying amount, the reporting unit's goodwill is not considered to be impaired. If the unit's fair value is less than its carrying amount, then goodwill impairment is a possibility, and the second step is required.

Under the second step, goodwill's implied value is calculated by subtracting the sum of the fair values of all of the tangible and other intangible assets less liabilities existing on the measurement date from the fair value of the reporting unit. The calculation of implied goodwill includes all assets and liabilities existing on the test date, whether or not they were previously recorded. If the implied, fair value of goodwill exceeds the carrying amount of goodwill, there is no impairment. If goodwill's carrying amount exceeds its implied value, goodwill is impaired and the difference must be written-off.

In addition to testing goodwill for impairment, FASB ASC 350 (SFAS No. 142) provides guidance on testing intangible assets that are not being amortized (indefinite-lived assets) for impairment. Intangible assets that are not currently being amortized, because their reaming useful life is not known, are tested for impairment at least annually. The test for impairment is rather simple. If the fair value as of the test date is less than their carrying value, the difference is the amount of impairment. If the fair value is greater than the carrying value, the asset is not considered impaired. The carrying value remains on the financial statements.

DELTA: GOODWILL IMPAIRMENT TESTING AND AN IMPAIRMENT CHARGE   One of the footnotes to Delta's December 31, 2008, Form 10-K states:

Goodwill reflects (1) the excess of the reorganization value of the Successor over the fair value of tangible and identifiable intangible assets, net of liabilities, from the adoption of fresh start reporting, adjusted for impairment, and (2) the excess of purchase price over the fair values of the tangible and identifiable intangible assets acquired and liabilities assumed from Northwest in the Merger. The following table reflects the change in the carrying amount of goodwill for the year ended December 31, 2008:

Balance as of December 31, 2007	$12,104
Impairment Charge	(6,939)
Northwest Merger	4,572
Other	(6)
Balance as of December 31, 2008	$ 9,731

During the March 2008 quarter, we experienced a significant decline in market capitalization driven primarily by record fuel prices and overall airline industry conditions. In addition, the announcement of our *intention to merge with Northwest established a stock exchange ratio based on the relative valuation of Delta and Northwest. For additional information about the Merger, see Note 2 of the Notes to the Consolidated Financial Statements. We determined that these factors combined with further increases in fuel prices were an indicator that a goodwill impairment test was required pursuant to SFAS No. 142, "Goodwill and Other Intangible Assets" ("SFAS 142"). As a result, we estimated fair value based on a discounted projection of future cash flows, supported with a market-based valuation. We determined that goodwill was impaired and recorded a non-cash charge of $6.9 billion for the year ended December 31, 2008. In estimating fair value, we based our estimates and assumptions on the same valuation techniques employed and levels of inputs used to estimate the fair value of goodwill upon adoption of fresh start reporting.*[27]

Issues in Measuring Fair Value When Testing for Impairment

Testing for impairment under FASB ASC 350, *Intangibles—Goodwill and Other* (SFAS No. 142), is complex and the statement is silent on several issues relevant to its implementation. These implementation issues presented within this section often require judgment on the part of the preparer. The preparer must evaluate the reasonableness of calculations and conclusion when performing impairment testing and focus on the goal of fairly presenting financial information.

COMPARING FAIR VALUE OF A REPORTING UNIT TO ITS CARRYING VALUE   As discussed previously, FASB ASC 350, *Intangibles—Goodwill and Other* (SFAS No. 142), describes the test of goodwill for impairment using a two-step method. The first step compares the fair value of a reporting unit with its carrying amount. Identification of the appropriate reporting unit is an important element in impairment testing. Any misidentification has the potential to change the outcome of the impairment test and the dollar amount of the impairment adjustment. In business combinations, acquired goodwill is assigned to a reporting unit. The reporting unit can be the entire acquired entity, a subset of the acquired entity, or the acquired entity can be combined with one of the acquirer's existing reporting units. Any new reporting units created in the business combination are consolidated and become part of the acquirer's operations. FASB ASC 350 describes a reporting unit as an operating segment, or a unit one level below an operating segment. A component of an operating segment is considered a reporting unit if there is discrete financial information about the component and if its operating results are regularly reviewed by segment management.[28] Determining the composition of a company's reporting units is not as straightforward as this description implies. However, it is a critical procedure because a reporting unit's level within a company's organizational structure has a tremendous impact on the outcome of goodwill impairment testing. When reporting units are more broadly defined, cash flows from other internally generated intangible assets and goodwill may be more than sufficient to counter-balance any negative cash flow impact from impaired goodwill. Under a narrow definition of the reporting unit, negative cash flow from the impaired goodwill would stand alone and require recognition in the financial statements.

Acquired assets and assumed liabilities are assigned to a reporting unit as of the business combination date. The carrying amount of a reporting unit equals the reporting unit's net assets after depreciation and amortization from the date of the business combination. FASB ASC 350-20-35 provides guidance for the assignment of acquired assets and assumed liabilities to reporting units. For the purpose of goodwill impairment testing, acquired assets and assumed liabilities are initially assigned to a reporting unit when both of the following two criteria are met:

1. The asset will be employed in or the liability relates to the operations of a reporting unit.
2. The asset or liability will be considered in determining the fair value of the reporting unit.[29]

Certain assets or liabilities are considered part of the corporate function rather than operating unit functions. However, even if an asset is considered a corporate asset, it should be assigned to a reporting unit if both of the above criteria are met. Examples of corporate items that might be assigned to a reporting unit are warranty liabilities and obligations related to noncompetition/employment agreements. Warranty liabilities and noncompete agreement obligations both relate to products produced at operating facilities, and would be included in the determination of the fair value of the operating unit. If corporate assets do not meet both of the above criteria, then they are not assigned to an individual reporting unit. An example would be the corporate headquarters facility. The assignment of acquired assets and assumed liabilities to reporting units applies to those viewed individually and to those viewed as part of a group of assets.

MEASURING THE FAIR VALUE OF A REPORTING UNIT   The "fair value hierarchy" described in FASB ASC 850 should be considered in measuring the fair value of a reporting unit for impairment purposes. According to FASB ASC 350 (SFAS No. 142), the best evidence for the fair value of a reporting unit is a quoted market price in an active market. Whenever quoted market prices are available, they should be used as the basis for the measurement of the reporting unit. When a quoted market price is not available, fair value should be based on the best information available. The valuation technique that is most commonly used when market prices are not available is a discounted cash flow analysis. A financial forecast prepared by the management of the reporting unit is the basis for a discounted cash flow analysis. Other valuation techniques that can be used to estimate the fair value of the reporting unit are the guideline company method and guideline transaction method under the market approach. FASB ASC 350-20-35 supports this method, saying, "In estimating the fair value of a reporting unit, a valuation technique based on multiples of earnings or revenue, or a similar performance measure may be used if that technique is consistent with the objective of measuring fair value."

FASB ASC 820-35-22 through 25 describes Determining the Fair Value of a Reporting Unit. There is significant diversion in practice about the appropriate interest to be measured when comparing the carrying value of a reporting unit to its fair value under step one of goodwill impairment testing. Many valuation specialists believe the appropriate interest to be measured is the invested capital of the reporting unit (equity plus interest bearing debt). The primary reason for this belief is that measuring invested capital eliminates any issues related to how debt is allocated to the reporting unit or how the entity actually financed it. Other valuation specialists take the position that the described in FASB ASC 820-35-22 is the equity of the reporting unit. This belief is based upon the description of quoted market prices provided within the statement itself. Other valuation specialists describe the interest being measured as net asset value.

Under most circumstances, the interest used as the basis for comparing carrying value and fair value under step one does not matter as long as the interest is used consistently in the measurement process. When there is a negative equity value, it is clear that invested capital should be the interest being measured. Another circumstance that requires further consideration when measuring a reporting unit on an entity or invested capital basis is when debt has a fair value below its carrying value. If the fair value of debt is below carrying value, then care should be taken in selecting an equity discount rate. The rate should reflect any additional risk to equity holders resulting from the remeasurement of the debt. If the entity's credit risk is such that the nonperformance risk increases and the fair value of debt is considered lower than the carrying value, then it is likely that market participants would require a higher equity return to reflect the potential risk of their investment.

CONTROL PREMIUM   A control premium issue sometime arises when using the guideline company method under the market approach. The question is whether a control premium should be added after applying a market multiple to a company's performance measure such as earnings or cash flows. A control premium is based on empirical evidence that acquirers of controlling interests in entities are often willing to pay more than quoted market prices since a controlling interest can permit them to take advantage of the ability to determine the entity's strategic direction. FASB ASC 350 describes control premiums in testing for impairment of goodwill by saying that:

> *The market price of individual security ... may not be representative of the fair value of the reporting unit as a whole. Substantial value may arise from the ability to take advantage of the synergies and other benefits that flow from control over another entity. Consequently, measuring the fair value of a collection of assets and liabilities that operate together in a controlled entity is different from measuring the fair value of that entity's individual equity securities. An acquiring entity often is willing to pay more for equity securities that give it a controlling interest than an investor would pay for a number of equity securities representing less than controlling interest. That control premium may cause the fair value of the reporting unit to exceed its market capitalization. The quoted market price of an individual equity security, therefore, need not be the sole measurement basis of the fair value of the reporting unit.[30]*

If a control premium is considered appropriate when estimating the fair value of a reporting unit under the guideline company method, then the data that is used to support the control premium must be relevant and reliable for its application under the methodology. The concept of premiums for control are further discussed in Chapter 5.

TESTING MANAGEMENT'S FORECASTS FOR USE IN A DISCOUNTED CASH FLOW ANALYSIS   In reviewing the assumptions underlying a discounted cash flow analysis used for impairment testing under FASB ASC 350 (SFAS No. 142), it may be helpful to review Chapter 7, "Reasonably Objective Basis," of the AICPA's *Guide for Prospective Financial Information*. The guide covers appropriate attributes of prospective financial information prepared using a "reasonably objective basis" and "appropriate assumptions." Those attributes include:

- Financial information is prepared by someone who has sufficient knowledge of the entity's business and industry to make appropriate judgments.
- Key factors on which the entity's future results depend such as sales, production, services, and financing activities have been identified.

- Assumptions have been developed for each key factor and they have an objective basis.
- Past performance supports key factor assumptions and they have been developed with realistic expectations about the future.
- Key factor assumptions are consistent with the entity's plans, consistent with each other, and they make sense when viewed together as a group.
- Key factor assumptions are consistent with industry trends and market conditions.
- The significance of key factors to the entity's future results has been evaluated.
- The sensitivity of future results to the assumption about the key factor has been evaluated.
- The discount rate is equal to the entity's cost of capital.
- The role of debt in the entity's capital structure has been considered.
- There is a rational relationship between the assumptions and the underlying facts modeled in the discounted cash flow analysis.
- The aggregate impact of individually insignificant assumptions has been considered.[31]

Deferred Tax Considerations

When recognizing and measuring the impairment of goodwill, questions have arisen about how an entity should account for the difference between the book and tax bases of assets and liabilities in determining the fair value of a reporting unit, the reporting unit's carrying value and the resulting implied fair value of goodwill under FASB ASC 350, *Intangibles—Goodwill and Other* (SFAS No. 142). In 2002, the FASB issued EITF Issue No. 02-13, *Deferred Income Tax Considerations in Applying the Goodwill Impairment Test in FASB Statement No. 142*, to clarify some of the goodwill impairment issues relating to deferred tax assets and liabilities.

EITF 02-13 identifies three issues related to deferred tax assets and liabilities:

Issue 1. Whether the fair value of a reporting unit should be estimated by assuming that the unit would be bought or sold in a nontaxable transaction versus a taxable transaction.

Issue 2. Whether deferred income taxes should be included in the carrying amount of a reporting unit for purposes of Step 1 of the Statement 142 goodwill impairment test.

Issue 3. For purposes of determining the implied fair value of a reporting unit's goodwill in Step 2 of the Statement 142 goodwill impairment test, what income tax bases an entity should use for a reporting unit's assets and liabilities in order to measure deferred tax assets and liabilities. That is, should an entity use the existing income tax bases or assume new income tax bases for the unit's assets and liabilities.[32]

The EITF clarified that the assumptions under Issue 1 are a matter of judgment that depend upon specific facts and circumstances. The assumption about whether the transaction is taxable or nontaxable should be consistent with the assumptions that market participants make when estimating fair value. A market participant would consider the feasibility of the tax structure and whether a prudent seller would utilize the particular tax structure to maximize value. Additional considerations would be tax regulations and corporate governance that may limit certain types of structures in the potential sale of the reporting unit.

In Issue 2, the EITF recommends that deferred taxes should be included in the carrying value of the reporting unit regardless of the assumption about the tax structure of the sale. The reporting unit's carrying value should include deferred taxes when performing step one under SFAS 142 impairment testing.

In Issue 3, the EITF recommends that the entity use the income tax bases in step 2 of SFAS 142 implicit in the assumed tax structure in estimating the fair value of the reporting unit in step 1. If the assumption under step 1 is a nontaxable transaction, then the entity should use the existing tax bases. If the assumption is a taxable transaction, then the reporting unit should use new tax bases.[33] When performing a test for impairment of goodwill FASB ASC 350, *Intangibles—Goodwill and Other*, management should make a determination whether the economic value would be higher in a nontaxable versus a taxable transaction under the facts and circumstances as of the test date.

EXAMPLE OF A NONTAXABLE TRANSACTION Blue Company is performing its annual goodwill impairment test as of June 30, 20X1. Blue has one reporting unit and the following fact pattern:

- Total assets of $235
- Tax basis of assets excluding goodwill and deferred income taxes of $125
- Goodwill of $75
- Net deferred tax liabilities of $25
- Corporate tax rate of 38 percent

Management of Blue believes that the entity could be sold and the transaction could be structured as either a stock sale (nontaxable) or an asset sale (taxable). The fair value of the entity assuming a stock sale is

$225, and due to tax ramifications, the fair value of the entity assuming an asset sale is $240. If the entity were sold in a nontaxable transaction, therefore, the tax impact would be approximately $25 as indicated by the deferred tax liability. If the entity were sold in a taxable transaction, the tax impact would be approximately $44 or [($240 − 125) * 38%].

Under EITF 02-13, Blue analyzes the economic impact of a nontaxable structure compared to a taxable structure as follows:

	Nontaxable	Taxable
Fair value	$225	$240
Less taxes paid	(25)	(44)
Economic value	$200	$196

Blue concludes that the entity's highest economic value would result from a nontaxable transaction, so management estimates the carrying value for step 1 of the testing goodwill for impairment under FASB ASC 350, *Intangibles—Goodwill and Other*, as:

Net assets (without goodwill and deferred taxes)	$185
Goodwill	75
Deferred taxes	(25)
Carry value	$235

Blue fails step 1 of the test of goodwill for impairment under FASB ASC 350 because its fair value is $225, which is less than its $235 carrying value. Therefore, Blue must perform a step 2 test. Management retains valuation specialists to assist with measuring the fair value of tangible and intangible assets as of the test date. The fair value of these assets was determined to be $190. The fair value of the goodwill as of the test date was measured as follows:

Fair value of Blue assuming nontaxable transaction	$225
Less: Fair value of net tangible and intangible assets	(190)
Plus deferred tax liabilities ($190 − 125) = 65 * 38% = $25	25
Fair value of goodwill	$ 60

The amount of impairment of the goodwill is therefore $15 = ($75 − 60).[34]

CARRYING FORWARD AN IMPAIRMENT TEST VALUATION   FASB ASC 350-20-35, *Intangibles—Goodwill and Other* (paragraph 27 of SFAS No. 142), provides guidance for carrying forward an impairment test valuation from a prior year, eliminating the need to do another valuation analysis. A detailed determination of the fair value of a reporting unit may be carried forward from one year to the next if all three of the following criteria have been met:

1. The assets and liabilities that make up the reporting unit have not changed significantly since the most recent fair value determination. A recent significant acquisition or a reorganization of an entity's segment reporting structure is an example of an event that might significantly change the composition of a reporting unit.
2. The most recent fair value determination resulted in an amount that exceeded the carrying amount of the reporting unit by a substantial margin.
3. Based on an analysis of events that have occurred and circumstances that have changed since the most recent fair value determination, the likelihood that a current fair value determination would be less than the current carrying amount of the reporting unit is remote.[35]

Accounting for the Impairment or Disposal of Long-Lived Assets Subject to Amortization

The accounting for long-lived assets generated in the absence of a business combination is inconsistent. Long-lived tangible assets such as plant and equipment are initially recorded at their cost and subsequently depreciated over the estimated useful life of the asset. Certain intangible assets are also considered long-lived assets. However, the costs of internally generated intangible assets are generally expensed as incurred. Intangible assets acquired in a business combination are recorded at their respective fair values either individually, or with a group of other assets.

TESTING FOR THE IMPAIRMENT OF LONG-LIVED ASSETS   FASB ASC 360-10-35, *Property, Plant, and Equipment* (paragraph 7 of SFAS No. 144), describes the testing for impairment of long-lived assets, both tangible assets subject to depreciation and intangible assets subject to amortization.

> *An impairment loss shall be recognized only if the carrying amount of a long-lived asset (asset group) is not recoverable and exceeds its fair value. The carrying amount of a long-lived asset (asset group) is not recoverable if it exceeds the sum of the undiscounted cash flows expected to result from the use and eventual disposition of the asset (asset group). That assessment should be based on the carrying amount of the asset (asset group) at the date it is tested for recoverability, whether in use or under development. An impairment loss shall be measured as the amount by*

which the carrying amount of a long-lived asset (asset group) exceeds its fair value.[36]

An important consideration in an impairment test for long-lived assets subject to depreciation or amortization is the measurement of assets in use with other assets. The Statement indicates that the test be applied to the lowest level where cash flows may be identified. As a practical matter, cash flows are associated with a group of assets such as a trade name, customer lists, and technology that relate to a particular product.

DELTA: IMPAIRMENT TESTING FOR LONG-LIVED ASSETS   Delta Airlines describes the testing for impairment of certain long-lived assets, particularly aircraft, as follows:

Our flight equipment and other long-lived assets have a recorded value of $20.6 billion on our Consolidated Balance Sheet at December 31, 2008. This value is based on various factors, including the assets' estimated useful lives and their estimated salvage values. In accordance with SFAS No. 144, "Accounting for the Impairment or Disposal of Long-Lived Assets" ("SFAS 144"), we record impairment losses on long-lived assets used in operations when events and circumstances indicate the assets might be impaired and the estimated future cash flows generated by those assets are less than their carrying amounts. If we decide to permanently remove flight equipment or other long-lived assets from operations, these assets will be evaluated under SFAS 144 and could result in impairment. The impairment loss recognized is the amount by which the asset's carrying amount exceeds its estimated fair value. In order to evaluate potential impairment as required by SFAS 144, we group assets at the fleet type level (the lowest level for which there are identifiable cash flows) and then estimate future cash flows based on projections of passenger yields, fuel costs, labor costs and other relevant factors. We estimate aircraft fair values using published sources, appraisals and bids received from third parties.[37]

Conclusion

Accounting for business combinations under SFAS 141(R), *Business Combinations*, improves financial reporting by eliminating inconsistencies previously allowed under APB 16's pooling and purchase methods of merger accounting. It introduces the acquisition method of accounting for business combinations and provides for a more accurate representation of identifiable assets acquired and liabilities assumed in a merger by establishing the acquisition date fair value as the measurement objective. It also improves the international comparability of financial statements through convergence with the International Accounting Standards Board and the simultaneous release of IFRS 3, *Business Combinations*.

Some of the more significant provisions of SFAS 141(R) are the requirement to identify the acquirer, the identification of all assets and liabilities, including intangible assets, recognition of a gain on a bargain purchase, recognition of contingent consideration, and the measurement of in-process research and development. In an effort to address concerns about the requirement to recognize contingent assets and liabilities existing on the acquisition date, the FASB issued FSP 141(R)-1. The Staff Position changes the previous requirement to recognize all contractual assets and liabilities and provides recognition guidance that is more consistent with FASB Statement No. 5, *Contingencies*.

Impairment testing for goodwill and other intangible assets is covered in either SFAS No. 142, *Goodwill and Other Intangibles*, or in SFAS No. 144, *Property, Plant and Equipment*. Goodwill and intangible assets with indefinite lives fall under SFAS No. 142 and are subject to impairment testing, annually, or sooner if indicated by a triggering event. Such events generally occur when there has been an adverse change in the business climate or a significant reorganization.

Goodwill impairment testing is a two-step process that identifies the existence of a potential impairment and then measures the amount of the impairment. Impairment testing for intangibles is a more straightforward comparison of fair value to carrying value. Impairment testing under SFAS 142 has nuances that include proper identification of the reporting unit, determining the order of testing, assessing any control premium, objective evaluation of valuation assumptions, and determining whether it is appropriate to carry forward an impairment test valuation from year to year.

Notes

1. SFAS 141(R), *Business Combinations,* paragraph 1. December 2007.
2. *Id.*
3. SFAS 142, paragraph B28.
4. SFAS 141, paragraph 39.
5. FASB issues FASB Statements No. 141(R), *Business Combinations,* and No. 160, *Noncontrolling Interests in Consolidated Financial Statements*, news release 12/04/07, www.fasb.org.
6. SFAS 141(R), *Business Combinations*, paragraph 7.
7. "Delta Air Lines, Northwest Airlines Combining to Create America's Premier Global Airline" Delta Newsroom, April 14, 2008, www.delta.com.
8. *Id.*

9. Delta Air Lines, Inc., Form 10-K, December 31, 2008, F-18.

10. FASB ASC 805, *Business Combinations* (SFAS 141(R)), paragraph 3k.

11. Delta Air Lines Inc., Form 10-K, December 31, 2008, page 47.

12. *Id.,* F-19.

13. *Id.,* page 49.

14. Statement of Financial Accounting Standards 141(R), *Business Combinations,* paragraph 3d, page 2.

15. *Id.,* paragraph 3e.

16. Delta Air Lines Inc., Form 10-K, December 31, 2008, page F–18.

17. FASB Staff Position No. 141(R)-1, *"Accounting for Assets Acquired and Liabilities Assumed in a Business Combination That Arise from Contingencies,"* April 1, 2009, paragraphs 6-9.

18. Id., paragraphs 10–12.

19. Summary of Statement No. 142, www.fasb.org.

20. *Id.*

21. FASB ASC 360-10-35-21.

22. FASB ASC 350.

23. *The International Glossary of Business Valuation Terms,* 2001, www. bvresources.com.

24. FASB Master Glossary, www.fasb.org.

25. SFAS No. 141(R), paragraph B313.

26. *Id.,* paragraphs B314 to B316.

27. Delta Air Lines Inc. Form 10-K, for the year ending December 31, 2008, page 49.

28. FASB ASC 350, paragraph 30.

29. SFAS 142, paragraph 32.

30. *Id.,* paragraph 23.

31. AICPA Audit and Accounting Guide, *Guide for Prospective Financial Information,* sections AAG-PRO 7.01–7.07. AICPA Audit and Accounting Guide, *Guide for Prospective Financial Information,* sections AAG-PRO 7.01–7.07.

32. EITF 02-13, paragraph 3.

33. Id., paragraph 7.

34. Id., paragraph 9 for additional examples.

35. FASB ASC 350-20-35 (SFAS No. 142, paragraph 27).

36. FASB ASC 360-10-35, www.fasb.org.

37. *Id.,* page 50.

CHAPTER 3

The Nature of Intangible Assets

One interesting aspect of fair value measurement in financial reporting is the increased recognition that intangible assets contribute value to an entity. Every entity, large and small, is made up of both tangible and intangible assets that work in conjunction to create value for the entity. Tangible assets are easily understood. They are assets with physical characteristics that we can typically see; inventory, machinery, and real estate are tangible assets that usually comprise a significant portion of the business enterprise. However, intangible assets are also a major component of a business enterprise. Intangible assets are unique because they generally cannot be observed or touched. Intangible assets typically lack physical substance, but they provide their owner with valuable rights and privileges. Estimating the fair value of these intangible properties creates challenges for those engaged in financial reporting.

The *International Glossary of Business Valuation Terms* defines intangible assets as "nonphysical assets such as franchises, trademarks, patents, copyrights, goodwill, equities, mineral rights, securities, and contracts (as distinguished from physical assets) that grant rights and privileges and have value for the owner."[1] The *Dictionary of Finance and Investment Terms* has a similar view of intangible assets, defining them as a "right or nonphysical resource that is presumed to represent an advantage to the firm's position in the market place. Such assets include copyrights, patents, trademarks, goodwill, computer programs, capitalized advertising costs, organization costs, licenses, leases, franchises, exploration permits, and import and export permits."[2] The accounting perspective provided by the Financial Accounting Standards Board (FASB) refers to intangible assets as "assets (not including financial assets) that lack physical substance."[3] The FASB's definition of intangible assets excludes goodwill, while the definition used by traditional corporate finance and valuation professionals includes goodwill in the broader definition of intangible assets.

History of Intangible Assets

Intangible assets represent the intellectual capital of an entity. As such, intangibles represent knowledge. Human history is predicated on development of knowledge. Intangible assets are not new phenomena; these assets have existed throughout human history. Changes in communications technology from the invention of the printing press in the 15th century and the telegraph in the 19th century, to the telephone, television, and the Internet in the 20th and 21st centuries, provide an example of how changes in technology impact mankind's development. The development of each of these new technologies created a significant number of new intangible assets and value for the assets' owners. As discussed previously, both the U.S. and global economies have undergone a tremendous shift, from an emphasis on "bricks and mortar" businesses to an emphasis on information-based businesses that require less investment in tangible assets such as machinery and buildings. Additionally, the globalization of international trade and the development of new information-based technologies in the last 20 years have contributed to recent recognition of the value that intangible assets add to an entity. As a consequence, a much greater percentage of global market capitalization is derived from intangible assets.

Governments have long protected the rights of owners of intangible assets, particularly intellectual property. Governments realize that to encourage innovation, the inventor's work has to be protected. One of the first declarations granting rights to inventors was the Statute of Monopolies declared by the King of England in 1623. The statute was written to promote competition and still protect the inventor. Written in the language of the time, the statute provides protection for the inventor for 14 years.

> *Provided alsoe That any Declaracion before mencioned shall not extend to any tres Patents and Graunt of Privilege for the tearme of fowerteene yeares or under, hereafter to be made of the sole working or makinge of any manner of new Manufactures within this Realme, to the true and first Inventor and Inventors of such Manufactures, which others at the tyme of makinge such tres Patents and Graunts shall not use, soe as alsoe they be not contrary to the Lawe nor mischievous to the State, by raisinge prices of Commodities at home, or hurt of Trade, or generallie inconvenient: the said fourteen yeares to be from the date of the first res Patents or Grant of such privilidge hereafter to be made, but that the same shall be of such force as they should be if this Act had never byn made, and of none other.*[4]

The Constitution of the United States grants the U.S. Congress the authority to "promote the progress of science and useful arts, by securing for limited times, to authors and inventors, the exclusive right to their respective writings and discoveries." Under this power, one of the first acts of the new Congress in 1790 was to adopt both patent and copyright laws. Originally, protection for trademarks was left to the individual states; however, Congress began passing the first federal trademark laws in 1870. Since then, Congress has amended the intellectual property statutes frequently in response to changes in technology and to advances in international commerce. Both houses of Congress have committees that are responsible for keeping intellectual property laws up to date.[5]

Although intellectual property creates value for an entity, the value added is sometimes difficult to quantify. The ability to quantify the fair value of the contribution of all assets to the entity is a fundamental concept in fair value measurements in financial reporting. An article on the World Intellectual Property Organization Web site quotes Sir William Thompson, Lord Kelvin, who spoke in the 19th century about the difficulty in measuring knowledge by saying, "When you measure what you are speaking about and express it in numbers, you know something about it, but when you cannot (or do not) measure it, when you cannot (or do not) express it in numbers, then your knowledge is of a meager and unsatisfactory kind."[6] Expressing similar thoughts, Galileo Galileli suggested, "Measure what is measurable, and make measurable what is not so."[7]

Economic Basis of Intangible Assets

Intangible assets create value for an entity in a number of ways. If intangible assets represent a knowledge advantage through some proprietary know-how, a relationship with important customers, or knowledge held by key employees, then the entity should be able to exploit that knowledge to achieve a competitive advantage in the market place. The knowledge advantage becomes an economic advantage through enhanced margins. For example, if an entity develops technology internally, then it does not have to license similar technology from an outside source and it does not have to pay licensing or royalty fees. Similarly, if the entity already has relationships with key customers, it will not have to incur as many marketing and selling expenses to attract new customers. Additionally, if the entity already has trained employees in its workforce, then it will not have to incur as many hiring and training expenses. Although the extent of the economic benefits provided by intangible assets varies by asset, the economic benefit generated by each intangible asset contributes to the value to the entity as a whole.

In *Intangibles: Management, Measurement, and Reporting,* Baruch Lev describes the fundamental value drivers unique to intangible assets. He calls them nonrivalry scalability and networking. Nonrivalry scalability refers to the ability to accommodate a multitude of users at any given time. Tangible assets, such as laptop computers, have a limit to the number of simultaneous users. Intangible assets, however, can be used by multitudes at once. The laptop can only be used by one person at time, but millions can simultaneously access eBay's Web site and use eBay's proprietary software technology. The use of an intangible asset typically does not have any physical limitations. The only limitation is the size of the market for that asset. Therefore, nonrivalry scalability described by Lev is a primary value driver for intangible assets.[8]

Another value driver described by Lev is the network effect of intangible assets. A network effect is simply that the value of the intangible asset increases as the number of users of the asset increases.[9] Adobe Systems Incorporated owns software that bridges the gap between computer images and print images. One of the most widely used Adobe products is Acrobat software, which allows the interface of electronic computer images with a printer. The Adobe Flash Player that utilizes this software is installed on 98 percent of Internet-connected desktops.[10] The widespread use of Flash Player makes this software the de facto industry standard and creates a competitive advantage for Adobe in marketing its other products.

The economic investment in intangible assets is substantial as the investment in specific intangible assets often creates a competitive advantage for the owner. A 2001 working paper by the Federal Reserve Bank of Philadelphia estimates that $1 trillion is spent annually on developing intangible assets in the United States alone. The $1 trillion annual investment equals the investment in tangible assets by those same businesses. The investment in intangible assets is likely to be even higher today. The same working paper also estimates that the capital stock of intangibles in the United States had an equilibrium market value of at least $5 trillion as of the year 2000.[11]

Identification of Intangible Assets

While economic benefits provide evidence as to the existence of intangible assets, the FASB provides specific criteria for recognizing an intangible asset in financial reporting. In a business combination, an intangible asset should be recorded on the balance sheet as of the acquisition date if it is considered identifiable. An intangible asset is considered identifiable if it is either:

- Separable, that is, capable of being separated or divided from the entity and sold, transferred, licensed, rented, or exchanged, either individually or together with a related contract, identifiable asset, or liability, regardless of whether the entity intends to do so; or if it

- Arises from contractual or other legal rights, regardless of whether those rights are transferable or separable from the entity or from other rights and obligations.[12]

According to the FASB, an intangible asset has substance that should be recognized in a company's financial statements if the intangible can be monetized or if it is created by a legal obligation. An intangible asset can be monetized by selling or licensing the asset to a market participant. A favorable contract is an example of a legal obligation that provides substance to an intangible asset.

Examples of Specific Intangible Assets

To understand how an intangible asset creates value within an entity, it may be helpful to examine the asset's place in the FASB's general classification of intangible asset. In *Business Combinations,* the FASB classifies intangible assets into groups of intangible assets that are marketing related, intangible assets that are related to establishing customer relationships, intangible assets that are considered artistic based, intangible assets that contribute to proprietary technology, and finally intangible assets that are the result of contractual obligations.[13]

Marketing-Related Intangible Assets

A number of intangible assets are used to create market awareness for an entity's products or services. Trade names and trademarks are used by companies to distinguish their products or services from their competitors. An apple is generally thought of as a fruit; however, when the logo of an apple with a bite taken out of it is attached to a laptop computer, the apple takes on an entirely different meaning. That difference represents the unique features of Apple's products and provides a competitive advantage for Apple Inc. by creating brand awareness in the marketplace.

Trade dress is another marketing-related intangible asset. Trade dress is a distinctive feature incorporated into the product or its packaging that identifies the entity that produced the product. Tiffany & Company uses a variation of the color turquoise called "Tiffany Blue" in its advertising and on boxes and shopping bags used in its stores. Tiffany itself describes the color as "Glimpsed on a busy street or resting in the palm of a hand, Tiffany Blue boxes and shopping bags epitomize the jeweler's great heritage of elegance, exclusivity and flawless craftsmanship."[14]

A marketing-related intangible asset that has become increasingly more important in the Internet age is the Internet domain name. A domain name that is obvious and easy to remember increases Internet traffic, and it is more valuable than a name that is difficult to remember. If you are wondering whether to bring an umbrella to work today, weather.com is an example of a domain name that certainly meets this criteria.

Another example of a marketing-related intangible asset is one that is not so obvious. A noncompete agreement is a marketing-related intangible asset that preserves market share by legally limiting potential competition from current or past employees. Noncompetition employment agreements are often executed when an employee is hired and when one company acquires another and are usually restricted to the specific industry within which the company operates. Trade names, trademarks, trade dress, and noncompete agreements enhance the value of a firm by supporting its marketing activities and by creating or preserving a competitive advantage.

Customer-Related Intangible Assets

Another group of intangible assets that adds value to an entity are those related to the development of customer relationships. Established customer relationships are a vital asset because the customers are a business entity's lifeblood, providing cash that the business needs to survive and grow. Customer relationships are physically represented in customer lists. A customer list is typically a database that includes information about the customers, such as their name, address, e-mail address, phone numbers, and contact names. It may also contain order histories and demographic information. Although a customer list generally doesn't provide any contractual or other legal rights, customer lists are often monetized by selling the contact information to another party. As such, a customer list acquired in a business combination normally meets the separability criterion for identifiably.[15]

How many of us have had a phone call as we are about to sit down to dinner from someone wanting to sell us something? It is likely that our telephone number and other contact information were sold to the dinner interrupter by another entity in order to monetize our contact information. Often customer relationships consist of both a contractual component and an additional relationship component. The value from the contract component is fairly self-evident. The value of the relationship component is derived from the possibility that the contract will be renewed, preserving the relationship and providing a future income stream.

Artistic-Related Intangible Assets

Artistic-related intangible assets such as works of art, books, plays, and musical scores derive value from their copyright protection. Since a copyright provides a legal protection, the copyright is considered identifiable and it meets the criteria for recognition in financial reporting. In addition, the holder of an artist-related intangible asset can transfer the copyright to another party through various means. It can be transferred in whole by assigning the right, or transferred in part through a licensing agreement that gives another party the right to use the asset for a specific period. Artistic-intangible assets can be recognized individually or recognized in conjunction with similar or related assets. If it is recognized in conjunction with other assets, the group of assets should have similar useful lives.[16] Artistic-related intangible assets are generally identified by entities within industries that produce or use artistic works, such as the music or publishing industries.

The NBC television and radio network started using a three-note chime to identify itself in the 1920s, and it continues to use its famous chime today. The chime was the first audio service mark registered with the U.S. Patent Office.[17] The familiar NBC chime is a valuable artistic intangible asset that is currently owned by the General Electric Corporation.

Contract-Related Intangible Assets

Contract intangible assets such as customer contracts, license agreements, franchise rights, and operating rights create value for an entity by allowing the entity to do something it otherwise would not be able to do, or by allowing the entity to do something with more favorable terms than current market conditions would allow. These types of intangible assets are inherently considered identifiable for financial reporting purposes because they meet the legal/contractual provision for recognition.

An example of a contract-related intangible asset would be a favorable lease. If an entity signs a long-term lease for a headquarters facility with a lease rate that is less than current market rates for a similar facility, then the lease is considered an intangible asset. The value of the intangible asset would be measured by determining the present value of the lease savings over the life of the lease.

A supply contract that provides for the conveyance of materials at lower than market rates would be another example of a contract-related intangible asset. Sometimes the value of a supply contract is derived from the assurance of an uninterrupted supply of materials when there are shortages in the market.

Another contract-based intangible asset would be a franchise agreement. Franchise agreements grant the right to distribute products, techniques, or trademarks in exchange for royalty payments or a share of revenues. Franchise agreements outline the obligations of the franchisor and franchisee and often include a geographical restriction or exclusivity clause.

An example of a franchise agreement would be the arrangement between an automobile dealership and the automobile manufacturer.

Technology-Related Intangible Assets

Technology-related intangible assets create value by applying technology to an entity's products or services. Technology assets are capable of providing unique benefits to the entity or to the entity's customers. Technology-related intangible assets include proprietary technology, such as patented and unpatented software, databases, trade secrets, and formulas. Technology-related intangible assets can be transferred and licensed, and increasingly are licensed as entities attempt to monetize their intellectual property. This transferability permits technology-related intangible assets to be considered identifiable and to be recognized in financial reporting.

Amazon recently issued Kindle2, a new version of their electronic book reader. Kindle2's proprietary technology makes the wireless downloading of electronic books possible using a high-speed 3G network that eliminates the need for connection to a computer.[18] Amazon named this technology Whispernet. The Whispernet technology used in Kindle2 creates a substantial advantage for Amazon by allowing it to create and dominate the electronic book reader market.

The general classification of intangible assets into the five major categories and specific example of intangible assets within those categories cited in SFAS 141(R) are summarized in Exhibit 3.1.[19] The exhibit also includes additional examples of intangible assets even though they are not specifically cited by SFAS 141(R).

Types of Intangible Assets

Intangible asset is a broad term that refers to any set of rights or nonphysical resources such as franchises, trademarks, patents, copyrights, goodwill, equities, mineral rights, securities, and contracts (as distinguished from physical assets) that provide an advantage to the owner.[20] This definition of intangible assets in general includes both intellectual property and goodwill. In measuring the fair value created from intangible assets, it is important to understand what distinguishes intellectual property from goodwill.

Intellectual Property

Intellectual property refers to creations of the mind such as inventions, literary and artistic works, and symbols, names, images, and designs used in commerce. Intellectual property can be protected legally.[21] Common legal

EXHIBIT 3.1 Identifiable Intangible Assets

Marketing-Related Intangible Assets

Trademarks	Trade names	Service marks
Collective marks	Certification marks	Trade dress
Newspaper mastheads	Internet domain names	Noncompetition
Brand names	Distribution rights*	agreements
Retail shelf space*	Subscription lists*	Distribution networks*
Cooperative ventures*		Supplier relationships*

Customer-Related Intangible Assets

Customer lists	Order backlogs	Customer contracts
Customer relationships	Noncontractual	Medical charts and
	relationships	records*

Artistic-Related Intangible Assets

Plays	Operas	Ballets
Books	Magazines	Newspapers
Literary works	Musical compositions	Song lyrics
Advertising jingles	Pictures	Photographs
Videos	Audiovisual material	Motion pictures
Films	Music videos	Television programs
Architectural drawings*	Blueprints*	Product designs*
Drawings*	Manuscripts*	Publications*
Slogans*	Film libraries*	

Contract-Based Intangible Assets

License agreements	Royalty agreements	Standstill agreements
Advertising contracts	Construction contracts	Management contracts
Service contracts	Supply contracts	Lease agreements
Construction permits	Franchise agreements	Broadcast rights
Operating rights	Servicing contracts	Employment contracts
Drilling rights	Water rights	Air rights
Timber rights	Route authorities	Airport gates*
Development rights*	Exploration rights*	FCC licenses*
Management contracts*	Mineral rights*	Permits*

Technology-Based Intangible Assets

Patented technology	Computer software	Computer mask works
Unpatented technology	Databases	Title plants
Trade secrets	Secret formulas	Processes
Recipes	In-process R&D*	Laboratory notebooks*
Patent applications*	Proprietary processes*	Technological
		documentation*

*Other examples not specifically mentioned in FASB ASC 805, *Business Combinations*, (SFAS 141 (R)).

protections for intellectual property are patents, copyrights, trademarks, trade names, service marks, and trade secrets. These legal protections prevent the use of the intellectual property by others.

The U.S. Patent and Trademark Office (USPTO) describes a patent as "a property right granted by the Government of the United States of America to an inventor to exclude others from making, using, offering for sale, or selling the invention throughout the United States or importing the invention into the United States for a limited time in exchange for public disclosure of the invention when the patent is granted."[22] Currently the term is 20 years from the date of application.

The USPTO distinguishes a trademark from a patent by describing a trademark as "protect(ing) words, names, symbols, sounds, or colors that distinguish goods and services from those manufactured or sold by others and to indicate the source of the goods. Trademarks, unlike patents, can be renewed forever, as long as they are being used in commerce."[23] A service mark is "a word, name, symbol or device that is to indicate the source of the services and to distinguish them from the services of others. A service mark is the same as a trademark except that it identifies and distinguishes the source of a service rather than a product. The terms 'trademark' and 'mark' are often used to refer to both trademarks and service marks."[24]

A copyright "protect works of authorship, such as writings, music, and works of art that have been tangibly expressed. The Library of Congress registers copyrights which last for the life of the author plus 70 years."[25]

Goodwill

Goodwill is a term that is sometimes used to refer to all of an entire entity's intangible assets, whether they are separately identifiable or not. However, goodwill also has an economic basis as a stand-alone asset. Goodwill represents the future economic benefits arising from all assets acquired in a business combination that are not individually identified and separately recognized. Goodwill is used specifically in accounting to refer to the excess price paid to acquire a business over and above the value of the acquired tangible and identifiable intangible assets. The *Dictionary of Finance and Investment Terms* describes goodwill as an "intangible asset representing going concern value in excess of asset value paid by a company for another company in a purchase acquisition."[26]

Exhibit 3.2 provides a graphical representation of the sources of company value for a hypothetical technology company. In the graph, goodwill's contribution to value is represented by the area between the goodwill line and the IPR&D line. Similarly, IPR&D's contribution to company value is represented by the area between the IPR&D line the intangible

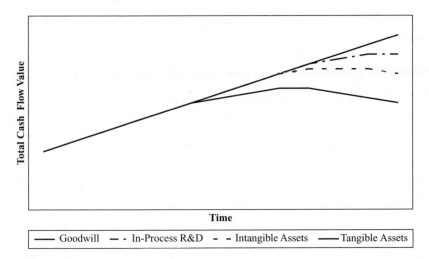

EXHIBIT 3.2 Sources of Company Value

asset line, and so forth. Over time, the relative contribution of tangible assets to company value declines while the relative contribution of all intangible assets increases. Mature companies often have significant going concern value over and above the value of their identifiable assets. Identifiable intangible assets and research and development efforts also have the potential to make significant contributions to a company's long-term success.

Useful Life of an Intangible Asset

The useful life of an intangible asset is an important consideration when estimating the fair value of the asset. The value of economic benefits generated by an intangible asset is directly related to the asset's useful life. The FASB defines the useful life as "the period over which an asset is expected to contribute directly or indirectly to future cash flows."[27] FASB ASC 350 (SFAS 142) further describes the importance of useful life to the recognition of intangible assets, saying:

> *The accounting for a recognized intangible asset is based on its useful life to the reporting entity. An intangible asset with a finite useful life is amortized; an intangible asset with an indefinite useful life is not amortized. The useful life of an intangible asset to an entity is the period over which the asset is expected to contribute directly or indirectly to the future cash flows of that entity.*

In a footnote, the FASB further clarifies the description of useful life, saying:

> *The useful life of an intangible asset shall reflect the period over which it will contribute to the cash flows of the reporting entity, not the period of time that it would take that entity to internally develop an intangible asset that would provide similar benefits. However, a reacquired right recognized as an intangible asset is amortized over the remaining contractual period of the contract in which the right was granted. If an entity subsequently reissues (sells) a reacquired right to a third party, the entity includes the related unamortized asset, if any, in determining the gain or loss on the reissuance.*[28]

The useful life of the asset is a component of each of the three valuation techniques that are used to measure fair value under SFAS 157, *Fair Value Measurement*. Under the income approach, the useful life of the intangible asset is directly related to the forecast of future cash flows that the asset is expected to generate. Under the market approach, the useful life of the intangible asset is inherently factored into the market prices for comparable guideline assets. Under the cost approach, the useful life of the asset is a concern when estimating its obsolescence.

FASB ASC 350 (SFAS 142) also describes several important factors that should be considered when estimating the useful life of an intangible asset for financial reporting purposes:

- Expected use of the asset
- Expected use of similar assets
- Legal, regulatory, and contractual provisions that may limit the useful life or enable renewal or extension
- The effects of obsolescence, demand, competition, and other economic factors
- Required future maintenance expenditures[29]

Estimating the useful life of an intangible asset is discussed further in Chapter 8.

Intangible Assets and Economic Risk

Intangible assets often have economic benefits such as nonrival scalability and network effects, but they are also characterized by a high level of risk. Intangible assets often have high development costs and low incremental costs once the intangible asset is developed. For example, a software program may take years to develop at a relatively high cost. Yet once developed, the software can be reproduced at a low marginal cost. High development costs create risk because there is no assurance that the initial investment will be recovered. High development costs with unknown benefits are risky.

The ease with which software can be reproduced is both a benefit and a detriment to the developer. The benefit is derived from low incremental costs and high profit margins as more units of the software are produced and sold. Ease of reproduction causes a detrimental impact in the form of lost revenue from the illegal use or copying of the asset (piracy). Another detrimental impact caused by the ease of reproduction is reengineering by a competitor to produce a similar product. The level of risk associated with intangible assets typically declines as the innovation process moves forward. Development stage intangible assets are far more risky than commercially developed intangible assets that benefit from legal protection through a patent or copyright.[30]

Economic Balance Sheet

Preparing an adjusted economic balance sheet can be a useful tool when analyzing a company's intangible assets. It helps determine the magnitude or aggregate value of all of the intangible assets owned by an entity. It also provides a structure to analyze the company's cost of capital and estimate the required rates of return for intangible assets.

The first step in preparing an adjusted economic balance sheet is to restate all the assets and noninterest-bearing liabilities recorded on the historic cost balance sheet and record them at their fair values. The second step is to subtract the fair value of current noninterest-bearing liabilities from the fair value of the current assets. The resulting fair value of debt-free working capital appears on the asset side of the balance sheet. The next step is to determine the fair value of the entity's invested capital (usually consisting of interest-bearing debt and equity). The fair value is estimated through traditional valuation methods such as the discounted cash flow method or the guideline company method, a market approach methodology. Once the value of invested capital is established, the value of the company's goodwill and intangible assets can be calculated in total. The difference between the fair value of invested capital on the right-hand side of the balance sheet and the sum of net working capital and tangible assets on the left side of the balance sheet equals the aggregate fair value of goodwill and intangible assets. After the fair values of all intangible assets have been identified and recorded, the remaining fair value is attributable to goodwill.

The economic balance sheet also provides the appropriate weights to be used in the calculation of the weighted average cost of capital. Since the weighted average cost of capital for the right side of the balance sheet should equal the weighted average return on assets for the left side of the balance sheet, the economic balance sheet provides information for calculating the required rates of return for individual classifications of assets. This topic will be covered in more depth in Chapter 6 in the discussion about the income approach to valuation. The top portion of Exhibit 3.3 shows a historic cost balance sheet and the middle section shows a fair value balance sheet. The economic balance sheet in the lower portion of Exhibit 3.3 highlights two important concepts. The entity's business enterprise value is equal to the amount of invested capital, and the weighted average return on assets required by the company's investors is equal to the cost of capital. The economic balance sheet is also based on the fair value of assets and liabilities.

Valuation Techniques

There are three general approaches to valuing any asset or interest in a business. The three approaches are commonly referred to as (1) the cost approach, (2) the market approach, and (3) the income approach. The FASB refers to the three approaches as valuation techniques.[31]

ASC 820, *Fair Value Measurements and Disclosures* (SFAS No. 157), requires the application of three valuation techniques to measure the fair value of an asset or liability. Paragraph 18 states, "Valuation techniques consistent with the market approach, income approach, and/or cost approach shall be used to measure fair value." Michael J. Mard and his co-authors Steven D. Hyden and Edward W. Trott get to the essence of the requirement in *Business Combinations with SFAS 141R, 157, and 160* by saying:

> *The objective is to use a valuation technique (or combination of techniques) appropriate for the circumstances but maximize the use of market inputs. Fundamentally, value is a function of economics and is based on the return on assets. The cost approach represents the replacement or reproduction of things owned or borrowed. The income approach quantifies the return these net assets can be expected to produce. The market approach reflects the market's perception of the things owned and borrowed and their expected returns.[32]*

These three valuation techniques are widely used by practitioners in the accounting, valuation, and appraisal industries. The *International Glossary of Business Valuation Terms* defines the cost, market, and income approaches to valuation as follows:

> *Cost Approach.* A general way of estimating a value indication of an individual asset by quantifying the amount of money that would be required to replace the future service capability of that asset.

Historic Cost Balance Sheet

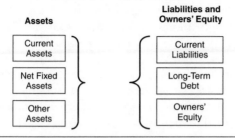

Fair Value Balance Sheet

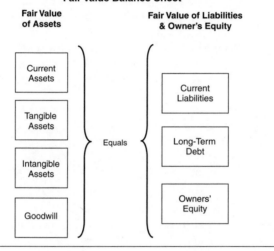

Economic Balance Sheet

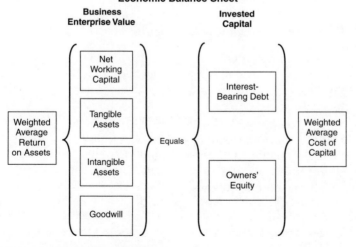

EXHIBIT 3.3 Economic Balance Sheet

Market Approach. A general way of determining a value indication of a
business, business ownership interest, security, or intangible asset
by using one or more methods that compare the subject to similar
businesses, business ownership interests, securities, or intangible
assets that have been sold.

Income Approach. A general way of determining a value indication of a
business, business ownership interest, security, or intangible asset
by using one or more methods that convert anticipated benefits to
a present single amount.[33]

Although SFAS 157's definitions of these valuation approaches are more
specific and apply only to measuring fair value for financial reporting they
are generally consistent with valuation approach definitions from the valuation profession. The SFAS 157 definitions and applications of the cost,
market, and income approaches are examined in more detail in subsequent
chapters.

Paragraph 19 of SFAS 157 goes on to say:

*Valuation techniques that are appropriate in the circumstances and for
which sufficient data are available shall be used to measure fair value. In
some cases, a single valuation technique will be appropriate ... In other
cases, multiple valuation techniques will be appropriate ... If multiple
valuation techniques are used to measure fair value, the results shall be
evaluated and weighted, as appropriate, considering the reasonableness
of the range indicated by those results. A fair value measurement is the
point within that range that is most representative of fair value in the
circumstances.*

The provisions for selecting and weighing valuation techniques in SFAS
157 are consistent with practices within the valuation industry. The American Institute of Certified Public Accountants (AICPA) issued Statement on
Standards for Valuation Services No. 1 "Valuation of a Business, a Business
Ownership Interest, Security or Intangible Asset" in June 2007, which represents generally accepted practices and procedures within the valuation
profession. According to the statement, the valuation analyst should use all
valuation approaches that are appropriate after considering the use of the
income, market, and asset-based (cost) approaches. In reaching a conclusion about the value, the analyst must correlate, reconcile, and assess the
reliability of the various value indications and determine whether the value
conclusion should be based on a single valuation method or a combination
of valuation methods.[34]

The American Society of Appraisers' Business Valuation Standards are
similar, saying:

The appraiser shall select and apply appropriate valuation approaches, methods and procedures. The conclusion of value reached by the appraiser will be based on value indications resulting from one or more methods performed under one or more appraisal approaches. The selection and reliance on appropriate methods and procedures depends on the judgment of the appraiser and not on any prescribed formula. One or more approaches may not be relevant to a particular situation, and more than one method under an approach may be relevant. The appraiser must use informed judgment when determining the relative weight to be accorded to indications of value reached on the basis of various methods, or whether the indication of value from a single method should be conclusive.[35]

The implementation guidance for SFAS 157 provides two examples of the use of multiple valuation techniques. They illustrate some of the factors that must be considered in determining fair value. Some key points are:

- When using multiple valuation techniques the goal is to determine the point within a range that is most representative of fair value in the circumstances.
- Sufficient data must be available to apply the valuation approach.
- A particular approach may not be appropriate to a specific fair value measurement.
- The fair value indicated by a particular approach will fall into a range.
- The relative weight ascribed to an approach depends on the relative reliability of the inputs.
- The number and subjectivity of the adjustments to inputs determines their relative reliability.
- The degree to which the ranges overlap should be evaluated.
- The reasonableness of the ranges must be considered.
- The width of the range and where the majority of data points fall within the range provides information to be considered.
- The attributes of the asset being valued may make the selection of one approach more appropriate to the exclusion of another.[36]

In the "Background Information and Basis for Conclusion" section of SFAS 157, the FASB emphasized that:

in many cases, multiple valuation techniques may not be appropriate or cost beneficial ... Consistent with existing valuation practice, valuation techniques that are appropriate in the circumstances and for which sufficient data are available should be used to measure fair value. The Statement does not specify the valuation technique that should be used in any particular circumstances. Determining the appropriateness of valuation techniques in the circumstances requires judgment. . . . The Board expects that in some cases a single valuation technique will be used. In other cases, multiple valuation techniques will be used, and the results of those techniques evaluated and weighted, as appropriate, in determining fair value. . . . However, in all cases, the objective is to use the valuation technique (or combination of valuation techniques) that is appropriate in the circumstances and for which there are sufficient data.[37]

A final requirement of SFAS 157 relating to valuation techniques used to measure fair value is that the technique must be consistently applied. Paragraph 20 states that a change in valuation technique or its application would be appropriate when the change "results in a measurement that is equally or more representative of fair value in the circumstances." Examples of situations when it would be appropriate to change techniques include when new markets develop, when new information becomes available, when information previously used is no longer available, and when valuation techniques improve. A change in the weighting of multiple valuation techniques would be considered a change in application. Changes in valuation techniques or the application of those techniques shall be accounted for as a change in estimate under FASB Statement No. 154, *Accounting Changes and Error Corrections*. The disclosure requirements of SFAS 154 are not applicable to changes in valuation techniques because the board did not consider them to be cost-beneficial.[38]

Conclusion

Although they lack physical substance, intangible assets are capable of contributing significant value to a business enterprise. Globalization and advances in technology have contributed to a shift in the relative value of many entities from primarily tangible assets to intangible assets. Legal protections such as copyrights and patents allow developers of intellectual property to benefit from their efforts, which also contribute to the shift in value to intangible assets. Intangible assets differ from tangible assets because these assets derive value from their ability to generate a competitive advantage in the form of higher profits. Nonrivalry scalability, or the ability to accommodate multiple users, and networking, a direct relationship between the number of users and value, are economic drivers of the value of intangible assets.

In a business combination, intangible assets should be recognized in financial reporting if they meet either the separable or the contractual criteria.

To help preparers identify intangible assets, the FASB introduced five broad categories for their classification. The categories are (1) marketing-, (2) customer-, (3) artistic-, (4) contractual-, and (5) technology-related intangible assets. For financial accounting purposes, goodwill has a specific meaning. It is the excess purchase price paid in a business combination over and above the fair value of the company's other tangible and intangible assets. As such, goodwill has an economic basis equal to the future benefits arising from all assets acquired in a business combination that are not individually identified and separately recognized.

Ascertaining an intangible asset's useful life is a fundamental step in determining the fair value of the asset. The useful life is the period over which the asset will contribute cash flows to the business entity. A clear understanding of the economic factors affecting a particular intangible asset such as its uses, substitutes, competition, demand, obsolescence, economic risks, and legal, regulatory, or contractual provisions is essential in determining the asset's useful life.

An economic balance sheet is another tool that may provide insight when determining the value of an intangible asset. The economic balance sheet allows the preparer to calculate the value of a company's intangible assets and goodwill in total. The economic balance sheet also helps calculate the required rate of return for tangible and intangible assets by using the company's weighted average cost of capital as a reference point.

ASC 820, *Fair Value Measurements and Disclosures,* requires the application of three valuation techniques to measure the fair value of an asset or liability: the cost, market, and income approach. These same three valuation methods are widely used in the valuation and appraisal industries. *Fair Value Measurement* says that the selection of an appropriate method or methods depends on the circumstances and the availability of data. In some cases, a single valuation technique would be appropriate, and in others case, multiple techniques would be appropriate. The selection and weighting of the techniques requires the use of judgment. Finally, *Fair Value Measurement* requires the consistent application of the valuation technique. The cost, market and income valuation techniques are the subjects of the next three chapters.

Notes

1. *International Glossary of Business Valuation Terms,* AICPA SSVS No. 1 Appendix B, www.aicpa.org (accessed April 16, 2009).
2. *Dictionary of Finance and Investment Terms,* 6th ed. (New York: Barron Educational Services, 2003).
3. FASB Glossary, www.fasb.org (accessed April 20, 2009).

4. Statute of Monopolies 1623, "The UK Statute Law Database Office of Public Sector Information," www.statutelaw.gov (accessed April 21, 2009).
5. "Intellectual Property," Microsoft Encarta Online Encyclopedia 2009, 1997–2009 Microsoft Corporation, http://encarta.msn.com (accessed April 19, 2009).
6. "Intangible Asset & Intellectual Property Valuation: A Multidisciplinary Perspective," World Intellectual Property Organization, www.wipo.int.
7. "Modern Metrix Measurement and Analytics in Marketing, Media and Political Research in XXI Century," http://mmx.typepad.com/mmx/.
8. Lev, Baruch, *Intangibles: Management, Measurement, and Reporting* (Washington, DC: Brookings Institution Press, 2001), 22.
9. *Id.*, page 26.
10. Adobe Systems Incorporated Corporate Overview, www.adobe.com (accessed April 21, 2009).
11. Nakamura, Leonard I, Working Paper No. 01-15. "What Is the U.S. Gross Investment in Intangibles? (at least) One Trillion Dollars a Year!" Federal Reserve Bank of Philadelphia, October 2001.
12. SFAS 141(R) *Business Combinations,* paragraph 3k.
13. *Id.*, paragraphs A29–A56.
14. "Tiffany Blue: A Color of Distinction," www.tiffany.com.
15. SFAS 141(R), paragraph A37.
16. *Id.*, paragraphs A44–A45.
17. Schneider, John, "The NBC Chimes Machine," www.bayarearadio.org/schneider/chimes.shtml.
18. "Wireless Access with Whispernet," www.amazon.com (accessed April 16, 2009).
19. SFAS 141(R), paragraphs A29–A56.
20. *International Glossary of Business Valuation Terms,* AICPA SSVS No.1 Appendix B, www.aicpa.org (accessed April 16, 2009).
21. "What Is Intellectual Property?" World Intellectual Property Organization, www.wipo.int (accessed April 16, 2009).
22. Glossary USPTO Web site, www.uspto.gov (accessed April 18, 2009).
23. *Id.*
24. *Id.*
25. *Id.*
26. *Dictionary of Finance and Investment Terms,* 6th ed. (New York: Barron Educational Services, 2003).
27. FASB Glossary, www.fasb.org (accessed April 17, 2009).
28. SFAS 142, footnote 9, page 142–10.
29. FASB ASC 350 (SFAS 142).
30. Lev, Baruch, *Intangibles: Management, Measurement, and Reporting* (Washington, DC: Brookings Institution Press, 2001), 37–45.
31. FASB ASC 820 (SFAS 157), paragraph 18.
32. Mard, Michael J., Steven D. Hyden, and Edward W. Trott, *Business Combinations with SFAS 141R, 157 and 160* (Hoboken, NJ: John Wiley & Sons, 2009), 21.
33. *International Glossary of Business Valuation Terms*, 2001.

34. Chiovari, Cory R., and Robert F. Reilly, "The Financial Adviser and the AICPA Statement on Standards for Valuation Services," *Insights* (Winter 2008).
35. American Society of Appraisers Business Valuation Standards BVS-I IV A, BVS-VI II B, III A & B, 2008.
36. FASB SFAS 157, paragraphs A13–A19.
37. FASB SFAS 157, paragraphs C54–C56.
38. *Id.*, paragraphs 20 and C57.

CHAPTER 4

The Cost Approach

The cost approach is one of the three valuation approaches used to measure fair value in financial reporting. The cost approach is often referred to as the asset approach, and the terms are used interchangeably. For instance, the American Society of Appraisers (ASA) Business Valuation Standards say that "in business valuation, the asset-based approach may be analogous to the cost approach of other appraisal disciplines."[1]

However, the *International Glossary of Business Valuation Terms* has separate definitions for the cost approach and asset approach. The glossary defines the cost approach as "a general way of estimating a value indication of an individual asset by quantifying the amount of money that would be required to replace the future service capability of that asset." Conversely, the glossary defines the asset approach as "a general way of determining a value indication of a business, business ownership interest or security by using one or more methods based on the value of the assets of that business net of liabilities."[2]

The difference between the two definitions is that the cost approach is more often used to describe the measurement of fair value of an individual asset while the asset approach is used to measure the fair value of a business, ownership interest, or security. Under the definition of the cost approach, fair value is measured as the cost to replace the service capacity of the asset. Under the definition of the asset approach, fair value measurement of an entity is the summation of individual asset and liability values determined by various other valuation methods.

According to the ASA Business Valuation Standards, using the asset approach to measure the fair value of an entity may not always be appropriate. Under most circumstances, the asset approach should not be the sole appraisal approach to value an operating entity that is a going concern. The asset approach is more appropriately used to value real estate holding companies or companies in liquidation.[3] The reason for this caution is that the

Thanks to Lynn Pierson for her assistance in writing this chapter.

basic form of the asset approach typically does not consider the fair value of unidentified assets, such as goodwill.

In the real estate profession, the cost approach is defined as "a set of procedures through which a value indication is derived for the fee simple interest in a property by estimating the current cost to construct a reproduction of, or replacement for, the existing structure plus any profit or incentive; deducting depreciation from the total cost; and adding the estimated land value."[4] This definition from the real estate profession is interesting in that it includes a "profit or incentive" as part of the costs included in the analysis.

In *Intellectual Property, Valuation, Exploitation, and Infringement Damages*, the authors Gordon Smith and Russell Parr describe the use of the cost approach to measuring fair value, which can be extended to intangible assets, by saying:

> *The cost approach seeks to measure the future benefits of ownership by quantifying the amount of money that would be required to replace the future service capacity of the subject intellectual property. The assumption underlying this approach is that the cost to purchase or develop new property is commensurate with the economic value of the service that the property can provide during its life . . . Using a cost approach to develop an indication of market value, however, requires consideration of economic obsolescence, and in this instance the appraiser must decide to what extent future economic benefits will support an investment at the indicated value.*[5]

The Cost Approach under FASB ASC 820, *Fair Value Measurements and Disclosures* (SFAS No. 157)

The valuation concepts in FASB ASC 820, *Fair Value Measurements and Disclosures* (SFAS No. 157), are similar to those previously described. In financial reporting the cost approach as presented in Paragraph 18c of *Fair Value Measurements and Disclosures* is defined as:

> *The cost approach is based on the amount that currently would be required to replace the service capacity of an asset (often referred to as current replacement cost). From the perspective of a market participant (seller), the price that would be received for the asset is determined based on the cost to a market participant (buyer) to acquire or construct a substitute asset of comparable utility, adjusted for obsolescence. Obsolescence encompasses physical deterioration, functional (technological) obsolescence, and economic (external) obsolescence and is broader than depreciation for financial reporting purposes or tax purposes.*[6]

The first element in the definition of the cost approach under FASB ASC 820, *Fair Value Measurements and Disclosures* (SFAS No. 157), is the concept of replacing the service capacity, or utility of an asset. The AICPA's Consulting Services Practice Aid 99-2, *Valuing Intellectual Property and Calculating Infringement Damages,* while not directly related to measuring fair value, still provides insight to this concept by saying:

> *Replacement cost contemplates the cost to recreate the functionality or utility of the subject discrete intangible asset, but in a form or appearance that may be quiet different from the actual intangible asset subject to appraisal. Functionality is an engineering concept that means the ability of the subject intangible asset to perform the task for which it was designed. Utility is an economics concept that means the ability of the subject intangible asset to provide an equivalent amount of satisfaction.*[7]

In economics, utility is a measure of happiness or relative satisfaction. Utility can also be thought of as a measure of economic returns that the investor expects the investment to generate.[8] Therefore, two very different assets could provide the same expected return on investment and thus the same utility.

The principle of substitution is a second element in the definition of the cost approach under FASB ASC 820, *Fair Value Measurements and Disclosures* (SFAS No. 157). Fair value is an exit price to a market participant. Under the principle of substitution, a seller can receive a price no higher than the price a buyer is willing to pay. The price a buyer is willing to pay is capped by what it would cost to purchase or construct a substitute asset of equal utility. This principle of substitution is also found in real estate appraisal. In *The Appraisal of Real Estate,* the Appraisal Institute describes the principle of substitution as:

> *The principle of substitution states that when several similar or commensurate commodities, goods or services are available, the one with the lowest price attracts the greatest demand and widest distribution. This principle assumes rational, prudent market behavior with no undue cost to delay. According to the principle of substitution, a buyer will not pay more for one property than for another that is equally desirable. Property values tend to be set by the price of acquiring equally desirable substitute property. The principle of substitution recognizes that buyers and sellers of real property have options; i.e., other properties are available for similar uses.*[9]

A third element in the definition of the cost approach under FASB ASC 820, *Fair Value Measurements and Disclosures,* and (SFAS No. 157) describes the potential obsolescence adjustments to reconcile the price of the substitute asset to the value of the subject asset. If the substitute asset provides greater utility, the buyer would pay more to purchase it. The replacement cost of the subject asset would be equal to the price a buyer would pay for a better substitute less an adjustment for the subject asset's obsolescence. The obsolescence factor would be equal to the excess utility of the replacement plus any other obsolescence in the subject asset. The AICPA's Practice Aid further describes the replacement concept under the cost approach by noting that:

> *Although the replacement intangible asset performs the same task as the subject intangible asset, the replacement asset is often better in some way than the subject asset. In that case, the replacement property may yield more satisfaction than the subject property. If this is true, the analyst should be careful to adjust this factor in the obsolescence estimation of the replacement cost analysis.*[10]

Obsolescence is a state that can be described as worn out, no longer in use, or outmoded in style, design, or construction.[11] The existence of obsolescence generally causes a reduction in the value of an asset. The three types of obsolescence mentioned specifically in FASB ASC 820, *Fair Value Measurements and Disclosures,* and (SFAS No. 157) are (1) physical deterioration, (2) functional obsolescence, and (3) economic obsolescence. Physical deterioration results from physical wear and tear caused by the asset's use or its aging. Functional obsolescence results when an asset is unable to perform the function for which it was originally intended. Advances in technology create technological obsolescence, which is a type of functional obsolescence. Economic obsolescence occurs when the asset is still able to function as it was originally intended, but not profitably. Economic obsolescence occurs when competitive market forces external to the entity reduce the asset's ability to earn a satisfactory return, thereby decreasing its value.[12,13]

One final point to emphasize about the definition of cost approach under FASB ASC 820, *Fair Value Measurements and Disclosures,* and (SFAS No. 157) is that the goal is to measure the fair value of an asset. The fair value is the price agreed on by market participants acting in their own self-interests. It is based on the assumptions that each market participant would use to price the asset. Under the cost approach, the seller assumes that the price cannot exceed an amount that the buyer is willing to pay. The buyer assumes that he will only pay an amount that is less than or equal to what it would cost to purchase or construct a similar asset. Therefore, under the cost approach, the price is a market price, the price at which the asset could be sold to a market participant.

Economic Foundation for the Cost Approach

Although the economic foundation of the cost approach was discussed in the previous section, they were not specifically identified. The economic foundation for the cost approach is concisely summarized in the AICPA's Practice Aid 99-2, *Valuing Intellectual Property and Calculating Infringement Damages*. According to the AICPA:

> *The theoretical underpinnings of the various cost approach valuation methods for valuing discrete intangible assets relate to the economic principles of substitution, supply and demand, and externalities.*
>
> - Substitution. *This principle affirms that no prudent buyer would pay more for a discrete intangible asset than the cost to construct an intangible of equal desirability and utility.*
> - Supply and demand. *Shifts in supply and demand cause costs to increase and decrease and cause changes in the need for supply of different kinds of discrete intangible assets.*
> - Externalities. *Gains or losses from external factors may accrue to intangible assets. External conditions may cause a newly constructed discrete intangible to be worth more or less than its original cost.*[14]

Cost versus Price versus Fair Value

Assuming that fair value is measured by the market price that a market participant would receive when selling an asset, and assuming that fair value is limited to the amount it would cost a buyer to purchase or construct a similar asset, then one might be tempted to conclude that cost equals price equals fair value. The conclusion may be appropriate, but first one must understand what distinguishes each of these terms and what other factors influence their relationship before concluding that cost can be used to measure fair value.

Cost refers to either the historic costs spent to create an asset or the amount that would be spent to re-create the asset as of the measurement date. Cost has a factual basis. Price also has a factual basis and is the amount paid to purchase an asset. Price is determined through a market transaction at a specific point in time. But the cost to create an asset under traditional cost approach methods and the price paid to purchase a similar asset would not be the same unless profitability and the cost of capital employed were also included as inherent costs of the asset under the cost approach.

When an entity develops an asset internally, it incurs direct costs for materials and labor. Other indirect costs such as employee benefits, administration, and utilities are typically allocated to the project, but the cost of capital and expected profit are not typically allocated to the project. However, when an entity purchases an asset, the acquisition price typically takes into consideration all the direct and indirect costs of producing the asset plus a markup. The markup provides the seller a reasonable profit and includes the seller's opportunity cost of capital. Entrepreneurial profit provides an incentive for the seller to be in business. The opportunity cost of capital provides the seller an incentive to direct resources to produce that specific asset to the exclusion of all other possible products. So the difference between the price to purchase an asset and the cost to create a similar asset can often be attributed to entrepreneurial profit and opportunity cost.

One of the shortcomings of the cost approach to measuring fair value is that traditionally entrepreneurial profit and opportunity costs have not often been included. There are two reasons for this. First, the historic costs on which the cost approach is based often tend not to measure entrepreneurial profit and incentive. This is particularly true for intangible assets as they are typically created or developed internally. Second, many valuation specialists do not adjust historic costs to include profit and incentive before using historic cost as the basis for the application of the cost approach to the measurement of fair value. There are inconsistencies in practice among valuation specialists and there is a lack of clear, authoritative guidance on the subject.

In a speech delivered at the 2005 AICPA National Conference on Current SEC and PCAOB Developments, Pamela Schlosser, at the time the Professional Accounting Fellow for the Office of the Chief Accountant of the U. S. Securities and Exchange Commission, briefly touched on the shortcomings of the cost approach to measure fair value while discussing customer-related intangibles. She said:

> *We are aware of questions regarding what valuation methodology should be used to estimate the fair value of intangible assets. Although the appropriateness of any valuation technique is highly dependent on individual facts and circumstances, I believe an income approach is generally the most appropriate method for estimating the fair value of customer-related intangible assets. Under this approach, the future benefits of those relationships can be quantified in the form of cash flows expected to be generated from incremental sales to those customers. On the other hand, the use of the cost approach has generally been challenged since, in the staff's experience, the models failed to capture all associated costs that would be necessary to rebuild that customer relationship and the resultant value was not deemed sufficient when compared to values derived by other approaches.*[15]

In essence, Schlosser is appropriately saying that the traditional cost approach methods generally fail to capture certain costs such as entrepreneur's profit and incentive. This limitation not only applies to measuring the fair value of customer relationships, but other assets using these methods as well. A potential solution to this problem is to adjust replacement costs by adding entrepreneur's profit and opportunity cost. If the entrepreneur's profit and incentive are included in the cost to create an asset, then the fully burdened historic cost would more closely resemble a historic market price and would serve as a better base from which to measure fair value under the cost approach. The resulting fair value measurement would be a close approximation of the fair value measurements using methods under the market and income approaches.

Some have asserted that the income approach is more appropriate to measure the fair value of certain intangible assets because it better captures the incremental future benefits associated with those intangibles. Although it is true that the income approach is preferred for the measurement of fair value when the asset is the primary asset associated with the generation of the entity's revenues, it would be incorrect to conclude that the cost approach to fair value measurement ignore future economic benefits, particularly if those methods consider entrepreneurial profits and the opportunity cost of capital.

The Role of Expected Economic Benefits in the Cost Approach

Although the cost approach to valuation traditionally does not directly measure the expected future benefits, the cost approach relies on an underlying assumption that future economic benefits are sufficient to cover the cost of the investment.[16] Economic benefits would take the form of an expected sales price, or future cash flows from revenues or reduced expenses. Entities often perform a cost versus benefit financial analysis to decide whether an investment in an entire entity, operating unit, or asset would be profitable. The cost of purchasing or creating the asset is compared to expected future benefits discounted at a project-specific rate of return, or hurdle rate. The rate of return would cover the cost of capital plus a risk premium specific to the asset, plus an amount to provide profit. The cost of capital is typically the entity's weighted average cost of capital. However, the valuation specialist may consider how the asset is typically financed when selecting the appropriate mix of debt and equity. The considerations are similar to those when calculating a required return under the income approach. If the expected future benefits discounted at the cost of capital exceed the cost of constructing or purchasing the asset, then the investment is considered worthwhile.

The relationship between the price to purchase the asset or the cost to develop the asset and its expected future benefit is relatively straightforward when the decision is made to invest in the subject asset. However, future economic benefits are also considered when determining the cost to reproduce or replace the subject asset on the valuation date. If future economic benefits are not sufficient to cover the cost to reproduce or replace the asset, then the subject asset is considered to be obsolete, and the subject asset's fair value is reduced by an amount equal to the shortfall in economic benefits. Economic obsolescence is covered in subsequent sections of this chapter.

Reproduction Cost versus Replacement Cost

Although paragraph 18c of FASB ASC 820, *Fair Value Measurements and Disclosures* (SFAS No. 157), specifically says that the cost approach is based on the amount that currently would be required to replace the service capacity of an asset (current replacement cost)," [17] understanding reproduction cost will provide a good foundation for understanding replacement cost. Reconciling reproduction cost to replacement cost will also provide a key to understanding and quantifying obsolescence.

The definitions of reproduction and replacement cost in *Valuing Intangible Assets* by Robert Reilly and Robert Schweihs are widely cited among valuation specialists because they so completely describe and differentiate the two concepts. According to Reilly and Schweihs, the valuation specialist must clearly understand the two approaches and decide which type of cost will be estimated from the start of the analysis.

> *Reproduction cost is the estimated cost to construct, at current prices as of the date of the analysis, an exact duplicate or replica of the subject intangible asset, using the same materials, production standards, design, layout, and quality of workmanship as the subject intangible asset. The reproduction intangible asset will include the same inadequacies, super-adequacies, and obsolescence as the subject intangible asset.*
>
> *Replacement cost is the estimated cost to construct, at current prices as of the date of the analysis, an intangible asset with equivalent utility to the subject intangible, using modern materials, production standards, design, layout, and quality workmanship. The replacement intangible asset will exclude all curable inadequacies, super-adequacies, and obsolescence that are present in the subject intangible asset.* [18]

Reproduction cost is the cost of creating an exact replica in today's dollars, and it is commonly referred to as "cost of reproduction new (CRN)."

The cost of replacement (COR) is the cost of purchasing or constructing an asset with equal utility in today's dollars. It is usually less expensive to replace an asset than it is to reproduce an asset. And the replacement is usually functionally superior to the original.

An important point to emphasize is that both reproduction and replacement cost are measured as of the valuation date. They are current costs, not historic costs. When calculating reproduction or replacement costs, any changes in the prices of labor or materials since the original asset was created would be incorporated into current costs. Efficiencies in the utilization of materials and labor would also be reflected in current costs.

The difference between the current cost to reproduce a replica and the current cost to replace it with a better substitute relates to obsolescence present in the original. Replacement cost is generally considered the most meaningful basis of value for fair value measurement under the cost approach. However, whether the starting point of a valuation analysis is from the cost of reproduction or from the cost of replacement, properly considering obsolescence will lead to the same value conclusion. The relationship can be summarized in the formula:

$$\text{Cost of Reproduction New (CRN)} - \text{Obsolescence}$$
$$= \text{Cost of Replacement (COR)}[19]$$

To illustrate the difference between reproduction cost and replacement cost, suppose a sixteenth-century European castle has been destroyed by fire. Even if it were possible to rebuild the castle using historic materials and similar craftsmanship, the cost in today's dollars would be staggering. Its modern replacement would be different in design and appearance, and would probably be a home or museum instead of a castle. The replacement would provide similar or superior utility and would have all the modern conveniences, such as running water, electricity, and central heat and air. The cost to build a lavish modern replacement would be significantly less than the cost to reproduce the castle. All the difference in materials, craftsmanship, and functionality would be attributable to the castle's obsolescence.

Components of Cost

Whether determining reproduction cost or replacement cost the valuation specialist should consider all relevant component costs associated with the subject asset. Relevant component costs may not be those incurred when constructing or creating the original asset, but would be those currently required to re-create or replace the asset. Reilly and Schweihs describe common component costs as material, labor, overhead, developer's profit, and entrepreneurial incentive.

Material costs generally represent a significant portion of a tangible asset's total costs. For a building project, material costs would include everything from the cost of the land to the cost of incidental supplies used in construction. Material costs are typically incidental to the creation of intangible assets and would include items such as data storage units, planning documents, laboratory notebooks, patterns, and technical documentation. All material costs relating to the subject asset, from the design phase to installation, would be included in the analysis of cost.

Labor costs would include all salaries and wages paid to employees while working on the project. Labor costs would also typically include payments to contractors involved in the project. Labor costs are usually the most significant component cost in the creation of intangible assets and they are often significant to tangible assets, as well.

Overhead costs such as payroll taxes and fringe benefits for development personnel, and utilities and operating expenses indirectly contribute to the production or development of the subject asset. An allocation of management and support personnel salary and wages would also be included in overhead costs. Project overhead allocations are commonly based on the percentage of time an employee dedicates to the project. Overhead costs are a component in the measurement of reproduction or replacement cost under the cost approach.

Entrepreneur's profit is essential to a smoothly functioning economy. It underlies the production of goods, the delivery of services, and the development of new products and intellectual property. A developer would not undertake a project unless he expected to receive a return sufficient to cover all the costs of the project and to make a profit on the project. The development of intangible assets is similar to the development of real estate with respect to developer's profit. In *The Appraisal of Real Estate,* the definition of entrepreneurial profit incorporates the concept that a profit component is needed to compensate the developer for risk associated with the development of the project.[20]

However, developer's profit has not traditionally been considered a component cost for intangible assets. Under the cost approach, entrepreneur's profit can be included in the fair value measurement by estimating a percentage markup on material, labor, and overhead, or by estimating a fixed dollar markup.[21] Developer's profit can be quantified as the profit that the developer would require if the project were sold to a market participant. Although developer's profit traditionally has not always been included in the measurement of fair value under a cost approach, its omission may understate the value, depending on the facts and circumstances of the measurement.

Opportunity costs are another component of cost that must be recovered in order to compensate a developer for undertaking a specific project. The time and effort devoted to a particular project are unavailable for profitable use elsewhere for the duration of the project. The developer forgoes the return from the next most attractive investment opportunity. Opportunity cost is sometime quantified by determining the cost of capital incurred in funding the project. Similar to entrepreneurial profit, opportunity cost must be recovered in order to compensate for the risk associated with the project. Omitting opportunity cost from the cost analysis may result in an understatement of fair value.

The consideration of developer's profit and opportunity cost appears to have achieved relatively widespread acceptance within appraisal of real estate. In fact, the analysis of cost for real estate goes even further to distinguish between project profit, contractor's profit, developer's profit, entrepreneurial profit, and entrepreneurial incentive (opportunity cost).[22]

Within the valuation profession the treatment of developer's profit and entrepreneurial incentive has been inconsistent in practice. However, these costs should be considered in the measurement of fair value under the cost approach. Entrepreneur's profit and opportunity cost should be considered regardless of whether the subject asset is purchased or developed internally and regardless of whether the subject asset is real estate, a tangible asset or an intangible asset. Omitting these costs could understate fair value.

Obsolescence

In previous sections, obsolescence was cited as the reason the subject asset is worth less than the cost of a modern replacement. Obsolescence is equal to the excess utility of the modern replacement. The difference between the cost to reproduce a replica and the cost of the modern replacement was attributed to the existence of obsolescence.

These general concepts can be expanded to improve understanding of the relationships between reproduction cost, replacement, and value and to introduce more specific forms of obsolescence. Understanding the types of obsolescence and how to measure them is critical in the fair value measurement of the subject asset. According to paragraph 18c of FASB ASC 820, *Fair Value Measurements and Disclosures* (FAS No. 157), all forms of obsolescence should be considered, including physical deterioration, functional (technological) obsolescence, and economic obsolescence. The following sections will discuss how each type of obsolescence relates to value, and how to recognize and quantify each form of obsolescence.

The Relationships among Cost, Obsolescence, and Value

Obsolescence is both curable and incurable from an economic perspective. An asset's deficiencies are curable if the expected economic benefits from the improvements exceed the current cost of improvements. Deficiencies are incurable if costs exceed benefits. The following formula is more specific about the types of obsolescence that distinguish reproduction and replacement cost:

> Reproduction Cost New − Curable Functional and Technological
> Obsolescence = Replacement Cost New

An additional formula provides the key to understanding how the cost of a new replacement can be used to measure fair value:

> Replacement Cost New − Physical Deterioration − Economic
> Obsolescence − Incurable Functional and Technological
> Obsolescence = Fair Value

Whether the starting point for the valuation is reproduction cost or replacement cost, the valuation specialist will arrive at the same fair value when all forms of obsolescence are adequately considered and measured.[23]

To illustrate various forms of obsolescence, the example of the sixteenth-century castle will be expanded. Suppose the sixteenth-century castle was being used as a museum to house a collection of early armaments when it was destroyed. Although the layout of the castle was not ideal for use as a museum, improvements had been made, including the additions of heat, electricity, restroom facilities, and emergency exits. Although most of the castle was in extraordinary condition considering its age, the northern wing had been permanently closed because it needed extensive structural work. The castle was surrounded by a moat and located in the heart of a medieval village. The castle and the village are protected by historic preservation laws. In the event a historic building is destroyed, the laws specify that any new building must conform to the footprint of the original building and any surviving structure must be preserved. Even though the museum is a popular tourist destination, it fails to cover its operating expenses.

In this example, reproduction costs would include all costs to rebuild a replica of the castle by using original historic materials and similar craftsmanship. The cost of any improvements made to date, such as the additions of electricity, heat, restrooms, and emergency exits, would also be included in the reproduction costs. All reproduction costs would be in today's dollars.

The original historic materials, antiquated craftsmanship, poor layout, and energy inefficiency are all examples of functional and technological obsolescence found in the original castle. Because these deficiencies would not be replicated in the modern replacement, they are considered curable. Therefore, curable obsolescence represents the difference between the cost of the castle's replica and the cost of a new modern replacement, calculated in today's dollars.

The modern replacement would be made of contemporary materials using the latest building technology. The museum's layout would be improved to provide more display space, a better flow from room to room, and better accessibility. And the replacement would be more energy efficient. However, the cost of a new replacement museum does not equal the fair value of the original castle. Additional adjustments are necessary to measure the fair value of the original castle, which is the subject asset in this example.

First, the castle's physical deterioration must be considered. The replacement is new, but the original is quite old. And a portion of the castle was not being used because of structural deficiencies. Both age and condition are elements of physical deterioration that must be deducted from the new replacement cost when measuring the original castle's fair value.

If it does not make economic sense to replace the castle with a modern replacement, then economic obsolescence is indicated. In this example, the museum's failure to cover its operating expenses is a sign of economic obsolescence. Economic obsolescence would equal the portion of the castle's replacement cost that would not be recovered over its economic life as a museum. Economic obsolescence must also be deducted from the new replacement cost when measuring the original castle's fair value.

In this example, incurable functional and technological obsolescence are present in the new replacement because historic preservation laws require that it be rebuilt following the same footprint as the original. Had the historic preservation laws not been in effect, the museum might be larger, smaller, or a different shape than the original. Because the moat survived the fire, according to law, it has to be incorporated into the replacement's design. A moat is functionally and technologically obsolete, and these incurable forms of functional and technological obsolescence are incorporated into the castle's replacement. The castle's replacement cost must be reduced by incurable obsolescence to arrive at the fair value of the original castle.

While understanding the relationships among reproduction cost, replacement cost, obsolescence, and fair value is important, being able to quantify each element is equally important when measuring fair value. Quantifying obsolescence is the subject of the next section.

Physical Deterioration

Decreases in an asset's value due to age or due to physical wear and tear are causes of physical deterioration. Physical inspection of tangible assets will help identify wear and tear, and examination of accounting records will help identify the age of the subject asset.

Physical deterioration can be estimated by determining the cost to cure the deficiency or based on observed depreciation.[24] Another common method to quantify physical deterioration is to calculate the percent of physical deterioration (%PD) based on the age and life expectancy of the asset, as follows:

$$\%PD = [EA/(EA + RUL)] \times 100 \text{ assuming:}$$

$$EL = EA + RUL \text{ where:}$$

EA is Effective Age = the age of the asset relative to a new asset of like kind, considering rebuilding and maintenance that will extend its service life

RUL is Remaining Useful Life = the estimated period during which an asset is expected to be profitably used for its intended purpose

EL is Economic Life = the estimated total life of the asset[25]

For example, suppose a sports drink manufacturer uses a mobile marketing trailer to promote its products at major sporting events. When it was originally built, the trailer was expected to have a 10-year life. Five years later, the company unveiled a new advertising campaign with new logos, colors, and slogans. As part of the new campaign, the trailer was redesigned and refurbished. The company plans to use the refurbished trailer for eight more years. What is the trailer's percentage of physical deterioration?

RUL = 8 years, as the company plans to use the trailer for 8 more years

EL = 10 years, because the estimated total life of a new trailer is 10 years

EA = 2 years, because the refurbished trailer service life has been extended to 8 years, which compares to a 10-year life for a new trailer

$$\%PD = [2/(2 + 8)] \times 100 = 20\%$$

Although it is not impossible for intangible assets to experience physical deterioration, this form of obsolescence is not usually applicable to intangible assets[26] because they rarely have physical form. And any deterioration in an intangible asset due to age would most likely be attributable to functional or economic obsolescence rather than physical deterioration.

Functional (Technological) Obsolescence

Functional obsolescence is a decrease in the subject asset's value due to its inability to perform the function for which it was designed. The intended function does not change; the subject asset's ability to perform the function has declined. Technological obsolescence is a type of functional obsolescence. It results when the function itself has become obsolete. Even though the function is obsolete, the subject asset is still able to perform the function.[27] For example, software in need of modification or enhancement might be considered functionally obsolete. But if the software were to be rewritten in a different programming language, using different hardware, operating systems, or utilities on the valuation date, then technological obsolescence would be indicated.[28]

Physical inspection is one method used to identify functional obsolescence. It is most effective for identifying functional obsolescence for tangible assets. Inefficient facility layout, structural deficiencies, excess capacity, and deficient capacity are all physical manifestations of functional obsolescence.

Comparative analysis is the other commonly used method to identify functional obsolescence, and it applies to technological obsolescence as well. To assess whether functional obsolescence exists, the subject asset is compared to a new version of itself. To assess whether technological obsolescence exists, the subject asset is compared to a new, ideal replacement. If continued use of the subject asset results in excess operating costs, maintenance costs, usage costs, or excess capital costs compared to a new replica or replacement, then obsolescence is indicated.

Measuring functional or technological obsolescence can be accomplished in a number of ways. One method is to calculate the cost to cure the functional or technical deficiency. The cost-to-cure method is most often used to measure obsolescence resulting from physical structural or capacity deficiencies. When there is excess capacity, a second method can be used to calculate the pro rata portion of capital costs attributable to the excess capacity. The pro rata excess capital costs would be a measure of obsolescence. A final method is to quantify excess operating costs attributable to the subject asset over its remaining useful life. This can be accomplished by using a one-period capitalization model[29] or a multiperiod discounted cash flow model. Capitalized or discounted excess costs would be a measure of the amount of obsolescence. The capitalized or discounted excess cost method is appropriate for calculating functional and technological obsolescence for both tangible and intangible assets.

Economic (External) Obsolescence

Economic obsolescence is the decrease in the value of an asset due to influences that are external to the subject asset. Economic obsolescence exists when the subject asset is unable to generate a sufficient rate of return over its expected remaining life based on its indicated value. Economic obsolescence is generally considered to be incurable.[30] Economic obsolescence typically cannot be determined through physical inspection, and it is broadly the same for tangible and intangible assets.

The American Society of Appraisers lists common external causes of economic obsolescence as:

- A declining industry
- Inability to get financing
- Loss of material or labor sources
- New legislation or ordinances
- Increases in the price of inputs without the ability to increase product prices
- Reduced demand for the product
- Increased competition
- Inflation or high interest rates[31]

In *Intellectual Property,* Smith and Parr describe four forms of economic obsolescence that can occur in trademarks: (1) event obsolescence, (2) technological obsolescence, (3) product obsolescence, and (4) cultural obsolescence. Each form of economic obsolescence prohibits the trademark from achieving its full potential because it reduces the trademark's capacity to contribute to the entity's earnings. All are considered economic obsolescence because they reflect factors external to the trademark itself.[32]

Smith and Parr further discuss the four forms of obsolescence by providing examples of each one. Event obsolescence occurs when unusual events reduce the potential value of a trademark. Product tampering might have caused the Tylenol trademark irreparable damage had the company not responded quickly and effectively. When a company's products become technologically obsolete, its trademark may also be damaged. The Betamax trademark has little value today because it is associated with obsolete home videocassette recording devices from the 1970s. Product obsolescence occurs when the value of a trademark associated with a product diminishes as the product goes out of use or is diminished in importance. In the 1940s and 1950s, automobile automatic transmissions were trademarked because they were highly prized and touted in company advertisements. Today, automatic transmissions are standard equipment and the trademarks have lost their value. Finally, cultural obsolescence occurs when religious, ethnic, or gender-related sensibilities inhibit the use of a trademark. The controversy over the use of Native American images and names in sports organizations is an example of cultural obsolescence.[33]

In order to determine whether economic obsolescence exists, a comparative analysis is helpful. The subject asset's economic performance is compared to its historical performance, to its budgeted performance, to a similar asset, or to an industry average. Common points of comparison are profit margins, returns on investment, unit selling price, unit cost of goods sold, and unit sales volume. Deficiencies in the comparative analysis would indicate that there is an economic shortfall with respect to the subject asset. Once identified, the economic shortfall is projected over the subject asset's remaining useful life and discounted to the present value. The present value of the economic shortfall is equal to economic obsolescence.

Another method to measure economic obsolescence is to compare the entity's business enterprise value to the total fair value of all its underlying assets, less liabilities. If the business enterprise value or fair value of the business is less than the sum of working capital, fixed assets, intangible assets, and other assets at fair value, the difference is attributable to economic obsolescence.[34]

Applying the Cost Approach

The cost approach is most often used to measure the fair values of both tangible and intangible assets that are not direct sources of cash flow generation for the entity. These contributory assets tend to be less significant to the entity's overall value. The cost approach is also used when the market or income approaches are not feasible. The cost approach is the preferable approach when the asset is readily replaceable and when the cost of reconstructing or replacing the subject asset with a similar asset can be reasonably determined.[35] The cost approach may also be preferable when valuing entities with heavy investments in tangible assets or when operating earnings are insignificant relative to the value of the underlying assets.[36]

While the application of the cost approach is more common in the valuation of tangible assets; the cost approach can be applied to intangible assets as well. The cost approach is more successfully applied to intangible assets when they are newer, when substitutes exist, and when estimating the fair value from the perspective of the current owner under an "in-use" premise. The cost approach is less applicable to unique intangibles that benefit from legal protection, such as trademarks and copyrights. It is also less applicable when estimating the value of intangibles using an "in-exchange" premise.[37] The American Society of Appraisers suggests that the cost approach is appropriately used to measure the fair values of the following intangible assets:

- Assembled workforce
- Internally developed and used software
- Mailing lists
- Engineering drawings
- Packaging designs[38]

In *Intellectual Property, Valuation, Exploitation, and Infringement Damages* by Smith and Parr, the authors describe three methods for applying the cost approach: historical cost trending, the unit cost method, and the unit of production method.

Historical Cost Trending

Historical cost trending is possible when the business entity has maintained records from the purchase, creation, or development of the subject asset. If the subject asset was purchased from another party in a market transaction, a historic price is available. The valuation specialist should consider whether market conditions existing on the historic transaction date are similar to market conditions existing on the valuation date. Market conditions would include market efficiency, the parties' relative negotiating strength, and the terms and conditions of the transaction such as price, timing, and other considerations.[39] If conditions are similar on the valuation date, then historic prices are suitable for cost trending. When the subject asset is created or developed internally, labor force market conditions would be applicable.

The historic prices for purchased assets and the historic costs of developed assets are expressed as current reproduction costs by applying an appropriate price index. Because the current costs represent the cost to reproduce a new replica of the subject asset and because the subject asset is not new, the current cost must be reduced by an amount equal to the subject asset's physical deterioration and functional and economic obsolescence, as appropriate.

For internally developed assets, the valuation specialist must also consider whether a similar amount of effort would be required to replicate the subject asset or whether new technology would permit a more efficient deployment of effort. The difference in the number of hours originally required to produce an asset and the number of hours required on the valuation date would indicate functional obsolescence in the original. The required number of hours required to replace the subject asset on the valuation date times the trended historical cost would result in an indication of the asset's fair value under the cost approach.

Exhibit 4.1 shows the fair value of customer order processing software measured using the replacement cost based on trending historic cost.

The Unit Cost Method

The unit cost method is simply a direct estimate of all the costs that would be incurred to create a similar replacement for the subject asset. The

EXHIBIT 4.1 ABC Corporation Customer Order Processing Software, Replacement Cost Based on Historic Cost Trending, as of June 30, 20X8

Year Cost Incurred	Price Index (1)	Historic Cost (2)	Index Adjustment Factor	Cost
20X0	168.9	1,124,800	210.3/168.9	$ 1,400,506
20X1	173.5	1,362,874	210.3/173.5	1,651,945
20X2	175.9	1,237,400	210.3/175.9	1,479,393
Trended Original Cost				4,531,843
Opportunity Cost: 15%, 26 months re-create (3)				1,472,849
Entrepreneur's Profit: 4% 26 months to re-create (3)				392,760
Reproduction Cost				6,397,452
Less: Obsolescence of 30% (3)				(1,919,236)
Before-Tax Replacement Cost				4,478,216
Less: Tax @ 38%				(1,701,722)
After-Tax Replacement Cost				2,776,494
Amortization Benefit Multiplier				1.16
Fair Value of Customer Order Processing Software, rounded				$ 3,221,000

Notes:
(1) Bureau of Labor Statistics—Urban Wage Earners

Base year—1984	100.0
20X0	168.9
20X1	173.5
20X2	175.9
Mid-year—20X8	210.3

(2) Historic costs include materials, direct labor, employment benefits, and overhead.
(3) Per management, opportunity cost is based on cost of capital; entrepeneur's profit is based on opertating margins; and obsolescence is based on discussions with programmers.

replacement would include improvements necessary to cure any functional or economic obsolescence in the subject asset. The replacement cost would be an aggregate of all applicable costs, such as:

- Salaries and benefits of employees involved in the project
- Amounts paid to outside consultants, engineers, etc.
- An allocation for the salary and benefits of managers and support personnel
- Materials
- Overhead costs including office space, utilities, and computer time
- Costs to create pilots, prototypes, or models
- Testing costs
- Documentation and implementation costs[40]

EXHIBIT 4.2 ABC Corporation Inventory Control Software, Replacement Cost Based on the Unit Cost Method, as of June 30, 20X8

	Estimate Hours to Replace	Hourly Rate	Materials	Direct Labor	Benefits, Overhead, Profit & Opportunity Costs (1)	Total Costs
Specification Development	500	$80.50	—	40,250	28,980	$ 69,230
Project Management	3,000	63.75	—	191,250	137,700	328,950
Analyst	12,200	48.50	—	591,700	426,024	1,017,724
Programmer	17,750	44.50	1,850	789,875	570,042	1,361,767
Documentation	2,300	38.75	725	89,125	64,692	154,542
Testing	1,500	34.50	—	51,750	37,260	89,010
Before-Tax Replacement Cost						3,021,223
Less Tax @ 38%						(1,148,065)
After-Tax Replacement Cost						1,873,158
Fair Value of Inventory Control Software, rounded						1.16
						$ 2,173,000

Note:
(1) Benefits of 33%, overhead of 20%, opportunity costs of 15%, and entrepreneur's profit of 4%.

The unit cost method can be used to estimate the costs of tangible assets such as buildings and production lines and intangible assets such as a company's operating software, its customer relationships, or its assembled workforce.

Exhibit 4.2 provides an example of fair value measured using the unit cost method to calculate the replacement cost for ABC Corporation's inventory control software.

The Unit of Production Method

The unit of production method is another replacement cost method. Within certain industries, rules of thumb exist for determining costs. The current unit cost to construct certain types of assets is well known, relatively standard, and widely used to estimate a project's total cost. For example, certain types of software can be developed within a specific range of cost per line of code, or employees in certain industries can be hired and become fully

EXHIBIT 4.3 ABC Corporation Auto Rental Franchise, Replacement Cost Based on the Unit of Production Method, as of June 30, 20X8

Franchise Location	Number of Automobiles	Replacement Cost per Auto (1)	Total Replacement
Gainesville, Florida	98	1,000	$ 98,000
Jacksonville, Florida	330	1,000	330,000
Tallahassee, Florida	168	1,000	168,000
Augusta, Georgia	74	1,000	74,000
Brunswick, Georgia	42	1,000	42,000
Savannah, Georgia	115	1,000	115,000
Charleston, South Carolina	248	1,000	248,000
Columbia, South Carolina	174	1,000	174,000
Hilton Head, South Carolina	229	1,000	229,000
Replacement Cost Before Obsolescence Adjustment			1,478,000
Less: Obsolescence of 10% (2)			(147,800)
Before-Tax Replacement Cost			1,330,200
Less: Tax @ 38%			(505,476)
After-Tax Replacement Cost			824,724
Amortization Benefit Multiplier			1.16
Fair Value of Auto Rental Franchise, rounded			$ 957,000

Notes:

(1) Per *Business Reference Guide*, 17th edition, automobile rental companies have a franchise value of $1,000 per auto. (Opportunity cost and entrepreneur's profit are assumed to be included.)

(2) Management estimate of overcapacity within local markets.

trained within a certain range of costs per employee. Within the beverage industry, franchise rights give the owner exclusive rights to bottle and distribute products within a certain geographic area. These franchise rights are often valued using rules of thumb based on the number of cases of product sold within the bottling territory in the most recent year.

The replacement cost for ABC Corporation's franchise rights are measured using the unit of production method in Exhibit 4.3. The value of the auto rental franchise is based on a $1,000 per automobile rule of thumb commonly used in the industry.

Applying each of these three methods results in an estimate of the subject's replacement cost, assuming it is new. Any physical depreciation in the subject must be measured and deducted from the cost of replacement. Similarly, any incurable functional or economic obsolescence in the subject must be measured and deducted from the cost of replacement. The resulting amount would measure the subject asset's fair value.

Taxes under the Cost Approach

The cost approach can either be applied on a pretax or after-tax basis, and there is divergence in practice among valuation professionals with respect to this issue. The lack of consensus within the profession is primarily a result of the complexity of the U.S. Tax Code. The tax structure of the entity and the tax structure of the transaction will influence the treatment of taxes under the cost approach. Whether the fair value is being measured as the result of a business combination, litigation, for estate tax purposes, or for some other reason can potentially affect the tax treatment. Finally, the tax-related assumptions that the hypothetical market participant makes should be considered when measuring fair value. These tax-related considerations are beyond the scope of this book.

When applying the cost approach on an after-tax basis, there are two components to calculate: the tax provision, and the tax benefit from depreciation or amortization. The tax provision includes the impact of federal and state taxes. The tax provision can be calculated using a marginal tax rate, an average statutory tax rate, or an actual tax rate based on the entity's tax returns. Selection of an appropriate tax rate should encompass information from several tax years because actual tax rates tend to vary from year to year.[41]

When applying the cost approach on an after-tax basis, an amortization benefit is added to the before-tax fair value. The amortization benefit reflects the additional value resulting from the ability to deduct amortization to the intangible asset over its tax life. The amortization benefit applies only to intangible assets that are deductible for tax purposes. If the subject asset were a tangible asset, a depreciation benefit would apply. The formula for the amortization benefit follows:

$$AB = PVCF \times [n/(n - \{[PV(r, n, -1) \times (1 + r)^{\wedge}0.5] \times T\}) - 1]$$

where:

$$AB = \text{Amortization benefit}$$
$$PVCF = \text{Present value of cash flows from the subject asset}$$
$$n = \text{Amortization period}$$
$$r = \text{Asset specific discount rate}$$
$$PV(r, n, -1) \times (1 + r)^{\wedge}0.5 = \text{Present value of an annuity of \$1 over } n \text{ years, at the discount rate } r$$
$$T = \text{Tax rate}[42]$$

Limitations of the Cost Approach

The cost approach has some limitations that make its application challenging. First, the approach is not as comprehensive as the other two approaches. Many of the factors that generate economic benefit and are important drivers of value are not directly incorporated into the technique. Information about the amount, timing, and trend of the subject asset's economic benefits is not considered. The risk associated with the realization of economic benefits is traditionally not factored into the measurement of cost. Second, the estimates used to develop reproduction and replacement costs are often subjective. As more time elapses between the date the subject asset is created and the date reproduction costs are estimated, the estimates become even more subjective. For a replacement asset, as the form of the replacement becomes more unlike the original asset, the replacement cost becomes more a matter of judgment. A third limitation is that obsolescence is sometimes difficult to quantify. Finally, there is divergence in practice among valuation specialists with regard to the treatment of taxes and developer's profit and entrepreneurial incentive.

Conclusion

Even though it has limitations, the cost approach is often used to measure the fair value. It is the preferred method when the asset is readily replaceable and when the cost of reconstructing or replacing the subject asset with a similar asset can be reasonably determined. And it is often used to measure the value of assets with indirect contribution to an entity's earning's stream, or when using other methods is not practical. The cost approach is sometimes used as a starting point or as a check for the value measured under the market or income approach.

The cost method provides a reasonable indication of value when all cost components are considered (materials, labor, overhead, developer's profit, and opportunity cost) and when cost is reduced for all forms of obsolescence (physical deterioration, functional or technological obsolescence, and economic obsolescence). Fair value can be measured under the cost approach using either a reproduction cost or a replacement cost as a starting point. The cost approach rests on the economic principles of substitution, supply and demand, and externalities. Substitution refers to the replacement of an asset's future service capability with another that provides similar utility. The cost of a substitute can indicate the fair value of an asset after considering whether future economic benefits will support investment in the replacement.

Notes

1. American Society of Appraisers, "ASA Business Valuation Standards," 2008, 9.
2. American Institute of Certified Public Accountants, American Society of Appraisers, Canadian Institute of Chartered Business Valuators, National Association of Certified Valuation Analysts, and the Institute of Business Appraisers, *International Glossary of Business Valuation Terms,* 2001, pages 2 and 4.
3. American Society of Appraisers, 9.
4. Appraisal Institute, *The Appraisal of Real Estate,* 12th ed., 2001, 349.
5. Smith, Gordon V., and Russell L. Parr, *Intellectual Property, Valuation, Exploitation and Infringement Damages* (Hoboken, NJ: John Wiley & Sons, 2005), 156.
6. Financial Accounting Standards Board (FASB) Statement of Financial Standards (SFAS) No. 157, *Fair Value Measurements,* FAS157-10.
7. Agiato, Joseph A. Jr., and Michael J. Mard, *Valuing Intellectual Property and Calculating Infringement Damages,* American Institute of Certified Public Accountants Consulting Services Practice Aid 99-2, 1999, 38–39.
8. Reilly, Robert F., and Robert S. Schweihs, *The Handbook of Business Valuation and Intellectual Property Analysis* (New York: McGraw-Hill, 2004), 282.
9. Appraisal Institute, 38–39.
10. Agiato and Mard, 39.
11. *Webster's II New College Dictionary* (Boston: Houghton Mifflin, 1995), 755.
12. American Society of Appraisers, *Valuation of Intangible Assets for Financial Reporting Purposes,* Business Valuation 301 Course Materials, 225–232.
13. Agiato and Mard, 40.
14. *Id.,* 38.
15. Schlosser, Pamela R., "Statement by SEC Staff: Remarks before the 2005 AICPA National Conference on Current SEC and PCAOB Developments," December 5, 2005, www.sec.gov/news/speech/spch120505ps.htm (accessed May 26, 2009).
16. Smith and Parr, 156.
17. FASB SFAS 157, 10.
18. Reilly, Robert F., and Robert S. Schweihs, *Valuing Intangible Assets* (New York: McGraw-Hill, 1999), 122.
19. Agiato and Mard, 40–41.
20. Appraisal Institute, 360
21. Reilly and Schweihs, *Valuing Intangible Assets,* 124–126
22. Appraisal Institute, 362.
23. Agiato and Mard, 40–41.
24. Willamette Management Associates, *Property Tax Valuation White Papers: Economic Obsolescence Is an Essential Procedure of a Cost Approach to Valuation of Industrial or Commercial Properties,* www.propertytaxvaluation.com/economic_obsolescence_essential_procedure.html (accessed 4/16/2009), 4–5.
25. Hitchner, James R., *Financial Valuation Application and Models, Second Edition* (Hoboken, NJ: John Wiley & Sons, 2006), 365.
26. Mard, Michael J., "Financial Factors: Cost Approach to Valuing Intellectual Property," *Licensing Journal* (August 2000): 27.
27. Willamette Management Associates, 4–7.

28. Reilly and Schweihs, *The Handbook of Business Valuation and Intellectual Property Analysis*, 486.
29. Willamette Management Associates, 4–7.
30. Agiato and Mard, 40.
31. American Society of Appraisers, 225.
32. Smith and Parr, 236–237.
33. *Id.*
34. American Society of Appraisers, 230.
35. *Id.*, 151.
36. Garuto, Loren, and Oliver Loud, "Taking the Temperature of Health Care Valuations," *Journal of Accountancy* (October 2001): 4.
37. Reilly and Schweihs, *Valuing Intangible Assets*, 120.
38. American Society of Appraisers, 153.
39. Reilly and Schweihs, *Valuing Intangible Assets,* 121–122.
40. Smith and Parr, 161–162.
41. Hitchner, 105–106.
42. Mard, Michael, et al., *Valuation for Financial Reporting: Intangible Assets, Goodwill and Impairment Analysis, SFAS 141 and 142* (Hoboken, NJ: John Wiley & Sons, 2002), 54.

CHAPTER 5

The Market Approach

Introduction

The market approach measures the fair value of an entity or an intangible asset by comparing market indications from actual transactions for the same or similar entity or intangible asset to the applicable economic parameter for the subject entity or intangible asset. The most common market approach methods apply earnings multiples or cash flow multiples from market transactions to the earnings or cash flows for the subject entity or intangible asset.

The market approach is one of the three basic valuation techniques specified for the measurement of fair value by FASB ASC 820, *Fair Value Measurements and Disclosures* (SFAS No. 157). Additionally, the market approach is often used to measure the fair value of a reporting unit when testing goodwill for impairment under FASB ASC 350, *Intangibles—Goodwill and Other* (SFAS No. 142). This chapter describes various market approach methods for estimating the fair value of an entity or a reporting unit. The later part of the chapter also discusses various market approach methods for measuring the fair value of individual intangible assets acquired through mergers and acquisitions, as required by FASB ASC 805, *Business Combinations* (SFAS No. 141(R)).

According to FASB ASC 820, *Fair Value Measurements* (SFAS No. 157), the market approach:

> *. . . uses prices and other relevant information generated by market transactions involving identical or comparable assets or liabilities (including a business). For example, valuation techniques consistent with the market approach often use market multiples derived from set of comparables. Multiples might lie in ranges with a different multiple for each comparable. The selection of where within the range the appropriate multiple falls requires judgment, considering factors specific to the measurement(qualitative and quantitative). Valuation techniques consistent*

with the market approach include matrix pricing. Matrix pricing is a mathematical technique used principally to value debt securities without relying exclusively on quoted prices for specific securities, but rather by relying on the securities' relationship to other benchmark quoted prices.[1]

The International Glossary of Business Valuation Terms (IGBVT) defines the market approach as "a general way of determining a value indication of a business, business ownership interest, security, or intangible asset by using one or more methods that compare the subject to similar businesses, business ownership interests, securities, or intangible assets that have been sold."[2] The market approach is most often applied to the measurement of a reporting unit's fair value unit using one of two common methods: (1) the guideline public company method, or (2) the guideline transaction method. The IGBVT describes the guideline public company method as "a method within the market approach whereby market multiples are derived from market prices of stocks of companies that are engaged in the same or similar lines of business and that are actively traded on a free and open market."[3] The glossary also describes the guideline transaction method as a "merger and acquisition method within the market approach whereby pricing multiples are derived from transactions of significant interests in companies engaged in the same or similar lines of business."[4] The distinction between the two methods is that the guideline public company method uses multiples derived from the market trading price of similar publicly traded companies, while the transaction method derives multiples from the acquisition price of similar companies that were recently acquired.

Conceptually, the market approach is easy to understand. Market approach methods for measuring the fair value of an entity employ market multiples based on an earnings parameter from market-based transactions for similar companies. The multiples are calculated based on trading prices for similar publicly traded companies or calculated based on the acquisition price of similar companies that have been recently sold. The other component of the market multiple is some measure of earnings for the guideline company. The price earnings ratio (P/E) is an example of a commonly used market multiple. Another example is the invested capital to earnings before interest, taxes depreciation, and amortization multiple (INVCAP/EBITDA).

Market multiples are typically classified as either equity multiples or invested capital multiples, depending on the ownership perspective for the underlying earnings used in the multiple. These will be discussed in greater detail in a subsequent section.

Applying the Market Approach in Measuring the Fair Value of an Entity or Reporting Unit of an Entity

The market approach is often used to measure the fair value of an entire entity or a reporting unit when testing goodwill for impairment under FASB ASC 350, *Intangibles—Goodwill and Other* (SFAS No. 142). The guideline public company method and guideline transaction method are commonly used for goodwill impairment testing. These methods can be applied to an entire entity as well as to a reporting unit of an entity. The following sections will describe the application of the guideline public company and guideline transaction methods to the fair value measurement of an entire entity. Their application to the measurement of the fair value of a reporting unit of an entity, while equally valid, is not presented.

Guideline Public Company Method

The guideline public company method uses multiples developed from similar publicly traded companies and is one of the more common methods used in estimating the fair value of an entity. The first step in applying the guideline public company method is to select a group of companies that are comparable. Comparable companies are similar enough to provide an indication as to the multiple(s) that the subject entity would trade, if it were also publicly traded. Once the guideline companies are selected, they are analyzed to determine the relative level of business and financial risk compared to the subject entity. Ratio analysis is commonly used to perform the analysis. After thorough analysis, market multiples from one or more guideline companies are selected to provide an indication of the fair value of the subject entity.

SELECTING GUIDELINE COMPANIES   One of the advantages of using the guideline public company method is that there is often an abundance of information about publicly traded companies from SEC filings and from the analysts who follow these companies. Guideline companies are typically found by relying on Standard Industrial Classification (SIC) or North American Industrial Classification System (NAICS) codes, which classify companies by their primary line of business. Comparable guideline companies are typically those that file governmental reports using the same SIC or NAICS code as the subject company. SIC codes can be found at the Securities and Exchange Commission's Web site at www.sec.gov. SIC codes are used when companies file SEC reports through its Electronic Data Gathering Analysis and Retrieval System (EDGAR). NAICS codes are used by the United States, Canada, and Mexico for collecting and publishing statistical economic data and can be found at the U.S. Census Bureau's Web site at www.census.gov.

There are no strict criteria for determining comparability for guideline companies. Accordingly, an analyst may consider companies outside the subject entity's primary line of business. The overarching consideration should simply be that the guideline companies' operations are subject to the same or similar macroeconomic factors. In other words, they face similar risks in the market place.

WW Wireless Inc. Example   The market approach concepts presented in this chapter will be illustrated using a wireless Internet company, WW Wireless Inc. The data sources that are referenced in the example are appropriate sources of information when measuring fair value under the market approach. However, the data, companies, and transactions provided in the example are not real. They are provided for illustrative purposes only.

WW Wireless Inc. is a privately held company that supplies wireless Internet services to small businesses using the domain name WirelessBus.com. Another wireless Internet service provider, Best Wireless Inc., acquired WW Wireless two years ago. The company is profitable, but its operating results have fallen short of premerger expectations. WW Wireless expects $125 million in revenues and $18.9 million in EBITDA in the period subsequent to the acquisition. The management of WW Wireless is testing its goodwill for impairment under FASB ASC 350 during this period. A valuation specialist has been hired to measure the fair value of the WW Wireless Inc. entity and to determine whether WW Wireless's goodwill is impaired. Company management provides historical and prospective financial statements for the analysis.

The valuation specialist decides to use the guideline public company method to measure WW Wireless's fair value. Yahoo Finance is a good source of guideline company information, so the valuation specialist searches for other comparable companies by looking in the Internet Service Providers and the Internet Software and Service Providers industry sectors. The industry browser allows the specialist to access a list of the public companies that make up each sector. The Web site includes a business summary for each company listed in the sector. The specialist scans each business summary, focusing on companies with operations in wireless Internet services. The specialist selects "wireless" companies with market capitalizations in the $100 million to $500 million range. Yahoo Finance also contains more detailed information about the guideline companies' market capitalization, key financial information, and analysts' views. A summary of the guideline publicly traded companies' financial information and multiples are presented in Exhibit 5.1.

EXHIBIT 5.1 WW Wireless Inc. Guideline Publicly Traded Company Multiples, as of December 31, 20X0

$ in thousands, except stock price and multiples

Company Name	WW Wireless Inc.	Alpha Inc.	Beta Inc.	Gamma Inc.	Delta Inc.	Epsilon Inc.	Average	Median
Ticker Symbol		AAA	BBB	GGG	DDD	EEE		
SIC Code	7379	7379	7379	7379	7379	7379		
	12/31/20XX	12/31/20XX	12/31/20XX	9/30/20XX	12/31/20XX	9/30/20XX		
Valuation Multiples								
Price/Earnings		(19.10)	28.24	19.16	26.92	40.88	19.22	26.92
Price/Book Value		46.96	1.60	0.86	13.54	1.75	12.94	1.75
BEV/Revenue		2.97	1.02	0.68	3.84	2.35	2.17	2.35
BEV/EBITDA		16.76	4.92	4.95	13.39	11.86	10.38	11.86
BEV/EBIT		67.29	9.13	8.87	16.69	18.96	24.19	16.69
Market Capitalization								
Stock Price		12.40	16.10	11.89	9.49	19.33		
Shares Oustanding		28,849.5	12,153.0	30,540.0	10,930.5	7,269.0		
Market Value of Equity		357,791.5	195,669.4	363,074.8	103,730.4	140,509.8		
Preferred Stock		—	—	—	—	—	—	—
Short-Term Debt		—	—	1,079.0	1,530.1	978.3	717.5	978.3
Long-Term Debt	85,000.0	189,248.3	69,000.0	67,500.0	227.9	199.2	65,235.1	67,500.0
Total Debt	85,000.0	189,248.3	69,000.0	68,579.0	1,758.0	1,177.5	65,952.5	68,579.0
Market Value of Invested Capital (with Cash)		547,039.7	264,669.4	431,653.8	105,488.4	141,687.2	298,107.7	264,669.4
Debt to MVIC		44.1%	40.0%	21.2%	1.7%	1.2%	21.6%	21.2%
Cash		118,360.2	92,120.6	107,827.5	2,580.0	40,617.0	72,301.1	92,120.6
Market Value of Invested Capital		428,679.5	172,548.8	323,826.3	102,908.4	101,070.2	225,806.7	172,548.8
Beta		0.84	0.70	0.92	1.56	1.74	1.15	0.92

(Continued)

EXHIBIT 5.1 (Continued)

Key Financial Information									
Revenue		102,537.4	144,260.3	169,789.5	474,314.4	26,785.8	43,098.2	171,649.6	144,260.3
EBITDA		16,460.9	25,575.6	35,087.6	65,444.2	7,683.1	8,523.4	28,462.8	25,575.6
Operating Income (EBIT)		6,247.3	6,370.9	18,905.0	36,503.6	6,167.2	5,332.0	14,655.8	6,370.9
Net Income		18,089.8	(18,734.6)	6,928.6	18,945.3	3,853.0	3,436.8	2,885.8	3,853.0
Total Book Value of Equity		200,252.9	7,619.3	122,576.0	420,778.7	7,660.8	80,180.7	127,763.1	80,180.7
Depreciation and Amortization		10,213.6	19,204.7	16,182.6	28,940.6	1,515.9	3,191.4		
Prior Year's Revenue		86,188	224,443	153,830	425,426	22,720	19,366		
Growth %		19.0%	−35.7%	10.4%	11.5%	17.9%	122.5%	25.3%	11.5%
Percentage of Debt in Capital Structure			30.0%	30.0%	20.0%	0.0%	0.0%		
Percentage of Equity in Capital Structure			70.0%	70.0%	80.0%	100.0%	100.0%		
Years in Business		6	8	12	11	4	5		
Analyst Estimates:									
Sales Growth (year/est)	Current QTR	−8.5%	11.5%	2.8%	15.6%	12.2%			
	Next QTR	−15.4%	9.3%	0.0%	19.1%	15.6%			
	Current YEAR	−9.9%	10.3%	1.6%	18.6%	13.8%			
	Next YEAR	1.9%	10.8%	6.9%	21.2%	20.4%			
EPS Growth Est	Current QTR	−13.8%	38.1%	7.7%	15.4%	−58.3%			
	Next QTR	−19.7%	24.0%	4.1%	20.0%	20.0%			
	Current YEAR	−11.4%	29.3%	−1.8%	34.6%	11.1%			
	Next YEAR	5.4%	23.4%	11.8%	24.3%	100.0%			
	Past 5 Years	17.6%	9.8%	19.8%	61.1%	68.2%			
	Next 5 Years	11.3%	15.4%	15.0%	27.1%	21.4%			

Source: Similar information is available at Yahoo! Finance. However, neither the companies nor the information presented in the exhibit is real.

ANALYZING GUIDELINE COMPANIES FOR COMPARABILITY   Once a set of companies is selected, each one is analyzed for comparability. The goal of the analysis is to determine whether the prospective guideline company is indeed subject to the same macroeconomic factors as the company being valued, then to determine an appropriate market multiple to apply to the subject entity's earnings parameter. The analysis usually involves a comparison of financial performance between the prospective guideline companies and the entity. Ratio analysis typically compares liquidity, working capital activity, leverage, and profitability for each prospective guideline company relative to the subject entity. Financial performance ratios and their trends over time are also used to make an assessment of the subject entity's relative risk as compared to the guideline companies.

Another important consideration when analyzing guideline companies for comparability and when selecting appropriate multiples is the expectation for cash flow growth for both the guideline companies and the subject entity. The market multiples of publicly traded companies reflect investors long-term growth expectations. Generally, publicly traded companies with higher growth expectations trade at higher multiples. Other factors such as the company's relative profitability and relative risk are also reflected in its market multiples.

WW Wireless Ratio Analysis   The valuation specialist decides to analyze the prospective guideline companies' financial statements by looking at key operating, profitability, liquidity, leverage, and activity ratios. Since these are publicly traded companies, financial statements are readily available at SEC.gov in the EDGAR database. The prospective guideline company ratio analysis is presented in Exhibit 5.2. Based on the financial ratios in the summary, the valuation specialist concludes that the guideline companies are indeed comparable and that they are suitable for use in measuring WW Wireless's enterprise value.

Invested Capital versus Equity Multiples

As discussed briefly in a previous section, there are two classifications of market multiples that can be used to measure the fair value of an entity. They differ with respect to the ownership perspective for the underlying earnings, and are either equity multiples or invested capital multiples. Equity multiples provide an indication of the fair value of the entity from the perspective of the equity shareholders, and are based on earnings available to shareholders. The applicable earning parameter would be earnings after the deduction of interest expense, as these are the residual cash flows that belong to the equity shareholders. Net income and free cash flow are examples of earnings parameters after interest has been deducted, and a

EXHIBIT 5.2 WW Wireless Inc., Guideline Publicly Traded Company Ratio Analysis, as of December 31, 20X0

Ratio	Alpha Inc.	Beta Inc.	Gamma Inc.	Delta Inc.	Epsilon Inc.
Operating Ratios					
Gross Profit Margin	18%	21%	14%	29%	20%
Operating Profit Margin	4%	11%	8%	23%	12%
Net Profit Margin	−13%	4%	4%	14%	8%
Profitability Ratios					
Return on Equity	−246%	6%	5%	50%	4%
Return on Assets	−69%	2%	1%	5%	1%
Liquidity Ratios					
Current Ratio	1.2	1.3	0.8	1.7	0.9
Quick Ratio	1.0	1.1	0.7	1.5	0.7
Leverage Ratios					
Debt to Total Invested Capital	44%	40%	21%	2%	1%
Debt to Equity Capital	2484%	56%	16%	23%	1%
Activity Ratios					
Accounts Receivable Turnover	4.5	3.9	5.3	6.1	4.2
Fixed Asset Turnover	1.2	1.8	2.1	1.5	1.7
Working Capital Turnover	8.4	6.9	8.9	10.6	7.3

	Best 1	Best Quartile	Mean	Median	Worst Quartile	Worst	WW Wireless Inc.
Operating Ratios							
Gross Profit Margin	29%	21%	20%	20%	18%	14%	16%
Operating Profit Margin	23%	12%	12%	11%	8%	4%	6%
Net Profit Margin	14%	8%	3%	4%	4%	-13%	18%
Profitability Ratios							
Return on Equity	50%	6%	-36%	5%	4%	-246%	9%
Return on Assets	5%	2%	-12%	1%	1%	-69%	6%
Liquidity Ratios							
Current Ratio	1.70	1.30	1.18	1.20	0.90	0.80	1.30
Quick Ratio	1.50	1.10	1.00	1.00	0.70	0.70	1.20
Leverage Ratios							
Debt to Total Invested Capital	1%	2%	22%	21%	40%	44%	30%
Debt to Equity Capital	1%	16%	516%	23%	56%	2484%	42%
Activity Ratios							
Accounts Receivable Turnover	6.10	5.30	4.80	4.50	4.20	3.90	3.90
Fixed Asset Turnover	2.10	1.80	1.66	1.70	1.50	1.20	1.60
Working Capital Turnover	10.60	8.90	8.42	8.40	7.30	6.90	7.40

P/E multiple is an example of a market multiple that indicates the fair value of equity.

Invested capital multiples are based on earnings available to both debt holders and equity shareholders. The applicable earnings parameter would be earnings before any deduction for interest expense. Examples of these earnings parameters are earnings before interest taxes depreciation and amortization (EBITDA), earnings before interest and taxes (EBIT), and debt free cash flow (DFCF). Therefore, an EBITDA, EBIT, or DFCF multiple indicates the fair value of invested capital. The fair value measurement of the invested capital can be reconciled to the fair value measurement of equity by deducting interest bearing debt from the fair value of invested capital.

Common Invested Capital Multiples

- Market value of invested capital/EBITDA (earnings before interest taxes, depreciation, and amortization)
- Market value of invested capital/EBIT (earnings before interest and taxes)
- Market value of invested capital/DFCF (debt-free cash flow)
- Market value of invested capital/DFNI (debt-free net income)
- Market value of invested capital/Revenue (sales)

Common Equity Multiples

- Market value of equity/earnings (price/earnings ratio)
- Market value of equity/free cash flow (net income plus noncash charges less capital expenditures less working capital additions)
- Market value of equity/carry value of equity (book value of equity)
- Market value of equity/net asset value (adjusted book value)

The application of each of the preceding multiples may not be necessary in every circumstance. A valuation specialist should use judgment in selecting the appropriate multiple(s) for a particular entity. The most commonly used multiples are MVIC/EBITDA (market value of invested capital to earnings before interest, tax, depreciation and amortization), MVIC/DFCF (debt-free cash flow), and P/E (price to earnings). However, other multiples may be just as appropriate in other circumstances. For example, many service entities are priced on a MVIC/revenue basis.

SELECTING THE APPROPRIATE MULTIPLES After analyzing the guideline companies by using ratio analysis and calculating the appropriate equity and invested capital multiples for each of the guideline companies, the next step is to select appropriate multiples to apply to each of the subject company's earnings parameters. The result will provide an indication of the fair value of the entity. Although significant judgment is required when selecting an appropriate multiple, there are certain statistical measures that may be helpful in the selection process.

STATISTICAL METHODS When measuring the fair value of an entity using the guideline company method, statistical analysis may provide information about the quality and usefulness of available market multiples. A valuation specialist will often begin analyzing prospective guideline company multiples by calculating the mean and the median. The mean and median are measures of central tendency. A simple or arithmetic mean is the sum of the observations divide the number of observations. For example, assume that four guideline companies have price/earnings multiples of 9, 10, 10.5, and 12. The mean would be 10.375, which equals $(9 + 10 + 10.5 + 12) / 4$. The median is simply found by arranging a list of numbers from highest to lowest and selecting the one in the middle. If there is an even number of observations, then the median is the average of the two middle numbers. The median P/E multiple in this example is 10.25.

Another statistical measure of central tendency is the harmonic mean. The advantage of the harmonic mean is that it gives equal weight to each of the observations, as opposed to the simple mean that gives more weight to observations with higher values.[5] The formula for the harmonic mean is:

$$1/H_y = 1/n \sum 1/Y_i$$

where:

H = harmonic mean, and $1/H$ is the inverse of the harmonic mean
n = number of observations, and $1/n$ is the inverse of the number
Σ = statistical symbol for summarization
Y = the value of each observations, and $1/Y$ is the inverse of the value

Calculating the harmonic mean for the four observations from the previous example:

$$1/H = 1/4 \, (1/9 + 1/10 + 1/10.5 + 1/12)$$
$$1/H = .25 \, (.111 + .1 + .095 + .083)$$
$$1/H = .097$$
$$H = 10.265$$

Note that the harmonic mean of 10.265 is less than the simple mean of 10.375. This is always the case.

Another statistical measure called the coefficient of variation is used to measure the degree of dispersion of a group of observations around their mean. It is often used in fair value measurement to assess the degree of dispersion for a set of market multiples from prospective guideline transactions within a certain industry. The degree of dispersion for multiples within an industry depends on market focuses within that industry and can vary widely from industry to industry. Consequently, when industry multiples are more tightly clustered (have less dispersion) they may deserve more consideration than multiples from industries that have wider dispersion. Tightly clustered multiples generally indicate that the market prices of companies within a particular industry are based to some extent on market participants' reliance on that multiple.[6] When that is the case, industry multiples are a valuable tool for measuring the fair value of a subject entity under the market approach.

The coefficient of variation for set of market multiple from prospective guideline industry transactions can be calculated by dividing the standard deviation of the multiples by their mean. A low coefficient of variation indicates a lower degree of dispersion, and it indicates that market multiples would be more appropriate to use in the guideline company method. A detailed discussion of standard deviation and the formula for calculating it are available in any statistics book; therefore, they are not presented in this chapter. Instead, understanding how the coefficient of variation is used to measure the dispersion of market multiples is the focus of this section.

WW Wireless: Selecting the Appropriate Multiple and a Preliminary Measure of Fair Value   Guideline publicly traded companies can be used to determine an appropriate market multiple. In this example, the enterprise value or invested capital of WW Wireless Inc. is calculated; therefore, a total invested capital multiple is appropriate as opposed to an equity multiple. Three multiples are considered: (1) market value of invested capital (MVIC) to sales, (2) MVIC to EBITDA, and (3) MVIC to EBIT. Statistical analysis of the coefficient of variation (standard deviation divided by mean) to assess the dispersion of the three multiples is employed to select the most appropriate multiple. The EBITDA multiple is the best multiple for measuring the entity's fair value because it has the lowest coefficient of variation and the tightest dispersion around the mean. Analysis of the three invested capital multiples, their coefficients of variation and the selected multiple is shown in Exhibit 5.3.

The calculation of fair market value is also shown in Exhibit 5.3 and is relatively straightforward. WW Wireless's expected $18.93 million EBITDA for the upcoming year is simply multiplied by the total invested capital to the EBITDA multiple of 11.86. A fair value for WW Wireless's invested capital of $224.5 million is indicated by the analysis.

Statistical analysis is useful when selecting an appropriate multiple under the guideline company method; however, the selection still requires some judgment. A valuation specialist should not simply pick the mean guideline company multiple as the multiple to use when measuring the fair value of an entity without considering the entity's risks and growth

EXHIBIT 5.3 WW Wireless Inc., Guideline Publicly Traded Company Method Summary, as of December 31, 20X0

Numbers in $000s

Guideline Companies	MVIC to			Revenue	EBITDA	EBIT	EBITDA%	EBIT%	Debt/MVIC
	Revenue	EBITDA	EBIT						
Alpha Inc.	2.97	16.76	67.29	144,260	25,576	6,371	17.7%	4.4%	44.1%
Beta Inc.	1.02	4.92	9.13	169,790	35,088	18,905	20.7%	11.1%	40.0%
Gamma Inc.	0.68	4.95	8.87	474,314	65,444	36,504	13.8%	7.7%	21.2%
Delta Inc.	3.84	13.39	16.69	26,786	7,683	6,167	28.7%	23.0%	1.7%
Epsilon Inc.	2.35	11.86	18.96	43,098	8,523	5,332	19.8%	12.4%	1.2%
WW Wireless Inc.				102,537	16,461	6,247	16.1%	6.1%	
Maximum	3.84	16.76	67.29	474,314	65,444	36,504	28.7%	23.0%	44.1%
Average	2.17	10.38	24.19	171,650	28,463	14,656	20.1%	11.7%	21.6%
Median	2.35	11.86	16.69	144,260	25,576	6,371	19.8%	11.1%	21.2%
Minimum	0.68	4.92	8.87	26,786	7,683	5,332	13.8%	4.4%	1.2%
Standard Deviation	1.32	5.28	24.51						
Coefficient of Variation	0.61	0.51	1.01						
Selected Multiple		11.86							
Expected 20X1 EBITDA		18,930							
Preliminary Fair Value of Business Enterprise		$224,472							

prospects compared to those for the guideline companies. A valuation specialist should understand each of the guideline companies' business models as well as the subject entity's business model. The focus of business model analysis and of any ratio and trend analysis should be on comparing the profitability, risk, and growth prospects of the guideline companies to the prospects of the subject entity. The fair value indicated by guideline company method is considered the value of the entity, assuming it is a publicly traded company. Since the subject entity may not be a stand-alone publicly traded entity, its lack of liquidity should be considered. A subject entity's lack of liquidity may result in an adjustment to the selected multiple or it may impact the selection of the multiple itself.

Control Premiums

In applying the guideline public company method to the measurement of fair value, the valuation specialist should consider whether the value indicated by applying guideline public company multiples should be adjusted to reflect a control premium. The theory behind the application of a control premium is that individual shares are traded on open exchanges on a minority interest basis. Minority interests are unable to control the entity's board of directors and management; therefore, they are unable to provide direction to the company. Direction refers to the development of a business model or plan, hiring of management, selling of assets, obtaining debt, incurring certain expenses, and making acquisitions. If one is unable to control the direction of the company, then investment risk increases. Additional investment risk is reflected in a lower price per share for guideline companies traded on the open exchange. The application of a control premium to the subject company reflects its lower investment risk relative to the guideline company resulting from the owner's ability to direct the company.

Acquisition premiums can be observed empirically. When a publicly traded company is acquired by another company, the acquirer often offers a premium above the price that individual shares are trading on an open exchange. This acquisition premium is the percentage that the tender offer price exceeds the traded price, just prior to the tender offer. Most valuation specialists believe a portion of the acquisition premium reflects the portion of the acquisition price that the acquirer is willing to pay to achieve control over the direction of the acquired company.

In a recent press release, Broadcom raised its all-cash tender offer for all of Emulex's outstanding shares from $9.25 per share to $11 per share. The $11 tender offer represents a 66 percent premium over Emulex's closing stock price on the day before Broadcom announced its initial offer. In a letter to Emulex's board of directors, Broadcom expresses its desire to complete the transaction on a "friendly, reasonable and expedited basis." Broadcom

EXHIBIT 5.4 MergerStat Industry Premiums, Industry Classification: Percent Premium Offered 20X0–20X4

Seller Industry	20X0	20X1	20X2	20X3	20X4
Computer Software, Supplies, and Services	52.7 (73)	35.9 (47)	34.5 (69)	30.9 (62)	37.4 (63)
Total	62.3 (371)	30.7 (322)	34.5 (391)	31.5 (454)	31.5 (491)

Source: The information is an abridged view from Mergerstat Review 2008. The premium offered is calculated by dividing the offer price per share by the seller's closing market price five days prior to the announcement of the transaction. May include foreign sellers, publicly traded sellers and divestitures. Excludes privately owned sellers and negative premiums. ( ) Denotes the number of transactions reporting by dollar value.

indicates that its high acquisition premium is designed to overcome anti-takeover defenses erected by Emulex's board.[7]

The acquisition premium can be empirically measured as the percentage the eventual acquisition price per share exceeds the publicly traded price per share, just prior to the acquisition's announcement. FactSet Research System Inc.'s Mergerstat Review tracks acquisition premiums for individual mergers and by industry. Acquisition premiums published by Mergerstat Review are often used as a basis for measuring control premiums that an acquirer would pay to obtain a controlling interest in an entity. Industry control premiums for the computer software, supplies, and services industry are from Mergerstat Review are presented in Exhibit 5.4.

However, care should be taken before concluding that an acquisition premium is attributable solely to a premium paid to achieve control. The premium that a company pays above the market price for another publicly traded company may be attributable to other factors. For example, data suggests that strategic buyers often pay a premium for the perceived synergies of the transaction. Synergies result in the creation of additional value through the combination of two companies.[8]

Broadcom's letter to the board of directors suggests that a portion of its acquisition premium is the result of perceived synergies. It says:

> *We believe combining our two companies will create significant value for our respective shareholders, employees and partners. We believe the best way to realize this value is to act now to capitalize on the opportunities our two companies could create together. . . . Together, the talented employees of our two companies could accelerate the convergence of Erthnet and Fibre Channel. Broadcom's technology, scale, track record of execution, and highly successful history of acquisitions, along with Emulex's considerable strengths today would make a terrific combination for our combined employees and customers.[9]*

Based on its letter and press release, it is reasonable to conclude that a portion of the acquisition premium contained in Broadcom's tender offer relates to a control premium and a portion relates to acquisition synergies.

The premium paid by the acquirer for synergies is different than the premium paid for control. Unfortunately, the transaction data compiled by Mergerstat Review does not distinguish between the portion of the acquisition premium paid for control and the portion paid for synergies. Determining the portion of the acquisition premium that is solely related to control is a matter of judgment supported by acquisition data. For example, a valuation specialist may analyze acquisitions premiums paid by financial buyers as opposed to strategic buyers, assuming financial buyers have little or no synergies. If a valuation specialist determines that a control premium may be warranted when applying the guideline company method, then the acquisition premium should be adjusted so that it only reflect the portion related to control. The valuation specialist should have a reasonable basis for making such an adjustment, particularly when it may have a material impact. A common situation when the addition of a control premium could have a material impact is when determining an entity's fair value for goodwill impairment testing.

However, many valuation specialists take the position that little if any of the acquisition premium is due to control. The reason for this position is that many publicly traded companies have already managed to maximize shareholder value. If the circumstances indicate that this is true for the guideline companies then there would be little or no additional value derived from controlling these entities since they are managed to maximize value already.

Activist institutional shareholders take a role in overseeing boards of Directors to manage these companies in a way to maximize value. As such, minority interests in these companies may already approximate controlling interest values.[10]

Guideline Transaction Method (Merger and Acquisition Method)

The guideline transaction method is similar to the guideline public company method except that instead of using per share prices of publicly traded companies in the numerator, the acquisition price per share for a recently acquired guideline company is used to develop the acquisition multiple. The guideline transaction method is often used in estimating the fair value of an entity when there are a number of relevant transactions for similar companies. The first step in the guideline transaction method is to select a group of companies that are similar enough to provide guidance as to the multiple(s) that the entity might expect if it were acquired in an arm's length transaction. Once guideline transactions are selected, they are analyzed to decide whether sufficient information is available to determine the relative business and financial risks for these guideline companies compared to the reporting unit. If the business and financial risks of the guideline and subject companies are considered comparable, then one or more multiples from the guideline company is selected to provide an indication of the subject entity's fair value. The guideline company multiple times the subject entity's earnings parameter equals the entity's estimated fair value.

One of the challenges in the application of the guideline transactions method is that except for the acquisition of a public company by another publicly traded entity, information may be limited. As acquisitions by private equity firms have become more prevalent in recent years, the overall availability of information for use as guideline transactions has decreased. The decrease in the amount of guideline transaction information available may limit the usefulness of the guideline transaction method for measuring the fair value of an entity.

Detailed financial information for guideline company transactions simply may not be publicly available. Even when the acquisition price is publicly available, other details about the transaction may not be. As a result, many valuation specialists do not consider the guideline transaction method to be the primary method for measuring fair value. Instead, they use this method as a reasonableness check for fair value measured using other methodologies.

WW Wireless: Guideline Transaction Method Now, assume that the valuation specialist decides to measure WW Wireless's enterprise value using the guideline transactions method, in addition to the guideline public company method. The company is classified in SIC code 7379—Other Computer Related Services, which is a broad category. A preliminary search for guideline company transactions is conducted using the Mergerstat BVR "Control Premium Study" database at www.bvmarketdata.com. The search yields 67 transactions in SIC code 7379 occurring in the last 10 years. Although 10 years is used in this example, a shorter time horizon may be used if it would yield more relevant information. The summary statistics from the Mergerstat search are shown in Exhibit 5.5.

Since the SIC code covers many different types of companies that provide computer services, the company descriptions are scrutinized and companies with the following key words are included: Internet, wireless, Web site, technology solutions, technology integration, mobile messaging, and online. Acquired companies with "consulting" or "programming" in their descriptions are eliminated. The group of potential guideline transactions is reduced to 18. After making another pass through the data to eliminate companies from countries other than the United States and Canada, transactions occurring prior to the year 2000, and one company without revenues, the field of potential guideline company transactions is reduced to nine.

EXHIBIT 5.5 WW Wireless Inc., Guideline Transactions, as of December 31, 20X0

Your search was executed 6/30/20X1
Your search results are based on this criteria: Target SIC Code 7379

Transaction Summary

Statistic	Count	Range	Mean	Median	Coefficient of Variation
Effective Date	67	last 10 years	N/A	N/A	N/A
Net Sales for Last Twelve Months (LTM) (US$)	67	$0–$1,476	$191	$79	N/A
EBITDA Cash Flow LTM (US $)	67	($808)–$92	($4)	$6	N/A
Deal Value (millions US$)	67	$2–$3,697	$298	$84	N/A
MergerStat Control Premium	67	−0.957–3.444	0.313	0.221	N/A
Implied Minority Discount	67	−22.072–0.775	−0.181	0.181	N/A
Price/Sales	62	0.040–9.321	1.879	1.082	1.148
Price/Income	33	0.700–39.046	17.927	17.766	0.589
Price/Book Value	52	0.010–9.172	2.725	2.036	0.849
Target Invested Capital/EBIT	38	1.323–33.994	16.155	15.266	0.550
Target Invested Capital/EBITDA	38	1.274–22.400	10.647	11.243	0.524

Source: Information adopted from the Mergerstat/BVR Control Premium Study Database, www.BvmarketData.com.

154

The companies' stock exchange and ticker symbols are part of the Mergerstat data; therefore, financial statement information is readily available from the SEC Web site. Financial ratio analysis for the nine companies and for WW Wireless Inc. is presented in Exhibit 5.6.

The ratio analysis indicates that WW Wireless is generally comparable to the average of the nine potential guideline companies. However, a further look at the ratios indicates that some of the companies may not be comparable. The Indigo Group and Osirus Corp have significant operating losses, while WW Wireless has been profitable for several years. The Indigo Group's and Osirus Corp's losses appear to be skewing the data. Another company, Butler Inc., appears to have an insignificant amount of debt. WW Wireless Inc.'s debt to total invested capital ratio is 30 percent. The valuation specialist decides to eliminate the Indigo Group, Osirus Corp, and Butler Inc. to see whether the ratios from the remaining companies are more comparable to WW Wireless's ratios. The ratio analysis for the remaining six companies is presented in Exhibit 5.7. The six companies appear to be comparable; therefore, market transactions for these companies provide a basis for measuring the fair value of our subject company.

Three market multiples indicated by recent transactions in guideline companies are considered for use: (1) MVIC to sales, (2) MVIC to EBITDA, and (3) MVIC to EBIT. Statistical analysis of the coefficient of variation (standard deviation divided by mean) to assess the dispersion of the three multiples is employed to select the most appropriate multiple. The EBITDA multiple is the best multiple to use in measuring the entity's fair value because it has the lowest coefficient of variation and the tightest dispersion around the mean. See Exhibit 5.8 for a calculation of the total invested capital to EBITDA multiple. However, note that valuation specialists may also consider the other multiples as well.

WW Wireless: Calculating the Preliminary Fair Value and Considering a Control Premium
The preliminary calculation of fair market value is relatively straightforward and it is also shown in Exhibit 5.8. WW Wireless's expected $18.9 million EBITDA for the upcoming year is multiplied by the total invested capital to EBITDA multiple of 14.2. A preliminary value of $269 million is indicated.

The Mergerstat transaction data indicates whether the acquisition creates a controlling interest. It also provides a calculation of the premium paid to achieve control. The data for our six guideline companies indicates that all six of the transactions resulted in a controlling interest, and the average control premium was 29.6 percent. Because WW Wireless's enterprise value is being measured and because it is wholly owned by Best Wireless Inc., the measurement of fair value is also for a controlling interest. Therefore, no adjustment is needed for any differences in control.

EXHIBIT 5.6 WW Wireless Inc., Guideline Transactions Company Ratio Analysis, as of December 31, 20X0

Ratio	Megabite Network Inc.	ACE Computer Technology Inc.	Butler Inc.	Techniscore Inc.	Indigo Group Inc.	Worldwide Website Corp.	Search Engine Matrix Inc.	Analog Applications Inc.	Osirus Corp.
Operating Ratios									
Gross Profit Margin	23%	21%	26%	19%	29%	18%	23%	31%	22%
Operating Profit Margin	5%	6%	7%	1%	−74%	7%	6%	5%	−18%
Net Profit Margin	1%	4%	4%	3%	−74%	7%	3%	3%	−15%
Profitability Ratios									
Return on Equity	1%	29%	11%	11%	−144%	28%	6%	29%	−36%
Return on Assets	0%	5%	11%	9%	−45%	6%	1%	3%	−32%
Liquidity Ratios									
Current Ratio	1.3	0.9	1.8	1.6	0.3	2.2	1.3	1.0	0.7
Quick Ratio	1.1	0.8	1.6	1.5	0.2	2	1.2	0.9	0.5
Leverage Ratios									
Debt to Total Invested Capital	61%	84%	2%	18%	68%	78%	78%	89%	10%
Debt to Equity Capital	160%	521%	2%	22%	217%	358%	350%	809%	11%
Activity Ratios									
Accounts Receivable Turnover	2.9	3.8	4.8	4.3	3.5	5.1	4.7	4.5	3.1
Fixed Asset Turnover	1.2	1.8	0.9	1.4	1.2	0.8	1.0	1.4	0.3
Working Capital Turnover	4.1	3.2	3.5	3.8	4.2	9.1	7.3	3.6	2.9

	Best	Best Quartile	Mean	Median	Worst Quartile	Worst	WW Wireless Inc.
Operating Ratios							
Gross Profit Margin	31%	26%	24%	23%	21%	18%	16%
Operating Profit Margin	7%	6%	–6%	5%	1%	–74%	6%
Net Profit Margin	7%	4%	–7%	3%	1%	–74%	18%
Profitability Ratios							
Return on Equity	29%	28%	–7%	11%	1%	–144%	9%
Return on Assets	11%	6%	–5%	3%	0%	–45%	6%
Liquidity Ratios							
Current Ratio	2.20	1.60	1.23	1.30	0.90	0.30	1.30
Quick Ratio	2.00	1.50	1.09	1.10	0.80	0.20	1.20
Leverage Ratios							
Debt to Total Invested Capital	2%	18%	54%	68%	78%	89%	30%
Debt to Equity Capital	2%	22%	272%	217%	358%	809%	42%
Activity Ratios							
Accounts Receivable Turnover	5.10	4.70	4.08	4.30	3.50	2.90	3.90
Fixed Asset Turnover	1.80	1.40	1.11	1.20	0.90	0.30	1.60
Working Capital Turnover	9.10	4.20	4.63	3.80	3.50	2.90	7.40

EXHIBIT 5.7 WW Wireless Inc., Revised Guideline Transactions Company Ratio Analysis, as of December 31, 20X0

Ratio	Megabite Network Inc.	ACE Computer Technology Inc.	Techniscore Inc.	Worldwide Website Corp	Search Engine Matrix Inc.	Analog Applications Inc.
Operating Ratios						
Gross Profit Margin	23%	21%	19%	18%	23%	31%
Operating Profit Margin	5%	6%	1%	7%	6%	5%
Net Profit Margin	1%	4%	3%	7%	3%	3%
Profitability Ratios						
Return on Equity	1%	29%	11%	28%	6%	29%
Return on Assets	0%	5%	9%	6%	1%	3%
Liquidity Ratios						
Current Ratio	1.3	0.9	1.6	2.2	1.3	1.0
Quick Ratio	1.1	0.8	1.5	2.0	1.2	0.9
Leverage Ratios						
Debt to Total Invested Capital	61%	84%	18%	78%	78%	89%
Debt to Equity Capital	160%	521%	22%	358%	350%	809%
Activity Ratios						
Accounts Receivable Turnover	2.9	3.8	4.3	5.1	4.7	4.5
Fixed Asset Turnover	1.2	1.8	1.4	0.8	1.0	1.4
Working Capital Turnover	4.1	3.2	3.8	9.1	7.3	3.6

	Best	Best Quartile	Mean	Median	Worst Quartile	Worst	WW Wireless Inc.
Operating Ratios							
Gross Profit Margin	31%	23%	23%	22%	20%	18%	16%
Operating Profit Margin	7%	6%	5%	6%	5%	1%	6%
Net Profit Margin	7%	3%	3%	3%	3%	1%	18%
Profitability Ratios							
Return on Equity	29%	28%	17%	19%	7%	1%	9%
Return on Assets	9%	6%	4%	4%	2%	0%	6%
Liquidity Ratios							
Current Ratio	2.20	1.53	1.38	1.30	1.08	0.90	1.30
Quick Ratio	2.00	1.43	1.25	1.15	0.95	0.80	1.20
Leverage Ratios							
Debt to Total Invested Capital	18%	66%	68%	78%	82%	89%	30%
Debt to Equity Capital	22%	207%	370%	354%	480%	809%	42%
Activity Ratios							
Accounts Receivable Turnover	5.10	4.65	4.22	4.40	3.93	2.90	3.90
Fixed Asset Turnover	1.80	1.40	1.27	1.30	1.05	0.80	1.60
Working Capital Turnover	9.10	6.50	5.18	3.95	3.65	3.20	7.40

EXHIBIT 5.8 WW Wireless Inc., Guideline Transaction Multiple, as of December 31, 20X0

(in millions)

Target Company	Business Description	Date	Target Invested Capital	Target Sales	Target EBITDA	Target EBIT	TIC/Sales	TIC/ EBITDA	TIC/EBIT
Megabite Networks Inc.	Provides Internet infrastructure services	10/24/20X8	295.813	68.703	18.282	3.232	4.31	16.18	91.52
ACE Computer Technology Inc.	Provides wireless technology, Internet-enabled management systems, software, and other services	3/1/20X4	73.967	97.333	11.225	5.856	0.76	6.59	12.63
Techniscore Inc.	Provides information technology solution services	7/23/20X2	40.636	134.700	3.420	1.740	0.30	11.88	23.35
Worldwide Website Corp.	Provides intranet, extranet, and Web site services and development for medium- and large-sized companies	3/1/20X0	36.486	33.570	2.820	2.510	1.09	12.94	14.54
Search Engine Matrix Inc.	Develops Internet strategies focusing on competitive advantages	4/19/20X1	219.430	81.690	9.790	4.980	2.69	22.41	44.06
Analog Applications Inc.	Provides network services for e-business applications	5/14/20X1	145.933	139.881	9.537	7.156	1.04	15.30	20.39
	Standard Deviation						1.51	5.24	30.14
	Mean						1.70	14.22	34.42
	Coefficient of Variation						0.89	0.37	0.88
	Selected Multiple (1)							14.22	
	Expected 20X1 EBITDA							18,930,000	
	Fair Value of Business Enterprise							$ 269,139,000	

Source: The information presented in this exhibit is typically available from the Mergerstat Transaction Database for the SIC Code 7379 (Other Computer Related Services).

(1) The EBITDA multiple was selected based on its coefficient of variation.

The concluded fair value measured for the invested capital of WW Wireless is $269 million.

The Application of the Market Approach in Measuring the Fair Value of Intangible Assets

Using the market approach to measure intangible assets is somewhat more difficult than using the market approach to measure the fair value of an entity. Information about the market price of guideline companies and guideline transactions is often readily available. However, information from transactions for individual intangible assets is often more difficult to obtain. The P/E multiple of publicly traded company can be easily obtained through various sources on the Internet such as Bloomberg or Yahoo Finance, or by simply looking it up in the *Wall Street Journal*. Multiples from the licensing of a patent or a trade name are not available from these sources. Fortunately, market approach methods can be adapted to make use of the limited market information available for specific intangible assets.

RELIEF FROM ROYALTY METHOD The relief from royalty method contains assumptions from both market and income approaches. The theory behind the relief from royalty method is that an entity that owns an intangible asset has a valuable right since the entity does not have to pay a third party a license fee for the right to use that intangible asset. The fair value of that right can be measured through an analysis of royalty rates charged by third parties for the use of similar intangible assets. Since the entity already owns the intangible asset, the entity is "relieved from" having to pay a third party a royalty for the use of the intangible asset.

The fair value of the intangible asset is measured as the present value of hypothetical royalty payments that the entity is relieved from paying by not having to license the use of the intangible asset from a third party.

The application of the relief from royalty method for measuring the fair value of an intangible asset involves three steps.

1. Analyze royalty rates from publicly available information for similar intangible assets.
2. Analyze the industry in which the entity owning the intangible asset operates.
3. Apply an appropriate royalty rate for licensing the intangible asset to the entity's prospective financial information (PFI). An appropriate royalty rate takes industry conditions and the terms of publicly available royalty data into consideration.

In applying the relief from royalty method to measure the fair value of an intangible asset, the first step is to analyze license agreements of transactions for the use of similar intangible assets. There are several commercially available sources for information about license agreements. The terms of the license agreements should be analyzed, which includes considering the royalty rate, the economic measure to which the royalty rate is applied, the geographic region to which the agreement applies, whether the agreement is exclusive or nonexclusive, and the length of time the agreement is in effect. Other aspects of the intangible license agreement require analysis to determine whether the agreement reflects similar risk and required rates of returns as the intangible asset under consideration. If not, then any differences in risk should be considered by adjusting the selected royalty rate.

The second step is to analyze the industry in which these license agreements fall. An understanding of the industry is important to provide a framework in determining a royalty rate derived from market transactions that are appropriate to apply to the intangible asset being valued. This process is similar to determining what the market would support if the intangible asset under consideration was licensed to a third party.

A topic that will be discussed further in Chapter 6, "The Income Approach," is a 25 percent to 30 percent rule of thumb for determining an appropriate royalty for intangible assets. The rule of thumb is rooted in actual license transactions and indicates that a royalty rate for a group of intangible assets would likely fall between 25 percent and 33 percent of operating income. It is important to consider normal industry margins in order to determine whether payment of a royalty is even feasible. A common error in the application of the relief from royalty method is the selection of a rate that cannot be supported by the entity's actual operating margins. Also, the analyst should understand the potential impact of substitute assets that would replace the intangible asset under consideration.

The third step in the relief from royalty method is to apply the selected royalty rate to the entity's applicable operating parameter. Most royalty rates are based on net sales. Net sales from the PFI would be multiplied by the royalty rate for each future year over a period of time that corresponds to the intangible asset's estimated remaining useful life. The results would be discounted at an appropriate rate, consistent with the entity's cost of capital and the relative risk of the intangible asset. The present value would be a measure of the intangible asset's fair value.

WW Wireless: Relief from Royalty Method   The valuation specialist has also been asked to measure the fair value of WW Wireless Inc.'s domain name "WirelessBus.com." The specialist decides to use the relief from royalty method and finds guideline royalty rates for the Internet industry in Royalty Source.

Exhibit 5.9 summarizes guideline royalty rates and shows the 1 percent selected royalty rate. The selected royalty rate is applied to WW Wireless's expected revenues as provided by management over the domain name's 30-year expected useful life. The present value of the royalty payments that WW Wireless is relieved from paying indicates that the fair value of the domain name is $6.5 million. Exhibit 5.10 contains the analysis.

Royalty Source's intellectual property transaction database is available at www.royaltysource.com. The Financial Valuation Group, an affiliation of business valuation and litigation support professionals, also provides an intellectual property transaction database that can be accessed at www.fairmarketvalue.com. Consor Intellectual Asset Management provides similar information at www.consor.com.

Another relatively new source of royalty rate information, ktMINE, offers access to thousands of intellectual property agreements and provides the ability to locate relevant agreements using search filters based on intellectual property agreement attributes. In addition to allowing a user to search the database using key words, ktMINE has search filters for the licensor, licensee, filing company, effective date, SIC Code, territory, exclusivity, agreement type, industry, and royalty rate. Searches can easily be refined and the pool of applicable agreements narrowed. Once the search has been completed, a results summary shows key licensing terms and royalty rates for each agreement. The user can view the agreements and quickly jump to the bookmarked royalty rate information.

A search using the key words "domain name" and filters for the travel industry and agreement exclusivity generated a results summary with four agreements. The summary for one of the agreements is presented in Exhibit 5.11. Detailed royalty rate information appears at the bottom of the summary.[11]

Guideline Transactions Method

A guideline transaction method is sometimes used to measure the fair value of an intangible asset when there is sufficient market information. The guideline transaction method is similar to the guideline transaction method that is used to measure the fair value of the equity or invested capital of an entity. A valuation multiple selected from guideline transactions for similar intangible assets is applied to a parameter of the subject intangible asset. Given its market-based nature, this method can be one of the most compelling indicators of value. Unfortunately, the lack of information about guideline transactions makes the guideline transaction method one of the more difficult methodologies to apply in practice.

The application of the guideline transaction method begins with an analysis of each individual transaction to understand its terms and

EXHIBIT 5.9 WW Wireless Inc., Internet Domain Names, as of December 31, 20X0

Licensor	Licensee	Date	Terms	Royalty	
				Low	High
Arlington Fulbright Inc.	Passion Technologies Inc.	May-0X	International	1.0%	2.0%
DigiWigiTech	TopTechNology.com	Dec-0X	Nontransferable	2.0%	4.0%
ThatName.com	Cottage Industry Inc.	Sep-0X	North America	2.0%	4.0%
ChaseHatMadden.com	Central Chemical Co	Jul-0X	NA	4.0%	4.0%
Technology Alliance Group	Titiens Technology GMBH	Apr-0X	International	0.1%	1.5%
Silverstein Jacobs LLC	Heartkind.com	Nov-0X	Exclusive	1.0%	1.0%
FirstPass.com	Sky Blue Sailing Inc.	Jun-0X	Exclusive	1.0%	2.0%
			High	4.0%	4.0%
			3rd Q	2.0%	4.0%
			Mean	1.6%	2.6%
			Median	1.0%	2.0%
			Ist Q	1.0%	1.8%
			Low	0.1%	1.0%
			Mode	1.0%	4.0%
			Selected Royalty Rate:		1.0%

Source: Royalty rates are available from *Royalty Source.* However, neither the companies nor royalty rates presented in this exhibit is real.

EXHIBIT 5.10 WW Wireless Inc., Valuation of Domain Name, as of December 31, 20X0

	20X1		20X2		20X3		20X4		20X5		20X1 + 30 Years	
Revenue	$125,000,000	100%	$131,250,000	100%	$140,437,500	100%	$150,268,125	100%	$159,284,213	100%	$343,510,942	100%
Growth				5%		7%		7%		6%		3%
Pre-Tax Royalty Savings	1,250,000	1%	1,312,500	1%	1,404,375	1%	1,502,681	1%	1,592,842	1%	3,435,109	1%
Less: Taxes	(475,000)	0%	(498,750)	0%	(533,663)	0%	(571,019)	0%	(605,280)	0%	(1,305,342)	0%
After-Tax Royalty Savings	775,000	1%	813,750	1%	870,713	1%	931,662	1%	987,562	1%	2,129,768	1%
Partial Period	0.06		1.00		1.00		1.00		1.00		1.00	
Period	0.03		0.56		1.56		2.56		3.56		29.56	
Present Value Factor	0.994		0.902		0.752		0.627		0.522		0.005	
PV of After-Tax Royalty Savings	48,556		734,363		654,807		583,870		515,752		9,716	

Sum of PV of Savings	5,603,327
Amortization Benefit Multiplier	1.15
Preliminary Value	6,438,222
Concluded Value, Rounded	$6,438,000

Assumptions	
Discount Rate	20.0%
Long-Term Growth Rate	3.0%
Tax Rate	38.0%
Royalty Rate	1.0%
Remaining Useful Life	30 years

Search Center | **Results Summary** | Agreement View | Analysis Center[(BETA)]

Filter to Narrow Results
Expand All
Exclusivity
☑ EXCLUSIVE
Agreement Types
Industries
Territory
Associated Keywords

4 Agreements found. Page [1] of 1   Start New Search | Refine Search

Save All Results as a Set   Save Search Steps   Modify Display   Export Results Summary

Agreement 4 of 4   Back to top

Synopsis
- Grant the right to advertise, market and sell Travel Products including but not limited to banners, text links, hotel bookings, flight bookings, tour bookings and travel insurance, on the Domain Name www.greatbritain.com.

		Actions
Agreement ID:	11961	View Agreement
Filling Company:	FREQUENTTRAVELLER.COM INC.	Comment on this Agreement
Licensor(s):	DOMAIN HOLDING INC.	**View Royalty Rate Text**
Licensee(s):	FREQUENTTRAVELLER.COM INC.	Add to Set...
Effective Date:	05/1/2005	**In Sets**
Type:	MARKETING INTANGIBLE	None
Industry:	ADVERTISING, CONSUMER SERVICES, INTERNET, TRAVEL AND RECREATION	
SIC Code:	—	
Territory:	N/A	
Exclusivity:	EXCLUSIVE	

Royalty Rate Summary[(BETA)] Tell us what you think.

Statistics Only   Actuals Only   Statistics and Actuals   View Royalty Rate Text

License Actuals	Value	Agreement Base	Modifier	Common Base
	5.00 %	NET REVENUES	generated during the calendar year by the Lessee; On portion up to $20 Million	NET SALES
	4.00 %	NET REVENUES	generated during the calendar year by the Lessee; On portion up between $20 Million & $40 Million	NET SALES
	3.00 %	NET REVENUES	generated during the calendar year by the Lessee; On the portion between $40 Million & $60 Million	NET SALES
	2.00 %	NET REVENUES	generated during the calendar year by the Lessee; On the portion between $60 Million & $80 Million	NET SALES
	1.00 %	NET REVENUES	generated during the calendar year by the Lessee; On the portion over and above $80 Million	NET SALES

EXHIBIT 5.11 ktMINE Agreement Summary

conditions. This analysis is important to determine whether any adjustments should be made to the guideline multiples to maximize comparability. After adjustments are made, the valuation multiples are applied to the subject intangible assets parameters.

WW Wireless: Guideline Transaction Method The valuation specialist also decides to measure the fair value of the "WirelessBus.com" domain name, using the guideline transaction method. Fortunately, there are several entities that provide services to buyers and sellers of Internet domain names. These entities provide a source of information about potential selling prices for similar names. The process is rather simple. Entering the domain name in the search engine on one of the service providers' Web sites it will provide list prices for similar names. The results of the valuation specialist's research on the name "WirelessBus.com" is presented as:[12]

Domain Name	Price
Wifimy.com	$2,500
Wifimy.net	$1,850
Wifii.com	$2,300
WiBus.com	$1,975
Wireless.net	$2,300

Comparable domain names seem to be offered for sale between $1,850 and $2,500. The valuation specialist also researches actual transactions for recent sales of similar domain names to determine whether actual sales between third parties are at, or below, their offer prices. The specialist notes that domain names with the .com extension appear to sell at a higher price. Since WiBus.com appears to be the most similar name, the specialist concludes that the fair value of the identified domain name is $2,000. The specialist also takes into consideration that these prices are offering prices not consummated by third-party transactions; therefore, the prices should be viewed as an "asking" price. The fair value indicated by these prices may require an adjustment since an asking price may not be the price that a market participant would be willing to pay for a particular asset.

SOURCES OF INFORMATION One of the challenges in using market approach methods to measure the fair value of intangible assets is that there are no public exchanges. Without public exchanges, there is little readily available information about guideline transactions. Another complicating factor is that most intangible assets are purchased or sold as part of a group of other assets. Exchanges of intangible assets usually occur through business combinations, rather than through individual purchases or sales. Consequently, finding appropriate information about transactions for individual intangible assets to provide a basis for measuring fair value is more difficult than finding information about transactions for an entire entity.

Although it is difficult to find transaction information for individual intangible assets, it may not be impossible as there are several alternatives ways to search for information. Many intangible assets are licensed. As discussed in the relief from royalty section of this chapter, there are commercially available sources of licensing data. Also, if one or both parties to the agreement is a publicly traded company, information about the licensing of intangible assets may be found in SEC filings or in summaries of transactions compiled and sold by commercial organizations. Royalty Stat is one of the organizations that provides an online database of royalty and license agreements compiled from the SEC's EDGAR archive.

SEC FILINGS   Another source of information about the licensing or sale of intangible assets is SEC filings for similar publicly traded companies. Competitors that are SEC registrants often file information in their SEC reports that describe licensing arrangements. The reports may provide enough information so that a guideline royalty rate can be determined and can be used when applying the relief from royalty method.

Information about royalty payments for Wendy's fast-food franchises can be found in the Meritage Hospitality Group Inc.'s 2007 Form 10-K filed with the SEC. The disclosure about franchise fees says:

> *The Wendy's Unit Franchise Agreement requires that the franchisee pay a royalty of 4 percent of gross sales, as defined in the agreement, from the operation of the restaurant. The agreement also typically requires that the franchisee pay the Company a technical assistance fee. In the United States, the standard technical assistance fee required under a newly executed Unit Franchise Agreement is currently $25,000 for each restaurant.*[13]

COURT CASES   Information about appropriate royalty rates within a certain industry and information about other intellectual property transactions may become public through intellectual property disputes. Reviewing decisions from certain U.S. tax court cases, particularly those involving transfer pricing issues, can yield valuable information. Civil cases involving patent and trademark infringement are also good sources of information when the case involves an intangible asset within the same or similar industry as the subject intangible asset. Court cases relating to a specific industry can be particularly useful when analyzing guideline transactions within that industry,

A recent example of a patent infringement court case that cites a royalty rate is NTP Inc. versus Research in Motion. In 2001, NTP Inc. filed suit against Research in Motion (RIM) alleging direct and indirect infringement of several patents owned by NTP. The patents enabled users to send and receive electronic mail messages from a mobile device. RIM manufactures and sells various devices and software under the BlackBerry name that provide their customers with mobile access to electronic mail. After a 13-day trial, the jury found RIM guilty of willful infringement of NTP patents. The jury awarded approximately $23 million in damages based on a reasonable royalty rate of 5.7 percent.[14,15]

The indicated royalty rate derived from a court case should be used with caution. Royalty rates from court cases may reflect a compromise reached by the court and may not be based on market participant assumptions.

INTELLECTUAL PROPERTY AUCTIONS   Many companies have intellectual property rights that they are not exploiting. The intellectual property rights may have been created as a by-product of another development effort. Or, while the technology covered by the intellectual property may still be viable, the company may no longer produce any products using the technology. When an intellectual property is not currently being exploited by its owner, the intellectual property may have value to another company. Companies are beginning to recognize that these dormant intellectual properties may have value and they are seeking ways to monetize intellectual property rights through sales to other parties.

Ocean Tomo, an investment bank specializing in intellectual property transactions, has begun assisting companies that would like to monetize dormant intellectual property rights by providing an auction for those rights. Ocean Tomo's first formal intellectual property rights auction took place in San Francisco in April 2006. The results of the first auction were mixed, but promising. Ocean Tomo organized the intellectual property into 78 "lots" of similar intellectual properties. Of the 78 lots, 26 sold for a total more than $3 million. The results of this first auction persuaded Ocean Tomo to proceed with the development of the intellectual property auction market.[16] Since then, Ocean Tomo has held eight auctions in Europe and the United States with $112 million in transactions. The investment bank notes that "The marketplace for IP transactions continues to evolve both as recognition of patents as an asset continues to grow and in response to the global recession."[17]

These types of transactions are expected to increase significantly in the future. For additional information about these auctions see www.oceantomoauctions.com.

The monetization of intellectual property through these newly formed intellectual property auctions may result in useful guideline transaction information for measuring the fair value of similar technology. The importance of intellectual property auctions as a source of information about market-based transactions for certain intangible assets is likely to increase in the future.

Conclusion

The market approach is one of the three basic approaches to measuring fair value. Methods under the market approach, such as the guideline public company method or the guideline transaction method are often used to measure the fair value of both an entity or a reporting unit of an entity. Other methods under the market approach, such as the relief from royalty, or the guideline transaction method, are often used to measure the fair value of identified intangible assets such as technology, trade names, or domain names.

Notes

1. SFAS 157, paragraph 18a.
2. *International Glossary of Business Valuation Terms,* Business Valuation Resources, www.bvresources.com/freedownloads/BVGlossary09.pdf (accessed July 10, 2009).
3. *Id.*
4. *Id.*
5. Pratt, Shannon, *The Market Approach to Valuing Businesses* (New York: John Wiley & Sons, 2001), 133.
6. *Id.*
7. "Broadcom Raises All-Cash Tender Offer for Emulex to $11.00 Per Share," press release dated June 29, 2009, posted by Mike Fratto, www.byteanswitch.com (accessed 7/23/2009).
8. "Assessing the Impact of Synergy on Value," Mark L. Zyla, CPA Expert (Fall 1999), www.AICPA.org.
9. Letter to the Board of Directors of Emulex Corporation from Scott A. McGregor, President and CEO of Broadcom dated June 29, 2009, posted by Mike Fratto, www.byteanswitch.com (accessed 7/23/2009).
10. Nath, Eric, "Control Premiums and Minority Interest Discounts in Private Companies," *Business Valuation Review*, Volume 9, No. 2, American Society of Appraisers, June 1990.
11. www.ktmine.com
12. While the information presented in this example is fictitious, the pricing of domain names can be found by Internet service companies such as Godaddy.com.
13. Meritage Hospitality Group Inc. Form 10-K, www.sec.gov.
14. United States Court of Appeals for the Federal Circuit (03-1615).
15. United States District Court for the Eastern District of Virginia, Richmond Division, Civil Action Number 3:01CV767, Memorandum of Opinion, filed 5/23/03.
16. "On the Block," Inside Counsel July 2006, www.insidecounsel.com.
17. IP Markets 2009 Featuring Ocean Tomo Live IP Auctions, www.oceantomo.com/ipmarkets2009.com.

CHAPTER 6

The Income Approach

Introduction

The income approach to fair value measurement estimates the fair value of an entity, intangible assets, or other assets and liabilities by calculating the present value of future cash flows that the entity or asset is expected to generate over its lifetime. The cash flows are discounted to the measurement date at a rate of return that is required to compensate for the risk associated with receipt of the future cash flows. The income approach is one of the three basic valuation techniques to measure fair value described in FASB ASC 820, *Fair Value Measurements and Disclosures* (SFAS No. 157). This chapter presents various methods used to estimate the fair value under the income approach. Although the income approach can be used to measure the fair value of entities, tangible assets, intangible assets, and liabilities, the focus of the chapter is on measuring the fair value of intangible assets that are recognized through business combinations. The chapter also includes a section on determining appropriate rates of return (discount rates) for those intangible assets.

The glossary to the Financial Accounting Standards Board (FASB) *Accounting Standards Codification* (ASC) incorporates the definition of the income approach originally provided by FASB ASC 820, *Fair Value Measurements and Disclosures* (SFAS No. 157). The FASB defines the income approach as "the use of valuation techniques to convert future amounts (cash flows or earnings) to a single present amount (discounted). The measurement is based on the value indicated by current market expectations about those future amounts."[1] *Fair Value Measurements and Disclosures* further describes several valuation techniques under the income approach. These valuation techniques or methods include present value models, option-pricing models, and the multiperiod excess earnings method. The Black-Scholes-Merton formula is an example of an option-pricing model that incorporates present value techniques. The multiperiod excess earnings method is a present value technique that is commonly used to measure the fair value of certain intangible assets.[2]

The International Glossary of Business Valuation Terms (IGBVT) defines the income approach as "a general way of determining a value indication of ... an intangible asset using one or more methods that convert anticipated benefits into a present single amount."[3] Both the FASB and IGBVT income approach definitions described the conversion of expected future cash flows to a single present amount, using various methods as a means to measure fair value.

Income approach methods fall into one of two categories. They are either single scenario methods or multiscenario methods. Single scenario methods are based on the entity's most likely cash flows, while multiscenario methods incorporate many different sets of possible cash flow outcomes. Single scenario methods are the most common methods used to determine fair value measurements in financial reporting. The advantage of using single scenario methods in fair value measurements is that these methods are more universally understood than multiscenario methods. Single scenario methods are also easier to audit since the results of the analysis are directly correlated to the underlying assumptions used in the analysis. The focus of this chapter will be on common single scenario methods under the income approach, including the Discounted Cash Flow analysis (DCF), the Multi-Period Excess Earnings Method (MPEEM), the Incremental Income/Cost Decrement Method, the Profit Split Method, and the Build-Out Method. Multiscenario methods include Real Option Techniques, Decision Tree Analysis, Monte Carlo Simulation, and DCF models using multiple forecasts.[4] A subsequent chapter will focus on more advanced multiscenario valuation methods.

Discounted Cash Flow Method

The basis for valuation methods under the income approach is a discounted cash flow analysis. Other valuation methods under the income approach are derived from this fundamental method. The DCF is simply defined in the *International Glossary of Business Valuation Terms* as "The present value of future expected net cash flows calculated using a discount rate."[5] The present value formula for the discounted cash flow analysis using a midyear convention is:

Fair Value = cash flow year $1/(1 + $ discount rate$)^{0.5} + $ cash flow year $2/(1 + $ discount rate$)^{1.5} + \cdots + $ [normalized cash flows year n/ (discount rate $-$ long-term growth rate)]$/(1 + $ discount rate$)^{n-0.5}$

The DCF method of estimating fair value requires three basic inputs: (1) the expected cash flows to be received over the explicit forecast period,

(2) the terminal value or perpetuity value that captures the value after the explicit forecast period, and (3) the discount rate, adjusted for the risk of actually receiving the cash flows. The exponents 0.5, 1.5 through $n-0.5$ are the number of years using a midyear convention assuming that cash flows are received evenly over the year.

The DCF is commonly used to measure the fair value of an entity when it is the acquisition target in a business combination. The DCF is used to determine the acquisition price and it becomes the foundation for recording the business combination under the acquisition method of accounting. The DCF is also used to measure the fair value of an entity or a reporting unit when testing goodwill for impairment.

There two most common forms of the DCF that are distinguished by the ownership perspective of the underlying cash flows. One is discounted cash flows to equity holders, and the other is debt-free cash flows to all holders of invested capital. This form includes equity and debt holders. As a result, there are variations in the specific income items to be considered as cash flows and variations in the selection of an appropriate discount rate for each form of DCF.

In the cash flows to equity form, relevant cash flows to equity holders are discounted back to the present at an equity rate of return. The formula to calculate each year's forecasted cash flows to equity holders in the DCF analysis is:

Net Income (including a deduction for interest expense)
Plus: Depreciation and amortization and other noncash expenses
Less: Capital expenditures required to support growth in revenue
Less: Change in working capital required to support growth in revenue
Plus: Additional borrowings
Less: Repayment of debt principal
Equals: Cash flows to equity holders

The cash flows to equity holders are discounted back to the present at the cost of equity, which is typically developed using a modified version of the Capital Asset Pricing Model (CAPM) or a variation of the CAPM commonly referred to as the Build-up method. (These models are discussed later in the chapter.) Discounting cash flows to equity holders at the appropriate cost of equity results in a present value that represents the fair value of the entity's equity ownership. The advantage of the equity form of the DCF is that it inherently uses the entity's own capital structure in measuring fair value. The disadvantage is that the entity's actual capital structure may not be similar to the hypothetical capital structure under a market participant assumption.

To illustrate the equity form of the DCF, assume that JT Austin Technology Inc. is acquired for $10.5 million on October 31, 20X1. The acquisition price consists of $8.5 million in cash and $2 million in debt with a 10 percent annual rate, due 12/31/20X5. A preliminary estimate of the fair values for the acquired asset and liabilities indicates that the fair value of intangible assets and goodwill is approximately $7.4 million. Based on the acquirer's projections for operating profit margins, depreciation expense, working capital requirements, capital expenditures, and taxes, the fair value of the equity holders' interest in JT Austin Technology Inc. is $7.9 million as presented in Exhibit 6.1. The DCF to equity holders is calculated using a 26 percent cost of equity for the discount rate. (The calculation of the cost of capital will be addressed in a later section.)

The cash flows to invested capital form of the DCF method is also referred to as the "debt free method." Under the debt-free method, cash flows to all investors, both debt holders and equity holders, are discounted back to the present at the weighted average cost of capital (WACC). When measuring fair value, the WACC is based on market participant assumptions. The formula to calculate each year's forecasted cash flows to investors under the debt-free form of the discounted cash flow is:

Net income
Plus: Tax affected interest expense
Plus: Depreciation and amortization and other noncash expenses
Less: Capital expenditures required supporting growth in revenue
Less: Working capital additions required to support growth in revenue
Equals: Debt-free cash flows (cash flows to holders of both debt and equity)

Debt-free cash flows are discounted back to the present using the WACC, and the resulting value represents the fair value of debt holders' and equity holders' interest in the entity; in other words, the fair value of invested capital. The fair value of the equity interest can be measured by subtracting the fair value of current interest-bearing debt from the total fair value of invested capital. The advantage of the debt-free method is that it can be used to measure fair value under a market participant assumption about capital structure. The disadvantage is that the measurement fair value depends on the calculation of WACC, which is often based on many assumptions. Deriving a WACC will be discussed later in the chapter.

An example of the invested capital form of the DCF is shown in Exhibit 6.2 using the same JT Austin illustration and assumptions from Exhibit 6.1.

The Weighted Average Cost of Capital (WACC) Compared to the Internal Rate of Return on the Investment (IRR)

One of the first steps in measuring the fair value of individual assets acquired in a business combination under FASB ASC 805, *Business*

EXHIBIT 6.1 JT Austin Technology Inc., Discounted Cash Flow Analysis to Equity Holders, as of October 31, 20X1

	20X1		20X2		20X3		20X4		20X5		Terminal Value	
Sales	$12,593,002	100%	$13,250,000	100%	$14,150,000	100%	$15,150,000	100%	$15,750,000	100%	$16,222,500	100%
Growth	5%		5%		7%		7%		4%		3%	
Cost of Sales	7,807,661	62%	7,685,000	58%	8,207,000	58%	8,787,000	58%	9,135,000	58%	9,409,050	58%
Gross Profit	4,785,341	38%	5,565,000	42%	5,943,000	42%	6,363,000	42%	6,615,000	42%	6,813,450	42%
SG&A Expenses	2,518,600	20%	2,385,000	18%	2,547,000	18%	2,727,000	18%	2,835,000	18%	2,920,050	18%
EBITDA	2,266,740	18%	3,180,000	24%	3,396,000	24%	3,636,000	24%	3,780,000	24%	3,893,400	24%
Less: Depreciation	275,830	2%	397,500	3%	424,500	3%	454,500	3%	472,500	3%	486,675	3%
EBIT	1,990,910	16%	2,782,500	21%	2,971,500	21%	3,181,500	21%	3,307,500	21%	3,406,725	21%
Less: Interest Expense	(200,000)	−2%	(200,000)	−2%	(200,000)	−1%	(200,000)	−1%	(200,000)	−1%	–	0%
EBT	1,790,910	14%	2,582,500	19%	2,771,500	20%	2,981,500	20%	3,107,500	20%	3,406,725	21%
Less: Taxes	(680,546)	−5%	(981,350)	−7%	(1,053,170)	−7%	(1,132,970)	−7%	(1,180,850)	−7%	(1,294,556)	−8%
Net Income	1,110,364	9%	1,601,150	12%	1,718,330	12%	1,848,530	12%	1,926,650	12%	2,112,170	13%
Plus: Depreciation	275,830	2%	397,500	3%	424,500	3%	454,500	3%	472,500	3%	486,675	3%
Less: Capital Expenditures (1)	(275,830)	−2%	(397,500)	−3%	(424,500)	−3%	(454,500)	−3%	(472,500)	−3%	(486,675)	−3%
Less: Incremental Working Capital (6)	(200,000)	−2%	(132,500)	−2%	(141,500)	−1%	(151,500)	−1%	(157,500)	−1%	(162,225)	−1%
Less: Repayment of Debt Principal (7)	–	0%	–		–	0%	–	0%	(2,000,000)	−13%	–	0%
Cash Flows to Equity Holders	910,364	7%	1,468,650	11%	1,576,830	11%	1,697,030	11%	(230,850)	−1%	1,949,945	12%
Terminal Value—in 20X5									8,541,524			
Partial Period	0.17		1.00		1.00		1.00		1.00		1.00	
Period	0.08		0.67		1.67		2.67		3.67		3.67	
Present Value Factor	0.981		0.858		0.682		0.542		0.431		0.431	
Present Value of Cash Flows to Equity	149,250		1,259,947		1,075,073		919,522		(99,408)		3,678,130	

Fair Value of Intangible Assets & Goodwill	7,400,000
15-Year Amortization Period	/15
Tax Amortization per Year	493,333
Tax Rate	× 38%
Annual Amortization Benefit	187,467
Sum of PV Factors 20X1 to 20Y6	5.03
Present Value of Amortization Benefit	942,676

Sum of PV of DFCF (20X1–20X5)	3,304,384	
PV of Terminal Value	3,678,130	
PV of Tax Benefit-Amortization of Intangibles (8)	942,676	
Preliminary Value	7,925,190	
Fair Value of Equity, Rounded	**$7,925,000**	

Assumptions		
Discount Rate	26%	(2)
Internal Rate of Return	24%	(3)
Tax Rate	38%	(4)
Long-Term Growth Rate	3%	(5)

Notes: (1) Makes the simplifying assumption that capital expenditures are equal to depreciation expense.

(2) Cost of equity capital per Exhibit 6.11.

(3) Implied rate that reconciles the future expected cash flows to equity holders to the fair value of the acquisition price less acquisition debt.

(4) Estimated corporate tax rate.

(5) Based on Management's projections, the growth prospects of the industry, and the overall economy.

(6) Based on industry average and management projections.

(7) This example assumes the repayment of all debt as a simplification. Any future borrowing would be added to cash flows to equity holders in the applicable period.

(8) Assumes the acquisition is an asset purchase.

EXHIBIT 6.2 JT Austin Technology Inc., Discounted Cash Flow Analysis—Total Invested Capital, as of October 31, 20X1

	20X1		20X2		20X3		20X4		20X5		Terminal Value	
Sales	$12,593,002	100%	$13,250,000	100%	$14,150,000	100%	$15,150,000	100%	$15,750,000	100%	$16,222,500	100%
Growth	*5%*		*5%*		*7%*		*7%*		*4%*		*3%*	
Cost of Sales	7,807,661	62%	7,685,000	58%	8,207,000	58%	8,787,000	58%	9,135,000	58%	9,409,050	58%
Gross Profit	4,785,341	38%	5,565,000	42%	5,943,000	42%	6,363,000	42%	6,615,000	42%	6,813,450	42%
SG&A Expenses	2,518,600	20%	2,385,000	18%	2,547,000	18%	2,727,000	18%	2,835,000	18%	2,920,050	18%
EBITDA	2,266,740	18%	3,180,000	24%	3,396,000	24%	3,636,000	24%	3,780,000	24%	3,893,400	24%
Less: Depreciation	275,830	2%	397,500	3%	424,500	3%	454,500	3%	472,500	3%	486,675	3%
EBIT	1,990,910	16%	2,782,500	21%	2,971,500	21%	3,181,500	21%	3,307,500	21%	3,406,725	21%
Less: Taxes	(756,546)	−6%	(1,057,350)	−8%	(1,129,170)	−8%	(1,208,970)	−8%	(1,256,850)	−8%	(1,294,556)	−8%
Debt-Free Net Income	1,234,364	10%	1,725,150	13%	1,842,330	13%	1,972,530	13%	2,050,650	13%	2,112,170	13%
Plus: Depreciation	275,830	2%	397,500	3%	424,500	3%	454,500	3%	472,500	3%	486,675	3%
Less: Capital Expenditures	(1) (275,830)	−2%	(397,500)	−3%	(424,500)	−3%	(454,500)	−3%	(472,500)	−3%	(486,675)	−3%
Less: Incremental Working Capital	(6) (200,000)	−2%	(132,500)	−1%	(141,500)	−1%	(151,500)	−1%	(157,500)	−1%	(162,225)	−1%
Debt-Free Cash Flows to Invested Capital	1,034,364	8%	1,592,650	12%	1,700,830	12%	1,821,030	12%	1,893,150	12%	1,949,945	12%
Terminal Value in 20X5											9,749,723	
Partial Period	0.17		1.00		1.00		1.00		1.00		1.00	
Period	0.08		0.67		1.67		2.67		3.67		3.67	
Present Value Factor	0.983		0.871		0.708		0.576		0.468		0.468	
Present Value of Cash Flows to Inv. Capital	169,902		1,387,211		1,204,420		1,048,405		886,119		4,563,511	

Sum of PV of DFCF (20X1–20X5)	4,696,057		Fair Value of Intangible Assets & Goodwill	7,400,000
PV of Terminal Value	4,563,511		15-Year Amortization Period	/15
PV of Tax Benefit-Amortization of Intangibles	1,018,655		Tax Amortization per Year	493,333
Preliminary Value	10,278,223		Tax Rate	38%
			Annual Amortization Benefit	187,467
Value of Invested Capital, Rounded	10,278,000		Sum of PV Factors 20X1 to 20Y6	5.43
Less: Debt	(2,000,000)		Present Value of Amortization Benefit	1,018,655
Fair Value of Equity, Rounded	$ 8,278,000			

Assumptions		
Discount Rate	23%	(2)
Internal Rate of Return	23%	(3)
Tax Rate	38%	(4)
Long-Term Growth Rate	3%	(5)

Notes:
(1) Makes the simplifying assumption that capital expenditures are equal to depreciation expense.
(2) Discounted at the weighted average cost of capital per Exhibit 6.11.
(3) Implied rate that reconciles the future expected cash flows to the fair value of acquisition price.
(4) Estimated corporate tax rate.
(5) Based on Management's projections, the growth prospects of the industry and the overall economy.
(6) Based in industry average and management projections.

Combinations (SFAS 141(R)), is to measure the fair value of the entire acquired entity. This fair value is also known as the business enterprise value (BEV). As mentioned, the most common method to measure the fair value of the acquired entity is the discounted cash flow method under the income approach. The entity's fair value indicated by the DCF can also be corroborated by other valuation techniques, such as the guideline company method under the market approach.

The BEV or the fair value of invested capital is measured by discounting debt-free cash flows to the present at the WACC. The fair value of the entity's equity is then measured by subtracting the fair value of debt from the BEV. A corollary to measuring the fair value of the equity using a DCF method at the WACC is to calculate the implied internal rate of return (IRR) on the investment. The IRR is the discount rate that makes the present value of the acquired entity's expected future debt-free cash flows to be equal to the acquisition price. In financial theory, the IRR should approximate the WACC. However, in practice there is often a difference, sometimes a substantial difference. If the WACC is greater than the acquired entity's IRR, then the acquirer may have paid more than the sum of the fair values of the identifiable assets. This situation results in the recognition of goodwill at a higher value than would otherwise be expected if the WACC were equal to the IRR. If the WACC is lower than the implied IRR, it is probable that the acquirer made a cost-effective acquisition and the resulting fair value of goodwill would be substantially lower than would otherwise be expected if the WACC were equal to the IRR. Valuation specialists often compare the entity's IRR to the WACC to gain insight about the prospective fair value of goodwill in an acquisition. The BEV in Exhibit 6.2 is calculated based on a 23 percent WACC. The IRR is 22.5 percent based on a $10.5 million acquisition price. In the JT Austin example, the difference between the implied IRR and the WACC is insignificant. When a significant difference between the two percentages exists, further analysis is needed. A significantly higher IRR may indicate the existence of a bargain purchase price that would potentially result in a gain. A significantly lower IRR may indicate the payment of a synergistic premium by the acquirer.

Multiperiod Excess Earnings Method

The Multiperiod Excess Earning Method (MPEEM) is a variation of the discounted cash flow analysis that is often used to measure the fair value of certain intangible assets. Unlike the DCF, which measures fair value by discounting cash flows for an entire entity, the MPEEM measures fair value by discounting expected future cash flows attributable to a single intangible asset. Typically, the single asset is the primary generator of cash flows for the entity. Customer relationships and technology are examples of intangible assets that are primary generators of cash flows and are therefore suitable for fair value measurement using the MPEEM.

To isolate cash flows attributable to a specific intangible asset, the portion of cash flows attributed to all other assets is deducted from total entity cash flows. The deduction of cash flows attributable to all other assets is accomplished through a contributory asset charge (CAC). The CAC is a form of economic rent for the use of all other assets in generating total cash flows. The CAC is composed of the required rate of return on all other assets, and an amount necessary to replace the fair value of certain contributory intangible assets. The amount necessary to replace the fair value of other contributory tangible assets is generally already taken into consideration in the total entity cash flows. The "return on" and "return of" concepts imbedded in contributory charges is similar to that for investment analysis. The Appraisal Foundation recently issued an Exposure Draft for *The Identification of Contributory Assets and the Calculation of Economic Rents* as part of a series entitled Best Practices for Valuations in Financial Reporting: Intangible Asset Working Groups. The Appraisal Foundation's Exposure Draft is the most comprehensive guidance within the valuation profession about contributory charges under the MPEEM.[6]

The origins of the MPEEM can be traced back to a "formula approach" found in the Internal Revenue Service's Committee on Appeals and Review Memorandum (ARM) 34, which was introduced in the 1920s when breweries and distilleries faced substantial losses due to their closure during Prohibition. The IRS issued ARM 34 to provide guidance to determine the value of intangible assets, including goodwill so that the owners of breweries and distilleries could be compensated for the closure of their businesses. ARM 34 presented formulas to determine the aggregate value of goodwill and intangible assets. The aggregate value was determined by deducting an economic charge on the value of working capital and tangible assets from the normalized net income of the entity. The residual earnings were called "excess earnings." The residual excess earnings were assumed to be attributed to the entity's intangible assets. These earnings were capitalized according to a formula using suggested capitalization rates. The capitalized aggregate value of goodwill and intangible assets was then added to the value of the entity's tangible assets to determine the entity's total value. Revenue Ruling 68-609 issued in 1968 provides additional guidance in estimating the value of an entity's intangible assets for tax reporting requirements.[7] Although they have many significant limitations, the methodologies presented in IRS ARM 34 and revised in Revenue Ruling 68-609 formed the basis for contributory charges under the MPEEM.

In December 2001, the AICPA issued a practice aid entitled *Acquired in a Business Combination to Be Used in Research and Development Activities: A Focus on Software, Electronic Devices, and Pharmaceutical Industries*

(No. 006609CPA12). The practice aid identifies best practices for defining, accounting for, disclosing, valuing, and auditing acquired assets to be used in R&D activities, including specific In-Process Research & Development (IPR&D) projects.[8] Although the practice aid only specifically covers acquired R&D, the concepts and methodologies provided in the practice aid are widely applied to other acquired assets. The AICPA's Fair Value Resource Group is currently in the process of updating this practice aid.

The MPEEM is one of the primary methods to estimate the fair value of IPR&D in a business combination covered by the practice aid. Expanding on the concepts introduced in ARM 34 and refined by RR 68-609 and by others, the practice aid provides a detailed description of the excess earnings methodology.[9] It extends the single period capitalization method found in the IRS ruling by applying the concept to a multiperiod analysis. The practice aid also provides improved guidance for calculating contributory charges so that the excess earnings methodology can be used to estimate the fair value of a single intangible asset instead of the aggregate value of all intangible assets. Guidance for determining appropriate rates of returns for various classes of assets can also be found in the practice aid. The AICPA's Fair Value Resource Panel has recently formed a task force to update the guidance found in the practice aid. The task force is expected to issue an exposure draft in 2010.

The fair value of JT Austin Technology Inc.'s patented technology is measured in Exhibit 6.3 to illustrate the multiperiod excess earnings method. The charge for the required return on contributory assets shown in Exhibit 6.3 (4.7 percent for 20X1, 4.5 percent for 20X2, and so on) is based on the fair values of contributory assets measured at either appraised value, replacement cost, or a DCF model, and is based on the required return calculations contained in Exhibit 6.4. Contributory charges are fully discussed in a subsequent section.

Applying the MPEEM

The MPEEM is one of the more common methods used to estimate the fair value of certain intangible asset in financial reporting. The concepts underlying the MPEEM are rather simple, but it is a complex multiperiod model that estimates cash flows over the intangible asset's estimate remaining useful life. When applying the MPEEM to the estimate of a specific intangible asset's fair value, there are numerous complexities that must be addressed. The first is to develop a fundamental understanding of the entity's operations and its value drivers. Although obtaining this insight may seem to be straightforward, it is sometimes difficult to achieve in practice. For example, the fair value of a technology-based entity may be driven by customer relationships, a trade or domain name, or by the technology itself. The task of

EXHIBIT 6.3 JT Austin Technology Inc., Valuation of Patented Technology, as of October 31, 20X1

		20X1	20X2	20X3	20X4	20X5	20X5 Plus 10 Years
Projected Companywide Revenue		$12,593,002	$13,250,000	$14,150,000	$15,150,000	$15,750,000	$21,166,683
Growth		5%	5%	7%	7%	4%	3%
Decay Factor	(3)	0.98	0.88	0.72	0.59	0.48	0.06
Surviving Company Revenues		12,384,292	11,594,988	10,137,992	8,886,879	7,564,118	1,375,756
EBITDA		2,229,173	2,782,797	2,433,118	2,132,851	1,815,388	330,182
Average EBITDA Margin		18%	24%	24%	24%	24%	24%
Less: Depreciation	(7)	271,259	347,850	304,140	266,606	226,924	41,273
EBIT		1,957,914	2,434,947	2,128,978	1,866,245	1,588,465	288,909
Less: Charge for Use of Trade Name		123,843	115,950	101,380	88,869	75,641	13,758
Adjusted EBIT		1,834,071	2,318,998	2,027,598	1,777,376	1,512,824	275,151
Less: Taxes		(696,947)	(881,219)	(770,487)	(675,403)	(574,873)	(104,557)
Debt-Free Net Income before Contributory Charge		1,137,124	1,437,778	1,257,111	1,101,973	937,551	170,594
Less: Contributory Asset Charge		(581,189)	(522,880)	(434,508)	(361,575)	(298,141)	(49,394)
Contributory Asset Charge as a % of Revenue		4.7%	4.5%	4.3%	4.1%	3.9%	3.6%
Debt-Free Cash Flow to Patented Technology	(5)	555,935	914,898	822,603	740,398	639,810	121,200
Partial Period		0.17	1.00	1.00	1.00	1.00	1.00
Period		0.08	0.67	1.67	2.67	3.67	13.67
Present Value Factor		0.983	0.871	0.708	0.576	0.468	0.059
Present Value of Debt-Free Cash Flows		91,316	796,884	582,516	426,262	299,473	7,157
Sum of PV of DFCF		2,861,019					
Amortization Benefit Multiplier	(6)	1.13					
Preliminary Value		3,225,051					

Concluded Value Patented Technology, Rounded $3,225,000

Assumptions		
Discount Rate	(1)	23%
Tax Rate	(2)	38%
Remaining Useful Life	(3)	5 years
Royalty Rate	(4)	1%

Notes:
(1) Weighted Average Cost of Capital per Exhibit 6.11.
(2) Estimated corporate tax rate.
(3) Based on 5-year life and the applicable decay factor with analysis truncated after 15 years. 98% of cash flows are captured in the first 15 years.
(4) Based on industry royalty rates.
(5) Charge for the use of the remaining assets that contribute to the cash flow forecast. See Contributory Asset analysis on Exhibit 6.4.
(6) Represents the present value of the estimated tax benefit derived from the amortization of the intangible asset, over the tax life (15 years) of the asset.
(7) Tax depreciation may be forecasted based on MACRS.

EXHIBIT 6.4 JT Austin Technology Inc., Required Return on Contributory Assets, as of October 31, 20X1

(000s)			20X1	20X2	20X3	20X4	20X5	Thereafter
Total Revenue			$ 12,593,002	$ 13,250,000	$ 14,150,000	$ 15,150,000	$ 15,750,000	$ 16,222,500
Growth			*5%*	*5%*	*7%*	*7%*	*4%*	*3%*
Total Revenue			12,593,002	13,250,000	14,150,000	15,150,000	15,750,000	16,222,500
Multiplied by: DFWC %			15.2%	15.2%	15.2%	15.2%	15.2%	15.2%
Debt-Free Working Capital Balance			1,914,136	2,014,000	2,150,800	2,302,800	2,394,000	2,465,820
Required Return on Working Capital	6.5%	(1)	124,598	131,098	140,003	149,897	155,834	160,509
Capital Expenditures (2)			275,830	397,500	424,500	454,500	472,500	486,675
Depreciation			275,830	397,500	424,500	454,500	472,500	486,675
Net Fixed Assets Balance	$ 1,175,200		1,175,200	1,175,200	1,175,200	1,175,200	1,175,200	1,175,200
Required Return on Capital Investment	7.0%	(3)	82,691	82,691	82,691	82,691	82,691	82,691
Noncompetition Agreement Beginning Value	$ 194,000							
Noncompetition Agreement Required Return	23.0%	(4)	44,620	44,620	44,620	44,620	44,620	—
Assembled Workforce Beginning Value	$ 530,000							
Assembled Workforce Required Return	23.0%	(4)	121,900	121,900	121,900	121,900	121,900	121,900
Customer Relationships Beginning Value	$ 865,000							
Customer Relationships Required Return	25.0%	(5)	216,250	216,250	216,250	216,250	216,250	216,250
Required Return on Contributory Assets (as a % of Revenue)			**4.7%**	**4.5%**	**4.3%**	**4.1%**	**3.9%**	**3.6%**

Notes:

(1) Assumes that DFWC would be financed with 15% equity and 85% debt at the prime rate of 3.5% plus a 1.5% premium, tax effected.

(2) Valuation specialists may make the simplifying assumption that capital expenditures are equal to depreciation expense, otherwise, based on management's forecasted capital expenditures and related tax depreciation.

(3) Assumes that capital expenditures would be financed with 15% equity and 85% debt at the prime rate of 3.5% plus a 2.5% premium, tax effected.

(4) WACC per Exhibit 6.11.

(5) WACC plus a 2% premium.

identifying the entity's primary value drivers falls to the management of the acquiring entity.

Other complexities in applying the MPEEM are isolating the actual cash flows that are attributable to the specific subject intangible asset and developing contributory charges. Understanding the difference between a "return of" the contributory asset and a "return on" that contributory asset is important to the successful development of contributory charges.

Returns on and of Contributory Assets

An entity is composed of a group of tangible and intangible assets that contribute to the generation of its total cash flows. The MPEEM separates cash flows attributable to the subject intangible asset by deducting contributory charges for all of the other assets that contribute to the entity's cash flows. After deducting these charges, the remaining residual cash flows are assumed to be attributable to the subject intangible asset.

The first component of the contributory charge represents a "return on" contributory assets. The "return on" contributory assets is based on the assumption that the entity pays a hypothetical economic rent or royalty for the use of the asset. It is a required rate of return on the fair value of all the contributory assets to compensate for the entity's use of those assets to produce economic benefits. The "return on" contributory assets is analogous to a royalty paid for the use of a technology in a product owned by another entity. The contributory charge includes a "return on" all contributory assets, including working capital, fixed assets, and intangible assets, excluding the subject intangible asset.

The second portion of the contributory asset charge is a "return of" contributory assets and is analogous to the return of principal that is part of each mortgage payment. However, the "return of" portion of the contributory charge is not for all contributory assets. It is only applicable to assets when the cost to replenish the asset is not already part of the cash flow analysis. For example, the cost to replace internally generated intangible assets such as assembled workforce and trade names are included in the cash flow analysis as expenses on the income statement. Similarly, a significant portion of the "return of" fixed assets is also already included as depreciation expense. When calculating initial cash flows prior to contributory asset charges, depreciation expense is therefore not added back as a noncash item since it reflects a "return of" the investment in fixed assets.

CLASSIFICATION OF CONTRIBUTORY ASSETS   There are four types of contributory assets that have distinct treatment when calculating contributory charges under the MPEEM. They differ with respect to how "return of" capital and "return on" capital are incorporated into the MPEEM.

1. Nonwasting assets replenish themselves indirectly through normal company operations. Working capital is an example of a nonwasting asset. It replenishes itself through normal operations and will increase or decrease with the growth or decline in company revenues. Nonwasting assets do not require a contributory charge for the "return of" the asset. However, a company does require a "return on" its working capital. Therefore, a contributory charge for a return on a nonwasting asset is appropriate.

2. Assets that are capitalized and deteriorate over time are considered wasting assets. Buildings, machinery, and equipment are examples of wasting assets that physically deteriorate over time. The physical deterioration is recognized in financial reporting as depreciation expense. Wasting assets must be replenished so that they can continue to support the expected cash flows of the entity. The return-of-capital charge should reflect the amount needed to maintain the viability of these assets throughout the MPEEM forecast period. There are two methods commonly used to capture the return of capital charge on wasting assets. One is to use depreciation expense as a proxy for the capital charge and the other is through the use of a hypothetical lease charge.

> *Depreciation Expenses as a Proxy.* In most DCF models, depreciation expense is added back to cash flows from operations because it is noncash operating expense. Planned capital expenditures are then subtracted to arrive at expected cash flows. An alternate treatment is based on the assumption that depreciation expense is a reasonable proxy for, or is equal to, the costs required to replenish the capital asset. Noncash depreciation expense would not be added back to operating cash flows as is typically done for other noncash expenses. Instead, the cash flows analysis would be burdened with depreciation expenses to fully reflect the "return of" capital charge for these assets. There would be no capital expenditures for the replenishment of these wasting assets in the MPEEM. Under this alternative, contributory charges would exclude a "return of" capital charge. However, wasting capital assets require a "return on" capital contributory charge to account for their contribution to the entity's cash flows. Therefore, the contributory charge under this alternative is a simple "return on" capital charge.
>
> *Hypothetical Lease Payment.* The other method is to treat wasting assets as though they are leased. The hypothetical lease payment is similar to payment of a royalty rate for an intangible asset. Since the assets are leased under this method, there is no

depreciation expense. The "return of" and "return on" capital charges are incorporated into the hypothetical lease payment and fully reflected in the contributory charge.

3. The costs to develop some assets are expensed when incurred. They receive recognition as assets through the acquisition method in a business combination. Examples of this type of asset would be an assembled workforce or existing customer relationships. After they are recognized as assets, any future costs to maintain the asset would be a normal part of operating expense. For example, hiring and training costs to maintain the workforce would be expensed as usual. Similarly, sales and marketing costs required to maintain existing customer relationships or to replace lost customers with new ones would be expensed. Since these costs flow through the income statement, the "return of" charge is already considered in operating cash flows that form the base for the MPEEM analysis. Therefore, the "return of" charge would not be included as a contributory asset charge. However, because all companies expect to earn a return on any costs incurred to train and hire a workforce or to build and maintain customer relationships, contributory charges would include a "return on" charge for these types of assets.
4. The contributory charge for some assets is more appropriately captured through market-based royalty rates. A trade name is a common example of this type of contributory assets. The value of the trade name may be disproportionate to the costs incurred to develop or maintain it. In this case, a market-based charge is more appropriate. Contributory charges for this type of asset can be reflected through a market royalty payment to a hypothetical owner of the asset. Both "return of" and "return on" charges are captured in the royalty rate since the hypothetical owner of the asset would have to be compensated for both of these charges.[10]

When using the MPEEM to measure the fair value of primary, revenue-generating assets, contributory charges should be calculated for all other operating assets that contribute to the entity's operating cash flows. The contributory asset charge includes a "return on" charge for all contributory assets. Sometimes the "return of" capital charge is included in the contributory asset charge and sometimes it flows through MPEEM operating cash flows. One must also consider the asset's remaining useful life when calculating contributory asset charges. For example, the contributory charge for a noncompetition agreement should be taken for the period of time the company expects to benefit from the agreement. Other assets such as fixed assets may require additions to the "return of" portion beyond depreciation expense if additional capacity is required to support forecasted revenue growth.

GOODWILL When measuring the fair value of a subject asset under the MPEEM, contributory charges are calculated for intangible assets that are recognized using the Acquisition Method to account for the business combination. Under FASB ASC 805, *Business Combinations* (SFAS 141(R)), the FASB requires the recognition of an asset in a business combination if it is identifiable. Recall that an intangible asset is considered identifiable if it meets one of two criteria:

1. *It is separable; that is, capable of being separated or divided from the entity and sold, transferred, licensed, rented, or exchanged, either individually or together with a related contract, identifiable asset, or liability, regardless of whether the entity intends to do so.*
2. *It arises from contractual or other legal rights, regardless of whether those rights are transferable or separable from the entity or from other rights and obligations.*[11]

Goodwill does not meet these criteria. Generally, goodwill represents the contribution of future assets and does not currently contribute to the entity's cash flows. When using the MPEEM to measure the fair value of the subject asset, a contributory charge is not typically taken for goodwill as a contributory asset. However, there are some exceptions. Some elements of goodwill are considered contributory assets and a contributory charge is appropriate. One common example is an assembled workforce. An assembled workforce is not specifically recognized as an identifiable intangible asset under FASB ASC 805, *Business Combinations*. The assembled workforce is included in goodwill. However, from an economic perspective, the workforce obviously contributes to the generation of cash flows. So the contribution of the assembled workforce should be considered when calculating contributory charges under the MPEEM.

In some industries, such as telecommunications and cable, there may be circumstances when some element of goodwill should be recognized as a contributory asset. This might be appropriate even when these assets do not meet the identifiably criteria under FASB ASC 805. The distinguishing characteristic of these industries is that their operations are dependent on the grant of a license or other similar authorization. SEC Staff Announcement Topic D-108, *Use of the Residual Method to Value Acquired Assets Other Than Goodwill*, describes the features of these assets and the difficulty in measuring their fair value using traditional valuation methods.[12] Examples of this type of assets are a nuclear power plant license, a cellular spectrum, a radio frequency license, and cable franchises. When applying the acquisition method, many SEC registrants allocated the entire residual amount from the business combination to these indistinguishable assets. In Topic D-108, the

SEC staff discusses the identification criteria under SFAS 141 (now FASB ASC 805, *Business Combinations*, SFAS 141(R)) and the residual nature of goodwill. D-108 requires that a direct valuation method be used to measure the fair value of these license types of assets and says that the residual method should only be used to measure goodwill.[13]

When calculating contributory charges under the MPEEM, there may be circumstances when a component of goodwill, such as a license, can be measured separately from goodwill. If so, a contributory charge can be taken for this component of goodwill in the MPEEM similar to the contributory charge for the economic contribution of an assembled workforce. However, these circumstances are rare given the difficulty in directly measuring the fair value of these indistinguishable assets.

The contributory asset charge calculation for JT Austin Technology is shown in Exhibit 6.4 to illustrate the application of these concepts. Note that the contributory charge percentages from Exhibit 6.4 are used in the fair value measurement of JT Austin's patented technology under the multi-period excess earnings method in Exhibit 6.3.

Note that this exhibit includes the simplifying assumption that JT Austin would not require an increased level of fixed assets, such as a new plant. The simplifying assumption means that capital expenditures are equal to depreciation expense in Exhibit 6.4. As a result, contributory charge percentages are relatively stable from year to year. If an additional investment in new assets is required during the life cycle of the technology, there would be a "stair step" effect resulting in an increase of the contributory charge in the year of the investment.

Prospective Financial Information (PFI)

Another important step in estimating the fair value of an intangible asset using the MPEEM is to determine the prospective financial information (PFI) that is appropriate to use in the analysis. Appropriate PFI are the revenue, expenses, and resulting cash flows associated with the subject intangible asset, and they should be directly tied to the remaining useful life of the subject intangible asset. Management typically provides PFI for the entire entity, which serves as a starting point for identifying the subject asset's PFI. Some valuation analysts prefer to analyze prospective financial information by breaking out fixed and variable expenses. The proportion of fixed to variable expense often is a reflection of the industry in which the company operates. Variable expenses tend to be more operational in nature and fixed expenses tend to be based on management's operating, investing, and financing decisions. Therefore, a thorough understanding of the entity's variable and fixed-cost structure leads to better identification of the PFI attributable to the subject intangible asset.

Since most intangible assets are wasting assets, the subject intangible asset's contribution to the entity's overall PFI typically declines over time. Therefore, the entity level PFI must be adjusted to reflect the economic life of the subject intangible asset. The resulting PFI for the subject intangible asset is used in the MPEEM.

MARKET PARTICIPANT ASSUMPTIONS IN THE PFI In a business combination measurement of fair value, the PFI should reflect those assumptions that a market participant would make rather than the assumptions that are specific to the acquiring entity. Recall that FASB ASC 820, *Fair Value Measurements and Disclosures* (SFAS No. 157), defines fair value as "the price that would be received to sell an asset or paid to transfer a liability in an orderly transaction between market participants at the measurement date."[14] Since the acquiring entity may be a frequent market participant, its assumptions may be similar to those assumptions made by market participants. FASB ASC 820 (SFAS 157) goes on to say that "the fair value of the asset or liability shall be determined based on the assumptions that market participants would use in pricing the asset or liability."[15] When developing fair value measurements, the FASB did not intend to identify specific individual market participants. FASB ASC 820 provides guidance about the market participant assumption by saying that the entity "should identify characteristics that distinguish market participants generally, considering factors specific to (a) the asset or liability, (b) the principal (or most advantageous) market for the asset or liability, and (c) market participants with whom the reporting entity would transact in that market."[16]

When developing the PFI, the market participant assumption should be made after considering the likely buyers for the entity or reporting unit. For example, likely buyers might be a small group of strategic buyers or a group of financial acquirers. If the business combination has many potential acquirers, each with similar bids, then the PFI prepared in conjunction with the acquisition would be more likely to reflect market participant assumptions and exclude synergies. Conversely, if the business combination has a limited group of potential strategic acquirers, then the assumptions underlying the PFI would be more entity-specific and be more likely to include synergies. If the market participant assumption incorporates synergies, then value of the synergies would be reflected in the value of the individual acquired intangible assets. If the market participant assumptions exclude synergies in individual intangible assets, the value of the entity-specific synergies would not be reflected in the value of the individual acquired assets, but would fall to goodwill. While FASB ASC 820, *Fair Value Measurements and Disclosures* (SFAS No. 157), does not require the identification of specific market participants, if they can be identified without undue cost or effort, then the assumptions used by these specific entities should be considered.

ANALYZING PFI FOR MARKET PARTICIPANT ASSUMPTIONS   Fair value is measured under the MPEEM using prospective financial information with market participant assumptions. However, market participant assumptions are often difficult to observe, leaving management with the difficult task of making assumptions appropriate for a hypothetical market participant. FASB ASC 820 (SFAS 157) describes the process determining market participant assumptions for unobservable inputs when management is developing PFI:

> *Unobservable inputs shall reflect the reporting entity's own assumptions about the assumptions that market participants would use in pricing the asset or liability (including assumptions about risk). Unobservable inputs shall be developed based on the best information available in the circumstances, which might include the reporting entity's own data. In developing unobservable inputs, the reporting entity need not undertake all possible efforts to obtain information about market participant assumptions. However, the reporting entity shall not ignore information about market participant assumptions that is reasonably available without undue cost and effort. Therefore, the reporting entity's own data used to develop unobservable inputs shall be adjusted if information is reasonably available without undue cost and effort that indicates that market participants would use different assumptions.*[17]

One of the important assumptions that management must make in developing the PFI using market participant assumptions is whether the market participant is a strategic or a financial acquirer. The choice is significant since market participant assumptions may be different for potential strategic and financial acquirers. Strategic acquirers have potential operating synergies related to revenue, expenses, and cost of capital. Revenue synergies may be experienced by using the acquirers existing distribution channels to sell the acquired entity's products. Additional revenue synergies may be found by combining complementary products within existing channels. Potential synergies relating to cost reductions are the result of economics of scale and the elimination of duplicate costs. Examples of cost-reduction synergies would be the elimination of redundant workforces and a reduction in fixed costs from combining manufacturing and distribution facilities. Finally, there may be synergies related to the reduced cost of capital of the combined entities. For example, a start-up may gain access to capital at a lower rate as part of a larger, more stable entity.

If there are synergies that can be realized by all market participants, then the synergies should be reflected in the PFI and in the fair value of the assets of the acquired entity. If synergies are specific to the business combination, and can only be realized by a few potential acquiring entities, then the PFI should be adjusted to exclude market synergies unavailable to other market participants. The resulting fair value of the acquired assets would exclude synergies. Instead, any value resulting from synergies would appear in goodwill.

ECONOMIC LIFE OF THE INTANGIBLE ASSET IN THE PFI Adjustments to the entity-wide PFI provided by management may be necessary because the time frame that it encompasses might not correspond to the subject asset's economic life. The assumption about the economic life of the subject asset must be considered when adjusting an entity-wide PFI for use in measuring the fair value of the specific intangible asset. The assumption about the economic life of a specific intangible asset depends on the nature of the intangible asset. There are two ways to estimate the economic life of an intangible asset when measuring its fair value. The American Society of Appraisers refers to these two methods as lifecycle analysis and attrition analysis.[18]

The lifecycle analysis is normally used for intangible assets that have an estimated product life such as developed technology sold to third parties. The economic life of an intangible asset is typically one of the considerations in the remaining useful life of the asset. FASB ASC 350, *Intangibles—Goodwill and Other* (SFAS No. 142), and FSP FAS 142-3 provide guidance about which factors should be considered when estimating the remaining life of the asset. The statement says that useful life shall be based on an analysis of all pertinent factors, with no one factor being more presumptive than the other. The six factors are:

1. The expected use of the asset by the entity.
2. The expected useful life of another asset or a group of assets to which the useful life of the intangible asset may relate.
3. Any legal, regulatory, or contractual provisions that may limit the useful life.
4. The entity's own historical experience in renewing or extending similar agreements (consistent with the intended use of the asset by the entity), regardless of whether those arrangements have explicit renewal or extension provisions. In the absence of that experience, the entity shall consider the assumptions that market participants would use about renewal or extensions (consistent with the highest and best use of the asset by market participants), adjusted for entity-specific factors in this paragraph.
5. The effects of obsolescence, demand, competition, and other economic factors (such as the stability of the industry, known technological advances, legislative action that results in an uncertain or changing regulatory environment, and expected changes in distribution channels).

6. The level of maintenance expenditures required to obtain the expected future cash flows from the asset (for example, a material level of required maintenance in relation to the carrying amount of the asset may suggest a very limited useful life).[19]

The economic life of the asset takes into consideration these factors and how they impact the expected positive cash flows specifically related to the use of the asset.

Attrition analysis is a statistical process for estimating the historical turnover for the subject intangible analysis. Historic turnover is applied to subject asset to estimate the future rate of loss due to the use of the intangible asset. An example of attrition analysis is examining historical customer turnover to estimate the likely turnover of customers would occur in the future.

ISSUES IN THE USE OF THE MPEEM   Due to the large number and complex nature of assumptions incorporated into the MPEEM, there are many divergent practices in the application of the method. The Appraisal Foundation's Best Practices on Contributory Assets recognizes these divergent practices and, where applicable, provides guidance about the best of the practices. Within the valuation profession, the more prevalent divergent practices relate to the use of contributory cross charges, the application of revenue splits, the selection of an appropriate level of contributory assets, and the inclusion of deferred revenue in the working capital contributory charge.

Contributory Asset Cross Charges   Typically, the MPEEM is used to measure the fair value of the intangible asset that is the primary value driver for the entity. The reason is that in most situations, the entity-wide set of PFI can only be adjusted to reflect the cash flows for one specific intangible asset. However, if these cash flows are generated by more than one significant intangible asset, it may be difficult to determine which asset is the primary asset. For example, suppose a software company sells prepackaged software that is acquired in a business combination. The entity has two identifiable intangible assets, developed software, and existing customer relationships.

A common method to determine which asset is the primary asset would be through discussions with management. The primary asset would be the subject asset whose fair value is determined using the MPEEM. Other methods such as a cost approach method or the relief from royalty method would be used to estimate the fair value of the second intangible asset. The fair value of the secondary asset would then be considered a contributing asset in the MPEEM.

The Appraisal Foundation's Exposure Draft on Contributory Charges discusses the diversity in practice for the simultaneous application of the

MPEEM to measure the fair value of two separate intangible assets. The simultaneous measurements can be accomplished by taking contributory cross charges in each MPEEM. For example, when measuring the fair value of the technology, a charge would be taken for the contribution of the customer relationships and when measuring the fair value of the customer relationships a charge would be taken for the contribution of the technology. There are some valuation specialists who believe the simultaneous application of the MPEEM using cross charges would measure the fair value of both intangible assets. Others believe this methodology is difficult to implement and is prone to overvaluation. Valuation specialists believe the simultaneous application of the MPEEM should be limited to situations where it is possible to identify distinct sets of cash flows generated by each intangible asset. Because of the problems associated with implementation of simultaneous MPEEM fair value measurements, the Appraisal Foundation Exposure Draft on Contributory Charges recommends against using this type of methodology.[20]

Splitting Revenues or Profits under the MPEEM A simple way to avoid the difficulties associated with using the MPEEM to simultaneously measure the fair value of two identified intangible assets is to split the entity's revenue and cash flows. The revenues and cash flows attributable to each of the two subject assets would be identified separately. For example, if the entity has two unique technologies that are used in two separate products, then the MPEEM can be used to measure the fair value of each technology by separating the cash flows by product line. Isolating the cash flows attributable to each technology avoids the problems associated with cross charges. The contributory assets would be those assets used exclusively with the subject technology to generate cash flows for the company. Contributory assets used in the generation of cash flows for both technologies would be allocated on a pro rata basis based on revenues. Thus, it would not be appropriate to take a charge for the other technology or any other asset exclusively used to produce the other product. If it is not possible to separate cash flows into those attributable to the two identified intangible assets, then the fair value of the primary assets can be measured using the MPEEM, but the fair value of the secondary asset must be measured by some other method.

Appropriate Level of Working Capital As discussed previously, working capital is considered a nonwasting asset that is replenished through the entity's normal operating cycle. However, an increased level of working capital would be required to generate cash flow growth. When this is the case, a "return on" the increased level of working capital should be included as a contributory charge under the MPEEM. The "return on" working capital contributory charge should be based on a normalized level of working capital that a market participant would require to support the cash flow generating ability of the subject asset.

Deferred Revenue   Deferred revenue is recorded when an entity receives cash for future products or services. The earnings process is not complete; therefore, the entity has an obligation to deliver additional products or services and revenue cannot be recognized. Examples of deferred revenues include a software vendor's maintenance obligation on prepaid maintained contracts, an airline's obligation to provide travel when tickets are purchased in advance, and magazine publisher's obligation to deliver magazines when subscriptions payments are received in advance. Sometimes, deferred revenues are included as a component of working capital when calculating contributory charges, and sometimes they are not. The Working Group of the Appraisal Foundation has discussed whether deferred revenue should be included in the computation of working capital as a contributory asset. Their conclusion is that deferred revenue should be included as a current liability in working capital if the PFI is developed using an accrual basis because the deferred revenue is a part of ongoing operations. Deferred revenue that is not considered part of ongoing operations may or may not be included as a component of working capital depending on the circumstances.[21]

Appropriate Level of Fixed Assets   The Appraisal Foundation describes two methods for calculating fixed asset contributory charges; one is the "Average Annual Balance" and the other is the "Level Payment" method.

The fixed asset contributory charge using the Average Annual Balance method is calculated as:

Debt-free net income
Plus: Accounting depreciation
Less: Measure of return of the fixed assets (may be accounting or tax depreciation as a proxy)
Less: Return on the average balance of the fixed assets
Less: Contributory asset charges on all other contributory assets
Equals: Cash flow to individual asset

As previously discussed, depreciation is often used as a proxy for the "return of" the fixed asset. Tax depreciation is the preferred proxy, but accounting depreciation is also used. This simplifying assumption may be appropriate in most circumstances; however, the valuation specialist should consider whether the level of fixed assets would remain constant throughout the forecast period of the MPEEM.[22]

The Level Payment method assumes that the contributory fixed asset is leased and the entity pays a market royalty for the use of the asset. The assumed lease or rent payment would include both a "return of" and "return on" the fixed asset because the hypothetical owner would charge an amount to cover the use of the fixed asset and to cover the cost to replenish the fixed asset.

The contributory charge using the Level Payment assumption is calculated as:

Debt-free net income
Plus: Accounting depreciation
Less: Rent contributory charge, which covers both return of and return on the asset.
Less: Contributory asset charges on all other contributory assets
Equals: Cash flow to individual asset[23]

The Level Payment assumption is similar to the relief from royalty method used to measure the fair value of certain intangible assets. An advantage of the Level Payment assumption is that it may do a better job of including market participant assumptions when comparable market rent data is available for similar assets. A disadvantage is that it may be difficult to obtain appropriate data.

FASB Concepts Statement 7

FASB Concepts Statement No. 7, *Using Cash Flow Information and Present Value in Accounting Measurements* (CON 7), provides guidance for using present value techniques to measure fair value, and it provides a framework for using estimated future cash flows in an accounting measurement. Uncertainties about the amount and timing of estimated future cash flows impact the measurement of an asset or a liability.

Typically, when an entity's management prepares PFI, they provide their "best estimate" of the future cash flows. CON 7 describes a "best estimate" as "the single most-likely amount in a range of possible estimated amounts. In statistics, this would be the mode. In the past, accounting pronouncements have used the term *best estimate* in a variety of contexts that range in meaning from 'unbiased' to 'most likely.'"[24] CON 7 also describes the "expected amount" as an alternative to the "best estimate." The best estimate is the single most likely amount, while the expected amount refers to the sum of probability-weighted amounts in a range of possible estimated amounts. It is the estimated mean or average.[25]

Under CON 7, there are two present value methodologies: (1) the traditional method and (2) the expected present value method. The traditional method uses the best estimate of the single, most likely set of cash flows.

This traditional method is the most common method for forecasting cash flows in PFI and is also commonly used in DCF methods to estimate the fair value of an entity. Under the traditional method, the risk associated with receiving estimated future cash flows is reflected in the risk-adjusted discount rate. A risk premium is added to the risk-free rate to account for the specific risk associated with estimated future cash flows.

According to CON 7, the expected cash flow is probably a more effective method than the traditional method. The expected cash flow method incorporates all of the expected outcomes for possible future cash flows instead of just a single, most-likely stream of cash flows. While theoretically preferable, the expected cash flow methodology is more difficult to implement in practice. Estimating all possible cash flows outcomes and assigning relative probabilities is a daunting task. However, in practice, the application of the expected cash flow approach is subject to cost-benefit constraints. The cost of obtaining additional information must be balanced against the additional reliability of that information. Therefore, it is not always necessary to apply the expected cash flow method using all possible cash flows. Instead, the expected cash flow method is often applied to a relatively small number of cash flow outcomes (or scenarios) using probabilities that capture the range of possible cash flows.

There are two basic versions of the expected cash flow method. They are similar in that both versions start with a set of expected cash flows determined using scenario analysis. The focus of scenario analysis is on direct analysis of the possible variations in the amount and timing of cash flows and on the underlying assumptions used in the development of the scenario. It is also necessary to estimate the likelihood or probability of each scenario. The expected set of cash flows is the probability weighted average of all the scenarios.

To illustrate the calculation of expected cash flows, assume that WXYZ Technology Inc. has recently agreed to license a trademarked logo to Buter Brothers Inc., an unrelated third party. In exchange for exclusive rights to use the logo, Buter Brothers Inc. has agreed to pay 2 percent of net revenues. The term of the agreement is through the end of 20X5, which corresponds with the remaining statutory life of the trademark protection. Buter Brothers Inc. has provided the revenue projections in Scenario 1. WXYZ's management believes the projections are optimistic. WXYZ's estimate of most likely revenues is included in Scenario 2. Management acknowledges that Buter Brothers' strategic marketing plan has the potential to succeed and that revenues could be higher. The most optimistic projections are included in Scenario 3. WXYZ management assesses the probability of Scenario 1 at 30 percent, Scenario 2 at 60 percent, and Scenario 3 at 10 percent. Assume in this example that these are the only potential outcomes. In reality, the outcomes may be much broader and require the use of statistical models such as Monte Carlo simulation. Expected license revenue is calculated in Exhibit 6.5.

The two versions of the expected cash flow method differ with respect to the method used to adjust for the systematic (market) risk associated with the expected cash flows. In the direct cash flow adjustment version, cash flows are directly adjusted for systematic market risk using market risk data. If market data is unavailable, a market premium from an asset pricing model can be used in the following formula to calculate the market risk adjustment:

$$MRA = CF - (CF \times (1 + R_f/1 + D)^\wedge P)$$

where:

MRA = market risk adjustment
CF = cash flow
R_f = risk-free rate
D = total discount rate, including the risk-free rate and a market risk premium
P = period

The market risk adjustment is deducted from expected cash flows. The resulting risk-adjusted expected cash flows are discounted at the risk-free rate to determine the fair value of the underlying asset. The fair value of the trademark using the direct adjustment version of the expected cash flow method is presented in Exhibit 6.6.

The other version of the expected cash flow method takes market risk into account through the discount rate. Expected cash flows are simply discounted at a discount rate that includes the risk-free rate and a market risk premium. Exhibit 6.7 shows the discount rate version of the expected cash flow method. Note that the resulting fair value for the trademark is the same under both methods. The version selected for use depends on the facts and circumstances in the situation, including the asset or liability being measured, the availability of data, and the application of judgment.[26]

Rates of Return under the Income Approach

A previous chapter introduced the concept of an adjusted economic balance sheet where the business entity value equals the business's invested capital. In the adjusted economic balance sheet, net working capital on a debt-free basis appears on the left-hand side with the fair value of all assets. The right

EXHIBIT 6.5 WXYZ Technology Inc.: Calculation of Expected License Revenues as of December 31, 20X1

	20X2	20X3	20X4	20X5	20X6
Scenario 1: Optimistic					
Expected Revenue	$ 35,387,500	$ 37,156,875	$ 39,014,719	$ 40,965,455	$ 43,013,727
Probability	30%	30%	30%	30%	30%
Scenario 1 Probability Weighted Revenue	10,616,250	11,147,063	11,704,416	12,289,636	12,904,118
Scenario 2: Most Likely					
Expected Revenue	32,600,000	33,578,000	34,585,340	35,622,900	36,691,587
Probability	60%	60%	60%	60%	60%
Scenario 2 Probability Weighted Revenue	19,560,000	20,146,800	20,751,204	21,373,740	22,014,952
Scenario 3: Very Optimistic					
Expected Revenue	38,926,250	40,872,563	42,916,191	45,062,000	47,315,100
Probability	10%	10%	10%	10%	10%
Scenario 3 Probability Weighted Revenue	3,892,625	4,087,256	4,291,619	4,506,200	4,731,510
Scenario 1 Probability Weighted Revenue	10,616,250	11,147,063	11,704,416	12,289,636	12,904,118
Scenario 2 Probability Weighted Revenue	19,560,000	20,146,800	20,751,204	21,373,740	22,014,952
Scenario 3 Probability Weighted Revenue	3,892,625	4,087,256	4,291,619	4,506,200	4,731,510
Expected Buter Brothers Revenue	34,068,875	35,381,119	36,747,239	38,169,577	39,650,581
Royalty Rate	2%	2%	2%	2%	2%
Expected License Revenue to WXYZ Technology	$ 681,378	$ 707,622	$ 734,945	$ 763,392	$ 793,012

EXHIBIT 6.6 Expected Cash Flow Method—Cash Flow Adjustment, WXYZ Technology Inc., Valuation of Trademark, as of December 31, 20X1

	Note	20X2	20X3	20X4	20X5	20X6
Expected License Revenue		$ 681,378	$707,622	$734,945	$763,392	$793,012
Less: Taxes		(258,923)	(268,897)	(279,279)	(290,089)	(301,344)
Expected License Cash Flows		422,454	438,726	455,666	473,303	491,667
Market Risk Adjustment	(1)	26,883	54,061	81,572	109,457	137,756
Expected Risk-Adjusted License Cash Flows		395,571	384,665	374,093	363,846	353,911
Period		1.00	2.00	3.00	4.00	5.00
Present Value Factor		0.971	0.943	0.915	0.888	0.863
PV of Risk-Adjusted License Cash Flows		384,049	362,583	342,348	323,272	305,287
Sum of PV of License Cash Flows		1,717,540				
Amortization Benefit Multiplier	(2)	1.25				
Preliminary Value		2,146,925				
Value of Trademark, rounded		**$2,147,000**				

Assumptions	Note	
Discount Rate	(3)	3.0%
Tax Rate	(4)	38.0%
Remaining Useful Life		5 years

Notes:

(1) Adjustment for systematic (market risk): Adjustment $= CF - (CF \times (1 + RF / 1 + D)^P)$, where CF is cash flow, RF is the risk-free rate, D is the total discount rate, including the risk-free rate plus a market risk premium, and P is the period. This example incorporates a 3% risk-free rate and a 7% market risk premium. The market risk adjustment is the amount of change in cash flow to equate risk-free and risk-adjusted discount rates.

(2) Represents the present value of the estimated tax benefit derived from the amortization of the intangible asset, over the tax life (15 years) of the asset. The amortization benefit multiplier is based on the 3% risk-free discount rate plus a 7% market risk premium.

(3) Risk-free rate of 3%.

(4) Estimated corporate tax rate.

EXHIBIT 6.7 Expected Cash Flow Method—Discount Rate Adjustment, WXYZ Technology Inc., Valuation of Trademark, as of December 31, 20X1

	20X2	20X3	20X4	20X5	20X6
Expected License Revenue	$ 681,378	$707,622	$734,945	$763,392	$793,012
Less: Taxes	(258,923)	(268,897)	(279,279)	(290,089)	(301,344)
Expected License Cash Flows	422,454	438,726	455,666	473,303	491,667
Period	1.00	2.00	3.00	4.00	5.00
Present Value Factor	0.909	0.826	0.751	0.683	0.621
PV of License Cash Flows	384,049	362,583	342,348	323,272	305,287

Sum of PV of License Cash Flows		1,717,540
Amortization Benefit Multiplier	(1)	1.25
Preliminary Value		2,146,925
Value of Trademark, rounded		$2,147,000

Assumptions	Note	
Discount Rate	(2)	10.0%
Tax Rate	(3)	38.0%
Remaining Useful Life		5 years

Notes:

(1) Represents the present value of the estimated tax benefit derived from the amortization of the intangible asset, over the tax life (15 years) of the asset.

(2) Risk-free rate of 3.0% plus a 7.0% market risk premium.

(3) Estimated corporate tax rate.

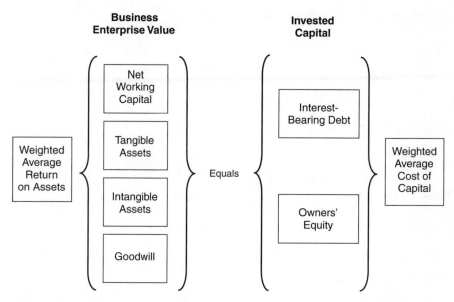

EXHIBIT 6.8 Economic Balance Sheet

side of the economic balance sheet shows how these assets are owned or financed. There is usually some combination of debt (both short term and long term) and equity. A simple adjusted economic balance sheet is presented in Exhibit 6.8.

The economic balance sheet is a useful tool for demonstrating how the entity finances its assets. It is also useful in determining appropriate required rates of return (or discount rates) for individual assets, particularly intangible assets. If the business enterprise value equals the invested capital and the weighted average cost of capital is the required rate of return on invested capital, then the weighted average required return on the assets must equal the weighted average cost of capital.

Examples of Required Returns on Contributory Assets

The required rates of return for individual assets should reflect the relative risk of that asset. The required return for individual assets can often be determined based on market-derived rates of return and based on the way the asset is typically financed. The required rate of return is the basis for the contributory charge under the MPEEM. The following chart provides an example of required rates of return for specific classes of contributory assets.

Asset	Basis of Contributory Charge
Debt-free working capital	After-tax short-term rates, which would be available to market participants. Examples include bank prime rates, commercial paper rates, and 30- to 90-day U.S. Treasuries. Each should be adjusted for entity-specific risk. Consideration should also be given to the mix of debt and equity financing required to fund working capital.
Fixed assets	Rates of "return on" would include financing rates for similar assets for market participants. Examples include observed vendor financing and bank debt available to fund a specific fixed asset. Consideration should be given to a blended mix of debt and equity financing if market participants typically fund these assets with a mixture of debt and equity.
Workforce, customer lists trademarks, and trade names intangible assets	Weighted average cost of capital for market participants, particularly entities with single-product assets, adjusted for the relevant mix of debt and equity. Most intangible assets are 100% funded with equity; therefore, an equity rate of return should be considered for those assets.
Technology-based intangible assets	Since most technology-based assets are funded with equity, the cost of equity is considered the base. It is adjusted upward for the increased relative risk of the technology-based asset compared to other company assets.
Other intangibles, including IPR&D assets	Rates should be consistent with the relative risk of the subject intangible asset. When market participant inputs are available, that information should be used in calculating a required rate of return. Riskier assets such as IPR&D should require higher rates of return.[27]

The Income Increment/Cost Decrement Method

The Income Increment/Cost Decrement method is an income approach that focuses on incremental cash flows attributable to the subject intangible asset. Incremental cash flows resulting from the use of the asset are estimated over the asset's remaining useful life and discounted to arrive at a present value. The incremental cash flow can be in the form of additional revenues or can be related to cost saving from the use of the assets. This method is sometimes referred to as the scenario method because it compares the operating results under two scenarios to measure the incremental cash flow benefit attributable to the use of the subject asset. The first scenario incorporates the assumption that the subject intangible asset is being used by the entity to generate incremental cash flows. The second scenario projects cash flows assuming the subject intangible asset is not available for use by the entity. The difference in the present value of cash flows from the two scenarios is the fair value of the subject intangible asset. The incremental income/cost decrement method is most often used to measure the fair value of noncompetition agreements and is sometimes referred to as the "with versus without" method.

The JT Austin Technology Inc. enterprise value, calculated using the total invested capital form of the discounted cash flow analysis from Exhibit 6.2, will be used as a basis for illustrating the "with versus without" method of measuring the fair value of a noncompete agreement. Assume that JT Austin's business enterprise value in Exhibit 6.2 includes the benefits from the previous owner's agreement not to compete. It is the "with" scenario. The new owners of JT Austin believe that without the agreement, they could potentially lose 25 percent of revenues in the remainder of 20X1, declining to a 10 percent revenue loss in 20X5. The new owners assess the probability of competition at 20 percent in all years.

Exhibit 6.9 reflects the adjustments for lost revenue due to competition and shows JT Austin's enterprise value "without" the noncompete agreement. The difference between the enterprise value "with" and "without" the noncompete agreement represents the preliminary value of the noncompete agreement. It is adjusted for the tax amortization benefit resulting from the recognition of the noncompete agreement as an intangible asset for tax purposes. The adjustment is made with an amortization benefit multiplier.

Profit Split Method

Another income approach method for measuring the fair value of an intangible asset is the profit split method. The theoretical basis for the profit split method is similar to the premise underlying the relief from royalty method under the market approach. The relief from royalty method assumes that the fair value of the subject intangible asset is based on what the company would have to pay a hypothetical third party to license the subject intangible asset if it were not already owned. The profit split method assumes that the fair value of the subject intangible asset is based on what the company would receive when licensing the subject intangible asset to a hypothetical third party. Under the profit split method, the company's revenues and profits are split into two groups: (1) revenues and profits attributable to the intangible asset based on a hypothetical license and (2) revenues and profits from the company's other operating assets. The percentage split profits

EXHIBIT 6.9 JT Austin Technology Inc., Analysis of Noncompetition Agreement, as of October 31, 20X1

	20X1		20X2		20X3		20X4		20X5		Terminal Value	
Revenue	$12,593,002		$13,250,000		$14,150,000		$15,150,000		$15,750,000		$16,222,500	
Growth	*5%*		*5%*		*7%*		*7%*		*4%*		*3%*	
Revenue Lost to Competition	(−) 3,148,251	25%	3,047,500	23%	2,830,000	20%	2,424,000	16%	1,575,000	10%	—	
× Probability of Competition	(−) 20%		20%		20%		20%		20%			
Adjusted Revenue	$11,963,352	100%	$12,640,500	100%	$13,584,000	100%	$14,665,200	100%	$15,435,000	100%	$16,222,500	100%
Cost of Sales	7,417,278	62%	7,331,490	58%	7,878,720	58%	8,505,816	58%	8,952,300	58%	9,409,050	58%
Gross Profit	4,546,074	38%	5,309,010	42%	5,705,280	42%	6,159,384	42%	6,482,700	42%	6,813,450	42%
SG&A Expenses	2,392,670	20%	2,275,290	18%	2,445,120	18%	2,639,736	18%	2,778,300	18%	2,920,050	18%
EBITDA	2,153,403	18%	3,033,720	24%	3,260,160	24%	3,519,648	24%	3,704,400	24%	3,893,400	24%
Depreciation	262,039	2%	379,215	3%	407,520	3%	439,956	3%	463,050	3%	486,675	3%
EBIT	1,891,365	16%	2,654,505	21%	2,852,640	21%	3,079,692	21%	3,241,350	21%	3,406,725	21%
Less: Taxes	(718,719)	−6%	(1,008,712)	−8%	(1,084,003)	−8%	(1,170,283)	−8%	(1,231,713)	−8%	(1,294,556)	−8%
Debt-Free Net Income	1,172,646	10%	1,645,793	13%	1,768,637	13%	1,909,409	13%	2,009,637	13%	2,112,170	13%
Plus: Depreciation	262,039	2%	379,215	3%	407,520	3%	439,956	3%	463,050	3%	486,675	3%
Less: Capital Expenditures	(262,039)	−2%	(379,215)	−3%	(407,520)	−3%	(439,956)	−3%	(463,050)	−3%	(486,675)	−3%
Less: Incremental Working Capital	(190,000)	−2%	(126,405)	−1%	(135,840)	−1%	(146,652)	−1%	(154,350)	−1%	(162,225)	−1%
Cash Flows to Invested Capital	982,646		1,519,388		1,632,797		1,762,757		1,855,287		1,949,945	

	20X1	20X2	20X3	20X4	20X5	
Cash Flows to Invested Capital	982,646	1,519,388	1,632,797	1,762,757	1,855,287	1,949,945
Terminal Value in 20X5						9,749,723
Partial Period	0.17	1.00	1.00	1.00	1.00	1.00
Period	0.08	0.67	1.67	2.67	3.67	3.67
Present Value Factor	0.983	0.871	0.708	0.576	0.468	0.468
Present Value of Cash Flows to Invested Capital	161,407	1,323,399	1,156,243	1,014,856	868,396	4,563,511

Sum of PV of DFCF (20X1 to 20X5)	4,524,302
PV of Terminal Value	4,563,511
PV of Tax Benefit-Amortization of Intangibles	1,018,655
Fair Value without Noncompetition Agreement	10,106,468
Value of Invested Capital with Noncompetition Agreement	10,278,000
Preliminary Value of Noncompetition Agreement	171,532
Amortization Benefit Multiplier (2)	1.13
Concluded Value of Noncompetition Agreement	$194,000

Fair Value of Intangible Assets & Goodwill	7,400,000
15-Year Amortization Period	/15
Tax Amortization per Year	493,333
Tax Rate	38%
Annual Amortization Benefit	187,467
Sum of PV Factors 20X1 to 20Y6	5.43
Present Value of Amortization Benefit	1,018,655

Assumptions:

Discount Rate	(3)	23%
Tax Rate	(4)	38%
Long-Term Growth Rate	(5)	3.0%
Term of Benefit from Noncompete Agreement	(6)	5 years

Notes:

(1) Based on discussions with management, direct competition would cause a 25% loss in revenue in 20X1, declining to 10% by 20X5, and would have no effect thereafter. Management estimates a 20% probability of competition for applicable years.

(2) Represents the present value of the estimated tax benefit derived from the amortization of the intangible asset, over the tax life (15 years) of the asset.

(3) Weighted average cost of capital per Exhibit 6.10.

(4) Estimated corporate tax rate.

(5) Based on Management's projections, the growth prospects of the industry and the overall economy.

(6) Per Noncompetition Agreement dated October 31, 20X1.

depends on the relative contribution the intangible asset makes to the entity's profitability.

To illustrate this method, assume that TTT Technology Inc. produces and sells microchips used in electronic toys. The company markets its products under the trade name "Total Teknology," which is widely recognized within the toy-making industry. Management of TTT Technology Inc. believes that it could license the trade name for an amount equal to 25 percent of profits. The company's projected annual revenues are $35.4 million. The fair value measurement of TTT Technology's trade name is presented in Exhibit 6.10.

The profit split method was developed years ago from guidelines used by independent parties when negotiating the use of intellectual property. Negotiations typically centered on determining an appropriate amount of consideration to pay based on the intellectual property's contribution to the development of a viable, commercial product. These guidelines recognized four steps in bringing a technology to market. The first step is to develop the technology itself. The second step is to incorporate the technology into a product that would have market acceptance. The third step is to manufacture the product. The fourth step is to sell the product in the market place.[28]

In negotiations for licensing the technology, each of these steps would be considered equally risky and would be weighted equally when considering the contribution to a profitable product. Therefore, the

EXHIBIT 6.10 TTT Technology Inc., Valuation of Trade Name Using the Profit Split Method, as of December 31, 20X1

Revenue	$ 35,400,000
Operating Margin	× 35% (1)
Profit before Tax	12,390,000
Less: Taxes @ 38%	(4,708,200)
Profit after Tax	7,681,800
Percentage Split	25% (3)
	1,920,450
Capitalization Rate	15% (4)
Concluded Value, Rounded	**$12,803,000**

Assumptions:		
Operating Margin	(1)	35%
Income Tax Rate	(2)	38%
Estimated Profit Split	(3)	25%
Long-Term Growth Rate	(1)	5%
Discount Rate	(5)	20%
Projected Life of Trade Name		Indefinite

Notes:
(1) Based on management projections.
(2) Estimated corporate tax rate.
(3) Based on management estimate of a hypothetical royalty rate of 5.4% of revenues.
(4) Discount rate less the long-term growth rate.
(5) Equals the weighted average cost of capital.

development of the technology contributes 25 percent of the profit margin from the sale of the product.

The profit split method is commonly used in the valuation of intellectual property such as patented technology. Under this method, the intellectual property's fair value is calculated based on 25 percent of the company's before-tax gross profits from sales of company's products in which the asset is used.[29] The fair value of the technology is estimated over the life of the technology assuming normal maintenance. Twenty-five percent of applicable profits are discounted back to the present at a risk-adjusted rate of return, or discount rate. The 25 percent rule and a 33 percent variation have emerged as commonly cited rules in articles on license agreements and in court cases involving intellectual property disputes. Therefore, the profit split method is widely recognized in the licensing and legal communities.

Although the profit split method is basically a rule of thumb, it does have a foundation based in economic realities. A licensee would be willing to pay a percentage of profits attributable to the successful commercialization of the licensed intangible asset. But the percentage would have an upper limit. The challenge for the valuation specialist is to estimate an appropriate gross profit "split" that would compensate the owner of the technology for its use. A 25 percent gross profit may be a good starting point. The percentage would be adjusted up or down based on the facts and circumstance unique to the measurement of fair value for the subject intellectual property. The adjustment would be based on the relative risk borne by the parties in the commercialization of the intellectual property.

The risks encountered in the commercialization of intellectual property are unique to the stage of development:

- Research and development risk. Is the technology viable?
- Manufacturability risk. Can the technology be included in a commercially viable product?
- Marketing risk. Is there a market for the product?
- Competitive risk. How will competitors react to the introduction of the new technology?
- Legal risk. Does the new technology infringe upon any third-party rights?[30]

Several recently published papers provide empirical support for the 25 percent profit split method. Kemmerer and Jiaqing's article entitled "Profitability and Royalty Rates across Industries: Some Preliminary Evidence" notes that while royalty rates across industries do not directly converge at the 25 percent rule, the rates generally fall between 25 percent of gross profit margins and 25 percent of operating profit margins. They conclude that the EBITDA (earnings before interest, taxes, depreciation and amortization) margin seems to be a "more reasonable base upon which to apply the 25 percent rule compared to the gross margin and EBIT margin."[31] In another study published in *les Nouvelles,* Goldscheider, Jarosz, and Mulhern analyzed licensee agreements from 347 companies and concluded that the median royalty rate applied to operating profit margins converged with the implied royalty rate from the 25 percent rule.[32]

Although the 25 percent rule appears to have an empirical basis, the profit split method is commonly used as a reference point when evaluating the reasonableness of a market royalty rate for use of comparable intellectual property. Because the profit split method is grounded in economic theory and is commonly used in practice, the percentage suggested by this method has implications for the range of royalty rates that would be viewed as reasonable. The profit split method can be used to support a royalty rate in the relief from royalty method under the market approach. The relief from royalty method is discussed in another chapter.

Build-Out Method, or "Greenfield Method" (With and Without)

Even though certain intangible assets are considered identifiable by FASB ASC 805, *Business Combinations* (SFAS 141(R)), it may be difficult to measure their fair value. Recall that an intangible asset is considered identifiable if it meets either the separable or contractual criteria.

In industries that require a government license or permit to operate, such as telecommunications, radio and television, or power generation, there has been a debate about appropriate methods to measure fair value. Recall that SEC topic D-108 suggests that the residual method only applies to goodwill and that these types of licensed intangible assets should be measured using a direct valuation method.

One such method is the build-out method, or "Greenfield method." The Greenfield method is an income approach method that is based on the assumption that the entity commences operations on the measurement date. Cash flows are forecasted assuming that the existing competitive situation continues within each market. The exception is that the subject entity's forecasted cash flows assume a start-up of operations. By assuming a start-up scenario, the analysis excludes any potential goodwill and going concern value. This allows the analyst to isolate the fair value of the licenses or permit to operate, and to measure the fair value of the license or permit directly.

Weighted Average Cost of Capital Calculation

As discussed previously, the weighted average cost of capital (WACC) is the appropriate rate for discounting debt-free cash flows. The WACC is the rate of return required by all investors, both debt and equity, to compensate them for the risk associated with their investment. The WACC is typically used to discount an entity's debt-free cash flows and to measure the fair value of the entity's invested capital.

In the WACC calculation, the required rate of return for each type of investor is weighted based on the fair value of the investment to derive a weighted average required rate of return. The formula for calculating the weighted average cost of capital (WACC) is:

$$WACC = k_e \times W_e + k_d \times W_d$$

where:

> k_e = Cost of equity (both common and preferred)
> W_e = Equity weight (value of equity/total invested capital)
> k_d = After-tax cost of debt (cost of debt × (1 − tax rate))
> W_d = Debt weight (interest-bearing debt/total invested capital)

Capital Structure

Theoretically, when measuring the fair value of an entity, a market participant's capital structure would be used to determine the relative weights of debt and equity in the calculation of the WACC. Estimating a hypothetical market participant's capital structure is often difficult due to limited information available for nonpublicly traded market participants. Consequently, valuation specialists typically rely on the capital structures of public companies as a proxy for the hypothetical market participant's capital structures. The weighting in the capital structure should be at market rather than carrying value.

Equity Rate of Return (k_e)

Appropriate rates for publicly traded preferred equity capital and debt can be objectively identified based on market yields and interest rates, but the identification of an appropriate cost of capital for privately held preferred and common equity is more subjective. Both rates are calculated based on empirical market data and required rates of return for investments with similar risk. Yields on privately held preferred equity are typically adjusted from market yields on similar, publicly traded shares. The cost of common equity is typically calculated using one of two models: (1) the Capital Asset Pricing Model or (2) a Build-Up Method. Another relatively new method is to estimate a required rate of return for equity by referring to studies on rates of return for venture capital investments.

CAPITAL ASSET PRICING MODEL   One method for estimating the cost of equity (k_e) is by using the Capital Asset Pricing Model (CAPM). The formula for a modified version of the CAPM is:

$$k_e = R_f + (RP_m \times Beta) + RP_s + RP_u$$

where:

Rf = Rate of return on a risk-free security

RP_m = Equity risk premium for the market

$Beta$ = Sensitivity of the specific asset return compared to the market returns

RP_s = Size risk premium over and above RPm

RP_u = Risk premium for unsystematic risk attributable to the specific company (company-specific risk premium)

Risk-free rate of return (R_f). The rate of return on a risk-free security is typically developed by analyzing the yields of U.S. Treasury securities. Ideally, the duration of the risk-free security selected should match the projected cash flow horizon of the subject asset or entity. One proxy for the risk-free rate is the yield on 20-year Treasury Constant Maturities as this is the duration that best approximates the duration of an entity.

Equity risk premium for the market (RP_m). The required return above the risk-free rate to reflect the additional risk associated with holding equities over a long horizon. Theoretically, the market risk premium is the rate of return for a market portfolio containing every possible equity investment in proportion to its relative market capitalization less the risk-free rate. In practice, the market risk premium is often based on the returns from a broad stock index such as the S&P 500 Composite Index less the risk-free rate. *The Stocks, Bonds, Bills and Inflation Valuation Edition Yearbook* published by Ibbotson Associates and Duff and Phelps, LLC Risk Premium Report are two excellent sources of equity risk premium data.

Beta (β). Beta is a measure of a specific security's sensitivity to the market. It is estimated using regression analysis to compare the security's historic excess returns over the risk-free rate to the historic market risk premium. Beta is the slope of the regression equation. Beta is also a measure of the security's systematic risk.[33]

Another method to estimate beta is based on published betas for publically traded guideline companies. Because published betas are based on overall market risks, they include operating and financial risks. Published, leveraged betas can be adjusted to remove the effects of financing decisions. Information about guideline companies' capital structures and tax rates is contained in their financial statement filed with the SEC. Using the formula following, an un-levered beta can be calculated for each guideline company:

$$\beta_U = \beta_L / (1 + (1-t) \times (D/E)), \text{ where}$$

β_U = unlevered beta
β_L = published levered beta
D = total debt
E = total equity capitalization
t = marginal tax rate

After selecting an appropriate unlevered beta, the unlevered guideline beta can be relevered to reflect the target company's capital structure using another version of the same formula:

where:

$$\beta_L = \beta_U \times (1 + (1-t) \times (D/E))^{34}$$

Size risk premium (RP$_s$). The risk premium associated with the required return on certain smaller size stocks above the required return on large capitalization stocks. Small company stocks typically have returns in excess of those that can be explained by their betas. These small company excess returns may occur when beta is calculated using a broad stock index such as the S&P 500 Composite Index. The market capitalization of the typical S&P 500 stock may be significantly larger than the market capitalization of the subject company. Size risk premiums can be calculated based upon empirical data. *Stocks, Bonds, Bills and Inflation Valuation Edition Yearbook* published by Ibbotson Associates and Duff and Phelps LLC Risk Premium Report are sources for determining appropriate size premiums.

Company-specific (unsystematic) risk (RP$_u$). The risk premium for un-systematic risk is designed to account for additional risk factors specific to the subject entity.

Firm specific risk factors may include:

- Small size relative to size premium group
- Leverage
- Industry risks
- Volatility of returns
- Other company-specific factors
  - Concentration of customer base
  - Key person dependence
  - Key supplier dependence
  - Abnormal present or pending competition
  - Pending regulatory changes
  - Pending lawsuits
  - Strengths/weaknesses of company management[35]

THE BUILD-UP METHOD   The other commonly used method to estimate the cost of equity (k_e) is the build-up method. It is similar to the modified version of the CAPM in that it seeks to estimate the cost of equity by starting with the risk-free rate and adding premiums for risks associated with the security. The formula for the build-up method is:

$$k_e = R_f + RP_m + RP_s + RP_u$$

The risk premium variables in the build-up formula are essentially the same as those found in the CAPM. The build-up method is flexible and can be customized for the attributes of the specific company being analyzed. Some versions of the build-up method use beta-adjusted risk premiums and others incorporate industry risk premiums.[36]

Debt Discount Rate (k_d)

The required return or cost of debt is usually defined as a market participant's marginal borrowing rate, less the tax benefit associated with the deductibility of interest expense. As a practical matter, the marginal borrowing rate can be identified by examining existing lending agreements, by interviewing current or prospective lenders, or by observing the current market rate for entities with similar credit ratings. The formula for the required rate of return for debt is:

$$k_d = \text{Marginal borrowing rate} \times (1 - \text{Marginal tax rate})$$

The calculation of JT Austin Technology's WACC is presented in Exhibit 6.11 to illustrate several of the concepts within this section. The cost of equity used in the WACC calculation is an average of the amounts derived from the Build-up Method and the CAPM. The cost of debt is a market rate for debt with a similar credit rating, adjusted for the tax benefit. Finally, the capital structure is an industry average for similar-sized companies. Thus, the WACC is calculated from the perspective of a market participant.

Venture Capital Rates of Return

An alternative way of determining an early stage entity's overall cost of capital is to use venture capital rates of return as a source for equity investor's required rate of return. This approach would be appropriate for entities in high-risk industries or those with unproven products. Some intangible assets such as developed technology, and particularly in-process research and development, have characteristics similar to venture capital investments. There is considerable risk and uncertainty associated with the products and target earnings for venture capital investments, developed technology, and in-process research and development. Venture capital rates may be the most

EXHIBIT 6.11 JT Austin Technology, Weighted Average Cost of Capital (WACC), as of October 31, 20X1

Cost of Equity:

Build-Up Method: $K_e = R_f + RP_m + RP_i + RP_s + RP_u$

	Ibbotson	Duff & Phelps	
Risk-Free Rate (R_f)	3.45% (1)	3.45%	(1)
Market Premium (RP_m)	7.10% (2)	4.85%	(9)
Industry Risk Premium (RP_i)	2.11% (2)	1.44%	(11)
Small Company Market Premium (RP_s)	5.82% (3)	6.91%	(10)
Company-Specific Risk Premium (RP_u)	8.00% (4)	8.00%	(4)
	$k_e = 26.48\%$	24.65%	

Capital Asset Pricing Model: $K_e = R_f + \beta(RP_m) + RP_s + RP_u$

	Ibbotson	Duff & Phelps	
Risk-Free Rate (R_f)	3.45% (1)	3.45%	(1)
Market Premium $\beta(RP_m)$ where $\beta = 1.17$ (5)	8.31% (2)	5.67%	(9)
Size Premium (RP_s)	5.82% (3)	6.91%	(10)
Company-Specific Risk Premium (RP_u)	8.00% (4)	8.00%	(4)
	$k_e = 25.58\%$	24.03%	

average $k_e = 26.03\%$

After-Tax Cost of Debt: $k_d = K_b(1-t)$

Borrowing Rate (K_b)	8.79% (6)
Tax Rate (t)	38.00% (7)
$k_d =$	5.45%

Weighted Average Cost of Capital (WACC)

	Capital Structure (8)	Cost	Weighted Cost
Equity	85.00%	26.03%	22.12%
Debt	15.00%	5.45%	0.82%
		WACC =	22.94%
		Rounded =	23.00%

Notes:
(1) 20-Year Treasury Bond as of October 31, 20X1; Federal Reserve Statistical Release.
(2) *Ibbotson: SBBI: Valuation Edition 20X1 Yearbook.*
(3) *Ibbotson: SBBI: Valuation Edition 20X1 Yearbook* (Long-Term Returns in Excess of CAPM Estimations for Decile Portfolios of the NYSE/AMEX/NASDAQ
(4) Based on discussions with Management and analysis of similar stage investments.
(5) Unlevered Adjusted Beta of 1.05: *Ibbotson Cost of Capital 20X1 Yearbook*. Relevered using the median capital structure of guideline companies (8) and the estimated corporate tax rate.
(6) Moody's Baa rate as of October 31, 20X1; Federal Reserve Statistical Release. (Proxy for marginal borrowing rate.)
(7) Estimated corporate tax rate.
(8) Based on median level of capital structure for the guideline public companies. *Morningstar 20X1 Cost of Capital Yearbook.*
(9) Market Premium, Duff & Phelps, *Risk Premium Report 20X1.*
(10) Size-specific equity risk premiums over CAPM are based on comparison of the Company to risk premium groups presented in the Duff & Phelps *Risk Premium Report 20X1.* (Smoothed Average Premium over CAPM).
(11) Converted Ibbotson IRP to D&P (New IRP=SBBI IRP*(D&P ERP/SBBI ERP)).

appropriate comparable rates available when estimating the discount rate to apply to the anticipated cash flows of an entity with unproven products or an intangible asset with unproven technology. The AICPA Practice Aid *Assets Acquired in a Business Combination to Be Used in Research and Development Activities: A Focus on Software, Electronic Devices, and Pharmaceutical Industries* refers to two studies on venture capital rates of return. One is the *QED Report on Venture Capital Financial Analysis,* published in 1987 by QED Research Inc. The other study is *A Method for Valuing High-Risk Long Term, Investments: The Venture Capital Method*, published in 1987 by the Harvard University Business School Press.[37]

The *QED Report* is a widely used source of data for determining an appropriate discount rate for investments in venture capital companies. The QED study is relatively comprehensive and includes information supplied by hundreds of venture capital investors.[38] For each stage in a start-up company's development, the report provides a range of required returns on investment. The QED study describes the stages that an entity goes through from start-up to harvest through an IPO or acquisition by another entity.

Start-up. Start-up investments are typically less than one year old. A start-up entity initially needs capital for product development, prototype testing, and test marketing (in experimental quantities to selected customers). This stage covers studying potential market penetration, bringing together a management team, and refining the business plan. The required rate of return for the start-up phase would be quite high, between 50 percent and 70 percent.

First stage. Investment proceeds through the first stage if prototypes are successfully developed and technical risk is considered minimal. Likewise, market studies must indicate that the product is viable and potentially profitable. The entity must have a modest manufacturing facility capable of producing and shipping the product in commercial quantities. First stage entities are unlikely to be profitable; therefore, they would have a required return in the 40 percent to 60 percent range.

Second stage. A second stage entity has shipped product to customers and has received real feedback from the market. Management is beginning to understand the time frame required to access markets but may not fully know the limits to potential market penetration. The entity is probably still unprofitable, or only marginally profitable. It probably needs capital to finance equipment purchases, inventories, and receivables financing. An appropriate required rate of return would be between 35 percent and 50 percent.

Third stage. Third stage companies experience rapid growth in sales and positive profit margins. Downside investment risk is minimal.

However, rapid expansion means more working capital is required than can be generated from internal cash flows. New venture capital investments would be used for the expansion of manufacturing facilities, expanded market reach, or for product enhancements. At this stage, banks may be willing to supply credit to the extent that it can be secured by fixed assets or receivables. Although credit may be more available at this stage, the required rate of return is still quite high in the 30 percent to 50 percent range.

Fourth stage. Entities at the fourth stage of development may still need outside cash to sustain rapid growth, but they are successful enough and stable enough so that the risk to outside investors is significantly reduced. The owners may prefer to finance growth with debt in order to prevent the dilution of their equity ownership. Commercial bank credit will play a more important role. Although the goal of many venture capital investors is to harvest their investment through a sale, public offering, or leveraged buy-out, the timing of the potential cash-out for stage four venture capital investors is still uncertain. A drop in the required rate of return to between 30 percent and 40 percent would be indicative of this stage of development.[39,40]

These stages describe the phases of development for a start-up company, but they can be also useful to identify the stages of development for an intangible asset since the intangible asset bears a similar risk profile. In addition, because their risk profiles are similar, the rates of return for venture capital investments provided in the QED study may be good proxies for required rates of return on certain intangible assets.

The following chart provides required rates of return from the QED study based on the various development stages of companies.

Stage	Mean Range	Median Range
Start-Up	49.2% to 75.4%	50.0% to 70.0%
First Stage	40.6% to 59.6%	40.0% to 60.0%
Second Stage	34.7% to 49.3%	35.0% to 50.0%
Third Stage	31.2% to 45.7%	30.0% to 50.0%
Fourth Stage	28.1% to 40.8%	30.0% to 40.0%
IPO	26.0% to 37.3%	25.0% to 35.0%

The Harvard Study recognizes the same stages of development and reaches similar conclusions about appropriate rates for each stage of investment. The Harvard Study notes that venture capital rates of return are extremely high, especially when compared to historical returns realized on a variety of other investments, including venture capital, stocks, real estate, foreign stocks, and gold. The Harvard Study cites several reasons for the high rate of return required by venture capitalists.

Venture capitalists perceive a high level of systematic risk associated with venture capital investments. Their investments are particularly vulnerable to market conditions when the time comes to liquidate the investment through a public offering or buy-out by a larger company. Venture capitalists expect to receive a higher return to compensate for this high level of systematic risk. Another factor contributing to a venture capital investment's risk and high required return is its illiquidity. Venture capital investments are often private companies with legal restrictions on the sale of their unregistered securities. Information about these companies is limited and the pool of potential buyers is small. A premium is needed to compensate for the illiquidity associated with venture capital investments. Another theory is that venture capitalists expect to be compensated for providing services to the portfolio company. A typical venture capitalist is an active investor who provides expertise and oversees management of the company. The return premium compensates the venture capitalist for the value he adds. The final reason cited by the Harvard Study for the high venture capitalist risk premium is that the return on a successful venture capital investment is offset by losses on other unsuccessful investments. Only about 25 percent of venture capital investments meet or exceed their forecasts. The venture capitalist expects this outcome. The high-risk premium is demanded to compensate for the fact that earnings forecasts are often unmet.[41]

The Harvard Study and the QED Study can be used by a valuation specialist to help determine an appropriate required rate of return or discount rate to use in a DCF model. As an entity or one of its intangible assets passes the hurdles to becoming a profit-generating business, its risk characteristics change. Thus, the valuation specialist should determine which stages of development the entity or intangible asset has passed through. The current stage of development will indicate an approximate range of returns that a hypothetical investor would expect for investing in a developing entity at that particular stage. The rate would be refined after considering the specific risk characteristics of the subject entity or individual asset as of the measurement date.

Conclusion

The income approach is one of the three basic valuation techniques described in FASB ASC 820 (SFAS 157) to measure fair value. The income approach measures fair value as the present value of the expected future cash flows that the entity generates or an intangible asset generates as part of an entity discounted for the risk of receiving those cash flows. The income approach provides a great deal of flexibility in measuring the fair value of an entity or a specific intangible asset in an entity.

Notes

1. Glossary (FASB), *Accounting Standards Codification* (ASC), www.fasb.org.
2. FASB ASC 820, *Fair Value Measurements and Disclosures* (SFAS No. 157).
3. *International Glossary of Business Valuation Terms*, www.fvs.aicpa.org (accessed May 17, 2009).
4. "Valuation of Intangible Assets for Financial Reporting Purposes," BV 301, American Society of Appraisers Course, www.bvappraisers.org.
5. *International Glossary of Business Valuation Terms*, www.fvs.aicpa.org (accessed May 17, 2009).
6. *The Identification of Contributory Assets and the Calculation of Economic Rents* Exposure Draft. The Appraisal Foundation, www.appraisalfoundation.org.
7. Trugman, Gary, "Evolution of Business Valuation Services," *A CPA's Guide to Valuing a Closely Held Business AICPA*, www.fvs.aicpa.org (accessed May 17, 2009).
8. "Practice Aid to Be Released on Business Combinations," *The CPA Letter,* AICPA, December 2001, www.aicpa.org (accessed May 17, 2009).
9. See Gooch, Lawrence B., ASA, "Capital Chares and the Valuation of Intangibles" *Business Valuation Review* (March 1992): 5–21, and Grabowksi, Roger, ASA, and Lawrence B. Gooch, ASA, "Advanced Valuation Methods in Mergers & Acquisitions," *Mergers & Acquisitions* (Summer 1976):15–29.
10. "Valuation of Intangible Assets for Financial Reporting Purposes," BV 301, American Society of Appraisers Course, www.bvappraisers.org, 448–454.
11. FASB ASC 805, *Business Combinations* (SFAS 141(R)), paragraph 3k.
12. *Use of Residual Method to Value Acquired Asses Other Than Goodwill*, Topic No. D-108, EITF Discussion Dates:, September 29–30 2004, www.fasb.org.
13. *Id.*
14. FASB ASC 820, *Fair Value Measurements and Disclosures* (SFAS No. 157), paragraph 5.
15. *Id.*, paragraph 11.
16. *Id.*
17. *Id.*, paragraph 30.
18. "Valuation of Intangible Assets for Financial Reporting Purposes," American Society of Appraisers Course BV301, www.bvappraisers.org, 422.
19. FASB ASC 350, *Intangibles—Goodwill and Other* (SFAS No. 142), paragraph 11.
20. *The Identification of Contributory Assets and the Calculation of Economic Rents,* The Appraisal Foundation, www.appraisalfoundation.org, paragraph 3.5.06.
21. *Id.,* paragraph 2.2.07.
22. *Id.,* paragraphs 3.4.06–3.4.08.
23. *Id.,* paragraphs 3.4.09–3.4.10.
24. Statement of Financial Accounting Concepts No. 7, *Using Cash Flow Information and Present Value in Accounting Measurements,* www.fasb.org.

25. *Id.*
26. FASB ASC 820, Appendix B, paragraphs B12–B18.
27. *The Identification of Contributory Assets and the Calculation of Economic Rents,* Exposure Draft, The Appraisal Foundation, www.appraisalfoundation.org, 25–26.
28. Razgaitis, Richard, *Valuation and Pricing of Technology-Based Intellectual Property* (NJ: John Wiley & Sons, 2003), 151.
29. Bishop, Jody C., "The Challenge of Valuing Intellectual Property Assets" *Northwestern Journal of Technology and Intellectual Property,* vol. 1, Issue 1 (Spring 2003).
30. Rowell, Simon, "Strategic Tips for Adding Value to Licensing Transactions," Current Partnering, www.currentpartnering.com/articles/1488 (accessed June 15, 2009).
31. Kemmerer, Jonathan E., and Lu, Jiaqing, "2008 Profitability and Royalty Rates Across Industries: Some Preliminary Evidence," *The Free Library* (March, 1) www.thefreelibrary.com, (accessed June 15, 2009).
32. Goldscheider, Jarosz, and Mulhern, "Use of the 25 Per Cent Rule in Valuing IP," *les Nouvelles,* (December 2002):123–133.
33. Pratt, Shannon P. and Roger J. Grabowski, *Cost of Capital: Applications and Examples,* 3rd ed. (NJ: John Wiley & Sons, 2008), 73–75.
34. Beneda, Nancy L., "Estimating Cost of Capital Using Bottom-Up Betas," *The CPA Journal,* www.nysscpa.org.
35. Pratt, Shannon P., and Roger J. Grabowski, *Cost of Capital: Applications and Examples,* 3rd ed. (NJ: John Wiley & Sons, 2008), 73–75.
36. *2008 Ibbotson Stock, Bond, Bills and Inflation Valuation Yearbook,* Morningstar Inc., Chicago, Illinois, pp. 37–44.
37. AICPA Practice Aid, *Assets Acquired in a Business Combination to Be Used in Research and Development Activities: A Focus on Software, Electronic Devises, and Pharmaceutical Industries* 2001, paragraph 5.3.88.
38. *QED Report on Venture Capital Financial Analysis,* QED Research, Inc. 1987.
39. *Id.*
40. AICPA Practice Aid, *Assets Acquired in a Business Combination to Be Used in Research and Development Activities: A Focus on Software, Electronic Devises, and Pharmaceutical Industries* 2001, paragraph 5.3.88.
41. Scherlis, Daniel R., and William Sahlman, *A Method for Valuing High Risk, Long Term, Investments: The Venture Capital Method* (Boston: Harvard Business School Publishing, 1987).

CHAPTER 7

Advanced Valuation Methods for Measuring the Fair Value of Intangible Assets

Introduction

Best practices for measuring the fair value of intangible assets continue to evolve. Professional organizations such as the American Institute of Certified Public Accountants (AICPA), the American Society of Appraisers, and the Appraisal Foundation have taken the lead in providing best practice guidance. The guidance extends to fair value measurement of intangible assets in financial reporting. Because of the unique nature of intangible assets, advanced financial theory can be applied to their fair value measurement. Advanced valuation techniques such as option-pricing methods, Monte Carlo simulations, and decision tree analysis are becoming more accepted as reliable tools for measuring the value of intangible assets. These methods may also be useful in measuring the fair value of contingent assets, contingent liabilities, and contingent consideration in a business combination. The purpose of this chapter is to explain several advanced methods for estimating fair value, particularly those methods that can be used in measuring the fair value of certain identified intangible assets.

Limitations of Traditional Valuation Methods

Previous chapters describe traditional valuation methods under the cost, market, and income approaches that are commonly used to measure the fair value of intangible assets in financial reporting. Although each of these methods is theoretically sound and widely accepted, they have limitations.

As discussed in Chapter 4, cost-approach methods may be limited because they often do not capture the opportunity costs and profit associated with measuring fair value. Also, cost-approach methods may not totally capture the risk of developing a particular asset. Additional adjustments may have to be made to capture these factors.

Chapter 5 discusses the limitations of the market approach. One salient issue in using market approach methods to measure fair value is that information about guideline intangible assets may be limited. Even if relevant information exits, it is often necessary to make adjustments to increase comparability.

The limitations of the discounted cash flow method were discussed in the CON 7 section of Chapter 6, "The Income Approach." One of the more significant limitations is that the discounted cash flow (DCF) method traditionally uses "most likely" cash flows from management's prospective financial information (PFI) as the basis for the analysis. The most likely future cash flow scenario is discounted to the present at an adjusted rate of return that reflects the uncertainty associated with the receipt of the cash flows. The most likely set of prospective cash flows and the required return are static, meaning that the PFI does not provide for future changes in assumptions once additional information becomes known.

The static assumptions in a traditional DCF reflect the normal, noncontingent PFI expectations as of the measurement date. Although a traditional DCF model is appropriate in most circumstances, it may be inappropriate in other circumstances because it fails to consider all of the factors that impact fair value. First, in the real world, cash flows are not static over the time horizon covered by PFI. Management receives information and makes decisions on a daily basis that impact cash flows. Second, uncertainty and risk are reduced with the passage of time as management receives information that either confirms or contradicts expectations.

Over time, management is better able to optimize future decisions as more information becomes known. Management's flexibility to react to incoming information when making decisions has a positive impact on the entity's value over time. For example, certain companies employ a "second to market" business strategy where the company relies on a competitor to develop and introduce a product. The company will wait to see whether the market accepts the product before making a decision to invest in a similar product.

This strategy can have advantages because the commercialization of a technology is capital intensive and risky. The competitor assumes all the risks of achieving market acceptance. The company will have insight about the market's positive and negative perceptions of the product before it decides to undertake the development and commercialization of a similar product. The disadvantage of this strategy is that the initial product may have such overwhelming acceptance that future products have difficulty in obtaining a foothold in the marketplace. The second to market strategy is common in the computer industry where manufacturers of desktop and laptop computers add new features to their models in response to market acceptance of competitors' innovations.

Flexibility in management decision making gives management the right, but not the obligation, to pursue the commercialization of a product. Having the right but not the obligation to do something is similar to owning a financial option on an underlying share of stock. A financial option gives the holder the right, but not the obligation, to buy (or sell) an underlying financial instrument. A call provides the option holder the right to buy the underlying equity shares at a certain price over a certain period of time, while a put provides the option holder the right to sell the underlying equity shares at a certain price over a certain period of time. The principles underlying the valuation of financial options can be extended and applied to situations where management's decision-making flexibility impacts the value of an intangible asset.

Real Options

Real options are often derived from the ownership rights of intangible assets; therefore, intangible assets are sometimes referred to as real options. They have many of the same characteristics as a financial option, including the right but not the obligation to do something. Options methodologies have the potential to capture the value created from this decision-making flexibility. Advanced valuation techniques such as option-pricing models can be used to estimate the fair value of certain intangible assets whose value is derived from, and therefore contingent on, actions by management. This methodology is sometimes referred to as a "real" option as the methodology measures the value resulting from specific operating decisions, rather than financial decisions. Real option valuation methods can be used to measure the fair value of certain intangible assets.

Although the application of options valuation techniques to assess the impact of managerial decision making is a relatively new topic in financial theory, its acceptance is becoming more widespread. The advantage of these methodologies is that they utilize models that more accurately reflect real-world decision making. Option pricing methodologies cannot only be used to quantify the additional value created by flexibility in decision making but they are useful tools for assessing the economic impact of contingent events. These techniques are applicable to the valuation of capital investments, specific tangible and intangible assets, to liabilities, and to the entity itself. Options valuation techniques are likely to assume a more prominent role in the measurement of fair value for financial reporting purposes in the future.

Option Basics

An option[1] is a contract that gives the owner the right to buy (or sell) an underlying asset from (to) the counterparty to the contract, at a certain price over a certain period of time. The option contract creates a right but it does not impose any obligation to buy or sell the underlying asset. Calls and puts, described in the previous section, are the most common types of options. Options are considered derivative securities because the value of the option is derived from the value of the underlying asset. Options are also considered contingent claims because the value of the option is contingent on the underlying asset achieving a certain benchmark value. The benchmark value is known as the exercise price. If the underlying asset fails to meet the exercise price, the option is worthless. The value of financial options is derived from the market prices of the underlying financial instruments or securities.

The value of an option is equal to the sum of its intrinsic value and its time value. The intrinsic value is equal to the difference between the price of the underlying share of stock and the exercise price of the option. Assume that an entity owns a call option on one share of PublicCo with an exercise price of $75 per share that expires in six months. If PublicCo is trading at $80 per share, then the intrinsic value of the call option is $5 per share. However, the intrinsic value is not necessarily the fair value of the option. If the option itself is publicly traded, then its fair value is most likely equal to the option's market price. The fair value of the option may be greater than its intrinsic value. This is most often the case when the option has a significant length of time before its expiration date. The value in excess of the intrinsic value is due to the time value of the option.

Suppose the entity wished to exercise the call option. The entity would have to pay the $75 exercise price to the option counterparty, and it would receive one share of stock from the counterparty. If the stock has a market value of $80, the entity would earn a profit of $5. However, the entity has six months to decide whether to exercise the option. It is possible that the price of the underlying share could increase even further, increasing the entity's profit. The value of the option related to the ability to wait to exercise the option is the time value of the option. Typically, options trade at a price higher than their intrinsic value when there is time remaining before the option expires. The difference between the market value of the option and its intrinsic value can be attributed to the time value of the option.

There are three factors that determine the time value of an option: (1) the volatility of the option, (2) the risk-free interest rate, and (3) the amount of time remaining until the option expires. Evaluating these three time value factors and the two intrinsic factors (the underlying share price and the exercise price) will provide sufficient information to determine the option's fair value.

For publicly traded stocks, the underlying share price is equal to the closing price on the option's measurement date. If the underlying shares are restricted shares, then the closing price must be adjusted for their lack of marketability. If the shares are in a privately held or thinly traded company, the value of the underlying shares is measured using one of the three traditional approaches to value (cost, market, and income approaches). Option-pricing models assume that the underlying share price is the same whether the stock is being bought or sold. The underlying share price is not necessarily a bid or ask price. Option-pricing models also assume that an unlimited number of shares can be bought or sold at the prevailing stock price without impacting the market price of the stock.

The exercise or strike price is the option's contract price. In the case of a call option, it is the price that the option holder can pay in exchange for the underlying shares of stock. In a put option, the exercise price is the amount of money that the option holder can receive in exchange for the underlying shares of stock. The intrinsic value of a call option is the underlying stock price minus the exercise price. If the underlying stock price is less than the exercise price, the option holder would have no reason to exercise the option. In that case, the option would be worthless. The intrinsic value of a put option is the exercise price minus the underlying price. If the exercise price is less than the underlying stock price, the option would have no reason to exercise the option and it is worthless.

The time remaining until expiration is the time from the option measurement date to the expiration date. In a financial option pricing model, the time remaining until expiration is expressed as a fraction with the number of days remaining until expiration in the numerator and 365 days in the denominator. Options pricing models are based on a 365-day year, as opposed to most financial models, which round to 360 days.

Volatility in a financial option is equal to the expected standard deviation of the underlying stock over the period of time until the option's expiration. As volatility increases, it is more likely that the price of the underlying stock will exceed the exercise price. Therefore, as volatility increases, so does the value of a call option. Similarly, as volatility increases it is more likely that the price of the underlying stock will be less than the option's exercise price. Therefore, as volatility of the underlying stock increases, so does the value of a put option.

When measuring the fair value of an option, volatility is calculated as the standard deviation of the underlying shares. Standard deviation is calculated for a period of time just before the measurement date. That period of time would be equal in length to the period of time from the measurement date to expiration. For example, if the option has 30 days to expiration, then the standard deviation of the underlying shares is calculated for the 30 days just prior to the measurement date. Volatility experienced just prior to the measurement date is expected to persist over the next 30 days.

However, if the option has a long-term expiration, then using volatility from a previous period may not be appropriate. If recent share prices reacted to some condition that is not expected to continue in the future, then recent volatility would not be representative of future volatility expectations. The standard deviation should be adjusted to reflect expectations for future performance when past experience is not considered relevant.

If the option's underlying shares are in a privately held or thinly traded company, then the implied volatility from publicly traded stock options of comparable companies can be used as a proxy. The implied volatility in publicly traded options can be calculated by solving for volatility using the Black-Scholes Options Pricing Model (discussed later in this chapter). The resulting measure of volatility represents the market's assumption about the volatility of the underlying shares of the publicly traded options.

The average volatility of guideline companies can also be used as a proxy for privately held companies. When using a group of guideline companies within the same industry as a proxy, caution should be exercised before drawing conclusions about the volatility of a single company based on the standard deviation of the guideline companies. For example, in modern portfolio theory, the standard deviation of the portfolio will reflect the diversification of the stocks in the portfolio and will likely result in a lower measurement of volatility than the average of the volatilities of individual shares that comprise the portfolio. This same limitation applies to the measurement of volatility in guideline companies. The lower volatility of a group of comparable companies in the same industry would not be indicative of the anticipated volatility of an individual stock.

The risk-free rate is the last component of an option's value. The risk-free rate represents the opportunity cost of capital assuming that the funds used to purchase the option could be used productively in other investment opportunities. The risk-free rate is the proxy for the opportunity cost of capital. A zero-coupon treasury bill of the same or close to the same maturity as the option would be an appropriate rate.

Using Option Pricing Methodologies to Value Intangible Assets

Although they were originally developed to measure the value of financial options, option pricing methodologies can be used to measure the fair value of intangible assets. They are often better than traditional valuation models that rely on the cost, market, and income approaches to measure fair value because they more fully capture the fair value of all the intangible asset's elements, particularly the value added by their flexibility. In other words, the option pricing models are better for estimating the fair value for intangible assets that have real options. Authors such as Chance and Peterson, and

Kodukla and Papudesu, describe seven types of real options that may add value to specific intangible assets. The real options described below are seven aspects in managerial decisions related to intangible assets that may not be capture by traditional methods but can be captured by option pricing models.

1. *Abandonment.* Management can choose to abandon a project before significant losses are incurred. This option is akin to the ability to discontinue an intellectual property research and development project if it appears the technology is not economically feasible.
2. *Expansions.* Management can choose to expand a product offering at a later date. This option is common in high-growth technology companies. For intangible asset, the choice may be whether to incorporate existing developed technology into new products.
3. *Contractions.* Management can choose to outsource certain functions such as manufacturing a product. An intangible asset example of this type of option would be licensing a technology or trade name from another party.
4. *Interactions.* These are options that may be connected to other options. Examples of interacting intangible assets are those that are considered to be "in use," such as a trade name, customer relationships, and technology. They interact with other intangibles to create value for the entity.
5. *Timing of entrances or exits.* Value may be created as a result of management's decision to wait to make an investment until market conditions become more certain. Waiting may reduce decision risk. An example of a timing option for intangible assets would be delaying the introduction of an intellectual property product until market acceptance is more readily determinable.
6. *Flexibility to switch.* Management can choose to abandon or expand depending on current market conditions. The ability to abandon a project may increase the fair value of certain assets by reducing the risk of a project through the potential reduction of fixed costs, if the project were to be abandoned. Management's flexibility to change the course of action, or to switch strategies in response to evolving business conditions, provides a real option that provides value over and above the option to abandon or expand.
7. *Barrier option.* An option where decision is made not solely on the underlying asset value but some other predetermined value. This option may be useful in the analysis of certain intangible assets such as a favorable lease where the terms may be fixed contractually. The "barrier" is the contractual obligation under the lease.[2,3]

Using Financial Option Models to Measure the Fair Value of Intangible Assets

When using financial option models to measure the fair value of intangible assets, the input parameters must be defined. The following table shows the inputs to financial option models, the definition of the input parameter as it relates to a financial option, and the definition as it relates to a real option.

Input Parameter	Financial Option	Real Option or Intangible Asset
S	The price of the underlying share of stock	The present value of the cash flows from the intangible asset
X	The strike or exercise price of the option	The present value of the opportunity cost either the delayed capital expenditure or future cost savings
R	The risk-free rate of interest that most closely matches the time horizon of the option	The risk-free rate or interest that most closely matches the time horizon of the decision
Σ	The volatility of the underlying share of stock	A proxy for the relative volatility of the intangible asset
T	Time to expiration of the option	The expected duration of the time period for the decision (i.e., expand, abandon)

Example of Using Option Pricing Methods to Estimate the Fair Value of an Intangible Asset

Suppose an entity is in the process of developing a new technology related to voice-activated cell phones.[4] The entity believes that this technology will be embraced as municipalities increase regulation and fines for the use of cell phones while driving. The entity is budgeting $2 million to develop the technology, which it estimates will take a year. Once the technology is developed, efforts to commercialize the technology would begin in the second year. However, because of uncertainties relating to commercialization of the product, management is uncertain about whether the initial $2 million investment would be recovered and whether it would generate positive returns.

Management initially calculates the return on the investment based on costs in the second year. Management is willing to incur the costs to develop the technology but is uncertain about incurring the costs for commercialization of the technology. The costs of commercialization are dependent on the degree of success achieved from the technology development phase. Management believes that the cost of commercialization will fall into one of three scenarios. In the first scenario, commercialization would cost $10 million because the technology development would result in exclusive rights and widespread use of the technology. In the second scenario, commercialization would cost $2 million because of nonexclusive rights to the technology and competing products. In the final scenario, commercialization would cost nothing because the entity would be unable to develop a viable technology.

The probability of the scenarios are 30 percent, 60 percent, and 10 percent, respectively. The cost of commercialization is a probability weighted average of the outcomes from the three scenarios, discounted from the second year back to the present. Assuming a 5 percent discount rate, management's analysis indicates the costs of developing and commercializing the technology would be equal to the $2 million initial cost to develop the technology plus the probability weighted average of the outcomes discounted at 5 percent, or:

$$\$2,000,000 + ((.30 \times \$10,000,000) + (.60 \times \$2,000,000) + (.10 \times \$0)/1.05)$$
$$= \$2,000,000 + ((3,000,000 + 1,200,000 + 0)/1.05)$$
$$= \$2,000,000 + (4,200,000/1.05)$$
$$= \$2,000,000 + 4,000,000$$
$$= \$6,000,000$$

Since management has already decided to invest $2 million to develop the technology, the development costs are considered sunk costs, and the only relevant costs in the commercialization decision are the costs that would be incurred in the second year. Management has the luxury of waiting until the end of the first year to make a decision whether to invest in the commercialization of the technology.

Assume the revenues from the commercialization of the technology are estimated to be 120 percent of the commercialization cost. If the commercialization of the technology is wildly successful, then the return would be much greater than it would be under the scenario with competition. Under the unsuccessful technology development scenario, there is no commercialization investment and, therefore, no return. The increase in revenue would be $12 million if the technology is widely successful, $2.4 million if there is competition, and $0 if the technology is not successful. The present value of the expected revenue is $4.8 million, calculated as follows:

Incremental Revenue	Probability	Expected Revenue
$12,000,000	30%	$3,600,000
2,400,000	60%	1,440,000
$ 0	10%	0
		$5,040,000

The present value of $5,040,000 discounted at 5 percent for one year is 5,040,000/1.05 = $4,800,000. The incremental benefit of undertaking just the commercialization investment for the new technology is $4,800,000 less $4,000,000, or $800,000. While the return is positive, intuitively it seems that the decision to invest is too close to call. Perhaps something is missing from this particular analysis. Is there additional value that management can achieve by waiting to decide whether to invest in the commercialization of the technology? Since management has the right but not the obligation to commercialize the technology assuming its development is successful, is there additional value that may be better captured through the use of a real option analysis?

The value of management's option to wait and decide whether to commercialize the technology can be estimated through real options analysis. The inputs into a real option pricing model are the same as the inputs when valuing a financial option.

- The value of the underlying asset is the incremental $5,040,000 revenue in year 2.
- The variance in the asset is expected to be 0.82. The variance is based on using a proxy for the variance of venture capital investments or the variance of the stock prices of smaller publicly traded companies, which have one significant technology.
- The time to expiration, which is the one-year development time frame
- The exercise price is the $4,200,000 cost of development.
- The risk-free rate of return of 5 percent

Inputting these variables into the Black-Scholes Option Model indicates that the option of waiting a year before deciding to commercialize this product is worth approximately $2 million.

Black-Scholes Option Pricing Model

There are two widely used option pricing models: the Black-Scholes Option Pricing Model and the Binomial Pricing Models, or Lattice Model. Of these two, the Black-Scholes model is the more widely used model. It is commonly known as the Black-Scholes Option Pricing Model, or simply Black-Scholes. Developed in 1973 by Fischer Black and Myron Scholes, and expanded on by Robert Merton, the Black-Scholes model was the first model to simplify the calculation of an option price. The model uses the five key factors described above in pricing an option: (1) the underlying stock price, (2) the exercise price, (3) volatility of the underlying stock, (4) time to expiration, and (5) the risk-free rate. Myron Scholes and Robert Merton received the 1997 Nobel Prize for their work in developing the option pricing model.[5]

The Black-Scholes formula measures the fair value of European options. European options are similar to American options except European options can only be exercised on the exercise date, while American options can be exercised any time before, or on, the exercise date. The Black-Scholes model's measurement of European options instead of American options can be thought of as a simplifying assumption. Since American options are more flexible than European options, they may be worth a little more. Therefore, the value of a European option can be thought of as a floor value for a similar American option. The Black-Scholes formula for a European call option is:

$$V = SN(d_1) - Xe^{-r(T-t)}N(d_2)$$

where:

$d_1 = \ln(S/X) + (r + (\sigma^2/2))(T-t)/\sigma((T-t)\hat{}1/2)$
$d_2 = d_1 - \sigma((T-t)\hat{}1/2)$
V = Value of call option
S = Market price of underlying stock
X = Exercise price
e = Base of natural logarithms
$N(d)$ = Cumulative density function (area under normal curve)
Ln = Natural logarithm
r = Current risk-free investment/maturity same as expiration of option
$T - t$ = Time to option's expiration, in years
σ = Standard deviation of the underlying stock

A Black-Scholes model can be accessed through a Microsoft Excel spreadsheet using the built-in Excel function. In addition, versions of the Black-Scholes models are available for use from many different sources on the Internet. Many of these Internet sites have expanded the model to cover the valuation of real options.[6] Of course, a bit of caution should be exercised when using models developed by others. It may be prudent to use two or three versions of the Black-Scholes model as a cross check for the results.

Example of a Real Option Measured with the Black-Scholes Options Pricing Model

Assume Sunrise Corporation (Sunrise) has a patent to develop a product that will harness wind energy more efficiently than other products on the market. The product is called Windergy. The product will be developed if the expected cash flows from the product will significantly exceed the cost of the development. If the costs of development exceed the expected cash flows, then management can decide to shelve the patent and not incur any further costs. Therefore, the patent can be viewed as a call option on the underlying product.

Based on an analysis of the market today, the present value of the cash flows that this new product is expected to yield is $100 million, before any consideration of the initial development cost. However, many analysts predict energy prices will rise dramatically within the next five years. The cost of developing the Windergy for commercial use is estimated to be $125 million. Sunrise has a patent on the product for the next five years. The current five-year Treasury bond rate is 3 percent, and the average earnings variance for publicly traded energy companies is 30 percent. The fair value measurement of the Windergy patent using the Excel version of the Black-Scholes Options Pricing Model is presented in Exhibit 7.1.

Note that the cost to develop the Windergy product is greater than the present value of the projected cash flow benefits that it will generate. Yet the patent still has value. The real option value is derived by the possibility that the patent could be used profitably in the future. The value of the patent is $23,676,720.

Binomial or Lattice Models

The Black-Scholes model is widely used because the resulting option price has been shown to be reliable. When comparing the theoretical option price generated by the Black-Scholes model to an actual trading price of a publicly traded option, the Black-Scholes results are similar to the publicly traded price in most situations. However, the Black-Scholes has some limitations and it has some simplifying assumptions.

Many financial instruments have complexities that exceed the capability of the model. In order to deal with more complexity, John Cox, Stephen Ross, and Mark Rubinstein developed a more robust option valuation model in 1979. Also used to price stock options, their model became known as the binomial model. The binomial model is similar to a decision tree where there are only two possible outcomes at each decision node. In spite of the limited number of outcomes for each period of time, the binomial model is considered more flexible than the Black-Scholes model because more decisions points or factors can be modeled. The binomial model's flexibility is also an advantage when using it to measure the fair value of intangible assets.

A binomial model is commonly used to price financial options such as calls or puts.[7] Binomial models are graphically represented as binomial

EXHIBIT 7.1 Sunrise Corporation, Valuation of Patents-Black-Scholes Options Pricing Method, as of December 31, 20X0

(USD$)	
Assumptions	
Current Patent Value (Present Value of Expected Cash Flows)	$ 100,000,000
Cost to Develop (Exercise Price)	125,000,000
Volatility	30%
Risk-Free Rate	3%
Time to Expiration of Patent	5 years
Exercise Price	$ 125,000,000
Years to Expiration	5
Days to Expiration	1,825
Volatility	30%
Risk-Free Rate r	3.00%
d_1 (1)	0.2264
$N(d_1)$	0.5895
$N(-d_1)$ or $[l - N(d_1)]$	0.4105
$d_2(1)$	(0.4444)
$N(d_2)$	0.3284
$N(-d_2)$ or $[l - N(d_2)]$	0.6716
Quarterly Dividend Rate	—
Dividend Yield	0.00%
Call Value (2)	$ 23,626,720

Notes:

(1) $N(d)$ = Cumulative density function (area under the normal curve) and d_1 and d_2 is as follows:

$$d_1 = \frac{\ln(\text{Market price/Exercise price} + ((r + ((\text{Volatility}^2/2)) * \text{years to expiration}}{\text{Volatility} * (\text{years to expiration})^{1/2}}$$

$$d_2 = d_1 - ((\text{volatility}) * (\text{years to expiration})^{1/2})$$

(2) Call Price = Market Price $* N(d_1) - [\text{Exercise Price} * e^{-r(\text{time to expiration})} N(d_2)]$

trees. Exhibit 7.2a shows what a binomial tree looks like before any of the values have been filled in.

The valuation date is on the left-hand side of the binomial tree at t_0 or time zero. S_0 represents the value of the underlying asset on the valuation date, at time zero. At the first branch, the value of the underlying asset can either go up to S_u or down to S_d. Each branch represents a time interval, or time step. Each node is associated with new values for S, at a specific point in time (t_1, t_2, etc.). At the next branch, S_u can go up to S_{uu} or down to S_{ud}, and likewise S_d can go up to S_{du} or down to S_{dd} at t_2. One of the model's simplifying assumptions is that at t_2, the values of S_{ud} and S_{du} are the same.[8]

The up and down changes in the value of the underlying asset are a result of the assets expected volatility. The volatility factor used in the

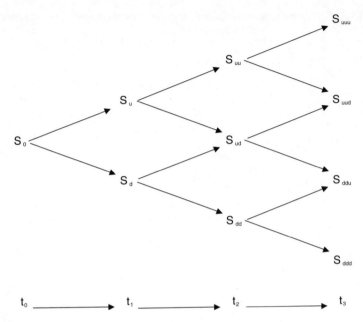

EXHIBIT 7.2a Binomial Tree

equations for an up or down move is the standard deviation of the logarithmic returns for the underlying asset. The volatility factor must be based on
the same time interval as those used in the model. Volatility is represented
by the σ symbol. A time step refers to the period of time over which one
change in underlying value occurs. Historic returns are often used as the
basis for expected volatility. U represents the upward change in value and
D represents a downward change in value.

Each branch of the binomial tree also has a probability associated with
it. An underlying assumption of the model is that the probabilities are risk
neutral. The symbol for the risk-neutral probability of an upward movement is P_u, and the symbol for the risk-neutral probability of a downward
movement is P_d. The formulas required to build a binomial model are:

$$U = e^{\sigma\sqrt{T}}$$
$$D = 1/U$$
$$P_u = e^{R_f T} - D/U - D$$
$$P_d = 1 - P_u, \text{where}$$
$$e = \text{log exponential function}$$
$$\sigma = \text{standard deviation of the underlying asset's logarithmic returns}$$
$$T = \text{the portion of a year in each time step (three months} = .25)$$
$$R_f = \text{the annual risk free rate}[9]$$

Example of a Real Option Measured with a Binomial Model

Suppose a movie producer is considering whether to purchase a screenplay. The screenplay is an adaptation of a recently released novel by a popular crime writer. The producer knows that the value of the screenplay is primarily dependent upon prospects for the novel's success. Owning the screenplay is similar to owning a call option on the movie. If the novel is successful, the producer can exercise his option to produce the movie. If the novel is unsuccessful, the producer can choose not to make the movie. The producer will make his decision after the novel has been in bookstores for one year.

The following assumptions are also part of this example. The binomial model input parameters are in parenthesis, where applicable. Many of these input parameters are similar to those for financial option models.

- The novel was released on January 1, 20X1.
- 200,000 copies were sold prior to March 31, 20X1. (S_0)
- An analysis of recent movies based on books indicates that expected movie revenues are $100 per copy of book sold in the fourth quarter after the book's release.
- It cost $20 million to produce a crime movie. (X)
- The screenplay is being offered for $1 million ($C_0$) on March 1, 20X1. ($t_0$)
- The producer will decide whether to invest in the movie on January 1, 20X2. (t_3)
- Industry research indicates that the standard deviation of the incremental number of crime novel copies sold during a quarter using a log scale is 40%. (σ)
- The applicable time frame for the binomial model is three-quarters. Each time step is one-quarter of a year. ($T = .25$)
- The annual risk free rate is 4 percent. (R_f)
- If the movie producer decides not to produce a movie on January 1, 20X2, the ownership of the screenplay reverts to the author (it is worthless).

In this example, the producer will decide whether to purchase the screenplay for $1 million. He will make his decision based on the value of the screenplay determined using a binomial model.

The first step in building a binomial tree is to solve for the upward change (U) and downward change (D) in the number of book copies.

$$U = e^{\sigma \sqrt{T}} = e^{.4 \cdot \sqrt{.25}} = 1.2214$$
$$D = 1 / U = 1 / 1.22 = .8187$$

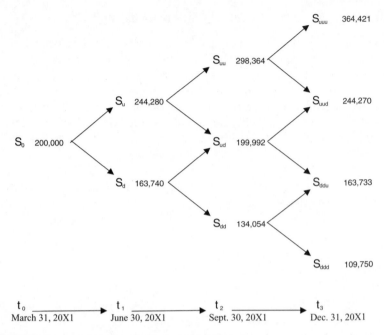

EXHIBIT 7.2b Binomial Tree with Underlying Values

The second step is to build the binomial tree by calculating the value of the underlying asset at each node. Recall that S_0 is 200,000 copies. Therefore $S_u = 200{,}000 \times 1.2214 = 244{,}280$, and $S_d = 200{,}000 \times .8187 = 163{,}740$. In the next time step, $S_{uu} = 244{,}280 \times 1.2214 = 298{,}364$, and so on. The binomial tree shown in Exhibit 7.2b includes the possible values for the underlying asset, which are number of book copies in this example. Based on the calculations in the binomial tree, the number of copies sold in the fourth quarter of 20X? will be between 109,750 and 364,421.

The third step is to calculate each of the possible options values on the exercise date, which is December 31, 20X1. There are four possible binomial tree outcomes for S at t_3. Recall that expected movie revenues are $100 times the number of book copies sold in the fourth quarter after release, and that it costs $20 million to produce a movie. The value of the screenplay, assuming 364,421 copies are sold (S_{uuu}), is $16,442,100 (364,421 copies × $100 less $20 million). Likewise, if 244,720 (S_{uud}) copies are sold, the screenplay value is $4,427,000.

At (S_{ddu}), book sales of 163,733 copies indicate that the movie would probably lose $3,626,700. The producer would decide not to make the movie. In other words, he would not exercise his option. The value of the screenplay is $0 at ($S_{ddu}$). At ($S_{ddd}$), the movie would lose even more money.

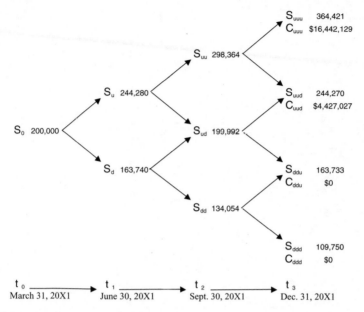

EXHIBIT 7.2c Binomial Tree with Terminal Values

The value of the screenplay is also $0 at this node. It is important to note that the option decision is made on the exercise date at t_3, and at no other time in this analysis.

At this point, the terminal call option values (C's) at t_3 can be added to the binomial tree. They are displayed directly underneath the S values. (See Exhibit 7.2c.)

The last step is to work backward from the option values at t_3, to find the option value at t_2, and to keep working backward to t_0. To do so, the risk-neutral probability formulas P_u and P_d for an upward and downward move will be used. The values for P_u and P_d are:

$$P_u = e^{Rf\,T} - D\,/\,U - D$$
$$= e^{(.04\,\times\,.25)} - .8187\,/\,1.2214 - .8187$$
$$= 1.010 - .8187\,/\,.4027$$
$$= .4752$$
$$P_d = 1 - P_u$$
$$= 1 - .4752 = .5258$$

The value of the option at any node is simply the probability weighted average of the up and down options values in the next time step, discounted at the risk-free rate using a log function. The formula to calculate the value of the option is:

$$C_t = ((P_u \times C_{u,\,t+1}) + (P_d \times C_{d,\,t+1}))\,/\,e^{Rf\,T}$$

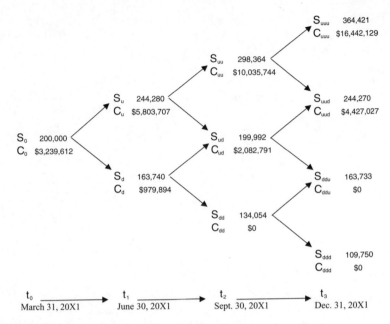

EXHIBIT 7.2d Binomial Tree with Real Option Values

The value of the option at node S_{uu} at t_2 is the probability weighted average of the option values C_{uuu} and C_{uud} at t_3, discounted at the risk-free rate using a log function.[10] The value of the option C_{uu} is \$10,035,744, which equals $(((\$16,442,129 \times .4752) + (\$4,427,027 \times .5248))/1.01)$. The value of each node in the binomial tree is calculated in a similar manner. The binomial tree with all the screenplay options values filled in is shown in Exhibit 7.2d.

According to the binomial tree analysis, the value of the screenplay is \$3,239,612 on March 31, 20X1. Therefore, the movie producer will purchase the screenplay for \$1 million.

Monte Carlo Simulation

The traditional DCF is a deterministic method, which means there is a single set of assumptions with one outcome. Monte Carlo simulations are stochastic techniques, which mean there are ranges of assumptions and outcomes. Monte Carlo simulation is useful in measuring fair value because the simulation allows for more complex scenarios with a greater number of variables than other valuation techniques.

Monte Carlo simulation is an advanced valuation method that can be useful in measuring the fair value of an intangible asset. Monte Carlo simulation is a statistical technique used to calculate the likely statistical distribution of possible outcomes based on multiple simulations, or trial runs. Each simulation uses random variables generated from statistical distributions of possible values for each of the variables. The model is also capable of considering correlations among variables.

Monte Carlo simulation is most commonly used for isolating one assumption, or variable, and estimating the range of probable outcomes and based on the distribution pattern for that particular assumption. Commercially available software products such as @Risk from Palisade Corporation and Crystal Ball from Oracle are two of the more widely used products that are available to run Monte Carlo simulations.[11]

Using commercially available software to run a Monte Carlo simulation is relatively straightforward. The first step is to determine the appropriate probability distribution for each assumption or variable. Probability distributions for variables can be a "normal" bell curve type of distributions, or they can be some other distribution pattern. Historical data is often used to determine the statistical properties of assumptions. The second step in the analysis is to identify the assumption, which is the input parameter. The assumption can be a growth rate, margin levels, or the remaining useful life of the intangible asset. In the third step, the software will run 1,000 or more times to simulate various outcome scenarios. Each trial uses a different value for the defined input assumption based on its statistical distribution in the model. Each trial has a different conclusion, and the conclusions are statistically summarized. The conclusion of the Monte Carlo simulation is a distribution of outcomes with a confidence level and with a most likely outcome.

Monte Carlo simulation can be applied to the measurement of fair value for intangible assets by quantifying uncertainties for assumptions in a discounted cash flow analysis that may not be captured through the use of a traditional discount rate. For example, when measuring the fair value of in-process research and development, the eventual unit sale price, the market demand, selling costs, and many other factors are all unknown. The traditional DCF makes the "most likely" assumption for these variables, but in reality they often have a wide range of possible outcomes. Sometimes assumptions like market demand and selling costs are interrelated. Monte Carlo simulations can be run for these types of complicated, interdependent assumption scenarios. Because it has the benefit of incorporating real-world complexities into assumptions and because it generates a thousand or more possible outcomes, the analysis is quite robust.

Monte Carlo Simulation Example

Assume that New Ideas Inc. has a patent with a remaining useful life of six years. A valuation specialist has been asked to measure the fair value of the patent. Management has provided information about the company's market share and the valuation specialist has researched the U.S. market and appropriate royalty rates. The information is summarized in the top portion of Exhibit 7.3.

The valuation specialist has calculated the net present value of the forecasted cash flows for the patent. Based on this discounted cash flow model, the valuation specialist estimates that the fair value of the patent is $1.5 million.

To support this value, the valuation specialist runs a Monte Carlo simulation, which provides a distribution of possible outcomes based on the assumptions input into the model and on 10,000 trial runs. In this simulation, the valuation specialist achieves a 95 percent confidence level (measured as two standard deviations from the mean) that the net present value falls within the range of $1.1 million to $2 million. The most likely result is $1.5 million. The output from the Monte Carlo simulation is presented in the lower portion of Exhibit 7.3 (output from Crystall Ball Software).

Decision Tree Analysis

Decision Tree Analysis can also be used to measure the fair value of various intangible assets. Decision Tree Analysis is easy to understand because it creates a pictorial example of the decision process. The name "decision tree" comes from its visual resemblance to the branches of a tree. A decision tree analysis incorporates the discounted cash flows for all possible outcomes and it assigns a probability to each outcome.

Example of a Decision Tree Analysis

The following example of a decision tree analysis is based on the fictitious company Florida Coastal Restaurants (FCR). FCR has a secret spice recipe for preparing fresh stone crab that is currently under development. FCR envisions developing the U.S. market for stone crabs prepared with secret spices by shipping the crabs via overnight delivery. Prior to investing in this marketing effort, management wants to estimate the value of its secret spice recipe. Since there are many possible future outcomes, a decision tree analysis is used to measure the value of the secret spice recipe.

FCR's management first identifies all the possible outcomes and the probabilities associated with them. Then it calculates the discounted cash

EXHIBIT 7.3 New Ideas, Inc., Forecasted Royalty Income—Static View

$ in millions

	20X1	20X2	20X3	20X4	20X5	20X6
U.S. Market	$ 100,000,000	$ 108,000,000	$ 118,800,000	$ 133,056,000	$ 146,361,600	$ 158,070,528
Subject IP's Market Share	5.0%	5.0%	5.0%	5.0%	5.0%	5.0%
Subject IP's U.S. Sales	$ 5,000,000	$ 5,400,000	$ 5,940,000	$ 6,652,800	$ 7,318,080	$ 7,903,526
Royalty Rate	6.0%	6.0%	6.0%	6.0%	6.0%	6.0%
Forecasted Royalty Income	$ 300,000	$ 324,000	$ 356,400	$ 399,168	$ 439,085	$ 474,212
Net Present Value—Royalty Income	$ 1,522,904					

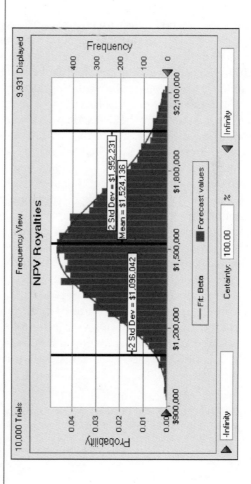

237

flows for each of the possible outcomes. Management believes that there is a 50 percent chance that its efforts to develop a U.S. market for stone crab prepared with the secret spices will be successful. Management is aware of another seafood restaurant based in the Northeast that has investigated overnight delivery for its lobsters. FCR expects successful outcomes and their probabilities to be no competition (30 percent probability), some competition (50 percent), and limited market acceptance (20 percent). If the project is unsuccessful, any investment made up to that date is lost. Management believes there are two potential unsuccessful scenarios: one in which the project is abandoned halfway through development (65 percent probability), and another where the project is abandoned right before it is ready to hit the market (35 percent).

FCR's management believes that a decision tree analysis would best measure the potential value of the market acceptance of stone crabs prepared with its secret recipe. Analysis of the potential market indicates expected future cash flows of $5 million assuming little to no competition, $2.5 million assuming some competition, and $1 million, assuming a limited market for the overnight delivery of stone crab. The first node (reading from right to left in this particular example) represents the decision whether the secret recipe is successful enough to market nationwide. Management will have invested $500,000 to develop the secret recipe. If FCR continues with its marketing plans but abandons the project at later date just prior to product introduction, FCR will have invested a total of $1 million. After the present value of the cash flows is measured for each unsuccessful scenario, the resulting cash flows are multiplied by their respective probabilities. The result of the decision tree analysis indicated the fair value of the secret recipe as part of a plan to market the stone crabs nationwide is approximately $1,137,500. Florida Coastal Restaurants's decision tree analysis is presented in Exhibit 7.4.

EXHIBIT 7.4 Florida Coastal Restaurants, Decision Tree Analysis, as of December 31, 20X0

Values Estimated Using Discounted Cash Flow Analysis

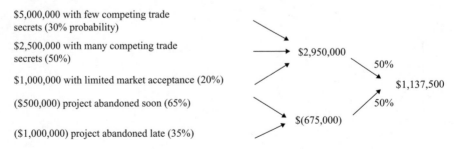

$5,000,000 with few competing trade secrets (30% probability)

$2,500,000 with many competing trade secrets (50%)

$1,000,000 with limited market acceptance (20%)

($500,000) project abandoned soon (65%)

($1,000,000) project abandoned late (35%)

$2,950,000

$(675,000)

50%

50%

$1,137,500

Conclusion

Options valuation techniques can be applied to assess the impact of managerial decisions. Known as real options, these elements create value by providing management flexibility. Real options include decisions relating to abandonment, expansions, contractions, interactions, timing of entrances and exits, flexibility to switch, and barrier options. They are similar to owning a financial option in that they give the owner a right to pursue a course of action, but they impose no obligation to do so; therefore, real options often have many of the same attributes as financial options. Real options are often derived from the ownership rights of intangible assets, and intangible as are sometimes referred to as real options.

Valuation methods using advance valuation techniques are being increasingly used to measure the fair value of certain intangible assets. Models based on advanced valuation theory such as option pricing models or real option, Monte Carlo simulations, and decision tree analysis can be readily applied to measuring the fair value in financial reporting. These methods may capture elements of value that are inherent in the intangible asset that traditional valuation methods may not recognize.

Notes

1. The fair value of financial options are measured in financial reporting under SFAS 123(R). Note that SFAS 123(R) expressly does not fall under the requirements of SFAS 157. The measurement standard under SFAS 123(R) is considered "fair value like," but not necessarily as fair value as defined under SFAS 157.
2. Kodukla, P., and C. Papudesu, *Project Valuation Using Real Options* (Ft. Lauderdale, FL: J. Ross Publishing Inc., 2006), 101–140.
3. Chance, Don M., and Pamela P. Peterson, *Real Options and Investment Valuation*, The Research Foundation of the AIMR (Charlottesville, VA: CFA Institute, 2002).
4. Cohen, Jeffery A., *Intangible Assets: Valuation and Economic Benefit* (New York: John Wiley & Sons, 2005), 85–87.
5. Fischer Black had died in 1995 and was ineligible for the award (see Chance and Peterson, page 9).
6. An excellent source of valuation models is Answarth Damodaran's Web site, Damodaran Online at http://pages.stern.nyu.edu/~adamodar/.
7. Cox, John C., Stephen Ross, and Mark Rubinstein, "Option Pricing: A Simplified Approach," *Journal of Financial Economics*, September 1979, p.2.
8. Chance, Don M., *Analysis of Derivatives for the CFA* Program (Charlottesville, VA: Association for Investment Management and Research, 2003), 200–207.
9. Kodukula, Prasa and Chandra Papudesu, *Project Valuation Using Real Options: A Practitioner's Guide* (Fort Lauderdale FL: J. Ross Publishing, Inc.), 74.
10. *Id.* 79.
11. www.palisade.com/risk/ and www.oracle.com/crystalball/index.html.

CHAPTER 8

Measuring the Remaining Useful Life of Intangible Assets in Financial Reporting

Introduction

Measuring the remaining useful life of an intangible asset is an important element in measuring the fair value of the asset in financial reporting. The useful life of an asset is often a significant factor contributing to its fair value. Intangible assets with longer lives typically have greater economic returns and higher values than similar, shorter-lived assets. The useful life of an intangible asset is also the principal factor for selecting the period over which the intangible asset is amortized.

FASB Guidance on Determining the Remaining Useful Life

The Financial Accounting Standards Board (FASB) Accounting Standards Codification (ASC) 850, *Fair Value Measurements and Disclosures* (SFAS No 157), describes the three basic valuation techniques (approaches) for measuring the fair value of an intangible asset. As discussed in previous chapters, useful life is a key consideration when measuring fair value using all three techniques. When measuring fair value using the income approach, the period of time covered by prospective financial information (PFI) for a specific asset should be equal in length to the asset's useful life. Under the market approach, the comparable intangible asset's useful life is one of the principle considerations when determining whether the asset is in fact comparable. The length of time covered by PFI is also a consideration for some market approach methods. In the cost approach, the useful life of the asset is a consideration when measuring the obsolescence of the asset.

FASB ASC 350, *Intangibles—Goodwill and Other* (SFAS No. 142), provides the following guidance about the useful life of an intangible asset:

The accounting for a recognized intangible asset is based on its useful life to the reporting entity. An intangible asset with a finite useful life is amortized; an intangible asset with an indefinite useful life is not amortized.[1] The useful life of an intangible asset to an entity is the period over which the asset is expected to contribute directly or indirectly to the future cash flows of that entity. The useful life is not the period of time that it would take that entity to internally develop an intangible asset that would provide similar benefits.[2]

Paragraph 11 of SFAS No. 142 also provides several factors that can impact the useful life of an intangible asset for financial reporting purposes:

- The expected use of the asset by the entity
- The expected useful life of another related asset or a group of related assets with which the intangible asset may be used
- Legal, regulatory, and contractual provisions that may limit the useful life or may permit the renewal or extension of the useful life
- The entity's own historical experience with respect to similar intangible assets
- The effects of obsolescence, demand, competition, and other economic factors
- The level of maintenance expenditures required to realize expected future cash flows from the asset[3]

These factors are useful in determining the useful life of an intangible asset, but it must be emphasized that the primary consideration is the period over which positive economic benefits flow from the intangible asset.

Indefinite-Lived Assets

Intangible-assets such as certain trade names, domain names, airport routes, and taxi cab medallions are not limited by contractual or other legal limitation, nor are they limited by economic factors. When that is the case, the intangible asset is considered to have an indefinite life. An indefinite life asset does not mean the life is perpetual, or that the useful life is indeterminable. It simply means that the life of the asset exists beyond the foreseeable time horizon as a contributor to the cash flow of the entity.[4] The lack of objective information about an asset's useful life would indicate that the intangible asset has an indefinite life. Indefinite lived assets should be rare in financial reporting. Although intangible assets such as trade names seem to have indefinite lives; a look at Fortune 100 companies from 1980 would indicate otherwise. Several Fortune 100 companies such as LTV, International Harvester, and Sperry have trade names that no longer enjoy widespread recognition.[5]

FSP FAS 142-3, *Determination of the Useful Life of Intangible Assets*

The FASB provided some clarify guidance about how contractual renewals and other extensions impact the useful life of an intangible asset. On April 25, 2008, the FASB issued FASB Staff Position (FSP) FAS 142-3, *Determination of the Useful Life of Intangible Assets.*

Prior to FSP FAS 142-3, there was variance in practice with respect to how renewal provisions for contractual intangible assets were treated when estimating the asset's useful life. For example, a one-year contractual customer relationship with a year-to-year renewed provision covering four additional years created confusion about whether the one-year contractual life or the five-year extended life should be considered the intangible asset's useful life. FSP FAS 142-3 provides clarification about what an entity should consider when estimating the useful life of an intangible asset. Of particular significance is that the FASB Board said that an entity can consider its own assumptions about the renewal or extension of contractual arrangements.

FSP FAS 142-3 describes the process for determining useful life when renewals or extensions are a factor, as follows. (The paragraph 11 factors it refers to are listed in a previous section.)

> *In developing assumptions about renewal or extension used to determine the useful life of a recognized intangible asset, an entity shall consider its own historical experience in renewing or extending similar arrangements; however, these assumptions should be adjusted for the entity-specific factors in paragraph 11 of Statement 142. In the absence of that experience, an entity shall consider the assumptions that market participants would use about renewal or extension (consistent with the highest and best use of the asset by market participants), adjusted for the entity-specific factors in paragraph 11 of Statement 142.*[6]

Under the FSP, the entity must disclose any intent to renew the contractual arrangement that has an impact on the useful life of the intangible asset. The FSP stipulates that "for a recognized intangible asset, an entity shall disclose information that enables users of financial statements to assess the extent to which the expected future cash flows associated with the asset are affected by the entity's intent and/or ability to renew or extend the arrangement."[7]

Considerations in Measuring Useful Lives of Intangible Assets

Assessing the useful life of an intangible asset requires considering several determinants of useful life. These determinants are independent of one another, so they should be considered individually when estimating an asset's useful life. In some situations, these determinants are interrelated with one another. A conclusion about the most appropriate useful life for the intangible asset is typically based on the determinant that indicates the shortest remaining useful life. This same conclusion about useful life should also be applied to the measurement of the intangible asset's fair value. Common determinants of useful life and examples of intangible assets for which they indicate a useful life are provided in the following chart.

Determinants to Consider in Useful Lives of Intangible Assets	Examples of Application to Intangible Asset
Legal Life of the Asset	Legal life of patents, trade names, and copyrights
Contractual Life	Contracts with customers, franchise agreements, and favorable leases
Economic Life	The period of time over which intangible asset such as developed technology or trade names generate a positive cash flow
Functional and Technological Obsolescence	Functionality obsolescence occurs when the asset is no longer able to efficiently perform the function for which it was intended. Technical obsolescence is a type of functional obsolescence caused by advances in technology. Obsolescence is a consideration for patents
Analytics	Analytics are a statistical measure of useful life based on actual historical data. Historical turnover can be used to determine the useful life of customer relationships

Applying the Determinants When Measuring Useful Life

LEGAL LIVES The legal life is an important determinant in measuring the fair value of intangible assets such as patents, trade names, trademarks, or copyrights, which provide legal protection from competition. A copyright on proprietary software provides legal protection from unauthorized copying for a period of time specified under copyright protection laws. Although the remaining time to the expiration of legal protections is one determinant of the asset's useful life, other factors such as the asset's potential economic benefit should also be considered. The duration of the asset's economic benefit is typically shorter than applicable legal protections, particularly for intangible assets in the technology sector.

Copyrights enjoy the longest legal protection of all intellectual property. A copyright lasts for the life of the author plus another 70 years. Typically the economic life of copyrighted software is much shorter than its legal life. Patent protection is granted for inventions that are new, useful, and not obvious. Patent protection can be granted for machines, tools, manufacturing processes, business processes, and new compositions of matter such as new drugs. The legal life of the patent depends on the type, and is either 14 years or 20 years. After the expiration of the patent, the invention becomes part of the public domain. Finally, trademarks have legal protection for 10 years, but the trademark can be renewed indefinitely.[8]

CONTRACTUAL LIVES   Contractual lives are similar to legal lives in that both are limited by agreement. A contractual agreement between two parties forms the basis of contractual lives while an agreement between the U.S. government and the registrant forms the basis for legal lives under statutory law. Contractual lives can be a determinant of an intangible asset's useful life, particularly if the intangible asset ceases to exist at the agreement's termination. Examples of intangible assets whose useful life may coincide with its contract life include favorable leases, favorable supplier agreements, and customer contracts. However, all of the facts and circumstances relating to the agreement should be considered, including contract terms, industry practices, and previous arrangements between the parties. As discussed previously, FSP FAS 142-3 acknowledges that some contracts are likely to be renewed and permits the use of the entity's own experience in measuring the useful life of the intangible asset, including the probability of renewal.

ECONOMIC LIVES   The economic life of an intangible asset is an important determinant in measuring its useful life. The economic life is the period over which the intangible asset contributes to an entity's cash flows. The fair value of an intangible asset is directly related to its economic life. An intangible asset with a longer economic life will have a higher fair value than a similar intangible asset with a shorter life.

Economic benefits attributable to a specific intangible asset can be estimated using one of the methods from the income approach to valuation.

The multiperiod excess earnings method (MPEEM) is particularly useful for this type of economic benefit analysis.

The MPEEM and other forms of the discounted cash flow methods capture factors that may influence the economic benefits derived from the intangible asset. If there is a contractual relationship, the MPEEM considers the probability of renewal. If the intangible asset is subject to certain functional or technological obsolesce, the MPEEM typically considers incremental costs associated with maintenance required to keep the intangible asset viable. The MPEEM also considers situations where the economic life of an intangible asset may differ from its legal or contractual life.

The first step in measuring the economic life of an intangible asset using the MPEEM is to estimate the remaining useful life through reference to some other determinate such as historical experience or information from other market participants.

The second step is to apply an economic decay curve to the PFI revenues in the MPEEM. An economic decay curve is a statistical technique used to determine the economic benefits from an intangible asset. The decay factor is applied to revenues attributable to a certain intangible asset in a MPEEM analysis. It quantifies the portion of economic benefit that is lost each year with the passage of time. The formula for the decay factor is:

$$e^{(\text{period}/-\text{remaining useful life})}$$

For example, if you assume a remaining useful life of 15 years, the decay factor for the first year is 0.9355, calculated using the following steps and a calculator with logarithmic functions: (1) divide 1 by negative 15 to get negative 0.0667; (2) depress the **2nd** and the **e^x** buttons on a logarithmic calculator to get 0.9355. The decay factors for years two and three are calculated in a similar manner and the results are 0.8752 and 0.8187, respectively. It is interesting to note that although the remaining useful life is 15 years, revenues attributable to a particular intangible asset using this decay factor will continue for approximately 30 years. For practical purposes, the economic benefits in the distant future are truncated in the analysis because they are immaterial. Typically the economic life is the time that the intangible has significant positive cash flows under the MPEEM. An example of a MPEEM showing the application of an exponential decay curve is shown in Exhibit 6.3.

An issue that should be considered when measuring the economic life of an intangible asset using the MPEEM is how fixed and variable costs are treated. As a simplifying assumption, many valuation specialists treat all costs as though they are variable costs. This approach may be appropriate in many circumstances. However, this simplifying assumption tends to result in longer economic lives than would be indicated if expenses were divided between fixed and variable costs. The relationship between total operating expense and the company's cost structure can be estimated statistically through a simple regression analysis, where:

Forecasted Operating Expense =

Total Fixed Costs + (Variable Cost per unit × # units of output).[9]

Some entities measure useful life using an 80 percent convention. The useful life is considered to be 80 percent of the intangible assets economic life. While the convention allows the entity to standardize the measurement, it also gives the estimate of fair value a conservative bias because the fair value of an intangible asset is directly related to the intangible asset's economic life.

FUNCTIONALITY AND TECHNOLOGICAL LIMITATIONS   One determinant that limits an intangible asset's useful life is obsolescence. Changes in an asset's functionality and changes in technology can impact useful life. Functionality describes how an entity uses the intangible asset. Various factors, both internal and external to the entity, may impact the intangible assets functionality. A common limitation to an intangible asset's functionality is technological change.

ANALYTICS (HISTORICAL TURNOVER)   FSP FAS 142-3 clarifies that the entity's own experience can be used to measure the useful life of an intangible asset in financial reporting. Statistical analysis of the entity's own historical trends is one way to quantify the entity's own experience for useful life analysis. Quantitative analysis of historical data related to the subject asset or similar assets can be used to statistically predict the useful life of the intangible asset. The expected useful life of customer relationships can be statistically measured by analyzing the historical customer turnover trends over a period of time. The time frame for analysis should be at least as long as the average length of time that current customers have been customers.

One statistical tool for measuring the useful lives of intangible assets is a survivor curve. Survivor curves are statistical tools that rely on the analysis of two forms of data to measure useful lives. First, the historical attrition rate of the intangible asset is measured by comparing the number that exists at the beginning of the period to the number remaining at the end of the period. Then, several periods are examined to determine an average attrition rate over time. The attrition rate is then compared or "fit" to a predetermined "survivor curve." The survivor curve is a statistical measurement based on observations from other assets with similar attrition characteristics.

Commercially available statistical software that uses this methodology can be employed to measure the useful life of an intangible asset. The measurement is based on the entity's own experience. Two common software programs available for estimating useful lives are the Iowa curve studies and the Weibull function.[10] These programs are based on statistical studies that were originally developed to measure the remaining useful life of fixed assets for tax-reporting purposes. The underlying statistical studies have been used for decades and have achieved widespread acceptance for tax-reporting purposes. Consequently, these statistical methods are valid for use in measuring useful lives of certain intangible assets in financial reporting.

A more detailed discussion of applying statistical analysis and survivor curves can be found in the American Society of Appraisers publication *Business Valuation Review*, in an article titled "Retirement Behavior and Customer Life Expectancy."[11]

Guideline Useful Lives

Another way to measure the useful life of intangible assets is based on useful lives reported by other market participants. Publicly available information such as SEC filings can serve as useful guidelines to measure the reaming useful life of intangible assets. The benefit of this guideline approach is that useful lives reported in public company filings have received SEC scrutiny for reasonableness. An example of potential guideline information for intangible asset's useful lives can be found in AT&T's most recent annual report. AT&T's footnotes describe the amortization of certain intangible assets based on the asset's useful lives.

> *Intangible assets that have finite useful lives are amortized over their useful lives, using a weighted average of 7.4 years. Customer relationships are amortized using primarily the sum-of-the-months-digits method of amortization over the expected period in which those relationships are expected to contribute to our future cash flows based in such a way as to allocate it as equitably as possible to periods during which we expect to benefit from those relationships.[12]*
>
> *It is our policy to capitalize certain costs incurred in connection with developing or obtaining internal use software. Capitalized software costs are included in "Property, Plant and Equipment" on our consolidated balance sheets and are primarily amortized over a three-year period. Software costs that do not meet capitalization criteria are expensed immediately.[13]*
>
> *A significant portion of intangible assets in our wireless segment are Federal Communications Commission (FCC) licenses that provide us with the exclusive right to utilize a certain radio frequency spectrum to provide wireless communications services. While FCC licenses are issued*

for a fixed time, renewals of FCC licenses have occurred routinely and at nominal cost. Moreover, we have determined that there are currently no legal, regulatory, contractual, competitive, economic, or other factors that limit the useful lives of our FCC licenses, and therefore the FCC licenses are an indefinite-lived intangible asset under the provisions of Statement of Financial Accounting Standards No. 142, "Goodwill and Other Intangible Assets."[14]

The information contained in this footnote and in the footnotes of other market participants provides a source of information about the useful life of similar assets. This guideline information can be used as a basis for measuring the useful lives of an entity's intangible assets.

Conclusion

The determination of an intangible asset's useful life is an important consideration in measuring the fair value of the asset in financial reporting. Intangible assets with longer lives typically have greater economic returns, which creates a higher fair value than shorter-lived assets. The intangible asset's useful life usually coincides with its financial statement amortization period.

The FASB outlined several determinants that should be considered when measuring the useful life of an intangible asset. Among these considerations are the entity's intended use for the asset, the useful lives of the group of assets with which the intangible may be used, legal or regulatory constraints on the use of the asset, the entity's own experience with the asset, the impact of obsolescence on the asset's ability to produce economic returns for the entity, and the level of maintenance required to retain the asset's functionality.

The useful lives of intangible assets can be measured using statistical analysis of the entity's own historical data, which is applied to the expectations of future use.

Another method to measure the expected useful life of an intangible asset is to analyze how other market participants measure the useful life of similar assets. Useful guideline information about how other market participants measure the useful lives of similar assets can often be found in public filings.

Notes

1. FASB ASC 350-30-35-1.
2. FASB ASC 350-30-35-2.

3. FASB ASC 350-30-35-3.
4. FASB ASC 350-30-35-5. 5. 5.
5. http://money.cnn.com/magazines/fortune/fortune500_archive/snapshots/1980/ 3547.html (accessed July 30, 2009).
6. FSP FAS 142-3, www.fasb.org.
7. FSP FAS 142-3, www.fasb.org.
8. Myer, Lisa M., "The Life of a Patent," www.ehow.com/about_5194971_life-patent .html.
9. Kennedy, G. William, "Using Statistical Measures in BVFLS Engagements," unpublished presentation to CPAAI, July 20–21, 2009.
10. Stout, William M., "A Comparison of Component and Group Depreciation For Large Homogeneous Groups of Network Assets," A Presentation to the Accounting Standards Executive Committee of the American Institute of Certified Public Accountants, August 28, 2002, www.aicpa.org/download/members/div/acctstd/ general/PPE.pdf (accessed July29, 2009).
11. Richard K. Ellsworth, "Retirement Behavior and Customer Life Expectancy," *Business Valuation Review*, Spring 2009, Volume 28, No. 1, pp. 36–38.
12. AT&T 2008 Annual report page 56, www.att.com/Common/about_us/annual_ report/pdfs/2008ATT_FullReport.pdf (accessed July 29, 2009).
13. *Id.*
14. *Id.*

CHAPTER 9

Fair Value Measurements of Private Equity and Other Alternative Investments

Introduction

Fair value measurement is currently one of the hottest topics for both investors in and management of private equity funds and other alternative investments. The American Institute of Certified Public Accountants (AICPA) considers alternative investments to be private investment funds that meet the definition of an investment company. In addition to private equity, some other common types of alternative investments include hedge funds, venture capital, real estate, fund of funds, and other similar types of investments. One of the challenges facing management of investment funds considered to be alternative investments is the appropriate measurement of value so that it can be reported to the fund's investors. Most investment funds require that the financial statements be reported under U.S. Generally Accepted Accounting Principles (GAAP), which requires that the assets held by the fund be measured at their respective fair values. Investments funds typically raise funds from sophisticated investors, as defined by the Securities and Exchange Commission (SEC), and in turn invest these funds in various types of investments. There are two salient issues in financial reporting related to the fair value measurements of alternative investments. The first issue is the fair value measurement of the fund's investments. These investments are recorded on the fund's financial statements as assets. The second issue is the fair value measurement of the investors' interests in the fund.

Previously, many funds reported the investment at historic cost and only made adjustments if there was an additional third-party transaction such as an add-on investment at different cost. Fair value measurements Financial Accounting Standards Board (FASB) Accounting Standards

Codification (ASC) 820, *Fair Value Measurements and Disclosures* (SFAS No. 157), significantly changes how investment managers measure and report the value of their investments. Fair value measurements are designed to provide consistency in measuring the value of investments. However, while providing consistency, fair value measurements also create some challenges in preparing the measurement for financial reporting.

AICPA's Alternative Investment Task Force

In order to provide additional guidance in financial reporting, in January 2009 the AICPA's Accounting Standards Executive Committee and the Alternative Investments Task Force released a draft issues paper to discuss the application of FASB ASC 820, *Fair Value Measurements and Disclosures* (SFAS 157), to the measurement of value for alternative investments. The draft issues paper notes that the determination of the appropriate accounting method to measure the investments depends on many factors, including the type of entity, the legal structure of the investment entity, and the percentage ownership being measured.[1] The AICPA paper focuses on the challenges of implementing fair value measurements to alternative investments that are not actively traded. Since these investments are not traded on an exchange, they are typically not registered with the SEC and financial information is unavailable. Potential investors are limited to those with a certain level of wealth and sophistication, which creates a narrow market for these interests. The lack of public information about the investments and infrequent transactions results in a lack of transparency for transactions of interest. The lack of transparency makes for some challenges in measuring their fair value.

The AICPA draft paper suggests that alternative investments can be classified into two types of investments: (1) those investments that have redeemable interests and (2) those investments that do not have redeemable interests. Investments with redeemable interests are those that allow investors opportunities to redeem their interests at certain times. These types of investments typically include hedge funds and bank trust funds. Investments with nonredeemable interests are typical of investments in private equity funds, venture capital funds, and real estate partnerships.

Due to the nature of alternative investments, the measurement of the fair value of these investments is challenging. Other than initial investment by third parties, there is often little market evidence as to the fair value of the interest. Even when there may be transactions for the same alternative investment, fund management may not provide transparent information about the transaction. However, management of the investment fund is responsible for the fair value measurement of the alternative investments present in the entity's financial statements. This is not to say the management cannot retain the services of an outside valuations specialist to assist them with the measurement. If fact, it is increasingly common for the fund's management to retain outside valuation specialists to assist in measuring not only the fair value of the underlying investments in the fund, which is used to determine the fund's net asset value, but also to assist management of the fund to measure the fair value of their investors' interest in the fund.

The purpose of the AICPA's draft issues paper is to provide assistance to fund management in implementing FASB ASC 820, *Fair Value Measurements and Disclosures* (SFAS 157), for the fair value measurement of their direct investments and their investments in other funds, which are often referred to as the fund of funds. The issues covered by the draft paper include the unit of account, the principal or most advantageous market for these investments, the net asset value in measuring fair value, and other issues unique to the measurement of fair value of alternative investments.

Unit of Account

In measuring the fair value of alternative investments, the draft paper notes that the appropriate unit of account is the interest in the investment fund, not necessarily the underlying assets of the fund. The investor owns an interest in the equity of the fund not an interest in the actual portfolio of assets less liabilities. This is an important concept. The investor usually does not have the ability to sell or dispose of individual assets of the fund, just as an investor in an operating entity lacks the ability to dispose of any particular operating asset. Additionally, the investor may be restricted from selling his interest in the investment fund either because the terms of the investment agreement prohibit such a transaction or because general market conditions limit the transferability of the interest. These limitations increase the risk of the investment beyond the risk incorporated into the measure of the fair value of the individual assets and liabilities. In measuring the fair value of the individual investor's interest in the investment fund, fair value measurement would include the factors that a market participant would consider, such as the structure of the investments, investor rights that are associated with the investment, and rights similar to those of other investors and lenders to the entity. Some examples of the factors that a market participant may consider are the ability to redeem the investment, any lock-up periods, additional required investments (capital calls), and restrictions on the transfer of the investment. In reviewing these features, a market participant may have the view that these features increase the relative risk of the investment and would therefore be taken into consideration when pricing the investment.

Principal or Most Advantageous Market for Alternative Investments

Alternative investments are unique in that most are not transferable without special permission from the fund management. Even if permission to transfer the investment is forthcoming, the market for alternative investments is limited since the investments are not registered with the SEC. Most alternative investments can be only transferred to "sophisticated investors" under SEC regulations.

If an interest in a fund is redeemable, then any potential market participant would have the ability to redeem the interest once it was acquired. In that case, the net asset value of the fund is a key starting point to the measurement of fair value of the interest in the fund. If there are restrictions as to the time period in which the interest may be redeemed, then that restriction should be considered when measuring fair value. Restrictions increase the investment's risk since they limit the ability to liquidate the investment. Thus, the fair value of an investment with restrictions would most likely be less than the investment's net asset value.

The fair value of a nonredeemable interest in alternative investments is even more difficult to measure. Even if there is a limited market for interests in nonredeemable funds, transactions in these limited markets may be somewhat problematic and may not be an indication of fair value. The reason is that information arising from the transaction may not be transparent or that information about the transaction may not be available to determine whether the transaction can be used as a relevant indication of fair value. Many of these transactions are a result of distressed sales, which are inappropriate for the use in the measurement of fair value.

The inputs in measuring the fair value of alternative investments under FASB ASC 820, *Fair Value Measurements and Disclosures* (SFAS 157), are the inputs that market participants would use in pricing the investment. If there are no actual market participants for the interest in the alternative investment, then the inputs should be inputs that the entity assumes market participants would use in pricing the investment. Inputs to measuring alternative investments typically include net asset value, transactions in external markets, and features specific to the investment. The underlying reason for transactions in nonredeemable interests may result in a transaction price that is not indicative of fair value. For instance, an investor may not want to or be able to make additional required capital contributions (capital calls) or they may seek further diversifications with other types of investments.

Net Asset Value

The net asset value of an investment fund is the difference between the sum of the assets' fair values of the fund less the fair value of the liabilities of the fund. Net asset value is often measured on a per share or per unit basis. Net asset values of investment funds are difficult to measure because the fund's assets (the fund's investments) are often illiquid and may constantly change over time. Net asset value per share or per unit is sometimes used as a proxy for the fair value of the investment by the fund's investors. However, diligence should be exercised before concluding that net asset value is the fund's fair value. Individual investments may have risk factors not considered in the fund's net asset value. These risk factors relate to the specific features of the investment.

Traditional industry practice had been to carry investments at the most recent transaction price for the underlying assets, which is either the cost when acquired or the value indicated by subsequent investments in the same asset. However, this measurement of net asset value is not necessarily the fair value as defined by FASB ASC 820, *Fair Value Measurements and Disclosures* (SFAS 157). The FASB's Valuation Resource Group (VRG) describes the relationship of net asset value to fair value as follows:

> *After the adoption of Statement 157, one might conclude that the net asset value (NAV) of a fund (per unit) may not be appropriate for subsequent measurements of investments in funds. Even though NAV is based on fair value of the underlying assets in the fund, it may not necessarily represent the price that would be received to sell an ownership interest in the fund in a transaction between market participants the measurement date.[2]*

In other words, net asset value is not necessarily fair value. However, net asset value should be considered, initially. In measuring fair value, "all relevant factor and attributes of the interest" should be considered, which may require some adjustments from the net asset value of the alternative investment.[3] In order to do so, first the net asset value should be analyzed to determine if the underlying assets and liabilities have been measured at their respective fair values or can be determined using some reasonable assumptions. Second, the attributes of the specific interest in the net asset value should be considered to determine whether any adjustments should be made to the specific interest.

There are several factors that may cause adjustments to net asset value, which measure the fair value of an interest in an alternative investment. In many circumstances significant time may have elapsed between the measurement date of the net asset value and the measurement date of the fair value of an interest in the alternative investment. Since the dates are different, then there may be changes in the fair value of the underlying assets of the portfolio, there may have been redemptions or distributions, general economic conditions may have changed, and the underlying asset mix of the portfolio may have changed.[4]

In other circumstances, the measurement standard may not be fair value as defined by FASB ASC 820 (SFAS 157). The fund may use different methods of accounting in calculating net asset values for redemption purpose than is used under *Fair Value Measurements and Disclosures*. For example, the fund may report debt at carrying value based on the original terms of the loan, which may not be at fair value as defined by the standard. Additionally, the specific rights and obligation of the alternative investment may impact the measurement of its fair value but may not be reflected in the net asset value of the portfolio of assets. If the underlying assets and liabilities are measured at standards other than fair value then further adjustments to the net asset value of the fund would be necessary before net asset value could be used as a proxy for fair value.

Features of an Alternative Investment

If net asset value is a starting point to measure the fair value of an interest in an alternative investment, then the features of the investment determine whether the fair value of the investment is equal to the net asset value, or at a premium to net asset value, or at a discount from net asset value. The AICPA's Draft Issue Paper segregates these features into two categories: (1) features that are considered in the initial due diligence of the investment and (2) those that are considered during the ongoing monitoring of the investment.

The features that a market participant would consider when acquiring an interest in the investment that may impact fair value are called due diligence features by the AICPA draft paper. Market participants consider the investment's due diligence features when determining what they would pay for the investment. As such, these due diligence features should be considered when determining whether the fair value of the interest would be equal to, at a premium to, or at a discount from net asset value.

The inclusion of each of these features both individually and collectively increases the risk of a market participant in an investment in the fund. Since a market participant would take these features into consideration when investing in a fund, these features should be considered when measuring the fair value of the interest. A perceived increase in risk would indicate that the investment would trade at a lower amount than its pro rata net asset value. Any perceived decrease in risk resulting from these features would indicate the interest would trade at a higher amount than its pro rata fair value.

Examples of Initial Due Diligence Features

Lock-Up Periods and Redemption Fees	Lock-up periods and redemption fees are sometimes included as part of the investment in an alternative. Lock-up periods are the amount of time that the investor must wait before redeeming the investment. The longer the lock-up period, the greater the risk to the market participant investor. Some funds allow an investor to redeem shares during a lock-up period if a fee is paid for the ability to redeem during this period.
Notice Periods	Notice period is the amount of time that any investor must give to the fund prior to redeeming shares in an alternative investment.
Holdbacks	During a redemption, the fund may retain the right to hold back a certain percentage of the redemption amount.
Suspension of Redemptions (sometimes referred to as "gates" in investment documents)	Some funds retain the right to suspend or defer redemptions. This right may impact fair value if it is likely the right may be exercised.
No Redemption Feature	Certain types of funds that invest in long-term assets with little liquidity, such as private equity, venture capital, and some real estate partnerships, may not allow investors to redeem their interest due to the lack of liquidity of the assets of these funds.
Approval of Fund Sponsor to Transfer Interests in the Investments	In most funds, investors may not transfer their interest without the written consent of the fund's management.
Use of Side Pockets	Side pockets are a way for redeemable funds to make investments in illiquid assets. Side pockets are separate accounts to track the investment in these illiquid assets. Any amount in the side pocket account cannot be redeemed until the illiquid asset is sold.[5]

Ongoing Monitoring Features

Other features that may influence the fair value of an investment in an alternative investment may occur after the initial investment. The AICPA draft paper refers to these features as ongoing monitoring features. Ongoing features are specific to different types of investments and may change as market conditions change. If these features are imposed by the fund's manager, then the fair value may not be equal to the net asset value since the net asset value likely does not reflect the risk of the investment in the portfolio. For example, the actual imposition of a gate (not just the ability to impose one) may change how a market participant would view the fair value of the investment. Or, for example, if there are many redemptions, the fund may be viewed by a market participants as having increasing risk since additional redemptions have the potential to create liquidity problems. Changes in general economic conditions may be another factor that may impact how market participants view the fair value of an alternative investment. Changes in general economic conditions may cause the fund to be unable to make additional profitable investments. Any other change in a market participant's perception of risk would likely impact the measurement of the interest's fair value.

Accounting Standards Update No. 2009–12, *Investments in Certain Entities That Calculated Net Asset Value per Share (or Its Equivalent)*

The purpose of Accounting Standards Update (ASU) No. 2009–12, *Investments in Certain Entities That Calculated Net Asset Value per Share (or Its Equivalent)*, is to provide additional authoritative guidance in applying the Statement 157 to investment companies and other forms of alternative investments. It provides guidance for measuring the fair value of investments in investment companies, which calculate net asset value under the AICPA's *Investment Companies Guide*. This Accounting Update is effective for interim and annual periods ending after December 15, 2009.

During its deliberations, the FASB noted that there are certain types of investments that allow investors to redeem or make distributions at the fund's net asset value. However, according to the AICPA's *Investment Companies Guide*, many of these funds are required to report net asset value by recording their underlying investments at fair value. The guide describes net asset value per share as follows:

> *Net asset value per share is the amount of net assets attributable to each share of capitals stock (other than senior equity securities, that is, preferred stock) outstanding at the close of the period. It excludes*

the effects of assuming conversion of outstanding convertible securities, whether or not their conversion would have a diluting effect. Net asset value per share should be disclosed for each class of shares.[6]

One of the issues is that investment in these types of funds are not traded on an exchange; thus they do not have a readily determinable fair value from market observations.

Prior to the implementation to FASB ASC 820, *Fair Value Measurements and Disclosures*, if there were no market observations, investors typically measured the fair value of their investments at their respective net asset value without any adjustments. In some circumstances, this made sense, particularly if the fund redeemed the investment at the respective net asset value. The problem arises when the investment has features that are not considered in net asset value that may change the risk of the investment and thus change how fair value would be viewed by a market participant.

In preparing this update, the FASB reviewed the AICPA's ASECS and Alternative Investments Tasks Force Draft Issues Paper, *FASB Statement No. 157 Valuation Considerations for Interest in Alternative Investments.* As discussed previously, the draft paper indicated that net asset value is a starting point when considering fair value of an alternative investment. However, it concluded that the investor must consider attributes and features of the investment to determine if an adjustment from net asset value should be considered when measuring fair value.

In the Proposed Financial Staff Position that was ultimately codified in ASU No. 2009–12, the FASB emphasized "that net asset value per share is the most relevant estimate of fair value available that would not require undue cost and effort for investments."[7] Furthermore, in the proposed FSP, the FASB determined that the fair value of an investment should be the net asset value per share with further adjustment if the net asset value per share is determined with AICPA *Audit and Accounting Guide, Investment Companies.*[8]

Requirements under ASU 2009–12

ASU 2009–12 applies to investments measured or disclosed at fair value when they do not have a readily determinable fair value and when they have investment activity, unit ownership, pooling of funds, and when the investment is the primary reporting entity. As a practical expedient, the update permits the reporting entity to measure the fair value of an investment on the basis of the net asset value per share. It requires disclosures about the following investment attributes by major category of investment:

- The nature of any restriction on the investor's ability to redeem the investment

- Any unfunded commitments
- The investment strategies

Major categories of investments are determined on the basis of the nature and the risks of the investment.[9]

Updated U.S. Private Equity Valuation Guidelines

The Private Equity Industry Guidelines Group (PEIGG) is a volunteer organization founded in 2002 to "debate and establish a set of reporting guidelines for the industry. Its mission is to promote increased reporting consistency and transparency while at the same time improving operating efficiency in the transfer of information among market participants by establishing a set of standard guidelines for the content, formatting and delivery of information."[10] The group is a combination of general partners, limited partners, and industry service providers of venture, buy-out, mezzanine, and other private equity investment firms that formed industry guidelines for the presentation of investments at fair value in financial reporting of private equity investment entities. The PEIGG is a volunteer organization, and while having widespread influence throughout the private equity industry, it is nonauthoritative.

The organization issued its first set of U.S. Private Equity Valuation Guidelines (Guidelines) in 2004 and updated them in 2007 for changes in fair value introduced by FASB ASC 820, *Fair Value Measurements and Disclosures* (SFAS 157).[11] The updated Guidelines are believed to be in conformance with fair value measurements under U.S. GAAP. Traditionally, the industry measured the value of investments either at the investment's cost or the implied value from the latest round of financing as an approximate to the fair value of the investment. The Guidelines provide a framework to measuring fair value using standard valuation approaches. However, after consideration of these approaches, the best indication of fair value still may be the cost or the value indicated by the most recent round of financing.

The PEIGG Guidelines note that the FASB's *Fair Value Measurements and Disclosures* describes three basic "techniques" to measure fair value. These techniques, more commonly known as approaches to value, are the cost, market, and income. Each of these techniques should be considered in the fair value measurement depending on the facts and circumstances of the interest being measured. The PEIGG Guidelines vary from this concept slightly by noting that the market approach using comparable company transactions or performance multiple inputs is the most appropriate for measuring the fair value of equity securities in private companies.[12] The guidelines do indicate that there are other methodologies under the cost and income approaches that may be appropriate in certain situations.

The guidelines note that the cost of the initial investment may be the investment's fair value (entrance versus exit price) since the fund making the investment typically considers near-term performance of the investment. However, certain factors such as related parties, duress, transaction costs, and different market conditions should be considered in measuring fair value since these factors may make the transaction not indicative of fair value concepts under FASB ASC 820. However, when there are additional rounds of financing for the investment, the fund should consider these rounds of financing when measuring fair value, even if the subject entity is not participating in the new financing. When the new round of financing is not yet complete, the pricing for the new round would be an indication of fair value if there is a high likelihood that it will be completed.

There are circumstances where the cost of the latest round of financing is not indicative of fair value. For example, as more time elapses from the most recent round of investment to the measurement date, the likelihood of a change in the investment's underlying economic circumstance increases. Naturally, company performance will be different than what was anticipated due to management's success or failure in implementing operating strategies and due to development of new technologies and/or products. Even the general market conditions for investment may have changed simply due to the passage of time. The more these conditions change then the less likely the cost of the latest round is determinative of current fair value of the investment.

Common Valuation Methodologies of Measuring the Fair Value of the Fund's Investment Portfolio

Most alternative investments funds such as private equity and venture capital funds invest in entities that are illiquid and considered by the fund to be a relatively long-term investment. When making the investment in a portfolio company, the fund's expectation is to provide the capital to support company growth to a point where the portfolio company can be sold through an initial public offering to another entity. The goal is to transform the portfolio company into an attractive acquisition target so that the investment fund exits profitably and is rewarded for the risk of the investment. The fair value of portfolio investment companies fund can be measured through methodologies under the three basic approaches to value: the cost, market, and income approaches discussed in previous chapters. However, due to the nature of portfolio investments and because portfolio investments are often in the early stage of their life cycle, certain valuation methodologies may be more appropriate than others when measuring fair value of the investment.

If there is an active industry market for the portfolio company, one method that may be appropriate for measuring the fair value is the guideline transaction method under the market approach. This method measures fair value through transactions of similar companies or investments in similar companies by unrelated third parties. The method uses the implied multiple from the pricing of the third-party transaction to some economic performance measure such as revenue or earnings before interest taxes, depreciation, and amortization (EBITDA), and applies the multiple to the same economic performance measure of the portfolio company as a measurement of its fair value.

Another method that may be used is the guideline public company method under the market approach. It is similar to the transaction method. Under this method, multiples of price to a certain economic performance measures of publicly traded companies are calculated. The multiples are then applied to the portfolio company to derive indications of the fair value of the investment. Under both transaction and public market methods, adjustments to the indicated multiple should be considered for differences in performance and relative risk of the fund's portfolio company.

Another commonly used method to estimate the fair value of an investment in a portfolio company is the discounted cash flow method (DCF) under the income approach. The DCF is often used in conjunction with one or both of the methods under the market approach or in circumstances where there may not be any comparable transactions or guideline public companies. The DCF is a particularly appropriate method in measuring the fair value of early-stage entities because the value from any future growth in cash flows is capture in the PFI. The discount rate used to discount the cash flows to the present should reflect the relative risk of the investment.

Conclusion

The implementation of fair value measurements in private equity and other alternative investments requires careful planning and attention to many different factors. There are two primary areas where fair value measurements impact investment funds. The first is in measuring the fair value of the portfolio assets themselves. Typically, traditional valuation methods under the three approaches to value can be used to measure the fair value of the portfolio investments. Prior to the implementation of FASB ASC 820, *Fair Value Measurements and Disclosures*, funds carried their investments at the cost of the investment unless there was an add-on investment, which provided a better indication of value.

The second area is measuring the fair value of the investors' interest in the fund. The AICPA recently issued a draft discussion paper, *Valuation*

Considerations for Interest in Alternative Investments, which provide guidance in measuring the fair value of the investors' interest in the fund. Traditionally, the fund's manager uses the net asset value as an indication of fair value when measuring an investor's pro rata interest in the fund. The AICPA paper notes that this may still be a good starting point if all the assets and liabilities of the fund have been appropriately measured at their respective fair values. However, the paper goes on to note that in measuring the fair value of an investor's interest, the fund should also take into consideration the features of the investment itself. These features may include such provisions as redemption rights, additional capital calls, lock-up periods, and others. The features of the particular investment affect that particular investments risk, thus its fair value.

As additional guidance, the FASB recently issued a proposed staff position, FSP FAS 157-g, "Estimating the Fair Value of Investments in Investment Companies That Have Calculated Net Asset Value per Share in Accordance with the AICPA Audit and Accounting Guide," *Investment Companies.* The proposed FSP suggests that net asset value may be an appropriate measure of the fair value of an investor's interest in the fund as long as the fund follows the AICPA's guidance in their draft paper when measuring fair value.

Finally, in addition to the accounting guidance, there are several organizations, such as the Private Equity Industry Guidelines Group, that issued guidelines as to the measurement of the value of underlying portfolio companies. The guidelines issued by the group were recently revised to conform to the FASB's requirements under FASB ASC 820, *Fair Value Measurements and Disclosures.*

Notes

1. Draft Issues Paper FASB Statement No. 157, *Valuation of Considerations for Interests in Alternative Investments*, AICPA, January 2009, page 2, www.aicpa.org.
2. Valuation Resource Group, July 2008, www.fasb.org.
3. Draft Issues Paper FASB Statement No. 157, *Valuation of Considerations for Interest in Alternative Investments*, AICPA, January 2009, page 10, www.aicpa.org.
4. *Id.*, page 12.
5. *Id.,* pages 14–17.
6. AICPA *Investment Companies Guide*, paragraph 7.39.
7. FSP FAS 157-g, paragraph 9, www.fasb.org.
8. *Id.*, A1.
9. Financial Accounting Standards Board, Accounting Standards Update No. 2009-12, *Investments in Certain Entities That Calculate Net Asset Value per Share (or Its Equivalent) to Topic 820*, September 2009, www.fasb.org, pp. 1–4.
10. www.peigg.org.
11. *Updated U.S. Private Equity Valuation Guidelines,* www.peigg.org.
12. *Id.*, paragraph 17.

CHAPTER 10

Fair Value Measurements under IFRSs

International Financial Reporting Standards (IFRSs) are accounting standards promulgated by the International Accounting Standards Board (IASB), an independent, privately funded standards setter whose goal is to provide the world's integrating capital markets with a common language for financial reporting. In 2001, the IASB replaced the International Accounting Standards Committee (IASC), the organization previously responsible for accounting standards primarily in the European Union. The IASB officially adopted the standards issued by the IASC, called International Accounting Standards (IAS). Thus, International Accounting Standards are the foundation of today's International Financial Reporting Standards. The European Union has officially adopted IFRSs and required publicly traded companies to use IFRSs for financial reporting beginning in 2005. Since the formation of the IASB in 2001, approximately 113 countries have adopted the standards to some extent. Several countries permit the use of IFRSs in some instances, and many are in the process of full convergence with IFRSs.[1,2]

Unlike U.S. Generally Accepted Accounting Principles (GAAP), IFRSs are based on principles rather than strict rules. Principles-based accounting permits a broader interpretation of accounting standards and it allows management to use more judgment in preparing financial statements that best represent the financial position of the entity. Since IFRSs require some assets and liabilities to be measured at fair value in certain circumstances, the concept of fair value measurement is clearly integral to the IASB's conceptual framework. In an effort to provide guidance so that preparers can improve the quality of fair value information included in their financial reports, the IASB has issued a discussion paper on the use of fair value measurements signaling its support for the concept. As a result of the IASB's acceptance of fair value measurement and as a result of the IASB's increasing global influence, fair value measurement is an increasingly important concept in international accounting standards.

Convergence of U.S. GAAP and IFRSs

As discussed in Chapter 1, the Financial Accounting Standards Board (FASB) in the United States and the IASB agreed to convergence of accounting standards in 2002. The agreement between the FASB and the IASB is called the Norwalk Agreement, named for the Connecticut town where the FASB is headquartered. In 2006, the boards jointly issued a Memorandum of Understanding in which "each acknowledged their commitment to the development of high quality, compatible accounting standards that could be used for both domestic and cross-border financial reporting. At that meeting, the FASB and the IASB pledged to use their best efforts (a) to make their existing financial reporting standards fully compatible as soon as is practicable and (b) to co-ordinate their future work programs to ensure that once achieved, compatibility is maintained."[3]

The Memorandum of Understanding between the FASB and IASB outlines the principles contained in the Norwalk Agreement. The principles are:

- Convergence of accounting standards can best be achieved through the development of high-quality, common standards over time.
- Trying to eliminate differences between two standards that are in need of significant improvement is not the best use of the FASB's and the IASB's resources—instead, a new common standard should be developed that improves the financial information reported to investors.
- Serving the needs of investors means that the boards should seek convergence by replacing standards in need of improvement with jointly developed new standards.[4]

In April 2008, the boards updated the Memorandum of Understanding to include milestones for 11 major joint projects in the convergence process. In 7 of the 11 joint projects, the boards have either issued common standards or are in the process of issuing common standards. The first common standard is *Business Combinations* issued by the FASB as SFAS 141(R) and by the IASB as Revised IFRS 3. Another of the projects is *Fair Value Measurements,* which was issued by the FASB in 2007 as FASB ASC 820, *Fair Value Measurements* (SFAS 157). The IASB issued a discussion paper in 2007, and after deliberations by the board, plans to issue a standard similar to SFAS 157.

As a result of the progress achieved by the boards toward convergence, the Securities and Exchange Commission (SEC) no longer requires reconciliation of IFRSs-based financial statement to U.S. GAAP for non-U.S. companies registered to issue securities in the United States. The European

Commission has a similar proposal for the European Union to eliminate the requirement to reconcile U.S. GAAP financial information to IFRSs, or to provide other compensating disclosures when U.S. companies have securities registered in European capital markets.[5] These developments effectively create two sets of somewhat similar but not completely convergent standards in the United States and Europe. These changes provide flexibility to foreign companies, but domestic corporations registered in the United States and the European Union currently do not have the ability to choose between the two sets of standards.

SEC Road Map to IFRSs

In 2008 the SEC issued a road map to advance the adoption of IFRSs for U.S.-based reporting entities, saying, "Because IFRSs has the greatest potential to become the global standard of accounting, we believe it is in the best interest of U.S. investors, U.S. issuers, and U.S. markets to consider mandating reporting under IFRSs in the United States as well."[6] The road map lists milestones to be achieved toward the goal of requiring that SEC registered companies use IFRSs for financial reporting purposes. If the milestones are met by 2011, the SEC plans to recommend the required use of IFRSs in a staged transition. Larger, accelerated filers would be required to use IFRSs for fiscal years ending on or after December 15, 2014. Accelerated filers would be required to use IFRSs in filing for fiscal years ending on or after December 15, 2015. Nonaccelerated filers, including smaller reporting companies, would be required to use IFRSs for fiscal years ending on or after December 15, 2016.[7] The SEC would like to see seven milestones accomplished before making its recommendation.

1. *Improvements in accounting standards.* The SEC supports the convergence process between the FASB and IASB outlined in the Norwalk agreement and the subsequent Memorandums of Understanding between the two boards. Under this first milestone, the SEC will evaluate the progress made by the boards in developing standards that are "high quality and sufficiently comprehensive."[8] The improvements are outlined in a joint work plan by the boards and are expected to be completed by 2011.
2. *Accountability and funding of the IASC Foundation.* The IASC Foundation is overseen by the IASC Foundation. Traditionally, the funding for the IASC has been on a voluntary basis from the participants in the capital markets, which have included companies, international organizations, central banks, and various governments. In 2006 the Trustees of

the IASC agreed to a plan to change the source of funding for the organization beginning in 2008. The new funding arrangement is supposed to be "broad based, compelling, open-ended, and country specific."[9] The plan includes levies to be paid by filers, imposed according to their home countries Gross National Product (GNP). The SEC also believes the IASC should have more oversight from securities authorities similar to the SEC's oversight of the FASB in the United States.

3. *Improvement in the ability to use interactive data for IFRSs reporting.* The SEC recently recommended that financial statement filers use eXensible Business Reporting Language (XBRL) to submit financial information to the SEC and to post information on corporate Web sites. XBRL will allow access to information in an interactive data format that will facilitate spreadsheet analysis and investment modeling. The SEC wants IFRSs financial statement preparers and users to have the ability to use a similar interactive data format.

4. *Education and training.* As U.S. GAAP is transitioned into IFRSs, the SEC recognizes that accountants, investors, auditors, and other users of the financial information will need to be retrained. Comprehensive IFRSs education would take place through professional organizations, colleges and universities, and government organizations, such as the Public Company Accounting Oversight Board (PCAOB). The SEC recognizes that this training effort would have to take place prior to the adoption of IFRSs in the United States.

5. *Allowance for limited early use of IFRSs where this would enhance comparability for U.S. investors.* The SEC has made several proposals for the early use of IFRSs by certain reporting entities where the adoption of IFRSs allows better comparison of financial data. One of the proposals allows U.S.-based entities to file early under IFRSs if the company is one of the 20 largest organizations with in its specific industry.

6. *Anticipated timing of future rulemaking by the commission.* The SEC plans to perform a comprehensive review of all SEC rules and to make recommendations for amendments to those rules so that IFRSs can be used for registration and reporting under the Exchange Act and the Securities Act. In addition, the Office of the Chief Accountant would need sufficient time to study the implications of IFRSs for investors and other market participants and to report its findings to the SEC.

7. *Implementation of the mandatory use of IFRSs.* The mandatory use of IFRSs would be implemented in stages, beginning in 2014. The SEC would require filers to provide three years of financial information in the first year of implementation. For example, large accelerated filers would be required to file financial statements using IFRSs for the fiscal years 2012 through 2014.[10]

The IASB's Fair Value Measurement Project

In November 2006 the IASB issued a discussion paper on fair value measurements in anticipation of eventually issuing an Exposure Draft of standards similar to the FASB's FASB ASC 820, *Fair Value Measurements* (SFAS 157). The Chairman of the IASB described the project by saying:

> *The use of fair value in financial reporting is of great interest to preparers, auditors, users and regulators. We believe that an essential ground-clearing step in the debate is to establish a clear international definition of fair value and a consistent framework for measuring it. This discussion paper is not about expanding the use of fair value in financial reporting, but about how to codify, clarify and simplify the guidance that is at present dispersed widely in IFRSs. We are therefore keen to receive views on the ideas set out in the paper.*[11]

The intent of the IASB's Fair Value Measurement Project is similar to the intent in FASB ASC 820, *Fair Value Measurements*. Both seek to clarify how to measure fair value consistently across all existing pronouncements, not to expand the use of fair value in financial reporting.

Based on the discussion paper and on comments letters received, the IASB plans to issue an Exposure Draft for a new fair value measurement standard during the second quarter of 2009. The IASB's Exposure Draft will address many of the same topics covered in the FASB's Statement on Fair Value Measurements, but the IASB's Exposure Draft is expected to have different wording and requirements. The objectives of the IASB's Fair Value Measurements project, however, are very similar to the FASB's objectives in issuing FASB ASC 820, *Fair Value Measurements*. The IASB's objectives are:

- To establish a single source of guidance for all fair value measurements required or permitted by existing IFRSs to reduce complexity and improve consistency in their application
- To clarify the definition of fair value and related guidance to communicate the measurement objective more clearly
- To enhance disclosures about fair value to enable users of financial statements to assess the extent to which fair value is used to measure assets and liabilities and to provide them with information about the inputs used to derive those fair values[12]

The IASB's Fair Value Measurement Project is a step toward the convergence of IASB and FASB standards, as was contemplated in the Memorandum of Understanding between the two governing bodies. In spite of the intent to reach convergence, there are some significant differences in fair value measurements between the IASB's project and the FASB's Statement, which are discussed in the following section.

Differences in the Definition of Fair Value

FASB ASC 820, *Fair Value Measurements* (SFAS 157), defines fair value as "the price that would be received to sell and asset or paid to transfer a liability in an orderly transaction between market participants at the measurement date"[13] This compares to IFRS's definition of fair value as "the amount for which an asset could be exchanged or a liability settled, between knowledgeable, willing parties in an arm's length transaction." There are three significant differences in the definitions of fair value between U.S. GAAP and IFRSs. The first difference is that fair value under FASB ASC 820, *Fair Value Measurements*, is an exit price, which is the price at which the asset can be sold or liability transferred. Under IFRSs, fair value is not defined as an exit price, nor is it defined as an entrance price (the price at which the asset is bought).

The second difference is that FASB ASC 820, *Fair Value Measurements*, refers to "market participants" where IFRSs refer to value from the perspective of "knowledgeable, willing parties in an arm's length transaction." The value perspective in IFRSs is similar to the concept of fair market value found in the U.S. Tax Code's Revenue Ruling 59-60.

The third difference in the two definitions relates to the fair value of liabilities. FASB ASC 820, *Fair Value Measurements*, describes the fair value of liabilities as the price at which the liability could be transferred. In other words, the obligation to the counterparty is assumed to continue. Under IFRSs, the fair value of liabilities is assumed to be a settlement amount between knowledgeable, willing parties in an arm's length transaction. The obligation to the counterparty does not continue; it is settled.[14]

TRANSACTION PRICE VERSUS FAIR VALUE AT INITIAL RECOGNITION FASB ASC 820, *Fair Value Measurements*, views an entry price and an exit price as different prices. In other words, the amount one would pay to buy an asset may not necessarily be equal to the amount one would receive when selling that asset to a market participant. The IASB considers the best evidence of fair value to be the transaction price. However, the IASB does recognize that there could be exceptions. Fair value may differ from the transaction price if there is evidence of fair value from other observable current market transactions for the same asset, or if there is evidence of fair value through the use of a financial model based solely on observable market inputs. The IASB discussion draft acknowledges two distinct views with respect to the appropriate fair value amount to initially recognize an asset or liability and seeks advice through the comment process.[15]

PRINCIPAL (OR MOST ADVANTAGEOUS) MARKET Under FASB ASC 820, *Fair Value Measurements*, there is an assumption that the measurement of fair value occurs through a sale to a market participant within the principal market, which is the market with the greatest volume for that particular asset or liability. In the absence of a principal market, the asset is assumed to be sold or the liability is assumed to be transferred in the most advantageous market, which is the market that would maximize the amount received or minimize the amount paid. Currently, IFRSs do not contain consistent guidance about the market assumption in fair value measurement. In the discussion draft, the IASB's Fair Value Measurement Project indicates that there is agreement with the market assumptions contained in FASB ASC 820, *Fair Value Measurements*.[16]

IN-USE VALUATION PREMISE VERSUS VALUE IN USE SFAS 157 assumes the highest and best use for an asset is "in-use" if the asset would provide maximum benefit to the owner through its use in combination with other assets as a group. Its fair value would be determined based on its sales price to a market participant as part of the group. The fair value is determined from the perspective of market participants. In contrast, the IASB refers to "value in use" as the asset's ability to generate cash for the entity, either on a stand-alone basis, or as part of an asset group. The asset's cash-generating value would be determined based on the amount, timing, and variation of expected future cash flows, the time value of money using an appropriate discount rate and other pertinent factors. The "value in use" is specific to the entity and is not a market-based measurement.[17]

IFRSs in Business Combinations and Impairment Testing

The application of fair value measurements to the assets and liabilities acquired in business combinations is one of the more common worldwide applications. According to the IASB's revised statement on Business Combinations, there were more than 13,000 merger and acquisition transactions worldwide in 2006. Almost half of the transaction value, approximately US$1.49 trillion, was reported using U.S. GAAP, while much of the remainder, about $1.82 trillion, was reported under IFRSs.[18] Consequently, one of the first Norwalk Agreement projects was to address the differences in accounting for business combinations under U.S. GAAP and IFRSs. The purpose of this initial convergence project was to increase the comparability of business combinations worldwide.

The revised IFRS 3, *Business Combinations*, incorporates several changes that bring the statement more in line with the FASB's FASB ASC 805, *Business Combinations* (SFAS 141(R)). In step acquisitions, goodwill is measured at the acquisition date as the difference between the fair value of the investment held before the acquisition, the fair value of the consideration transferred, and the fair value of the net assets acquired. If an acquirer obtains control without acquiring 100 percent of the equity of the entity, then the portion not acquired can be measured at fair value. Costs incurred to make the acquisition are expensed rather than capitalized.[19]

Differences between Revised IFRS 3 and SFAS 141(R)

Although revised IFRS 3 and FASB ASC 805, *Business Combinations* (SFAS 141(R)), were the first jointly issued statements by the IASB and the FASB and although most of the accounting requirements are the same, there are two differences with respect to accounting for business combinations. The first difference relates to noncontrolling interests. Revised IFRS 3 permits the measurement of the noncontrolling interest in the acquiree at either its fair value or at the value of its proportionate share of the acquirer's identifiable net assets. FASB ASC 805, *Business Combinations*, requires the noncontrolling interest in an acquiree to be measured at fair value.

The other difference between the two statements relates to three disclosure items. FASB ASC 805, *Business Combinations*, and IFRS 3 have different definitions of control because of differences in consolidation standards between the two boards. As discussed above, revised IFRS 3 uses an exchange value and U.S. GAAP uses an exit value to determine fair value. Initially, the statements had slightly different criteria for the initial measurement and recognition of contingent assets and liabilities. IFRS 3 recognizes contingencies when they can be reliably measured, but SFAS 141(R) uses a "more likely than not" criteria for recognition.

However, the FASB subsequently revised the accounting for contingent assets and liabilities arising in a business combination with the issuance of FASB FSP 141(R)-1. Now, the fair value of the contingent asset or liability is measured at fair value when it is probable that the contingent asset or liability had been incurred at the measurement date and when the fair value can be reasonably estimated under the guidance in Statement 5.[20]

Differences between GAAP and IFRS in Testing Goodwill and Other Intangible Assets for Impairment

As discussed in Chapter 2, the accounting requirements for goodwill and intangible assets with indefinite lives are outlined in FASB ASC 350,

Intangibles—Goodwill and Other (SFAS No. 142). Under SFAS 142, goodwill acquired through a business combination is assigned to specific relevant reporting unit(s) for annual impairment testing. If certain "triggering events" occur, goodwill must be tested for impairment immediately.

Goodwill impairment testing is a two-step process under FASB ASC 350, *Intangibles—Goodwill and Other Intangibles*. The first step is to compare the reporting unit's test date fair value to its carrying value. If the fair value of the reporting unit is greater than its carrying value, then goodwill is not considered to be impaired and the carrying amount of goodwill on the balance sheet does not have to be written down. However, if the fair value of the reporting unit is less than its carrying value, then the second step is performed to quantify the possible goodwill impairment.

The second step is a comparison of the implied fair value of goodwill on the test date to the carrying amount of goodwill. Implied goodwill is measured using a process similar to the measurement of goodwill in a business combination. The fair value of the implied goodwill is equal to the difference between the fair value of the reporting unit and the sum of the fair values of all of the other assets that exist on the measurement date, whether previously recognized. If the fair value of the implied goodwill is less than its carrying amount, the difference is recognized as impaired and is written off.

FAS 142 is silent as to exactly what interest in the reporting unit should be tested for impairment. There are differences in interpretation as to whether the fair value of the reporting unit relates to its equity, its invested capital, or its net assets. The interest selected for testing may have an impact on whether the reporting unit passes the first impairment testing step. Most valuation specialists believe that the appropriate interest is the reporting unit's invested capital because testing at the invested capital level provides a more comprehensive view of the entity's ownership interest. The entity's assets are financed by some mix of both debt and equity. The economic balance sheet in Chapter 3 provides a graphic illustration of this point. The economic balance sheet shows the fair value of the entity's assets on the left-hand side (starting with debt-free working capital and ending with goodwill) and the right-hand side of the balance sheet represents the fair value of the capital provided and typically includes both short-term and long-term interest-bearing debt and equity.

Under IFRS, testing goodwill for impairment is slightly different. Goodwill is assigned to a cash-generating unit (CGU) or allocated among a group of CGUs at initial recognition. IAS 36 describes a CGU as "the smallest identifiable group of assets that generates cash inflows that are largely independent of the cash inflows from other assets or groups of assets."[21] Testing for impairment under IAS 36 utilizes a one-step approach rather than the two-step process required under FASB ASC 350, *Intangibles—Goodwill and*

Other Intangibles. The IAS 36 test is a comparison of the estimated recoverable amount of the CGU or Group of CGUs to the carrying amount of the CGU or Group of CGUs. The recoverable amount is the higher of the CGU's fair value less cost to sell or the CGU's value in use.

Fair value less costs to sell is best exemplified by a binding agreement to sell the asset in an arm's-length transaction adjusted for costs that would be incurred to dispose the assets. If there is no binding agreement, but a similar asset is traded in an active market, then the fair value less costs to sell would equal the similar asset's trading price less costs to dispose of the asset. In absence of either a binding agreement or a trading price for a similar asset, fair value less costs to sells is estimated based on the best information available about the amount the entity could obtain in an arm's-length transaction after deducting the costs of disposal. The arm's-length transaction is assumed to be between willing, knowledgeable parties and is not assumed to be a forced sale, unless management is under some compulsion to sell immediately.[22]

Fair value less costs to sell is compared to value in use to estimate the recoverable amount under the standard. Value in use can be thought of as a value determined through a form of discounted cash flow analysis related to the asset or group of assets. IAS 36 describes estimating the future net cash flows to be derived from the asset's continued use. The cash flows include an amount from its ultimate disposal. An appropriate risk adjusted discount rate is applied to the future cash flows to compensate for the risk associated with the receipt of the cash flows. Certain elements should be reflected in the value in use, including:

- Estimate of future cash flows derived from the asset
- Expectation about variation in the amount of cash flows and their timing
- The time value of money as reflected in the risk-free rate
- The price for the risk of uncertainty in receiving the cash flows

Other factors, such as the asset's lack of liquidity, that market participants would consider when pricing the asset's expected future cash flows should also be reflected in value.[23] It is noteworthy to point out that estimates of future cash flows under IAS 36 do not include *cash inflows or outflows from financing activities or income tax receipts or payments.*[24] (Emphasis added.)

An impairment loss is recognized if the recoverable amount of an asset is less than its carrying amount. The difference represents the amount of impairment, and the carrying amount is reduced to its recoverable amount. The impairment is allocated to the carrying amounts of the CGU by first allocating to goodwill until it is depleted, and then to the other assets of the CGU on a pro rata basis.[25]

A significant difference between GAAP and IFRS is the subsequent treatment of impairment losses. Under IFRS, impairment losses may be reversed in subsequent periods if certain conditions are met. If there has been a change in the estimates that were used in determining the asset's recoverable amount since the impairment loss was originally taken, then revised estimates can be used to recalculate a new recoverable amount. The carrying amount can be adjusted to the new recoverable amount. For an individual asset, the new carrying amount cannot exceed the original carrying amount prior to the recognition of the impairment loss. Similarly, an impairment loss to a CGU can be reversed by allocating the adjustment to the recoverable amount on a prorate basis to the assets of the carrying unit. Although IAS 38 generally allows the reversal of impairment losses, it does not permit the reversal of impairment losses to goodwill.[26] U.S. GAAP does not permit the reversal of impairment losses due to a subsequent recovery for any asset.

IAS 38 Intangible Assets

IAS 38 provides guidance about when to recognize and how to measure intangible assets that do not fall under any other International Accounting Standards. The statement defines an intangible asset as:

> *an identifiable non-monetary asset without physical substance. An intangible asset is a resource that is controlled by the enterprise as a result of past events (purchase or self-creation) and from which future economic benefits are expected. The three critical attributes of an intangible asset are identifiability, control (power to obtain benefits from the asset) and the existence of future economic benefits (such as revenues or reduced future costs).[27]*

IAS 38 has the same two criteria for determining whether an intangible asset is identifiable that FASB ASC 805, *Business Combinations* (SFAS 141(R)), has. Intangible assets are considered identifiable when they are separable or when they arise from contractual or other legal rights. One significant difference between the IASB and FASB treatment of intangible assets is their recognition criteria. IAS 38 requires an entity to recognize an intangible asset if it is probable that the future economic benefits that are attributable to the asset will be received by the entity and if the cost of the asset can be measured reliably. Intangible assets are recognized under IAS 38 whether they are purchased or self-created.[28]

IAS 38 incorporates the criteria for recognition of an intangible asset in a business combination from the revised IFRS 3. The statement assumes that the existence of future economic benefits is inherently probable for an intangible asset identified in business combination.

Internally Generated Intangible Assets

Under U.S. GAAP, research and development costs are expensed as incurred with a few expectations. One exception is the treatment of software development costs for products to be sold to third parties. Another exception is the treatment of software developed for internal use. The costs that can be capitalized differ for each type of software.[29] Except for these limited situations, internally generated intangible assets are not capitalized under U.S. GAAP.

Under IFRSs, costs incurred in the creation of intangible assets are separated into two classes: research and development. Costs associated with research are expensed. Costs associated with development are capitalized if all of the following criteria are met:

- The intangible asset is technically feasible.
- The entity intends to complete the development of the intangible asset.
- The entity developing the intangible asset has the ability to use or sell the asset to a third party.
- The entity has a plan to receive future economic benefits from the intangible asset once developed.
- The entity has sufficient resources to complete the development.
- There is an ability to track expeditors related to the development of the intangible asset.[30]

There are some exceptions to the rules for capitalizing internally generated intangible assets under IFRSs. Certain internally generated assets such as mastheads, publishing titles, customer lists, and similar items are believed to be undistinguishable from the business as a whole and the cost of developing them cannot be capitalized.[31]

Impairment of Intangible Assets Held for Use

Under U.S. GAAP the impairment of long-lived assets falls under FASB ASC 350-30 (SFAS No. 144) if the asset is held for use by the entity and it is currently being depreciated or amortized. The test for impairment is simply to compare the sum of future undiscounted cash flows associated with the asset to the asset's carrying value. If the sum of undiscounted cash flows is greater than the carrying value, the long-lived asset is not assumed to be impaired. If the sum of the undiscounted cash flows is less than the carrying value, then the asset is assumed to be impaired. When impairment exists, the fair value of the intangible asset is determined through standard valuation techniques for fair value as described in FASB ASC 820, *Fair Value Measurements* (SFAS 157). The impairment is an amount equal to the difference between the asset's carrying value and its fair value.

IAS 36, *Impairment of Assets*, describes the accounting treatment for the potential impairment of assets, particularly the subsequent accounting treatment of those assets recognized in a business combination. IFRSs have a different impairment test for assets held for use by the entity. IAS 36 calls for a one-step impairment test where the carrying amount of an asset is compared with the recoverable amount of the asset. IFRS 36 describes the recoverable amount as the higher of the fair value of the asset less costs to sell, or the asset's value in use.

The IAS 36 concept of recoverability as the "fair value less cost to sell" does not have a counterpart within FASB statements. Fair value less cost to sell is the "the amount obtainable form the sale of an asset or cash-generating unit in an arm's length transaction between knowledgeable, willing parties less the costs of disposal."[32] An example of a recoverable amount would be the price contained in a binding sale agreement that is an arm's-length transaction, adjusted for incremental costs related to the sale of the asset.[33]

"Value in use" would be determined using a discounted cash flow model. The calculation would include an estimate of future cash flows attributable to the asset and it would include expectations about possible variations in the amount or timing or the future cash flows (i.e., it would assign probabilities to those cash flows). The calculation of "value in use" would also consider the time value of money by estimating the risk-free rate and an additional risk premium for uncertainly inherent in the asset.

International Valuation Standards Council

The International Valuation Standards Council (IVSC) is an independent not-for-profit private organization whose objectives are to:

- Create and ensure an independent and transparent international valuation standards setting process
- Develop and maintain a highly effective comprehensive set of high-quality international valuation standards that are understandable, practical to implement, and protect the public interest
- Identify where local or regional standards differ from the international valuation standards, and work toward greater compatibility and harmonization between local or regional requirements and the International Valuation Standards

- Contribute to the development of the global valuation profession and protect the public interest by encouraging high-quality best practices by the global valuation profession
- Be the international voice of the valuation profession[34]

The IVSC was formed more than 25 years ago as an unincorporated association of valuation organizations under a single constitution. In 2003 the IVSC was incorporated in the United States as a not-for-profit entity, although its headquarters is in London, England. Currently the IVSC represents more than 50 countries with professional valuation organizations that have member or observer status. The Appraisal Institute, which is the credentialing body for real estate appraisers, and the American Society of Appraisers, a multidisciplinary appraisal origination, are members representing the United States.

International Valuation Standards

The IVSC was formed because professional bodies from around the world realized that there needs to be uniformity in valuation approaches used in real estate markets. The first IVSC standards were for the valuation of real property. In the last 10 years, the IVSC standards have evolved and expanded to include many types of assets, including machinery and equipment, intangible assets, and interests in business enterprises. The IVSC has created standards for specific purposes, such as financial reporting and lending by financial institutions. In 2007 the IVSC established a Critical Review Group to review all existing standards. The IVSC also radically restructured its organization. The goal was to transform the IVSC into an organization with robust and open procedures for setting and interpreting international valuation and reporting standards. The IVSC envisions its role in shaping valuation standards as similar to the IASB's role in shaping international accounting standards. In describing the organization's goals, Michel Prada, the new chairman of the restructured organization, said:

> Now more than ever, there is a global need for clarity around valuation standards, across all business sectors. Standardized valuation, delivered under the auspices of an independent and global body, is vital for reducing investment risk, adding confidence to financial reporting, and providing a consistent approach to portfolio and asset valuation . . . Unless such standards are established through a strong global standard setter there is a . . . (risk of) . . . ending up with multiple sets of standards—for different asset classes and for different purposes. The IVSC intends to work in close cooperation with other standard setters and international regulatory organizations.[35]

IFRS for Small and Medium Size Entities (SME)

On July 9, 2009, the IASB issued IFRS for Small and Medium Size Entities. The purpose of the statements are to simplify accounting standards for smaller and medium-size entities. The statements however are applicable to any privately held entity. IFRS for SMEs continues to extend fair value accounting to smaller and medium-sized entities with a few simplifying concepts. SME does still have to record identifiable assets at their respective fair values in business combinations, for example. The identified assets are amortized over their useful life, *including goodwill*. If the useful life cannot be determined then the identified assets and goodwill are amortized over ten years. Intangible assets are considered impaired if their recoverable amount is less than their carrying amount. The recoverable amount is the greater of fair value less cost to sell and value in use. If the circumstances that led to impairment no longer exist, then the impairment is reverse.[36]

Conclusion

U.S. GAAP is well on its way toward converging into International Financial Reporting Standards. The convergence into IFRS is being directed by the FASB through the Convergence Project and by the SEC through its oversight of the FASB and through its recent issuance of the Roadmap to Convergence for public registrants. The IASB and FASB are issuing accounting pronouncements jointly, including those that require fair value measurement. However, there are still some differences. As convergence progresses, preparers of financial statements using fair value measurement will need to understand the impact of the differences between the two sets of standards.

Notes

1. "Who We Are and What We Do," International Accounting Standards Board, www.iasb.org (accessed April 22, 2009).
2. "Roadmap for the Potential Use of Financial Statements Prepared in Accordance with International Financial Reporting Stands by U.S. Issuers," Securities and Exchange Commission Release No. 33-8982, www.sec.gov (accessed April 21, 2009).
3. Completing the February 2006 "Memorandum of Understanding: A Progress Report and Timetable for Completion," (September 2008). IASB www.iasb.org (accessed April 21, 2009).
4. *Id.*
5. *Id.*

6. "Roadmap for the Potential Use of Financial Statements Prepared in Accordance with International Financial Reporting Stands by U.S. Issuers," Securities and Exchange Commission Release No. 33-8982, www.sec.gov, page 33 (accessed April 21, 2007).
7. *Id.,* page 35.
8. *Id.,* page 23.
9. "Who We Are and What We Do," International Accounting Standards Board, www.iasb.org (accessed April 23, 2009).
10. "Roadmap for the Potential Use of Financial Statements Prepared in Accordance with International Financial Reporting Stands by U.S. Issuers," Securities and Exchange Commission Release No. 33-8982, www.sec.gov, pages 20–37 (accessed April 21, 2009).
11. Discussion Paper on Fair Value Measurements, IASB, www.iasb.org (accessed April 24, 2009).
12. "Fair Value Measurement: Where Are We in the Project," IASB, www.iasb.org (accessed April 21, 2009).
13. SFAS 157 *Fair Value Measurements,* paragraph 5.
14. Discussion Paper, "Fair Value Measurements Part 1: Invitation to Comment and relevant IFRS guidance," IASB, November 2006, page 8.
15. *Id.,* pages 15–16.
16. *Id.,* page 18.
17. *Id.,* page 21.
18. International Accounting Standards Board, "Business Combinations Phase II Project Summary and Feedback Statement," January 2008, page 4, www.iasb.com (accessed April 20, 2009).
19. *Id.,* page 9.
20. *Id.,* page 10.
21. IAS 36, paragraph 6.
22. *Id.,* paragraphs 25–28.
23. *Id.,* paragraph 30.
24. *Id.,* paragraph 50.
25. *Id.,* paragraph 104.
26. *Id.,* paragraphs 117–125.
27. IAS 38, paragraph 8.
28. *Id.,* paragraph 21.
29. FASB ASC 350-40-25-2.
30. IAS 38.
31. *Id.*
32. IAS 36, paragraph 6.
33. *Id.,* paragraph 25.
34. "About the International Standards Valuation Council (IVSC)," www.ivsc.org (accessed May 1, 2009).
35. "Global Standards for Valuation Process Reach New Phase," Press Release 3, March 2009, www.ivsc.org (accessed May 1, 2009).
36. International Accounting Standards Board, *International Financial Reporting Standards for Small and Medium-Sized Entities,* July 2009.

CHAPTER 11

Disclosures in Fair Value Measurements

Introduction

Financial statement disclosures consist of footnotes and other supplementary information that accompany financial statements. Footnotes are an integral part of financial statements that provide additional information to the users of the financial statements. Disclosures are required by various Financial Accounting Standards Board (FASB) standards. One of the purposes of disclosures is to provide information about accounting methods, assumptions, and estimates. This additional information is included in footnotes to provide users with information so that they can assess the amounts, timing, and uncertainty of estimates incorporated into the financial statements.

The Security and Exchange Commission (SEC) also requires disclosures to increase the transparency of financial statements in public filings. Public registrants also provide other supplementary information in their financial reporting that is contained in public companies' 10-Q quarterly reports and 10-K annual reports as required by the SEC. The supplementary information required by the SEC includes management's discussion and analysis ("MD&A"), information about the lines of business of the entity, any legal proceedings, changes in auditors, as well as supplemental schedules for such things as bad debt reserves, valuation allowances, real estate, accumulated depreciation, and mortgage loans.[1]

Finally, the Sarbanes-Oxley Act of 2002 requires enhanced financial disclosures for material off-balance sheet liabilities, obligations, or transactions, and for material correcting adjustments identified by the company's auditors. Sarbanes-Oxley also imposes the requirement that management furnish a financial statement certification and a report that addresses the adequacy and effectiveness of internal controls supporting financial reporting.[2]

Thanks to Lynn Pierson for her assistance in developing this chapter.

The Role of Disclosures

Financial statements are the primary source of information that an investor relies on to assess an investment's potential reward and risk. Disclosures are considered by the FASB as an integral part of an entity's financial statements. Disclosures supplement the information contained within financial statements by providing additional transparency for the investor's benefit. A discussion about information provided by financial statements should include a discussion about the information contained in the disclosures in the statements.

The CFA Institute Center for Financial Market Integrity (CFA Center) is a worldwide organization that represents investment portfolio managers, investment analysts, and investment advisors. Its mission "is to promote fair and transparent global capital markets and to advocate for investor protections."[3] One of the CFA Center's primary goals is to promote high-quality financial reporting and disclosures that benefit investors.

In *A Comprehensive Business Reporting Model: Financial Reporting for Investors,* the CFA Center discusses the role of financial statements and disclosures by noting:

> *Corporate financial statements and their related disclosures are fundamental to sound investment decision making. The well-being of the world's financial markets, and of the millions of investors who entrust their financial present and future to those markets, depends directly on the information financial statements and disclosures provide. Consequently, the quality of the information drives global financial markets. The quality, in turn, depends directly on the principles and standards managers apply when recognizing and measuring economic activities and events affecting their companies' operations.*
>
> *Financial statements should serve the needs of those who provide capital to a company and bear risk as a result; common shareowners are the residual risk bearers in a company. Hence we believe that one of the primary objectives of financial reporting and disclosure must be to provide all of the information that the owners of common equity require to evaluate their investments. Common shareowners use information to make forecasts of future cash flows, evaluate the sustainability of the company's business model, and assess its cash-generating ability. This information is used to estimate the investment's value and its future value.*[4]

The purpose of financial statement disclosures is to complement financial statements so that when considered together, there is sufficient information for an investor to determine the value of the investment and the future potential of that investment. As described by the CFA Center, value is the key consideration in the decision-making process of current and future investors.

In addition, the CFA Center is also a strong advocate of fair value measurement in financial reporting and a critic of today's mixed-attribute reporting model that combines items measured at historic cost and those measured at fair value in the same report. The CFA Center cites the mixed-attribute reporting model as a source of complexity in financial reporting, saying that such reports do not reflect the underlying business economics. In addition, the lack of adequate disclosures for items reported at historical costs hampers analysts' ability to fully utilize valuation models to make investment decisions. The CFA Center blames the mixed-attribute system for undermining comparability among entities and confounding investor's abilities to discern the effects of and exposures to market price changes. The CFA Center's goal is to move financial reporting to a model based on fair value measurements that will improve transparency in both measurement and disclosure.[5]

Disclosures under FASB ASC 820, *Fair Value Measurements and Disclosures* (SFAS No. 157)

In the introductory summary of FASB ASC 820, *Fair Value Measurements and Disclosures* (SFAS No. 157), the FASB says that the statement will improve financial reporting by expanding fair value measurement disclosures and provide financial statement users with better information about the extent to which fair value measurements are used to measure recognized assets and liabilities, the inputs used to develop the measurements, and the effect of certain measurements on earnings (or changes in assets) for the period.[6] Understanding the extent to which fair value measurement is used to recognize assets and liabilities in the financial statements is particularly important because not all of the assets and liabilities recognized in U.S. Generally Accepted Accounting Principles (GAAP) financial statements are recorded at fair value. Some are reported at historical cost and some are reported at fair value in a mixed-attribute reporting system. The mixed-attribute reporting system is even further complicated by companies' ability to select fair value measurement on an asset-by-asset basis under SFAS No. 159, *Fair Value Option for Financial Assets and Liabilities.*

Disclosure of the inputs used to develop fair value measurements is accomplished using the fair value hierarchy to categorize inputs into groups based on the extent to which they are observable in the marketplace. Recall that Level 1 inputs are based on quoted prices in active markets for identical assets. Level 2 inputs are based on market-corroborated information. These inputs can be based on indirectly observable market data or direct quotes for similar assets. Level 3 inputs are unobservable inputs used when other forms of observable data are not available. These inputs are developed based on the best information available and can include the reporting unit's own data. Full disclosure of the inputs to fair value measurement allows investors to understand the nature and relative objectivity of those measures.

Finally, improved disclosures allow the investor to understand how changes in fair value measurements flow through the entity's financial statements. Changes in fair value from one reporting period to the next create unrealized gains and losses, which can be included in earnings or they can flow through equity as comprehensive income. Gains and losses can also be realized through the sale of an asset, investment, reporting unit, or entity.

Required Disclosures

Under *Fair Value Measurements and Disclosures,* the purpose of disclosures is to provide users of financial statements with information to assess the inputs used to develop the fair value measurement. Inputs to the measurement of fair value are categorized into Levels 1, 2, and 3 based on their relative marketplace observability. And assets and liabilities are either measured on a recurring basis or a nonrecurring basis subsequent to their initial recognition. Under FASB ASC 820, the required disclosures depend on whether the assets or liability is measured on a recurring or nonrecurring basis. Trading securities would be an example of an asset measured on a recurring basis, while impaired assets would be an example of an asset measured on a nonrecurring basis.

Recurring Measurements

In addition to providing financial statement users with information to assess the inputs to a fair value measurement, disclosures for Level 3 recurring fair value measurements allow users of financial statements to understand how changes in the net assets' fair value is reflected in earnings. The following disclosures are required for assets and liabilities measured on a recurring basis. They are required in each interim and annual period, and for each major category of asset and liability.

- The fair value measurements at the reporting date
- The level within the fair value hierarchy in which the fair value measurements in their entirety fall, segregating fair value measurements by level

- For fair value measurements using significant Level 3 inputs, a reconciliation of the beginning and ending balances, separately presenting changes attributable to:
  - Total gains or losses for the period (realized and unrealized), segregating those included in earnings (or changes in net assets) and a description of where they are reported in the income statement
  - Purchases, sales, issuances, and settlements, net
  - Transfers in and out of Level 3
- The amount of total gains or losses for the period from above included in earnings (or changes in net assets) that are attributable to the change in unrealized gains or losses relating to those assets and liabilities still held at the reporting date and a description of where those unrealized gains or losses are reported in the statement of income
- In annual reports, disclose the valuation techniques used to measure fair value and a discussion of changes of valuation techniques, if any[7]

Exhibit 11.1 shows the quantitative, tabular disclosures required for all assets measured at fair value on a recurring basis. Exhibit 11.2 provides an example of the additional required disclosures for Level 3 assets measured at fair value on a recurring basis. Any quantitative disclosures for recurring fair value measurements should be made in a tabular format. Similar schedules would be required for any liabilities measured at fair value on a recurring basis.[8]

EXHIBIT 11.1 Assets Measured at Fair Value on a Recurring Basis

($ in 000s)		Fair Value Measurements at Reporting Date Using		
Description	12/31/X1	Quoted Prices in Active Markets for Identical Assets (Level 1)	Significant Other Observable Inputs (Level 2)	Significant Unobservable Inputs (Level 3)
Trading securities	$345	$315	$30	
Available-for-sale securities	225	225		
Derivatives	180	75	45	$60
Venture captial investments	30			30
Total	$780	$615	$75	$90

EXHIBIT 11.2 Assets Measured at Fair Value on a Recurring Basis Using Significant Unobservable Inputs (Level 3)

($ in 000s)	Fair Value Measurements Using Significant Unobservable Inputs (Level 3)		
	Derivatives	Venture Capital Investments	Total
Beginning balance	$42	$33	$75
Total gains or losses (realized / unrealized)			
Included in earnings (or changes in net assets)	33	(9)	24
Included in other comprehensive income	12		12
Purchases, issuances, and settlements	(21)	6	(15)
Transfers in and/or out of Level 3	(6)		(6)
Ending balance	$60	$30	$90
The amount of total gains or losses for the period included in earnings (or changes in net assets) attributable to the change in unrealized gains or losses relating to assets still held at the reporting date	$21	$6	$27

Gains and losses (realized and unrealized) included in earnings (or changes in net assets) for the period (above) are reported in trading revenues and in other revenues as follows:

	Trading Revenues	Other Revenues
Total gains or losses included in earnings (or changes in net assets) for the period (above)	$33	($9)
Change in unrealized gains or losses relating to assets still held at reporting date	$21	$6

Nonrecurring Measurements

For assets and liabilities measured on a nonrecurring basis after initial recognition, the following should be disclosed for each annual and interim period and for each major category of assets and liabilities:

- The fair value measurements recorded during the period and the reasons for the measurement
- The level within the fair value hierarchy in which the fair value measurements in their entirety fall, segregating fair value measurements by level
- For Level 3 measurements, a description of the inputs and the information used to develop inputs
- In annual reports, disclose the valuation techniques used to measure fair value and a discussion of changes of valuation techniques, if any

Any quantitative disclosures for nonrecurring fair value measurements should be made in a tabular format.[9] Exhibit 11.3 provides an example of the tabular disclosure required for nonrecurring fair value measurements.[10]

EXHIBIT 11.3 Assets Measured at Fair Value on a Nonrecurring Basis

($ in 000s)		Fair Value Measurements Using			
Description	12/31/X1	Quoted Prices in Active Markets for Identical Assets (Level 1)	Significant Other Observable Inputs (Level 2)	Significant Unobservable Inputs (Level 3)	Total Gains (Losses)
Long-lived assets held and used	$225		$225		($75)
Goodwill	90			90	(105)
Long-lived assets held for sale	78		78		(45)
					($225)

In accordance with the provisions of Statement 144, long-lived assets held and used with a carrying amount of $300 million were written down to their fair value of $225 million, resulting in an impairment charge of $75 million, which was included in earnings for the period.

In accordance with the provisions of Statement 142, goodwill with a carrying amount of $195 million was written down to its implied fair value of $90 million, resulting in an impairment charge of $105 million, which was included in earnings for the period.

In accordance with the provisions of Statement 144, long-lived assets held for sale with a carrying amount of $105 million were written down to their fair value of $78 million, less cost to sell of $18 million (or $60 million), resulting in a loss of $45 million, which was included in earnings for the period.

Fair Value Disclosures in Business Combinations and in Subsequent Impairments of Goodwill and Other Intangibles

FASB ASC 850, *Business Combinations* (SFAS No.141(R)), and FASB ASC 350-20-35, *Goodwill and Other Intangible Assets, Subsequent Measurement* (SFAS No. 142), require the disclosures of fair value information for just a few specific situations. *Business Combinations* requires the disclosure of the acquisition date fair value of the total consideration transferred to the seller and the fair value of each major class of consideration transferred. When the acquirer holds less than 100 percent of the acquiree, then the fair value of the noncontrolling interest, the valuation technique, and significant inputs used to measure the fair value of the noncontrolling interest must be disclosed. When a business combination is achieved in stages, the fair value of the equity interest should be disclosed along with any gain or loss recognized resulting from the remeasurement of the equity interest. Finally, the fair value of certain acquired receivables must be disclosed.

Goodwill and Other Intangible Assets requires fair value disclosures when impairment losses are recognized. When a goodwill impairment loss is recognized, the amount of the impairment loss and the method of determining the fair value of the associated reporting unit must be disclosed. The disclosure should specify whether the fair value of the reporting unit is determined based on quoted market prices, prices of comparable businesses, a present value or other valuation technique, or a combination of valuation techniques. When an impairment loss is recognized for an intangible asset, the amount of the impairment loss and the method for determining the fair value of the intangible asset must be disclosed.

Although the specific fair value disclosures required by the accounting standards for business combinations and goodwill and intangible asset impairments are somewhat limited, the disclosure requirements of FASB ASC 820, *Fair Value Measurements and Disclosures* (SFAS No. 157), apply to business combinations and impairments. Business combinations and impairments result in the measurement of assets and liabilities at fair value on a nonrecurring basis during the period; therefore, the "nonrecurring" disclosure requirements of *Fair Value Measurements and Disclosures* should be applied.

As an example of required disclosures in fair value measurements, Delta Airlines' SEC Form 10-K for 2008 presents required fair value measurement disclosures in Note 3. The footnote provides separate sections for assets and liabilities measured at fair value on a recurring basis and a nonrecurring basis. Delta merged with Northwest Airlines in 2008. It also recognized impairment losses on goodwill and other intangible assets during the year. As a result, its fair value measurement footnote provides a comprehensive example of the application of FASB ASC 820 to a business combination and to impairment losses. Exhibit 11.4 shows Delta's

EXHIBIT 11.4 Note 3. Fair Value Measurements

Upon emerging from bankruptcy, we adopted SFAS 157, "Fair Value Measurements" ("SFAS 157"), which defines fair value, establishes a consistent framework for measuring fair value and expands disclosure for each major asset and liability category measured at fair value on either a recurring or nonrecurring basis. SFAS 157 clarifies that fair value is an exit price, representing the amount that would be received to sell an asset or paid to transfer a liability in an orderly transaction between market participants. As such, fair value is a market-based measurement that should be determined based on assumptions that market participants would use in pricing an asset or liability. As a basis for considering such assumptions, SFAS 157 establishes a three-tier fair value hierarchy, which prioritizes the inputs used in measuring fair value as follows:

- *Level 1.* Observable inputs such as quoted prices in active markets;
- *Level 2.* Inputs, other than the quoted prices in active markets, that are observable either directly or indirectly; and
- *Level 3.* Unobservable inputs in which there is little or no market data, which require the reporting entity to develop its own assumptions.

Assets and liabilities measured at fair value are based on one or more of three valuation techniques noted in SFAS 157. The three valuation techniques are identified in the tables below. Where more than one technique is noted, individual assets or liabilities were valued using one or more of the noted techniques. The valuation techniques are as follows:

a) *Market approach.* Prices and other relevant information generated by market transactions involving identical or comparable assets or liabilities.
b) *Cost approach.* Amount that would be required to replace the service capacity of an asset (replacement cost).
c) *Income approach.* Techniques to convert future amounts to a single present amount based on market expectations (including present value techniques, option-pricing and excess earnings models).

Assets and Liabilities Measured at Fair Value on a Recurring Basis

(in millions)	December 31, 2008	Quoted Prices in Active Markets for Identical Assets (Level 1)	Significant Other Observable Inputs (Level 2)	Significant Unobservable Inputs (Level 3)	Valuation Technique
Cash equivalents	$ 4,020	$ 4,020	$ —	$ —	(a)
Short-term investments	212	—	—	212	(c)
Restricted cash equivalents	128	128	—	—	(a)
Long-term investments	121	—	—	121	(c)
Hedge derivatives liability, net	(1,109)	—	(18)	(1,091)	(a)(c)

(continued)

EXHIBIT 11.4 *(Continued)*

Due to uncertainty regarding the timing of the distribution of our current holdings in the Primary Fund and the amount we will receive from the distribution, we changed our valuation technique for the Primary Fund to an income approach using a discounted cash flow model during the September 2008 quarter. Accordingly, our short-term investments at December 31, 2008, comprised of these securities, changed from Level 1 to Level 3 within SFAS 157's three-tier fair value hierarchy since initial valuation upon acquisition earlier in 2008.

Our fuel hedge option derivative contracts are valued under the income approach using option-pricing models. During 2008, we reevaluated the valuation inputs used for our option contracts. As a result, we reclassified these contracts from Level 2 to Level 3 within SFAS 157's three-tier fair value hierarchy since valuation at December 31, 2007.

Assets Measured at Fair Value on a Recurring Basis Using Significant Unobservable Inputs (Level 3) *2008*

(in millions)	Short-Term Investments	Long-Term Investments	Hedge Derivatives Liability, Net
Balance at December 31, 2007	$ 107	$ —	$ —
Redesignation	(107)	107	—
Assets acquired and liabilities assumed from Northwest	246'	45	(567)
Transfers to Level 3	831	—	53
Change in fair value included in earnings	(13)	(24)	(203)
Change in fair value included in other comprehensive income	—	(7)	(1,298)
Purchases and settlements, net	(852)	—	924
Balance at December 31, 2008	$ 212	$ 121	$ (1.091)
Losses included in earnings attributable to the change in unrealized losses relating to assets still held at December 31, 2008	$ (13)	$ (24)	$ (96)

Losses included in earnings above for the year ended December 31, 2008, are recorded on our Consolidated Statement of Operations as follows:

(in millions)	Fuel Expense and Related Taxes	Other (Expense) Income
Total losses included in earnings	$ (176)	$ (64)
Change in unrealized losses relating to assets still held at December 31, 2008	$ (91)	$ (42)

EXHIBIT 11.4 *(Continued)*

Assets and Liabilities Measured at Fair Value on a Nonrecurring Basis *2008*
Assets Acquired and Liabilities Assumed from Northwest

(in millions)	October 29, 2008	Significant Other Observable Inputs (Level 2)	Significant Unobservable Inputs (Level 3)[1]	Valuation Technique
Flight equipment	$ 7,954	S 7,954	$	(a)
Other property and equipment	598	598	—	(a)(b)
Goodwill[2]	4,572	—	4.572	(a)(b)(c)
Indefinite-lived intangible assets[2]	2,631	—	2,631	(a)(c)
Definite-lived intangible assets[2]	71	—	71	(e)
Other noncurrent assets	261	181	80	(a)(b)
Debt and capital leases	6,239	6,239	—	(a)(c)
WorldPerks deferred revenue[3]	2,034	—	2.034	(a)
Other noncurrent liabilities	224	224	—	(a)

[1] These valuations were based on the present value of future cash flows for specific assets derived from our projections of future revenue, expense and airline market conditions. These cash flows were discounted to their present value using a rate of return that considers the relative risk of not realizing the estimated annual cash flows and time value of money.

[2] Goodwill represents the excess of purchase price over the fair value of the tangible and identifiable intangible assets acquired and liabilities assumed from Northwest in the Merger. Indefinite-lived and definite-lived intangible assets are identified by type in Note 5. Fair value measurements for goodwill and other intangible assets included significant unpbservable inputs which generally include a five-year business plan, 12-months of historical revenues and expenses by city pair, projections of available seat miles, revenue passenger miles, load factors, and operating costs per available seat mile and a discount rate.

One of the significant unobservable inputs underlying the intangible fair value measurements performed on the Closing Date is the discount rate. We determined the discount rate using the weighted average cost of capital of the airline industry, which was measured using a Capital Asset Pricing Model ("CAPM"). The CAPM in the valuation of goodwill and indefinite-lived intangibles utilizing a 50% debt and 50% equity structure. The historical average debt-to-equity structure of the major airlines since 1990 is also approximately 50% debt and 50% equity, which was similar to Northwest's debt-to-equity structure at emergence from Chapter 11. The return on debt was measured using a bid-to-yield analysis of major airline corporate bonds. The expected market rate of return for equity was measured based on the risk free rate, the airline industry beta, and risk premiums based on the Federal Reserve Statistical Release H. 15 or Ibbotson® Stocks, Bonds, Bills, and Inflation® Valuation Yearbook, Edition 2008. These factors resulted in a 13% discount rate. This compares to an 11% discount rate used at emergence by Northwest.

[3] The fair value of Northwest's WorldPerks Program liability was determined based on the estimated price that third parties would require us to pay for them to assume the obligation for miles expected to be redeemed under the WorldPerks Program. This estimated price was determined based on the weighted-average equivalent ticket value of a WorldPerks award which is redeemed for travel on Northwest, Delta or a participating airline. The weighted-average equivalent ticket value contemplates differing classes of service, domestic and international itineraries and the carrier providing the award travel.

(continued)

EXHIBIT 11.4 *(Continued)*

Goodwill and Other Intangible Assets at December 31, 2008

(in millions)	December 31, 2008	Significant Unobservable Inputs (Level 3)	Total Impairment	Valuation Technique
Goodwill [1]	$ 9,731	$ 9,731	$ 6,939	(a)(b)(c)
Indefinite-lived intangible assets[2]	4,314	4,314	314	(a)(c)
Definite-lived intangible assets	630	630	43	(c)

[1] In evaluating our goodwill for impairment we first compare our one reporting unit's fair value to its carrying value. We estimate the fair value of our reporting unit by considering (1) our market capitalization, (2) any premium to our market capitalization an investor would pay for a controlling interest, (3) the potential value of synergies and other benefits that could result from such interest, (4) market multiple and recent transaction values of peer companies and (5) projected discounted future cash flows, if reasonably estimable.

[2] We perform the impairment test for our indefinite-lived intangible assets by comparing the asset's fair value to its carrying value. Fair value is estimated based on recent market transactions, where available, or projected discounted future cash flows.

At December 31, 2007, we had goodwill of $12.1 billion, indefinite-lived intangible assets of $2.0 billion and definite-lived intangible assets of $809 million. During the year ended December 31, 2008, we recorded non-cash impairment charges of $6.9 billion for goodwill, $314 million for indefinite-lived intangible assets and $43 million for definite-lived intangible assets.

fair value measurement disclosures in Note 3 (2007 information is not shown).[11]

SEC Suggested Disclosures

In March 2008, the SEC sent letters (Dear CFO letters) to certain public companies with significant amounts of asset-backed securities, loans (carried at fair value or at the lower of cost or market), and derivative assets and liabilities reported in their financial statements. The letter states that inputs to fair value measurements must be classified as Level 3 measurements when fair value is measured using valuation models that rely on significant unobservable inputs. Given that judgment must be applied when using unobservable inputs to determine fair value, and given the potential for fair value measurements to materially affect the results of operations, liquidity, and capital resources, the material use of Level 3 inputs would indicate a need for further Management Discussion and Analysis (MD&A) disclosure.

The SEC asked the recipients of the letter to address the following items in their MD&A:

- How Level 3 inputs are determined
- How the fair values of assets and liabilities measured using Level 3 inputs and how changes to those values would impact
  - Results of operations
  - Liquidity
  - Capital resources
- The amount of Level 3 assets and liabilities as a percentage of total assets and liabilities measured at fair value
- The amount and reason for any material increase or decrease in Level 3 asset and liabilities resulting from a transfer from or into Level 1 or 2
- If assets or liabilities are transferred into Level 3, discuss the significant inputs no longer considered observable and any material gain or loss recognized
- Whether realized and unrealized gains (losses) affected the results of operations, liquidity, or capital resources and if so, how
- The reason for material declines or increases in fair value
- Whether the company anticipates fair values to diverge from anticipated amounts from settlement or maturity, and if so, why

The SEC also asked the companies to consider providing the following information in MD&A for all assets and liabilities within the SFAS 157 hierarchy (Levels 1, 2, and 3):

- For all asset-backed security (all levels), the nature and type of any assets underlying the security, the years of issuance, the asset's current credit rating, and potential changes to the credit rating
- A description of the valuation technique or model, and material changes to the technique or model
- How relevant market indices are included in the technique or model
- A discussion of how the technique or model is validated
- A discussion of how sensitive the fair values are to significant inputs (consider providing a range of fair values)
- A discussion of how increases and decreases in fair value of assets and liabilities may affect liquidity or capital resources[12]

In September 2008, the SEC sent a follow-up letter to those recipients. The purpose of the letter was to encourage clearer and more transparent fair value measurement disclosures particularly for financial instruments that are not actively traded. The focus of the letter was on the judgments and assumptions underlying fair value measurements and the sensitivity of those measurements to the assumptions. The letter made the following suggestions for disclosure in MD&A:

- Judgments made when classifying a particular financial instrument in the fair value hierarchy
- An explanation of how credit risk is incorporated into the fair value measurement
- When disclosing gains and losses on financial instruments required to be carried at fair value, including derivatives, explain how credit risk and counterparty risk affected the valuation and resulting gain or loss.
- Criteria used for determining whether a market for a financial instrument is active or inactive (illiquid)
- How the lack of liquidity is factored into the valuation technique and fair value of financial instruments
- When brokers or pricing services are used to assist in determining fair value, provide information about the nature and amount of assets, the classification in the fair value hierarchy, the number of quotes used, whether quotes were adjusted, how quotes were adjusted, the extent to which brokers or pricing services rely on observable or unobservable inputs, whether quotes are binding or not, and procedures performed to validate prices.[13]

Although the suggested disclosures in the SEC's March and September 2008 letters are not required, they provide significant guidance to preparers of financial statements when reporting assets and liabilities at fair value.

FAS 157—Improving Disclosures about Fair Value Measurements

At the February 18, 2009, meeting, the FASB announced the addition of a new project intended to improve the application guidance for disclosures about fair value measurements. This project was added in response to recommendations contained in the Securities and Exchange Commission's study on mark-to-market accounting, as well as in response to input provided by the FASB's Valuation Resource Group.

The FASB stated project objective is to improve disclosures about fair value measurements, noting that the project may consider additional disclosures, such as the sensitivity of fair value measurements to changes in assumptions and transfers between the three levels of the fair value hierarchy.

As of May 27, 2009, the board had already made the following tentative decisions:

1. *Level of disaggregation.* FASB Statement No. 157, *Fair Value Measurements,* currently requires separate disclosures for each *major category* of assets and liabilities, which is often interpreted in current practice to be equivalent to a line item in the statement of financial position. The board decided that the level of disaggregation generally should be greater than the line items for assets and liabilities in the statement of financial position. Additional guidance on disaggregation will be discussed at a future board meeting.
2. *Inputs.* Paragraph 32(e) of Statement 157 requires a discussion of the valuation techniques used to measure fair value. The board decided to clarify that this discussion should include descriptive disclosures about significant inputs for both Level 2 and Level 3 estimates.
3. *Effect of reasonably possible alternative inputs.* For Level 3 estimates, entities should disclose any significant effect of reasonably possible alternative inputs and how the effect was calculated.
4. *Transfers between levels.* Entities should disclose any significant transfers between Levels 1, 2, and 3 during the reporting period and the reasons the transfers were made.

The FASB has asked its staff to undertake field visits to obtain feedback from preparers about the operationality of the proposed disclosures, particularly those relating to the level of disaggregation and the effect of reasonably possible alternative inputs for Level 3 estimates. The FASB expects to release a FSP to conclude this project, which is expected to be effective for fiscal years beginning after 2009.[14]

In August 2009, the FASB issued an Exposure Draft on a proposed Accounting Standards Update that is intended to improve disclosures about fair value measurements under FASB ASC 820-10. Specifically, the proposed new disclosures would require the preparer of financial statements to:

- State the effect of reasonably possible alternative Level 3 inputs
- Disclose significant transfers in and out of Levels 1 and 2 and provide the reasons for those transfers
- Inform financial statement users about activity in Level 3 fair value measurements

The exposure draft will amend existing disclosures by:

- Applying judgment to the appropriate level of disaggregation in the classification of assets and liabilities

- Providing disclosures as to the valuation techniques and inputs used for fair value measurement in Level 2 or Level 3

The FASB is accepting comments on the exposure draft through October 12, 2009.

Conclusion

Financial statements are the primary source of information that an investor relies on to assess an investment's potential reward and risk, and disclosures are an integral part of a company's financial statements. They supplement the information contained within financial statements providing additional transparency for the investor's benefit. *Fair Value Measurements and Disclosures* expands fair value measurement disclosures in order to provide financial statement users with better information about the extent to which fair value measurements are used to measure recognized assets and liabilities, the inputs used to develop the measurements, and the effect of certain measurements on earnings (or changes in assets) for the period. Understanding the extent to which fair value measurements is used to recognize assets and liabilities in the financial statements is particularly important because not all of the assets and liabilities recognized in U.S. GAAP financial statements are recorded at fair value. Some are reported at historical cost and some are reported at fair value in a mixed-attribute reporting system.

Disclosure of the inputs used to develop fair value measurements is accomplished using the fair value hierarchy to categorize inputs into groups based on the extent to which they are observable in the market place. Level 1 inputs are based on quoted prices in active markets for identical assets, Level 2 inputs are based on market-corroborated information, and Level 3 inputs are unobservable inputs used when other forms of observable data are not available. Disclosures also allow the investor to understand how changes in fair value measurements flow through the entity's financial statements. Changes in fair value from one reporting period to the next create unrealized gains and losses, which can be included in earnings or they can flow through equity as comprehensive income.

The required disclosures for fair value measurements under FASB ASC 820, *Fair Value Measurements and Disclosures* (SFAS No. 157), depend on whether the assets or liability is measured on a recurring or nonrecurring basis. Trading securities would be an example of an asset measured on a recurring basis. Business combinations and impairments result in the measurement of assets and liabilities at fair value on a nonrecurring basis during the period. Finally, in its March and September 2008 sample letters to public companies, the SEC provided significant guidance to preparers of financial statements about appropriate disclosures when reporting financial assets and liabilities at fair value.

Notes

1. White, Gerald I., Ashwinpaul C. Sodhi, and Dov Fried, *The Analysis and Use of Financial Statements,* 2nd ed. (New York: John Wiley & Sons, 1994), 20–21.
2. "Sarbanes-Oxley Executive Summary, Orrick Securities Law Update," Corporate Department of Orrick, Herrington & Sutcliffe LLP, August 2002, www.orrick.com (accessed 6/23/09).
3. CFA Institute Center for Financial Market Integrity, "Comment Letter on FSP 157-e: Determining Whether a Market is Not Active and a Transaction is Note Distressed," addressed to Robert Herz, Chair of the FASB, dated March 30, 2009.
4. CFA Institute Center for Financial Market Integrity, *A Comprehensive Business Reporting Model: Financial Reporting for Investors,* July 2007, 4 and 7, www.cfapubs.org (accessed 6/22/09).
5. CFA Institute Center for Financial Market Integrity's comment letter on "The Progress Report of the SEC Advisory Committee on Improvement to Financial Reporting," March 31, 2008, 3–4.
6. Financial Accounting Standards Board, *Original Pronouncements as Amended,* Statement of Financial Accounting Standard No. 157, *Fair Value Measurements,* 5.
7. *Id.*, paragraph 32.
8. *Id.*, Appendix A, paragraph A34–A35.
9. *Id.*, paragraphs 33–34.
10. *Id.*, Appendix A, paragraph A 36.
11. Delta Airlines, Inc. Form 10-K for fiscal year ended December 31, 2008, p. F–15, www.sec.gov/Archives/edgar/data/27904/000119312509042726/d10k.htm (accessed 6/22/09).
12. Senior Assistant Chief Accountant of the U.S. Securities and Exchange Commission, "Sample Letter Sent to Public Companies on MD&A Disclosure Regarding the Application of SFAS 157 (Fair Value Measurements)," March 2008, www.sec.gov/divisions/corpfin/guidance/fairvalueltr0308.htm (accessed 6/22/09).
13. Senior Assistant Chief Accountant of the U.S. Securities and Exchange Commission, "Sample Letter Sent to Public Companies on MD&A Disclosure Regarding the Application of SFAS 157 (Fair Value Measurements), September 2008, www.sec.gov/divisions/corpfin/guidance/fairvalueltr0908.htm (accessed 7/16/09).
14. "Project Update FAS 157—Improving Disclosures about Fair Value Measurements, Financial Accounting Standards Board," www.fasb.org/fas157_improving_disclosures_about_fvm.shtml (accessed July 19, 2009).

CHAPTER 12

Auditing Fair Value Measurements

Introduction

The increase in the amount of fair value measurements in financial reporting creates a challenge for auditors. As discussed in previous chapters, fair value measurement often includes inputs that are based on judgment and other assumptions made by preparers of financial statements. In many situations, the preparer of the financial statement may retain an outside valuation specialist to assist with the measurement. The judgment aspect of fair value measurement creates complexity in auditing those measurements. The role of the auditor is to obtain sufficient competent audit evidence to provide reasonable assurance the fair value measurements are in conformity with Generally Accepted Accounting Principles (GAAP). These challenges are faced by auditors in the United States and worldwide as fair value measures become more extensive in financial reporting internationally. The International Auditing and Assurance Standards Board (IAASB) describes some of the challenges that auditors face in fair value accounting in obtaining sufficient competent audit evidence to opine as to the conformity of the measurements to accounting standards. Some of the audit challenges recognized by the IAASB include:

- Fair value measurements that are expressed in terms of the value of a current transaction or financial statement item based on conditions prevalent at the measurement date (rather than a historical cost)
- The need to incorporate judgments concerning significant assumption that may be made by others such as valuation specialists engaged by the preparer
- The availability (or lack thereof) of information or evidence and its reliability in the fair value measurement
- The breadth of assets and liabilities to which fair value accounting may be, or is required to be, applied

- The choice and sophistication of acceptable valuation techniques and models
- The need for appropriate disclosure in the financial statements about measurement methods and uncertainty, especially when relevant markets are illiquid as experienced in the current credit crisis[1]

At the very least, fair value measurements in the presentation of financial statements adds an additional layer of complexity to the audit of those statements.

The Audit Process

In order to better understand how to audit fair value measurements, it may be helpful to provide a brief overview of the audit process itself. The American Accounting Association defines auditing as "a systematic process of objectively obtaining and evaluating evidence regarding assertions about economic actions and events to ascertain the degree of correspondence between those assertions and established criteria and communicating the results to interested users."[2] Montgomery's *Auditing* suggests further breaking down this definition into five parts:

1. Assertions about economic actions and events
2. Degree of correspondence between assertions and established criteria
3. Objectively obtaining and evaluating evidence
4. Systematic process
5. Communicating the results to interested users

A graphical representation of the audit process is presented in Exhibit 12.1.

Assertions about Economic Actions and Events

Evaluating management's assertion about fair value measurements included in the presentation of a financial statement must be incorporated into the audit of the financial statements. For example, management may include the fair value of technology acquired in a business combination on the company's balance sheet at $10 million as of December 31, 200X. Since technology is measured at its fair value under SFAS 157, the measurement inherently contains assumptions about economic actions and events most likely to occur in the future. These assumptions and events must be quantified to be audited for reasonableness. Quantification is typically through a valuation model or a combination of valuation models using various valuation

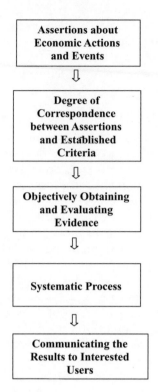

EXHIBIT 12.1 The Audit Process

methods. First, the auditor determines whether the methodology and model are appropriate for the fair value measurement. Next, the auditor makes a determination as to the reasonableness of the assumptions underlying the measurement.

Degree of Correspondence between Assertions and Established Criteria

The primary objective of an audit is to provide an opinion about management's assertions that economic actions and events are represented fairly in the financial statements. When auditing financial statements, GAAP is the established accounting standard against which these economic actions and events are measured for conformity. The Auditing Standards Board of the American Institute of Certified Public Accountants (AICPA) issued AU Section 328, SAS No. 101, *Auditing Fair Value Measurements and Disclosures,* to provide additional guidance specifically in the auditing of fair value measurements. SAS 101 is effective for periods after June 15, 2003. On December 10, 2007, the PCAOB issued Staff Audit Practice Alert No. 2, *Matters Related to Auditing Fair Value Measurements of Financial Instruments and the Use of Specialists,* to provide further guidance to auditors of public entities. Both SAS 101 and Staff Audit Practice Alert No. 2 provide general criteria, which an auditor must consider when auditing fair value measurements.

Objectively Obtaining and Evaluating Evidence

The objective in auditing fair value measurements is to obtain and evaluate evidence that will support the auditor's opinion that management's fair value measurement conforms to GAAP. Audit evidence may be the work product of an outside valuation specialist retained by management to assist with the fair value measurement process. Although management maintains responsibility for the fair value measurement's presentation in the financial statements, the valuation specialist's work product may be used as audit evidence in the audit of the fair value measurement. Going back to the example of the technology acquired in a business combination, assume management retains a valuation specialist to assist them with the measurement of the fair value of the technology as of the date of the acquisition. The valuation specialist can use one or more of the various methods under the three standard valuation techniques (cost, market, or income approaches) to estimate the fair value of the acquired technology. The valuation specialist will issue a report describing the methods and assumptions used to estimate the fair value of the developed technology and provide supporting schedules showing calculation of the $10 million value. Management can provide the valuation specialist's report to the auditor to be used as audit evidence supporting the assertion that the fair value of the technology is $10 million on the date of the business combination.

Systematic Process

The term "systematic process" conveys the point that there is a process to auditing fair value measurements. Consequently, planning the audit is a vital part of the audit process. A carefully conceived audit strategy must provide a plan to test the reasonableness of management's assumptions incorporated into the fair value measurement. This unique aspect of auditing fair value measurements requires auditing judgment. Montgomery's *Auditing* goes as far as describing the phrase "systematic process" as one that uses at least in part the "scientific method." Although the term "scientific method" probably conveys a much more rigid approach to obtaining a conclusion than is possible or warranted in most audits, it does provide the notion that an audit is a structured process.[3] In our business combination example, the process may involve using valuation specialists as part of the audit team to audit the fair value of the developed technology. The audit team's valuation specialist would systematically analyze the work product of management's outside valuation specialist. He would evaluate the reasonableness and reliability of their conclusion that the fair value of the acquired technology is $10 million.

Communicating the Results to Interested Users

The purpose of an audit is to provide assurance to users of financial statements that those financial statements meet the requirements of GAAP. Management asserts that a company's financial statements are prepared in accordance with GAAP. The auditor's report provides conclusions as to whether management's assertions are accurate and whether the financial statements conform to GAAP. If they do not conform to GAAP, the report provides the reasons why. The audit report provides a level of comfort to the users of the financial statements. In the acquired technology example, the $10 million fair value is but one component of the company's entire financial statements. Though not specifically stated, the auditor's report should provide assurance that the fair value measurement at least conforms to FASB ASC 820, *Fair Value Measurements and Disclosures* (SFAS No. 157), and to FASB ASC 805, *Business Combinations* (SFAS No. 141(R)), among other accounting standards. Exhibit 12.2 is an example of an auditor's report.

Auditing Estimates in Fair Value Measurements

An estimate is often the basis for a fair value measurement. Prior to any specific auditing standard specifically related to fair value measurements, such as AU Section 328, SAS No. 101, *Auditing Fair Value Measurements and Disclosures*, auditors referred to AU Section 342 formerly the Statement on Auditing Standards No. 57 (SAS 57), *Auditing Accounting Estimates,* for guidance on auditing the estimates that are sometimes a part of a fair value measurement.[4] Accounting estimates are defined under generally accepted auditing standards (GAAS) as "an approximation of a financial statement element item or account."[5] The nature of fair value measurement gives rise to numerous accounting estimates in the measurement process. Often these measurements are derived from expectations about future events for which there may not be relevant historical experience.

AU Section 342, formerly the Statement on Auditing Standards No. 57 (SAS 57), *Auditing Accounting Estimates,* outlines the management's responsibility for accounting estimates and provides guidance to auditors in "obtaining and evaluating sufficient competent evidential matter to support significant accounting estimates in an audit of financial statements."[6] According to *Auditing Accounting Estimates,* management has the responsibility for making the accounting estimates incorporated in financial statements, including fair value measurements. The statement points out that "estimates

EXHIBIT 12.2 Report of Independent Registered Public Accounting Firm

Board of Directors and Shareowners

The Coca-Cola Company

We have audited the accompanying consolidated balance sheets of The Coca-Cola Company and subsidiaries as of December 31, 2008, and 2007, and the related consolidated statements of income, shareowners' equity, and cash flows for each of the three years in the period ended December 31, 2008. These financial statements are the responsibility of the Company's management. Our responsibility is to express an opinion on these financial statements based on our audits. We conducted our audits in accordance with the standards of the Public Company Accounting Oversight Board (United States). Those standards require that we plan and perform the audit to obtain reasonable assurance about whether the financial statements are free of material misstatement. An audit includes examining, on a test basis, evidence supporting the amounts and disclosures in the financial statements. An audit also includes assessing the accounting principles used and significant estimates made by management, as well as evaluating the overall financial statement presentation. We believe that our audits provide a reasonable basis for our opinion. In our opinion, the financial statements referred to above present fairly, in all material respects, the consolidated financial position of The Coca-Cola Company and subsidiaries at December 31, 2008, and 2007, and the consolidated results of their operations and their cash flows for each of the three years in the period ended December 31, 2008, in conformity with U.S. generally accepted accounting principles. As discussed in Notes 1 and 17 to the consolidated financial statements, in 2007 the Company adopted FASB Interpretation No. 48 related to accounting for uncertainty in income taxes. Also as discussed in Notes 1 and 16 to the consolidated financial statements, in 2006 the Company adopted SFAS No. 158 related to defined benefit pension and other postretirement plans We also have audited, in accordance with the standards of the Public Company Accounting Oversight Board (United States), The Coca-Cola Company's internal control over financial reporting as of December 31, 2008, based on criteria established in *Internal Control—Integrated Framework* issued by the Committee of Sponsoring Organizations of the Treadway Commission and our report dated February 26, 2009 expressed an unqualified opinion thereon.

/s/ Ernst & Young L.L.P.
Atlanta, Georgia
February 26, 2009[7]

are based on subjective as well as objective factors and, as a result, judgment is required to estimate an amount at the date of the financial statements. Management's judgment is normally based on its knowledge and experience about past and current events and its assumptions about conditions it expects to exist and courses of action it expects to take."[8]

Auditing Accounting Estimates further describes how management should develop a process for preparing accounting estimates. The process does not have to be formal. However, when measuring fair value based on an accounting estimate, management should be able to provide a reasonable basis for:

- Identifying situations for which accounting estimates are required in the fair value measurement
- Identifying the relevant factors that may affect the accounting estimate, particularly unobservable inputs
- Accumulating relevant, sufficient, and reliable data on which to base the estimate. The estimate then may be used in a valuation model using one of the valuation techniques to estimate fair value of the asset or liability.
- Developing assumptions that represent management's judgment of the most likely circumstances and events with respect to the relevant factors
- Determining the estimated amount based on the assumptions and other relevant factors
- Determining that the accounting estimate is presented in conformity with applicable accounting principles and that disclosure is adequate,[9] particularly giving consideration to the guidance for measuring fair value under FASB ASC 820, *Fair Value Measurements and Disclosures* (SFAS 157)[10]

In auditing accounting estimates that are a factor in the fair value measurement, the auditor is responsible for evaluating the reasonableness of management's accounting estimate in the context of the financial statements taken as a whole. Since accounting estimates consist of both subjective as well as objective factors, management may have difficulty in establishing appropriate controls over the estimate. Subjective factors may be unobservable inputs as described in FASB ASC 820, *Fair Value Measurements and Disclosures* (SFAS 157). Objective factors may be estimates that are observable in the marketplace as described in *Fair Value Measurements* (SFAS 157).

The auditor should become comfortable that management's estimation process involves competent personnel using relevant and reliable data, whether those personnel are part of management or are outside specialists. Even with competent personnel and appropriate use of date, there is potential for management bias in some of the subjective factors. When planning and performing the audit procedures to evaluate management's accounting estimates, *Auditing Accounting Estimates* suggests that auditors should consider "with an attitude of professional skepticism, both the subjective and objective factors."[11]

AU Section 328 (SAS 101), *Auditing Fair Value Measurements and Disclosures*

Auditing fair value measurements, however, requires more than just auditing management's estimates. When market prices are not available, management estimates fair value by using valuation techniques, which require inputs that market participants would use in estimating value. The Auditing Standards Board (ASB) believed this added complexity required additional guidance in auditing management's fair value measurement beyond the guidance for just auditing estimates. The ASB provided this additional guidance through SAS No. 101, *Auditing Fair Value Measurements and Disclosures*.

The statement, a codified section of the AICPA Professional Standards, AU Section 328, (SAS No. 101), *Auditing Fair Value Measurements and Disclosures,* became effective for audits of financial statements providing fair value measurements for periods beginning on or after June 15, 2003. The purpose of AU Section 328 (SAS No. 101) is to establish standards and provide guidance on auditing fair value measurements and disclosures contained in financial statements.[12] In particular, AU 328 (SAS 101) addresses audit considerations relating to the measurement and disclosure of assets, liabilities, and specific components of equity presented or disclosed at fair value in financial statements. These considerations are particularly relevant when fair value measurements change from period to period after the initial measurement of the asset or liability.[13]

AU 328 (SAS 101) is designed to provide a general framework for auditing all fair value measurements. The standard does not provide guidance as to auditing specific types of fair value measurement. The general framework begins with understanding management's process for developing the measurement of fair value. After understanding management's process, the auditor makes a determination whether the measurement conforms to GAAP. Audit procedures are used to assess management's assumptions, the suitability of the valuation method, to test the inputs and to test the valuation model itself.

Management is responsible for the presentation and disclosures of fair value measurements included in the company's financial statements. In order to present the fair value measurement fairly, management should establish an accounting and financial reporting process for determining when fair value measurements and disclosures are required, selecting the appropriate methods for measuring fair value under the three basic approaches to value, identifying and adequately supporting any significant assumptions used in the fair value measurement, preparing the valuation internally or with the assistance of an outside valuation specialist, and finally ensuring that the presentation and disclosure of the fair value measurements are in accordance with GAAP.[14]

When obtaining an understanding of the entity's process for determining fair value measurements and disclosures, the auditor should consider, for example:

- Controls over the process used to determine fair value measurements, including controls over data and the segregation of duties between those committing the entity to the underlying transactions and those responsible for undertaking the valuations
- The expertise and experience of personnel determining the fair value measurements
- The role that information technology has in the process
- The types of accounts or transactions requiring fair value measurements or disclosures (for example, whether the accounts arise from the recording of routine and recurring transactions or whether they arise from nonroutine or unusual transactions)
- The extent to which the entity's process relies on a service organization to provide fair value measurements or the data that supports the measurement. When an entity uses a service organization, the auditor must consider the requirements of SAS No. 70, *Service Organizations* (AU Section 324), as amended.
- The extent to which the entity engages or employs specialists in determining fair value measurements and disclosures
- The significant management assumptions used in determining fair value
- The documentation supporting management's assumptions
- The process used to develop and apply management assumptions, including whether management used available market information to develop the assumptions
- The process used to monitor changes in management's assumptions
- The integrity of change controls and security procedures for valuation models and relevant information systems, including the approval processes
- The controls over the consistency, timeliness, and reliability of the data used in valuation models[15]

AU328 (SAS 101) provides guidance on understanding management's process for developing fair value estimates and evaluating whether the measurement conforms to GAAP. The Auditing Standards Board issued AU 328 (SAS 101) because estimates of fair value are unique when compared to other accounting estimates. In estimating fair value when market prices are not readily available, management must estimate fair value using a valuation technique. The valuation technique has as inputs, assumptions that under FASB ASC 820, *Fair Value Measurements and Disclosures* (SFAS No. 157), should reflect those that market participants would make. This aspect of fair value measurement often requires some form of judgment. Because of the convergence of U.S. GAAP with international accounting standards, among other factors, there are an increasing number of accounting standards that require fair value measurements and disclosures. The standards are also becoming more complex in their requirement for the measurement of fair value. As an example, FASB ASC 825-10-25 (SFAS 159), *The Fair Value Option,* has increased the complexity of the measurement process. The significance of these measurements in the financial reporting process requires further auditing guidance that is specific to such measurements. AU 329 (SAS 101) is the first of that additional guidance.[16]

Testing Management's Fair Value Measurements

As with any financial statement assertion, the auditor should test management's fair value measurements and disclosures. Auditing a fair value measurement can be complex. The goal of the audit is to test management's evidence to see if it supports the assertion of the fair value measurement and ensure that the assertion is free from material misstatement. In order to determine if the assertion is free from material misstatement the auditor should perform substantive tests of the measurement using management's audit evidence. These substantive tests of the fair value measurements may include testing management's significant assumptions, testing the valuation model, and testing the underlying data.

Some fair value measurements are much more complicated than others. The level of complexity is due to the nature of the item being measured at fair value and the degree of sophistication of the valuation method itself. For example, If the equity of a reporting unit under SFAS 142 is not publicly traded, the fair value of the equity may be estimated by using valuation methods such as the discounted cash flow method or the guideline public company method. Complex fair value measurements normally are characterized by greater uncertainty regarding the reliability of the measurement process. This greater uncertainty may be a result of:

- The length of the forecast period
- The number of significant and complex assumptions associated with the process
- A higher degree of subjectivity associated with the assumptions and factors used in the process

- A higher degree of uncertainty associated with the future occurrence or outcome of events underlying the assumptions used
- Lack of objective data when highly subjective factors are used[17]

Proper audit procedures for fair value measurement require the auditor to understand management's process for determining fair value measurements and to assess the risk of material misstatement of the fair value measurement. Audit procedures are designed based on the assessment of management's process for determining fair value measures and on the risk of material misstatement. AU 328 (SAS 101) provides some examples of situations an auditor might encounter and procedures that an auditor might consider when auditing fair value measurements.

When the fair value measurement is made at a date other than the financial statement reporting date, the auditor should obtain evidence that management has taken into consideration any differences that may impact the fair value measurement between the date of the fair value measurement and the reporting date. This may occur when an outside valuation specialist conducts the analysis as of a different date due to information constraints or timing constraints for the engagement.

When collateral is an important aspect in the fair value measurement of an investment, the auditor should obtain sufficient appropriate audit evidence that the features of the collateral have been considered by management in estimating its fair value. Certain types of investments in debt instruments measured at fair value have collateral assigned to them. When testing for impairment, possible impairment of the collateral must also be considered. In certain circumstances, the auditor should perform additional procedures, such as a visual inspection of an asset. A detailed inspection of the asset may reveal information about the current physical condition of the asset, which may impact its fair value. An inspection of a security or other asset may reveal a limitation as to its marketability, which may affect its value.[18]

A critical step in determining appropriate audit procedures is gaining an understanding of the process used by management to determine fair value measurement. When the auditor tests managements' fair value measurements, the evaluation process should consider the basis that management used in the fair value measurement. Management's assumptions in the fair value measurement should be reasonable and consistent with information available from the market. If market information is not available, the fair value measurement should be estimated using an appropriate valuation model for that particular asset or liability. Management should use all of the relevant information available on the date of measurement when determining an asset or liability's fair value.

Testing Management's Significant Assumptions, the Valuation Model, and the Underlying Data

Once the auditor gains confidence as to the reliability of the process used by management to determine fair value measurement, the next step is to test management's assumptions, the valuation model, and underlying data used in the model. Some considerations in auditing fair value measurements are:

- Management's assumptions are reasonable and are consistent with assumptions made by market participants.
- Management uses an appropriate valuation model to estimate the fair value measurement.
- Management uses known or knowable market participant assumptions that are available on the measurement date.

One simple indication of the reliability of management's processes is to compare the current fair value measurement to prior periods. Significant swings in value might be evidence that management's process is unreliable. However, the auditor should also take into consideration that the estimate of fair value may be impacted by market or economic changes from the prior period.

Testing the Reliability of Management's Assumptions

When testing management's assumptions, the auditor should evaluate whether significant assumptions used by management in measuring fair value provide a reasonable basis for the fair value measurements. Assumptions are an essential component of valuation methods, particularly in detailed valuation models. For example, a discounted cash flow analysis under the income approach is commonly used to measure fair value. A discounted cash flow model incorporates assumptions about expected future cash flows within a discrete forecast period, assumptions about the cash flows after the discrete forecast period, and even more assumptions about the rate of return required to compensate for the uncertainty associated with the future receipt of those cash flows. Auditors should pay particular attention to the assumptions incorporated into a discounted cash flow model and evaluate whether those assumptions are reasonable and are consistent with market participant information.

In evaluating evidence to support the assumptions used by management in fair value measurement, the auditor must consider the source and reliability of the evidence and take into consideration historical and market information related to the evidence.

Management should identify assumptions that are significant to the fair value measurement. The auditor then focuses on the evidence that supports the significant assumptions that management has identified. Significant assumptions are those that materially affect the fair value measurement, such as:

- Assumptions that are sensitive to variation or are uncertain in amount or nature. For example, assumptions about a discount rate may be susceptible to significant variation compared to assumptions about long-term growth rates in cash flow.
- Assumptions that may be susceptible to misapplication or bias and can be easily manipulated in the fair value measurement. An example would be the selected royalty rate in the relief from royalty method used to estimate the fair value of a trade name.[19]

In considering the sensitivity of the fair value measurement to variation in significant assumptions, the auditor may ask management to use techniques such as sensitivity analysis to help identify sensitive assumptions. If management has not identified particularly sensitive assumptions, the auditor should consider whether to employ sensitivity analysis to identify those assumptions that may be significant to the measurement.

Assumptions used in fair value measurements should have a reasonable basis individually and when used with other assumptions. An assumption may appear to be reasonable individually but many may not be reasonable when used in combination with other assumptions. For example, in a fair value measurement that use a discounted cash flow valuation method, management may assume that the company's revenue will grow 5 percent each year for the next five years. If the company has historically grown 5 percent per year, this assumption may appear to be reasonable, at first. However, the forecast may also assume that management is curtailing certain operating expenses and capital expenditures for the next year due to borrowing constraints. The assumption of 5 percent growth may not be reasonable if management does not have the cash available to support growth in revenue as it had in the past.

To test the reasonableness of assumptions in a fair value measurement, the assumptions have to be reasonable individually and in combination with other assumptions. For the fair value measurement to be considered reasonable, AU 328 (SAS 101), *Auditing Fair Value Measurements,* suggests that assumptions have to be consistent with these factors as well:

- The general economic environment, the economic environment of the specific industry, and the entity's economic circumstances
- Existing market information

- The plans of the entity, including what management expects will be the outcome of specific objectives and strategies
- Assumptions made in prior periods, if appropriate
- Past experience of, or previous conditions experienced by, the entity to the extent currently applicable
- Other matters relating to the financial statements, for example, assumptions used by management in accounting estimates for financial statement accounts other than those relating to fair value measurements and disclosures
- The risk associated with cash flows, if applicable, including the potential variability in the amount and timing of the cash flows and the related effect on the discount rate.[20]

A fair value measurement generally has two types of assumptions. The first type of assumption is based on historical information such as past financial performance. If a company's revenue has grown at 5 percent per year for the past five years, it may be reasonable to forecast 5 percent growth for the next five years. However, the reasonableness of this assumption should be considered in conjunction with other assumptions. The second type of assumption used in a valuation model is not based on historical information.

In auditing the reasonableness of an assumption, the auditor should consider whether the assumption is consistent with management's plans and past experience. For example, management may rely on historical financial information as a basis for the assumption in the fair value measurement. If overall conditions remain consistent with the past then this assumption may be reasonable. If management changes strategies or other conditions change, the assumption may not be reasonable.

In a fair value measurement based on a valuation model, the auditor should first review the model and evaluate whether the model is appropriate for the fair value measurement. If it is appropriate, then the auditor should evaluate the significant assumptions used in the model for reasonableness. For example, it may be inappropriate to use the guideline company method under the market approach to estimate the fair value of an early-stage equity investment when there are limited revenues to support normalized earnings and cash flow due to the company's stage of development.

Finally, if the auditor believes that the valuation model and the assumptions used in the model are appropriate, then the auditor should test the underlying data used in the valuation model. For example, if the guideline company method is used to estimate the fair value of a reporting unit, the auditor should test the data by comparing it to similar data from publicly traded guideline entities. The comparison should test data for "accuracy, completeness and relevancy."[21]

Should an Auditor Engage a Valuation Specialist?

Since fair value measurements may require special skill and independent judgment, management often engages an outside valuation specialist to assist with the fair value measurement. The company's auditor may have the skill and knowledge to plan and perform procedures related to audit of management's fair values measurement. Conversely, the auditor may also decide to include the work of a valuation specialist on the audit team to assist in obtaining sufficient audit evidence to support management's assertions about fair value measurements.

The valuation specialist may be used as part of the audit process in a number of ways. The valuation specialist can evaluate the assumptions and methodologies used by management or those used by an outside valuation specialist engaged by management.

Often, the valuation specialist is asked to test assumptions underlying the fair value measurement. The tests that a valuation specialist included as part of the audit team may include procedures such as:

- Verifying the source of the data
- Mathematical recomputation of inputs
- Reviewing of information for internal consistency
- Comparing the methods and assumptions used in the fair value measurement to professional "best practices." Many of the best practices for valuations in financial reporting are being developed by both the AICPA and the Appraisal Foundation.
- Developing independent fair value estimates for corroborative purposes. An independent valuation analysis or "shadow valuation" may use the same valuation technique with different assumption or another valuation technique altogether to test the fair value representation on the financial statements.[22]

The auditor's valuation specialist then will issue what is sometimes termed, a "SAS 73 memo" giving their conclusions as to the reasonableness of the fair value assertions, including the valuation analysis that may be performed by management's outside valuation specialist.

PCAOB Staff Audit Practice Alert No. 2, *Matters Related to Auditing Fair Value Measurements of Financial Instruments and the Use of Specialists*

The PCAOB issued Staff Audit Practice Alert No. 2, *Matters Related to Auditing Fair Value Measurements of Financial Instruments and the Use of*

Specialists, on December 10, 2007. The PCAOB focuses on the audits of publicly traded companies. The PCAOB said the purpose of this alert is to remind auditors of their responsibility for auditing fair value measurements of specifically financial instruments. Although the descriptions provided in the alert can also be applied to auditing the fair value of nonfinancial instruments. The alert also describes the existing standards of the PCAOB when auditing the work of management's outside valuation specialists.

There are specific factors that are likely to increase audit risk related to the fair value of financial instruments. One particularly relevant factor currently is the changing economic environment. The PCAOB specifically asks the auditor to focus on certain areas in the implementations of FASB ASC 820, *Fair Value Measurements and Disclosures* (SFAS No. 157). The alert describes the auditor's responsibilities when management uses the work of an outside valuation specialist. The alert provides additional guidance as to the auditor's responsibility to evaluate the appropriateness of using the specialist's work for the fair value measurements. Staff Audit Practice Alert No. 2 has four sections:

1. Auditing fair value measurements
2. Classification within the fair value hierarchy under SFAS No. 157
3. Using the work of valuation specialists
4. Use of a pricing service

Auditing Fair Value Measurements

The PCAOB alert specifically mentions AU Sec. 328 (SAS No. 101), *Auditing Fair Value Measurements and Disclosure*, as providing guidance to the auditor on evaluating whether the fair value measurement conforms to GAAP. In planning for audit procedures to assess the risk associated with auditing the fair value measurements, the auditor should assess management's process for determining the measurements.

- Consider whether management's inputs into the fair value measurement are "reasonable and reflect, or are not inconsistent with, market information." For example, if management is forecasting significant sales growth during a period where other market participants are not experiencing the same growth, then the auditor should evaluate whether the growth forecast is reasonable under the circumstances at the measurement date.
- Conversely, if management uses historical financial information in the development of an input, the auditor should consider whether the reliance is appropriate for the fair value measurement. Historical information might not be the best indication of future conditions or events. For

example, an auditor should evaluate whether a company's use of historical profit margins in a cash flow forecast is justified in an economic environment where sales are declining.

■ Evaluate whether management's method for determining fair value measurements are applied consistently. If management uses the same methods and similar assumptions as in the past, then the auditor should consider whether changes in the environment or circumstances affecting the company warrant consistent treatment or whether the methodology or assumptions should be revised. For example, in estimating the fair value of developed technology that was estimated using a relief from royalty method in previous years, the market information may not be as relevant as in previous years. Consequently, the auditor may consider asking management to revise its measurement to include some other form of the income approach or some other change in the model.[23]

Classification within the Fair Value Hierarchy under FASB ASC 820, *Fair Value Measurements and Disclosures* (SFAS No. 157)

FASB ASC 820, *Fair Value Measurements and Disclosures*, describes three levels within a fair value hierarchy. The purpose of the fair value hierarchy is to provide guidance as to the relative reliability as to the input in its measurement. The fair value hierarchy level within which a fair value measurement is classified is based on the lowest level input that is significant to the fair value measurement in its entirety.

In an article entitled *SFAS 157 Fair Value Measurements: Implementation Challenges for the Alternative Investment Industry*, author Chris Mears says, "Unfortunately the term 'significant' is not defined by the Standard. In assessing the significance of a market input, the fund should consider the sensitivity of the fair value to changes in the input used. Assessing the significance of an input will require judgment considering factors specific to the financial instrument being valued. The tone from the top should be one of conservatism in assigning level designations to securities with unobservable inputs."[24]

The article goes on to provide clarifying examples for designating appropriate fair value levels for disclosure. In one example, Level 2 is assigned to a total return swap where the underlying notational position is an actively traded (Level 1) security. The rationale is that the unit of measure is the total return swap, not the underlying stock.

Another example shows how options could be classified as Level 1, 2, or 3 under SFAS 157. Options traded on an exchange in an active market would be classified as Level 1. Those traded on an exchange, but not in an active market, would be Level 2. Options valued using widely accepted models with observable inputs would also be considered Level 2. Finally, options priced using models with unobservable inputs and significant adjustments and judgments would be assigned to Level 3.[25]

The PCAOB Alert notes that because the risk of material misstatement is higher using lower levels of inputs, there are different disclosures associated with each of the three levels of the fair value hierarchy. The auditor should consider whether management has misclassified the level of measurement within the fair value hierarchy.

Using the Work of a Valuation Specialist

As required in performing an audit, the auditor needs to honestly evaluate his or her own skills, knowledge, and ability to plan and perform audit procedures related to fair value measurements. If the auditor believes he does not have the necessary skill and knowledge to perform that portion of the audit adequately, the auditor can use the work of an outside specialist. AU Section 336 (SAS 73), *Using the Work of a Specialist,* describes circumstances when an auditor may involve a specialist as part of the audit engagement team. A specialist is someone who has specialized skills or knowledge outside of accounting and auditing. If the auditor uses the work of a specialist as part of the audit process, the auditor has certain responsibilities concerning the uses of the specialist work in the audit. The auditor is responsible for obtaining an understanding of the methods and assumptions used by the specialist, making appropriate tests of data provided to the specialist, and evaluating whether the specialist's findings support the related assertions in the financial statements.[26] The specialist's job is to test management's fair value measurements in financial statements so that the auditor may provide an opinion as to whether those measurements are prepared in conformity with GAAP.

Use of a Pricing Service

The valuation of certain types of financial assets and liabilities are extremely complex. Often the value of these instruments is measured by using outside pricing services that have created complex models to price the financial asset and/or liability. When management uses a pricing service to measure fair value, the auditor should first understand the nature of the information used by the pricing service in making the fair value measurement. The nature of the information would include whether the inputs are from quoted prices of the same or similar assets or liabilities traded in the market, or whether the inputs are based on a financial model. If a financial model is used, then the auditor should evaluate whether the assumptions used by the pricing service reflect market participant assumptions. Under FASB ASC 820, *Fair Value Measurements and Disclosures* (SFAS No. 157), the financial model should reflect the price to sell the asset or paid to transfer the liability in the principal market or most advantageous market if the company has no principal market. If the pricing service valuation is based on actual trades or quotes of the same or similar assets or liabilities, the auditor should evaluate whether those traded or quoted prices meet the definition of fair value in FASB ASC 820, *Fair Value Measurements and Disclosures.* The primary question is whether the traded or quoted price on which the fair value measurement is based would be available in a principal market or most advantageous market, if there is no principal market. For example, a pricing service might provide a fair value measurement of an investment-grade corporate bond. The auditor should understand how the pricing service determined the market price for the bond. If the price is based on a market that is not available to the holder of the bond, then that price may not be an appropriate measure of fair value under *Fair Value Measurements and Disclosures.*

SEC Audit Guidance

The Securities and Exchange Commission (SEC) has also provided guidance in auditing fair value measurements. The SEC's Division of Corporation Finance sent a letter in September 2008 to certain public companies identifying a number of disclosure items that should be included when preparing Management's Discussion and Analysis (MD&A). Some of the specific items relating to fair value measurement disclosure that the SEC letter described included:

- Significant judgments made in classifying a particular financial instrument in the fair value hierarchy
- An explanation of how credit risk is incorporated and considered in the valuation of assets or liabilities
- The criteria used to determine whether the market for a financial instrument is active or inactive
- Which financial instruments are affected by the lack of market liquidity and how the lack of liquidity impacted the valuation techniques used
- If using brokers or pricing services, the extent to which, and how, the information was obtained and was used in developing fair value measurements

Nonauthoritative Guidance

The AICPA has issued additional nonauthoritative guidance to assist an auditor in auditing fair value measurements, including a toolkit practice aid available on the AICPA's Web site titled "Auditing Fair Value Measurements and Disclosures."[27] Although the toolkit predates SFAS 157 and SFAS 141(R), it still contains some relevant information to assist the auditor in understanding fair value measurement.

In addition, the AICPA has recently formed a strategic Fair Value Resource Panel to provide guidance to its members and others on issues related to fair value measurements. The panel identified four immediate projects to begin its mission.

1. "Update the Assets Acquired in a Business Combination to Be Used in Research and Development Activities: A Focus on Software, Electronic Devices & Pharmaceutical Industries Practice Aid," which was first issued by the AICPA in 2001 and has not yet been updated for accounting pronouncement since it was first published.
2. Update the *Valuation of Privately-Held-Company Equity Securities Issued as Compensation* practice aid, which was first issued by the AICPA in 2004 and has not yet been updated for accounting pronouncement since it was first published.
3. Create a new practice aid on the issue of impairment of assets in financial reporting. The practice aid will address impairment of goodwill and finite-lived intangible assets. This new practice aid will also provide guidance on how to measure fair value under FASB ASC 350, *Goodwill and Other Intangible Assets* (SFAS 142), and SFAS 144, *Testing for Impairment of Long Lived Assets*. The practice aid will also address how to determine useful lives of acquired assets.
4. Develop a new practice aid on valuation of hedge funds. Hedge funds have a tremendous amount of valuation issues. Examples of some of the issues are lock-up provisions, sale restrictions, and developing the net asset value of the fund itself. The new practice aid will provide guidance on how to value a hedge fund. The practice aid would be relevant for a number of other types of entities other than hedge funds as well, including not-for-profit organizations, employee benefit plans, health care companies, investment companies, and broker-dealers all of which invest in hedge funds.

The practice aids will provide nonauthoritative guidance to auditors on more specific issues in auditing fair value measurements and should be available by the middle of 2010.

The Appraisal Foundation

The Appraisal Foundation, authorized by the U.S. Congress, is a nonprofit educational organization dedicated to the advancement of the valuation profession. Founded in 1987, the organization was formed as a direct result of the government's intervention into the Savings and Loan crisis of the mid-1980s. Its purpose is to provide a source of appraisal standards and qualifications. The foundation is not an individual member organization but rather one that is composed of other organizations.[28]

In addition to its other services, the foundation sponsors and facilitates Business Valuation Working Groups, which are charged with developing best practices for specific valuation issues in financial reporting. The first working group issued an exposure draft in February 2009 titled "The Identification of Contributory Assets and the Calculation of Economic Rents," which describes "the preferred methods of addressing certain situations in the valuation of intangible assets using the Multi-Period Excess Earnings Method."[29] The final version of the document is expected to be issued in November 2009.

The Appraisal Foundation also sponsored a second working group, which discussed issues related to the valuation of customer relationships in financial reporting. In September 2009, the working group issued an exposure draft for a toolkit to be used with "The Identification of Contributory Assets and the Calculation of Economic Rents." The toolkit is intended to serve as an example for the proper calculation and reflection of contributory asset changes. Comments will be posted to the Web site.[30]

Appraisal Issues Task Force (AITF)

The Appraisal Issues Task Force (AITF) is a voluntary group of valuation specialists who focus on improving valuation practices in financial reporting. The specialists understand that the FASB and the SEC are increasingly looking for information regarding the development and implementation of Fair Value Measurements. Prior to the issuance of Financial Accounting Standards Board (FASB) *Accounting Standards Codification* (ASC) 805, *Business Combinations* (SFAS 141(R)), and FASB ASC 350, *Intangibles—Goodwill and Other* (SFAS No. 142), there was a lack of both authoritative and nonauthoritative guidance regarding best practices in fair value measurement. As a result, the valuation specialist often had to rely on his or her own professional judgment in developing the fair value measurement in financial reporting. Valuation specialists with comparable skills and training often came to different conclusions as to appropriate valuation methods and assumptions.

The AITF was formed to help valuation specialists understand guidelines that existed at the time for valuations for financial reporting. As part of the process of establishing more consistent practices in the valuation profession, the AITF communicated directly with representatives from the FASB, the SEC, and the PCAOB to evaluate proposals and recommend methodologies, assumptions, and approaches. The meetings of the AITF are open to all interested parties and have often included observers from the SEC and the PCAOB, as well as the FASB.[31] As part of its mission to improve the practice of valuations in financial reporting, the AITF formed a subcommittee in 2006 that developed a list of financial reporting valuation issues that needed further discussion and debate.[32] At the time, this list was considered the valuation profession's view as to which areas of valuation required additional guidance for application to financial reporting. The AITF's recommendations predated the FASB's Valuation Resource Group, which was organized by the FASB to provide recommendations and clarifications to the FASB staff about fair value measurements from an accounting perspective. The AITF's recommendations were used by the Appraisal Foundation in determining the subject matter for the first Business Valuation Working Group. The AITF continues to meet on a regular basis to discuss salient issues in valuations for financial reporting. The group's discussions and conclusions are nonauthoritative, but they provide a forum for the profession to express its views.

Conclusion

Since fair value measurements often include assumptions that are based on judgment or other nonmarket-based information, auditing the fair value measurements is complex. When there is not a market price available, the fair value measurement is often based on the work of an outside valuation specialist. The work of the outside specialist is also used to provide audit evidence to the auditors. Even though the measurement is performed by the valuation specialist, management still has the responsibility for the fair value measurement reported on the financial statements. The company's outside auditors audit the financial statements, which include the work of an outside specialist providing audit evidence.

Fair value measurements create an interesting new dynamic between the management of the company who prepares the financial statement, the company's independent auditor who audits the financial statements for conformity to GAAP, and an outside valuation specialist retained by management to develop the fair value measurements that are a part of the statements. One key to success is effective and early communication among management, the outside valuation specialist, and the company's independent auditing firm about the assumptions and methods used in determining fair value.

The Auditing Standards Board of the AICPA issued AU Section 328, SAS No. 101, *Auditing Fair Value Measurements and Disclosures,* to provide additional guidance specifically in the auditing of fair value measurements. SAS 101 is effective for periods after June 15, 2003. The guidance in SAS 101 suggests that the auditor evaluate significant assumptions used by the specialist, consider whether the valuation model is appropriate, and test the underlying data used in the analysis.

Reviews of fair value measurements by the Public Company Accounting Oversight Board have increased during the past few years. The PCAOB issued Staff Audit Practice Alert No. 2, *Matters Related to Auditing Fair Value Measurements of Financial Instruments and the Use of Specialists.*

Notes

1. "Challenges in Auditing Fair Value Accounting Estimates in the Current Market Environment, International Auditing and Assurance Standards Board," October 2008.
2. "The Report of the Committee on Basic Auditing Concepts," The American Accounting Association, *Accounting Review,* vol. 47.
3. O'Reilly, Vincent M. et al., *Montgomery's Auditing,* 12th ed. (New York: John Wiley & Sons, 1998), paragraph 1.5(d).
4. AU Section refers to the Codified Section of AICPA Professional Standards.
5. SAS 57, *Auditing Accounting Estimates.*
6. AU 342.01, *Auditing Accounting Estimates,* www.aicpa.org.
7. The Coca-Cola Company Form 10-K, December 31, 2008, page 146, www.thecoca-colacompany.com.
8. *Id.*
9. AU 342.05.
10. *Id.*
11. *Auditing Accounting Estimates,* www.aicpa.org.
12. AU Section 328, *Auditing Fair Value Measurements and Disclosures* AU 328.01
13. *Id.*
14. "Auditing Fair Value Measurements and Disclosures: A Toolkit for Auditors," AICPA, paragraph 7, www.aicpa.org.
15. AU §328.12, www.aicpa.org.
16. Menelaides, Susan L., Lynford E. Graham, and Gretchen Fischbach, "Auditor's Approach to Fair Value," *Journal of Accountancy,* AICPA (June 2003), www.aicpa.org.
17. AU 328.24.
18. AU 328.25.
19. AU 328.33.
20. AU 328.36.
21. *Id.*
22. AU 328.39.
23. Staff Audit Practice Alert No. 2, "Matters Related to Auditing Fair Value Measurements of Financial Instruments and the Use of Specialists," PCAOB, December 10, 2007, 4–5.
24. "SFAS 157 Fair Value Measurements: Implementation Challenges for the Alternative Investment Industry," Chris Mears, Principal in Charge of Rothstein Kass, September 2008, www.rko.com/pdfilb/SFAS_157_Fair_Value.pdf., p. 3.

25. *Id.*, p. 26.
26. Staff Audit Practice Alert No. 2, page 7.
27. "Auditing Fair Value Measurements and Disclosures," AICPA, www.aicpa.org.
28. "Our Mission & Vision," The Appraisal Foundation, www.appraisalfoundation. org.
29. Business Valuation Best Practices Working Group, "The Identification of Contributory Assets and the Calculation of Economic Rents," Exposure Draft, dated February 25, 2009, The Appraisal Foundation, page 5, www.appraisalfoundation.org.
30. Business Valuation Best Practices Working Group, "The Identification of Contributary Assets and the Calculation of Economic Rents: Toolkit," Exposure Draft, dated September 10, 2009. The Appraisal Foundation, p. 1, www.appraisalfoundation.org.
31. www.aitf.info.
32. *Illustrated Valuation Issues*, Appraisal Issues Task Force, February 6, 2006, www.appraisalfoundation.org.

CHAPTER 13

Fair Value Measurement Case Study

Learning Objectives

Software[2] Inc. is a fictional company. The narrative and exhibits in this case study include concepts under the Financial Accounting Standards Board's (FASB) Accounting Standards Codification (ASC) 820, *Fair Value Measurements and Disclosures* (SFAS 157), FASB ASC 805, *Business Combinations*, (SFAS 141 (R)) and FASB ASC 350, *Intangibles—Goodwill and Other* (SFAS 142). The case study is intended to provide an integrated illustration of a valuation engagement using the acquisition method and subsequent impairment analysis to illustrate points and provide examples. They are not intended to be used for any other purpose. Although the case has been prepared using commonly accepted valuation techniques, there is variation among practitioners within the profession. Others may choose different valuation methods and assumptions than the ones presented in the case study.

The case study is written with questions and exhibits intermingled throughout the fact pattern, so that the reader can test their understanding of the concepts presented throughout the text. Suggested answers can be found in Appendix 13A.

After reading this material, the reader should be able to apply the concepts presented in the FASB ASC 820, *Fair Value Measurements and Disclosures* (SFAS 157) ASC 805, *Business Combinations* (SFAS 141 (R)), and ASC 350, *Intangibles—Goodwill and Other* (SFAS 142). The case study will help the reader understand how a valuation specialist applies valuation techniques to estimate fair value, how to use the acquisition method of accounting, how to test for impairments of goodwill and other intangible assets, and how to calculate any impairment charge.

Business Background and Facts—Software

Software Squared Inc. (Software[2]) is an independent provider of graphic design and project-planning software primarily to architecture and engineering firms. Its revolutionary graphic design software allows firms to design in three dimensions. Second-generation upgrades to the graphic design software have recently been granted copyright protection. Recently Software^2 decided to shift the company's strategic focus away from graphic design software toward project-planning software. Management believes that the effort required to stay ahead of technological advancements in the graphic design field is too great, and that its flagship graphic design product's life is limited to a five-year horizon. In accordance with the new strategic focus, Software^2 is in the process of developing its own line of project management software for new market segments. It also plans to continue marketing third-party project management software to existing market segments. The project-planning software produced by outside vendors currently accounts for 15 percent of Software^2's sales. Software^2 plans to introduce its own project management software in January 20X3.

Software^2's graphic design software attracted the attention of Arch Span Technology Inc.'s (Arch Span) CEO who purchased the assets of the company on December 8, 20X1. Arch Span agreed to pay $18.2 million in cash and $1 million in Arch Span stock at closing. Arch Span is publicly traded on the NASDAQ exchange. The closing price was $31.25 per share on December 8, 20X1.

In addition to the cash and stock consideration, Arch Span will assume a $2 million obligation to JAX Industrial Supply (JAX), one of Software^2's suppliers. The $2 million JAX assumed note is due June 30, 20X4, and has a 10 percent annual interest rate with quarterly interest payments of $50,000. The 10 percent interest rate is considered to be a market rate. All operating liabilities will be assumed by Arch Span, as well.

Arch Span will also pay contingent consideration to Software^2's founder Ben Owen for the next four years based on the dollar amount of Software^2's revenues. If revenues exceed 110 percent of base 20X1 revenues, Owen will receive $100,000. If revenues fall between 100 percent and 109 percent of base revenues, Owen will receive $50,000. And if revenues fall below the base level, Owen will receive nothing. Each outcome is considered equally likely for all future years. Software^2's founder Ben Owen also signed an employment agreement with Arch Span containing a noncompetition clause.

Arch Span incurred $215,000 in legal fees and other due diligence costs associated with the acquisition of Software^2.

---

1. You have been engaged by Arch Span Technology Inc. to perform an acquisition date intangible asset valuation under the acquisition method. Discuss the acquisition method. What are the steps in the acquisition method? What is the measurement date of the business combination? What would cause the measurement date to differ from the closing date?

2. What information will you typically need to gather in order to perform an intangible asset valuation under the acquisition method? How does a valuation specialist obtain the requisite information?

Exhibit 13.1 contains a summary of Software[2]'s historic income statements. Common size calculations show each line item as a percentage of total sales. Exhibit 13.2 contains prospective financial information (PFI) and common-size calculations.

---

3. When using management forecasts as a basis for fair value measurement under income approaches, does a valuation specialist need to analyze management forecasts? Under what circumstances would it be appropriate to make adjustments to management projections? How are common-size statements used?

Exhibit 13.3a shows Software[2]'s business enterprise value (BEV) assuming the business combination is a stock acquisition. It excludes the recognition of goodwill and intangible assets resulting from the business combination. Therefore, it excludes the tax benefit from the deduction of amortization expenses relating to intangible assets. Exhibit 13.3b shows an alternate calculation of the BEV, including the tax benefit from deducting amortization expense on intangible assets and goodwill resulting from the business combination. The BEV in 13.3b is typical of business combinations structured as asset purchases. The acquisition of Software[2] by Arch Span is structured as an asset purchase.

---

4. What does business enterprise value mean, and why is it calculated? What are the common methods to calculate the BEV? When is it appropriate to include tax benefits in the calculation of BEV? How does the market participant assumption influence the BEV? Why would a valuation specialist calculate the BEV under the acquisition method?
5. How does the acquisition price compare to each of the business enterprise values in Exhibits 13.3a and b, and what does this generally indicate? How does the implied internal rate of return (IRR) compare to the discount rate? How does the inclusion of the tax benefits impact the IRR?
6. Discuss the following elements of the BEV in Exhibit 13.3a and b:

   - Calculation of the terminal value
   - What are the alternatives for calculating the terminal value?
   - How is debt treated, and what are the alternatives to this treatment?

The business enterprise value is calculated using a discount rate of 18 percent. Exhibit 13.4 shows the calculation of the 18 percent weighted average cost of capital (WACC) and is based on prevailing market rates on December 8, 20X1. The notes contained on the exhibit provide additional source information.

EXHIBIT 13.1 Software Squared: Historical Income Statements and Common-Size Income Statements, as of December 8, 20X1

	For Year Ended December 31								Last Twelve Months	
	20W7		20W8		20W9		20X0		11/30/20X1	
Graphic Design Software Sales	$ 7,641,747	53%	$ 8,809,511	57%	$ 9,123,394	54%	$17,232,208	78%	$25,217,769	85%
Project Planning Software Sales	6,689,598	47%	6,565,439	43%	7,661,960	46%	4,870,658	22%	4,450,195	15%
Discounts	(12,112)	0%	(4,148)	0%	(12,324)	0%	(10,291)	0%	(9,407)	0%
Sales	14,319,233	100%	15,370,802	100%	16,773,030	100%	22,092,575	100%	29,658,557	100%
Growth	*19%*		*7%*		*9%*		*32%*		*34%*	
Cost of Sales	9,959,506	70%	9,963,743	65%	10,880,565	65%	13,321,228	60%	18,112,952	61%
Gross Profit	4,359,727	30%	5,407,059	35%	5,892,465	35%	8,771,347	40%	11,545,605	39%
SG&A Expenses	3,179,116	22%	4,181,520	27%	4,186,296	25%	5,400,908	24%	5,700,813	19%
EBITDA	1,180,611	8%	1,225,539	8%	1,706,169	10%	3,370,439	15%	5,844,792	20%
Depreciation	218,142	2%	250,204	2%	410,076	2%	370,960	2%	331,844	1%
EBIT	$ 962,469	7%	$ 975,335	6%	$ 1,296,093	8%	$ 2,999,479	14%	$ 5,512,948	19%

Notes: Provided by Management.

EXHIBIT 13.2 Software Squared: Projected Income Statements and Common-Size Income Statements, as of December 8, 20X1

	For Year Ending December 31									
	20X1		20X2		20X3		20X4		20X5	
Graphic Design Software Sales	$ 22,149,309	85%	$ 23,256,689	85%	$ 21,956,990	75%	$ 20,361,410	65%	$ 19,923,241	60%
Project Planning Software Sales										
Third-Party Planning Software	3,908,702	15%	4,104,122	15%	2,927,599	10%	3,132,525	10%	3,320,540	10%
Software² Planning Software	—	0%	—	0%	4,391,398	15%	7,831,312	25%	9,961,620	30%
Discounts	(16,010)	0%	(16,810)	0%	(17,987)	0%	(19,246)	0%	(20,401)	0%
Sales	26,042,000	100%	27,344,000	100%	29,258,000	100%	31,306,000	100%	33,185,000	100%
Growth	*18%*		*5%*		*7%*		*7%*		*6%*	
Cost of Sales	15,625,000	60%	17,227,000	63%	18,433,000	63%	19,723,000	63%	20,906,000	63%
Gross Profit	10,417,000	40%	10,117,000	37%	10,825,000	37%	11,583,000	37%	12,279,000	37%
SG&A Expenses	5,504,000	21%	5,195,000	19%	5,559,000	19%	5,948,000	19%	6,306,000	19%
EBITDA	4,913,000	19%	4,922,000	18%	5,266,000	18%	5,635,000	18%	5,973,000	18%
Depreciation	353,944	1%	355,000	1%	380,000	1%	407,000	1%	431,000	1%
EBIT	$ 4,559,056	18%	$ 4,567,000	17%	$ 4,886,000	17%	$ 5,228,000	17%	$ 5,542,000	17%

Notes: Provided by Management.

EXHIBIT 13.3a Software Squared: Discounted Cash Flow Analysis—Assuming a Stock Purchase, as of December 8, 20X1

	20X1		20X2		20X3		20X4		20X5		Terminal Value	
Sales	$26,042,000	100%	$27,344,000	100%	$29,258,000	100%	$31,306,000	100%	$33,185,000	100%	$33,848,700	100%
Growth	*18%*		*5%*		*7%*		*7%*		*6%*		*2%*	
Cost of Sales	15,625,000	60%	17,227,000	63%	18,433,000	63%	19,723,000	63%	20,906,000	63%	21,324,120	63%
Gross Profit	10,417,000	40%	10,117,000	37%	10,825,000	37%	11,583,000	37%	12,279,000	37%	12,524,580	37%
SG&A Expenses	5,504,000	21%	5,195,000	19%	5,559,000	19%	5,948,000	19%	6,306,000	19%	6,432,120	19%
EBITDA	4,913,000	19%	4,922,000	18%	5,266,000	18%	5,635,000	18%	5,973,000	18%	6,092,460	18%
Less: Depreciation	353,944	1%	355,000	1%	380,000	1%	407,000	1%	431,000	1%	439,620	1%
EBIT	4,559,056	18%	4,567,000	17%	4,886,000	17%	5,228,000	17%	5,542,000	17%	5,652,840	17%
Less: Taxes	(1,732,441)	−7%	(1,735,460)	−6%	(1,856,680)	−6%	(1,986,640)	−6%	(2,105,960)	−6%	(2,148,079)	−6%
Debt-Free Net Income	2,826,615	11%	2,831,540	10%	3,029,320	10%	3,241,360	10%	3,436,040	10%	3,504,761	10%
Plus: Depreciation	353,944	1%	355,000	1%	380,000	1%	407,000	1%	431,000	1%	439,620	1%
Less: Capital Expenditures	(415,240)	−2%	(436,000)	−2%	(475,000)	−2%	(517,000)	−2%	(555,000)	−2%	(439,620)	−1%
Less: Incremental Working Capital	(718,769)	−3%	(236,955)	−1%	(348,335)	−1%	(372,723)	−1%	(341,966)	−1%	(120,789)	0%

		8%	9%	9%	9%	9%	10%
Cash Flows to Invested Capital		2,046,550	2,513,585	2,585,985	2,758,637	2,970,074	3,383,972
Terminal Value in 20X5							21,149,824
Partial Period		0.06	1.00	1.00	1.00	1.00	1.00
Period		0.03	0.56	1.56	2.56	3.56	3.56
Present Value Factor		0.995	0.911	0.772	0.654	0.554	0.554
Present Value Cash Flows to Invested Capital		128,290	2,289,934	1,996,519	1,804,929	1,646,837	11,727,088
Sum of PV of CF		7,866,509					
PV of Terminal Value		11,727,088					
Preliminary Value		19,593,596					
Enterprise Value, Rounded		**$19,594,000**					

Assumptions			
Discount Rate	(1)	18.0%	
Internal Rate of Return	(2)	16.6%	
Tax Rate	(3)	38.0%	
Long-Term Growth Rate	(4)	2.0%	
Debt-Free Working Capital %	(5)	18.2%	

Notes:
(1) Weighted average cost of capital per Exhibit 13.4.
(2) Implied rate that reconciles the future expected cash flows to the fair value of acquisition price.
(3) Estimated corporate tax rate.
(4) Based on Management's projections, the growth prospects of the industry, and the overall economy.
(5) Per Exhibit 13.21.

EXHIBIT 13.3b Software Squared: Discounted Cash Flow Analysis—Including Tax Benefits, Assuming an Asset Purchase, as of December 8, 20X1

	20X1		20X2		20X3		20X4		20X5		Terminal Value	
Sales	$26,042,000	100%	$27,344,000	100%	$29,258,000	100%	$31,306,000	100%	$33,185,000	100%	$33,848,700	100%
Growth	18%		5%		7%		7%		6%		2%	
Cost of Sales	15,625,000	60%	17,227,000	63%	18,433,000	63%	19,723,000	63%	20,906,000	63%	21,324,120	63%
Gross Profit	10,417,000	40%	10,117,000	37%	10,825,000	37%	11,583,000	37%	12,279,000	37%	12,524,580	37%
SG&A Expenses	5,504,000	21%	5,195,000	19%	5,559,000	19%	5,948,000	19%	6,306,000	19%	6,432,120	19%
EBITDA	4,913,000	19%	4,922,000	18%	5,266,000	18%	5,635,000	18%	5,973,000	18%	6,092,460	18%
Less: Depreciation	(6) 353,944	1%	355,000	1%	380,000	1%	407,000	1%	431,000	1%	439,620	1%
EBIT	4,559,056	18%	4,567,000	17%	4,886,000	17%	5,228,000	17%	5,542,000	17%	5,652,840	17%
Less: Taxes	(1,732,441)	–7%	(1,735,460)	–6%	(1,856,680)	–6%	(1,986,640)	–6%	(2,105,960)	–6%	(2,148,079)	–6%
Debt-Free Net Income	2,825,615	11%	2,831,540	11%	3,029,320	10%	3,241,360	10%	3,436,040	10%	3,504,761	10%
Plus: Depreciation	353,944	1%	355,000	1%	380,000	1%	407,000	1%	431,000	1%	439,620	1%
Less: Capital Expenditures	(415,240)	–2%	(436,000)	–2%	(475,000)	–2%	(517,000)	–2%	(555,000)	–2%	(439,620)	–1%
Less: Incremental Working Capital	(713,769)	–3%	(236,955)	–1%	(348,335)	–1%	(372,723)	–1%	(341,966)	–1%	(120,789)	0%

	8%	9%	9%	9%	9%	10%
Cash Flows to Invested Capital	2,046,550	2,513,585	2,585,985	2,758,637	2,970,074	3,383,972
Terminal Value in 20X5						21,149,824
Partial Period	0.06	1.00	1.00	1.00	1.00	1.00
Period	0.03	0.56	1.56	2.56	3.56	3.56
Present Value Factor	0.995	0.911	0.772	0.654	0.554	0.554
Present Value Cash Flows to Invested Capital	128,290	2,289,934	1,996,519	1,804,929	1,646,837	11,727,088
Sum of PV of CF	7,866,509					
PV of Terminal Value	11,727,088					
PV of Tax Benefit—Amortization of Intangibles	2,622,192					
Preliminary Value	22,215,788					
Enterprise Value, Rounded	**$22,216,000**					

Present Value of Tax Benefit—Amortization of Intangibles: (7)

Fair Value of Intangible Assets and Goodwill	16,000,000
15-Year Amortization Period	/ 15
Tax Amortization Expense per Year	1,066,667
Tax Rate	38.0%
Annual Amortization Benefit	405,333
Sum of PV Factors 20X1 to 20Y6	6.47
Present Value of Amortization Benefit	2,622,192

Assumptions		
Discount Rate	(1)	18.0%
Internal Rate of Return	(2)	18.6%
Tax Rate	(3)	38.0%
Long-Term Growth Rate	(4)	2.0%
Debt-Free Working Capital %	(5)	18.2%

Notes:

(1) Weighted average cost of capital per Exhibit 13.4.

(2) Implied rate that reconciles the future expected cash flows to the fair value of the acquisition price.

(3) Estimated corporate tax rate.

(4) Based on Management's projections, the growth prospects of the industry, and the overall economy.

(5) Per Exhibit 13.21.

(6) No adjustment was made to depreciation expense resulting from $407,000 step up of tax basis of fixed assets. The impact is considered immaterial to Enterprise Value.

(7) Estimated based on acquisition price of $21.4 million less $3.9 million working capital and less $1.8 million appraised value of fixed assets.

EXHIBIT 13.4 Software Squared: Weighted Average Cost of Capital (WACC), as of December 8, 20X1

Cost of Equity:

Build-up Method: $K_e = R_f + RP_m + RP_s + RP_u$

Risk-Free Rate (R_f)	3.45%	(1)
Market Premium (RP_m)	7.10%	(2)
Small Company Market Premium (RP_s)	5.82%	(3)
Company Specific Risk Premium (RP_u)	2.00%	(4)
$k_e =$	18.37%	

Capital Asset Pricing Model: $K_e = R_f + \beta(RP_m) + RP_s + RP_u$

Risk-Free Rate (R_f)	3.45%	(1)
Market Premium $\beta(RP_m)$, where $\beta = 1.14$	8.12%	(5)
Small Company Market Premium (RP_s)	5.82%	(3)
Company Specific Risk Premium (RP_u)	2.00%	(4)
$k_e =$	19.39%	
average $k_e =$	18.88%	

After-Tax Cost of Debt: $k_d = K_b(1 - t)$

Borrowing Rate (K_b)	8.79%	(6)
Tax Rate (t)	38.00%	(7)
$k_d =$	5.45%	

Weighted Average Cost of Capital (WACC)

	Capital Structure (8)	Cost	Weighted Cost
Equity	90.00%	18.88%	16.99%
Debt	10.00%	5.45%	0.54%
		WACC =	17.53%
		Rounded =	18.00%

Notes:
(1) 20-Year Treasury bond as of December 8, 20X1; Federal Reserve Statistical Release.
(2) Ibbotson: *SBBI: Valuation Edition 20X1 Yearbook*. Many valuation specialists add an industry adjustment factor per Ibbotson; however, the adjustment is controversial and there is wide diversity in practice.
(3) Ibbotson: *SBBI: Valuation Edition 20X1 Yearbook* (Long-Term Returns in Excess of CAPM Estimations for Decile Portfolios of the NYSE/AMEX/NASDAQ. Typically, from judgment using either the 9th or 10th deciles.
(4) Based on discussions with Management.
(5) Unlevered Adjusted Beta of 1.07: Ibbotson *Cost of Capital 20X1 Yearbook*. Relevered using median capital structure of guideline companies (8) and estimated corporate tax rate.
(6) Moody's Baa rate as of December 8, 20X1; Federal Reserve Statistical Release (proxy for marginal borrowing rate).
(7) Estimated corporate tax rate.
(8) Based on median level of capital structure for the guideline public companies. *Morningstar 20X1 Cost of Capital Yearbook.*

7. What is a weighted average cost of capital? How are the weights determined? Is the 18 percent weighted average cost of capital for Arch Span, Software[2], the combined entity, or some other hypothetical entity? What are the alternative methods for calculating the cost of equity? Why is the WACC appropriate in calculating the BEV for use in the acquisition method?

Fair Value of the Acquisition Price

Under FASB ASC 805, *Business Combinations*, (SFAS 141(R)) purchase consideration is the aggregate fair value of assets transferred from, liabilities incurred, and equity interests issued by the acquirer to the target company and its previous owners. It includes cash, other assets, a business or subsidiary of the acquirer, contingent consideration, common or preferred equity, options, warrants, and member interests of mutual entities. Determining the fair value of the acquisition price is the starting point when valuing intangible assets using the acquisition method.

8. Calculate the fair value of the acquisition price.
9. How is the contingent consideration treated in the fair value acquisition price under FASB ASC 805 (SFAS 141(R))? How does this treatment differ from previous accounting for business combinations?
10. What is an alternative to calculating the fair value of the consideration paid under the acquisition method?

Exhibit 13.5 shows the calculation of the fair value of the acquisition price.

Adjustments to the Closing Balance Sheet

When a valuation specialist is engaged to perform a valuation of intangible assets under the acquisition method, the specialist typically relies on management to provide the fair value of certain other assets and liabilities as of the acquisition date. The acquirer also typically retains appraisers to determine the fair value of real estate and other tangible assets.

Exhibit 13.6 presents Software[2]'s historic cost balance sheet on the closing date of the acquisition—December 8, 20X1.

As you analyze Software[2]'s closing date balance sheet, several items come to your attention:

- Cash and equivalents include a $100,000, one-year T-bill, recorded at its purchase price of $90,196. The T-bill matures in early 20X2 and is worth $98,778 on December 8, 20X1.

- An analysis of the accounts receivable aging reveals two customers with severely delinquent accounts. Further investigation indicates both customers are insolvent and the likelihood of repayment is remote. The $125,000 in receivables for these two customers is reflected at 25 percent in the allowance for doubtful accounts. A 100 percent provision is considered appropriate as of December 8, 20X1.
- Software[2]'s product line includes project planning and management software. Although it is developing its own project management software, Software[2] sells and distributes software from outside vendors. One of the vendors, Target Project Management, has recently gone out of business and its software is considered obsolete. Sixteen copies of Target Project Management Software are included in inventory at $65,000 each.
- The land, building, and machinery and equipment were appraised for $150,000, $250,000, and $800,000, respectively. Office equipment's depreciated cost is considered to be a close approximation of its fair value. Accumulated depreciation for office equipment is $230,000.
- Analysis of Software[2]'s sales contracts indicates the company offers an 18-month warranty for all its products. In the past, all warranty costs have been expensed at the time of payment. Further analysis indicates a $735,000 warranty liability is appropriate on December 8, 20X1.
- Arch Span's tax accountant examined Software[2]'s financial statements and tax returns. He agrees that the $150,000 deferred tax asset is appropriately recorded. However, he believes that some aggressive positions were taken, and he estimates the deferred tax liability to be $100,000.
- Software[2] is in the process of installing software for two of its customers. Although the company has received full payment for the software, the customers have not signed off on the installations. Under the terms of the sales contracts, the customers can return the software within 60 days if they are not completely satisfied. Software[2] has recorded the $450,000 received from these two customers as deferred income.

---

11. Why is it necessary for the valuation specialist to analyze the company's preliminary acquisition balance sheet? What are the implications for fair value measurement if the balance sheet is misstated?

12. Why is the "highest and best" use assumption important in the fair value measurement of intangible assets?

13. How does the analysis of deferred tax assets differ from deferred tax liabilities? What is the central issue for deferred tax assets?

14. Why is revenue recognition an important consideration when performing an acquisition method valuation?

EXHIBIT 13.5 Software Squared: Fair Value of Acquisition Price, as of December 8, 20X1

Cash		$18,200,000
Equity Consideration—Arch Span	(1)	1,000,000
Contingent Consideration—Owen	(2)	174,850
Note Payable to JAX Industrial Supply	(3)	2,037,363
Acquisition Costs	(4)	—
Fair Value of Acquisition Price		**$21,412,213**

Notes:
(1) 32,000 shares at closing price on 12/8/X1 of $31.25 /share.
(2) The fair value of expected contingent consideration is recognized at acquisition date, as part of the purchase price per FASB ASC 805 (SFAS 141(R)).
   A. Calculate the expected payment.
      $(33.3\% \times \$100,000) + (33.3\% \times \$50,000) + (33.3\% \times \$0) = \$50,000$
   B. Present value on December 31, 20X1
      PMT = 50,000
      N = 4
      I/Y = 5.456%
      Computed PV = 175,436
   C. Present value on December 8, 20X1
      FV = 175,436
      N = 23/365
      I/Y = 5.456%
      Computed PV = 174,850
(3) The note payable to JAX Industrial Supply includes accrued interest.
(4) Acquisition costs are excluded from fair value of acquisition price because deal-related transaction costs are expensed under FASB ASC 805 (SFAS 141(R)).

The required adjustments to Software²'s December 8, 20X1, balance sheet have been made as shown in Exhibit 13.7. It represents the preliminary acquisition balance sheet prior to recording goodwill and intangible assets.

Identifying and Valuing Intangible Assets

15. How does a valuation specialist typically identify an acquired company's intangible assets? What are the likely acquired intangible assets in this case study?
16. What are the two criteria for recognizing intangible assets under FASB ASC 805 (SFAS 141(R))? Who is responsible for identifying the intangible assets? How does this occur in practice?
17. What are the three broad approaches to valuing intangible assets and specific methods within those approaches that you would use to value Software²'s intangible assets? What are the advantages and disadvantages of each of the approaches?

EXHIBIT 13.6 Software Squared: Historic Cost Balance Sheet, as of December 8, 20X1

Assets		Liabilities & Stockholders' Equity	
Current Assets		**Current Liabilities**	
Cash & Equivalents	296,526	Accounts Payable	878,168
Trade Receivables	2,975,097	Accrued Liabilities	191,431
Allowance—Doubtful Accounts	(50,000)	Deferred Income	450,000
Inventories	3,832,377	Income Taxes Payable	77,296
Prepaid Expenses	291,136		
		Total Current Liabilities	1,596,895
Total Current Assets	7,345,136		
		Deferred Income Tax Liability	61,000
Other Assets			
In Process R&D	91,718	**Long-Term Debt**	
Software Development Costs, Net	3,256,000	Notes Payable—Jax Industrial Supply	2,000,000
Organization Costs, Net	59,390		
Deferred Taxes	150,000	Total Long-Term Debt	2,000,000
Total Other Assets	3,557,108		
		Stockholders' Equity	
Property and Equipment		Common Stock—$1 Par	22,000
Land	341,776	Additional Paid-In Capital	1,638,000
Building	1,534,502	Retained Earnings	4,388,644
Machinery and Equipment	2,525,687	Year to Date Earnings	2,622,105
Office Equipment	863,487		
	5,265,452	Total Equity	8,670,749
Less-Accum. Depreciation	3,839,052		
Net Property and Equipment	1,426,400		
Total Assets	12,328,644	Total Liabilities & Equity	12,328,644

EXHIBIT 13.7 Software Squared: Preliminary Balance Sheet—Acquisition Method without Intangible and Goodwill Adjustments, as of December 8, 20X1

		Adjustments		
Assets	Unadjusted	Debit	Credit	Adjusted
Current Assets				
Cash & Equivalents	296,526	8,582		305,108
Trade Receivables	2,975,097			2,975,097
Allowance—Doubtful Accounts	(50,000)		93,750	(143,750)
Inventories	3,832,377		1,040,000	2,792,377
Prepaid Expenses	291,136			291,136
Total Current Assets	7,345,136			6,219,968
Other Assets				
In-Process R&D	91,718		91,718	—
Software Development Costs, Net	3,256,000		3,256,000	—
Organization Costs, Net	59,390		59,390	—
Deferred Taxes	150,000			150,000
Total Other Assets	3,557,108			150,000
Property & Equipment				
Land	341,776		191,776	150,000
Building	1,534,502		1,284,502	250,000
Machinery & Equipment	2,525,687		1,725,687	800,000
Office Equipment	863,487		230,000	633,487
	5,265,452			1,833,487
Less-Accum. Depreciation	3,839,052	3,839,052		—
Net Property & Equipment	1,426,400			1,833,487
Total Assets	12,328,644			8,203,455
Liabilities & Stockholders' Equity				
Current Liabilities				
Accrued Interest—N/P			37,363	37,363
Accounts Payable	878,168			878,168
Accrued Liabilities	191,431			191,431
Deferred Income	450,000			450,000
Income Taxes Payable	77,296			77,296
Warranty Liability			735,000	735,000
Total Current Liabilities	1,596,895			2,369,258
Deferred Income Tax Liability	61,000		39,000	100,000
Long-Term Debt				
Notes Payable	2,000,000			2,000,000
Total Long-Term Debt	2,000,000			2,000,000
Stockholders' Equity				
Common Stock—$1 Par	22,000			22,000
Additional Paid-In Capital	1,638,000		2,074,197	3,712,197
Retained Earnings	4,388,644	4,388,644		—
Year-to-Date Earnings (Loss)	2,622,105	2,622,105		—
Total Equity	8,670,749			3,734,197
Total Liabilities & Equity	12,328,644	10,858,383	10,858,383	8,203,455
Adjusted Debt-Free Working Capital Calculation				3,888,073

On the acquisition date, Software^2's unadjusted, closing balance sheet contained capitalized software development costs of $3.256 million and in-process research and development of $91,718. The capitalized software development costs included costs related to the graphic design software. The in-process R&D costs are for the project management software that has been in development for one year.

Although many of the costs associated with the graphic design software and the project management software were appropriately expensed as incurred, Software^2 has kept meticulous records from the inception of these projects. The records include the number of hours to create these software projects by employee and the hourly salaries for each employee involved in the projects. Management estimates that benefits and overhead cost an additional 33 percent and 15 percent, respectively. For software projects, management believes the opportunity cost is equal to the company's weighted average cost of capital of 18 percent, and expects to make a 5 percent profit.

---

18. Graphic design software is Software^2's most important asset, and it was the reason for Arch Span's acquisition of Software^2. What additional consideration does this situation warrant? What alternative approaches can be used to value graphic design software?

19. When performing a valuation using the cost approach, which costs would you likely consider? What are the alternative treatments of taxes and the tax benefit from amortization? Why do some valuation specialists apply the cost approach on a before-tax basis and others apply it on an after-tax basis?

Exhibits 13.8a and b show calculations of the graphic design software's reproduction cost and replacement cost under alternative tax applications and Exhibits 13.9a and b show calculations of IPR&D replacement cost under alternative tax applications.

---

20. What is the difference between reproduction cost and replacement cost? Obsolescence is deducted from the reproduction cost to arrive at the replacement cost. What types of obsolescence would the valuation specialist consider? Based on the facts in this case study, does a 25 percent obsolescence factor seem appropriate?

21. Why would an opportunity cost of development and entrepreneurial profit be included as part of the costs? How are these percentages determined?

As a result of its sophisticated marketing efforts, Software^2 has attracted a broad customer base within its specific market niche. Its software products have a relatively high unit cost that is usually treated as a capital expenditure by customers. Therefore, customer relationships tend to last for several years. Existing customers provide a captive market for graphic design software upgrades and for cross-selling the company's project management software. Software[2] has 69 customers, including the 31 projected new customers for full year 20X1. Software[2] estimates that it has spent $1.28 million to attract 147 new customers in the last five years. The marketing director believes that it would take two and a half years to build a customer base from scratch.

Exhibits 13.10a and b show the valuation of customer relationships under the cost approach using alternative tax applications.

EXIIIBIT 13.8a Software Squared: Valuation of Graphic Design Software, Including Tax Benefits, as of December 8, 20X1

	Productivity		
	Lines of Code	Lines per Hour	Estimated Hours to Re-create
Module A	96,000	2	48,000
Module B	150,000	3	50,000
Module C	120,000	3	40,000
Module D	9,800	4	2,450
	375,800		140,450
Fully Loaded, Hourly Rate (1)			73.87
Reproduction Cost			10,375,042
Less: Obsolescence based on remaining useful life		25%	(2,593,760)
Replacement Cost			7,781,281
Less: Tax		38%	(2,956,887)
After-Tax Value before Amortization Benefit			4,824,394
Amortization Benefit Multiplier (2)			1.16
			5,575,700
Fair Value of Graphic Design Software, Rounded			**$5,576,000**

Note:
(1) The fully loaded, hourly rate includes:

Blended hourly salary		$43.29
Benefits	33%	14.28
Overhead	15%	6.35
Opportunity cost of development	18%	7.79
Entrepreneurial profit	5%	2.16
		$73.87

(2) Amortization Benefit Multiplier based on a 19% required rate of return.

EXHIBIT 13.8b Software Squared: Valuation of Graphic Design Software, Excluding Tax Benefits, as of December 8, 20X1

	Productivity		
	Lines of Code	Lines per Hour	Estimated Hours to Re-create
Module A	96,000	2	48,000
Module B	150,000	3	50,000
Module C	120,000	3	40,000
Module D	9,800	4	2,450
	375,800		140,450
Fully Loaded, Hourly Rate (1)			73.87
Reproduction Cost			10,375,042
Less: Obsolescence based on remaining useful life		25%	(2,593,760)
Replacement Cost			7,781,281
Fair Value of Graphic Design Software, Rounded			**$7,781,000**

Note:

(1) The fully loaded, hourly rate includes:

Blended hourly salary		$43.29
Benefits	33%	14.28
Overhead	15%	6.35
Opportunity cost of development	18%	7.79
Entrepreneurial profit	5%	2.16
		$73.87

22. The fair value measurement of customer relationships includes opportunity costs and entrepreneur's profit. Why is there a time frame included in this calculation?

23. Exhibit 13.10a includes an amortization benefit factor of 1.15. What is an amortization benefit factor? What is the purpose of this adjustment? How is it calculated?

24. What are the alternatives to using the replacement cost method to estimate the fair value of customer relationships?

EXHIBIT 13.9a Software Squared: Valuation of In-Process Research and Development, Including Tax Benefits, as of December 8, 20X1

Cost of In-Process R&D (1)		$1,485,600
Opportunity Cost (2)	18%	267,408
Entrepreneur's Profit (2)	5%	74,280
Total Replacement Cost		**1,827,288**
Less: Taxes	38%	(694,369)
After-Tax Replacement Cost		1,132,919
Amortization Benefit Multiplier (3)		1.12
Total Replacement Cost After-Tax Benefits		1,267,186
Fair Value In-Process R&D, Rounded		**$1,267,000**

Notes:
(1) Information provided by management.
(2) Assumes a one-year period applies to the opportunity costs to develop and to entrepreneurial profit.
(3) Amortization Benefit Multiplier based on a 26% required rate of return.

EXHIBIT 13.9b Software Squared: Valuation of In-Process Research and Development, Excluding Tax Benefits, as of December 8, 20X1

Cost of In-Process R&D (1)		$1,485,600
Opportunity Cost (2)	18%	267,408
Entrepreneur's Profit (2)	5%	74,280
Total Replacement Cost		1,827,288
Fair Value In-Process R&D, Rounded		**$1,827,000**

Notes:
(1) Information provided by management.
(2) Assumes a one-year period applies to the opportunity costs to develop and to entrepreneurial profit.

Software^2 has 43 dedicated employees, including 19 highly qualified graphic designers and programmers. Several of the graphic designers and programmers are considered to be indispensable, as they are the creative force behind the company's product development. In addition to payroll information, Software^2 files contain information on direct hiring and training costs. Software^2 also estimates inefficiency costs for new employees based on effectiveness percentages ranging from 70 percent to 90 percent and on a three- to six-month period required to achieve full productivity.

Exhibits 13.11a and 13.11b show the valuation of Software^2's assembled workforce under alternative tax approaches.

EXHIBIT 13.10a Software Squared: Valuation of Customer Relationships, Including Tax Benefits, as of December 8, 20X1

Year	Total Selling and Marketing Expense	% of Cost from New Customers	Selling Costs for New Customers	Number of New Customers
20X1 (1)	$299,860	71.2%	$ 213,500	31
20X0	417,074	59.3%	247,325	26
20W9	418,415	68.4%	286,196	42
20W8	464,830	62.8%	291,913	27
20W7	407,286	59.8%	243,557	21
Total			$1,282,491	147

Total Selling Costs for New Customers	$ 1,282,491
Divided by Total New Customers	147
Cost per New Customer	8,724
Times the Number of Customers on Dec. 8, 20X1	69
Total Selling and Marketing Cost for Existing Customers	601,986

Opportunity Cost / Years to Re-create	2.5 (2)	18% (2)	270,894
Entrepreneur's Profit / Years to Re-create	2.5 (2)	5% (2)	75,248

Before-Tax Replacement Cost of Existing Customers	948,127
Less: Tax @ 38%	(360,288)
After-Tax Replacement Cost of Customers	587,839
Amortization Benefit Multiplier (3)	1.15
Fair Value of Customer Relationships	675,483
Fair Value of Customer Relationships, rounded	$ 675,000

Notes:
  (1) 20X1 is projected full year.
  (2) Per Management.
  (3) Amortization Benefit Multiplier based on a 20% required rate of return.

EXHIBIT 13.10b Software Squared: Valuation of Customer Relationships, Excluding Tax Benefits, as of December 8, 20X1

Year	Total Selling and Marketing Expense	% of Cost from New Customers	Selling Costs for New Customers	Number of New Customers
20X1 (1)	$299,860	71.2%	$ 213,500	31
20X0	417,074	59.3%	247,325	26
20W9	418,415	68.4%	286,196	42
20W8	464,830	62.8%	291,913	27
20W7	407,286	59.8%	243,557	21
Total			$1,282,491	147

Total Selling Costs for New Customers	$ 1,282,491
Divided by Total New Customers	147
Cost per New Customer	8,724
Times the Number of Customers on Dec. 8, 20X1	69
Total Selling and Marketing Cost for Existing Customers	601,986

Opportunity Cost / Years to Re-create	2.5 (2)	18% (2)	270,894
Entrepreneur's Profit / Years to Re-create	2.5 (2)	5% (2)	75,248

Before-Tax Replacement Cost of Existing Customers	948,127
Fair Value of Customer Relationships, rounded	**$ 948,000**

Notes:
(1) 20X1 is projected full year.
(2) Per Management.

25. Is assembled workforce an identifiable intangible asset under the acquisition method? Why would the fair value of an assembled workforce be determined under the acquisition method? Why are opportunity costs and entrepreneur's profit excluded? Can other methods be used to value the assembled workforce?

EXHIBIT 13.11a Software Squared: Valuation of Assembled Workforce, Including Tax Benefits, as of December 8, 20X1

Employee Classification	Average Annual Salary (1)	Fringe Benefits (1)	Average Annual Salary with Benefits	Total Hiring Cost per Employee (2)	Number of Employees as of Valuation Date (1)	Total Hiring Cost
Executive	113,575	12,239	125,814	25,163	4	100,651
Sales	89,191	10,295	99,486	19,897	8	159,177
Graphic Designers	65,780	546	66,326	13,265	10	132,651
Administrative	22,958	3,837	26,795	5,359	5	26,795
Programmers	46,344	4,465	50,809	10,162	9	91,456
Warehouse	26,073	2,089	28,162	5,632	7	39,427
					43	550,157

Employee Classification	Average Salary with Benefits	Percent Effective (1)	Number of Months Until Full Productivity (1)	Inefficiency Training Costs	Direct Training Costs (3)	Total Training Costs per Employee	Number of Employees as of Valuation Date (1)	Total Training Cost
Executive	125,814	90%	6.0	3,670	3,621	7,291	4	29,162
Sales	99,486	90%	3.0	1,658	1,699	3,357	8	26,857
Graphic Designers	66,326	90%	3.0	1,105	1,241	2,346	10	23,464
Administrative	26,795	90%	3.0	447	1,135	1,582	5	7,908
Programmers	50,809	80%	3.0	1,694	1,320	3,014	9	27,123
Warehouse	28,162	70%	3.0	1,408	618	2,026	7	14,183
							43	128,697

Subtotal	678,854
Less: Income Tax Expense	(257,964)
Total	420,889
Plus: Amortization Benefit (4)	1.16
Fair Value of Assembled Workforce	489,472
Rounded to	489,000

Notes:

(1) Information provided by Management.

(2) Estimated to be 20% of average annual salary and benefits, based on discussions with management.

(3) Estimated by Human Resources based on recent costs for classes and materials.

(4) Amortization Benefit Multiplier based on an 18% required rate of return.

EXHIBIT 13.11b Software Squared: Valuation of Assembled Workforce, Excluding Tax Benefits, as of December 8, 20X1

Employee Classification	Average Annual Salary (1)	Fringe Benefits (1)	Average Annual Salary with Benefits	Total Hiring Cost per Employee (2)	Number of Employees as of Valuation Date (1)	Total Hiring Cost
Executive	113,575	12,239	125,814	25,163	4	100,651
Sales	89,191	10,295	99,486	19,897	8	159,177
Graphic Designers	65,780	546	66,326	13,265	10	132,651
Administrative	22,958	3,837	26,795	5,359	5	26,795
Programmers	46,344	4,465	50,809	10,162	9	91,456
Warehouse	26,073	2,089	28,162	5,632	7	39,427
					43	550,157

Employee Classification	Average Salary with Benefits	Percent Effective (1)	Number of Months Until Full Productivity (1)	Inefficiency Training Costs	Direct Training Costs (3)	Total Training Costs per Employee	Number of Employees as of Valuation Date (1)	Total Training Cost
Executive	125,814	90%	6.0	3,670	3,621	7,291	4	29,162
Sales	99,486	90%	3.0	1,658	1,699	3,357	8	26,857
Graphic Designers	66,326	90%	3.0	1,105	1,241	2,346	10	23,464
Administrative	26,795	90%	3.0	447	1,135	1,582	5	7,908
Programmers	50,809	80%	3.0	1,694	1,320	3,014	9	27,123
Warehouse	28,162	70%	3.0	1,408	618	2,026	7	14,183
							43	128,697

Replacement Cost of Assembled Workforce   678,854

Fair Value of Assembled Workforce   679,000

Notes:

(1) Information provided by Management.

(2) Estimated to be 20% of average annual salary and benefits, based on discussions with management.

(3) Estimated by Human Resources based on recent costs for classes and materials.

345

Prospects for future sales are enhanced by Software^2's widespread name recognition within the industry. When its graphic design software was introduced to the market four years ago, the marketing director created a sensation at the industry's largest trade show. That introduction was followed up by an award-winning, targeted advertising campaign. As a result, Software^2's marketing research indicates that more than 33 percent of industry participants recognize the Software^2 name and logo and associate it with graphic design software.

Royalty rates for licenses within the design and engineering software industry are presented in Exhibit 13.12, and Software^2's trade name is valued using the relief from royalty method, as shown in Exhibit 13.13.

---

26. The fair value of the trade name is determined using a royalty savings rate of 1 percent based on comparable industry rates. What factors should the valuation specialist consider when selecting an appropriate industry royalty rate? What are some of the challenges in applying the relief from royalty method?

27. Is the relief from royalty method a market or an income valuation approach? What assumptions are incorporated into this valuation? The valuation of the trade name is presented after taxes and includes the tax benefit of amortization. Why is the after-tax application preferred in the relief from royalty method? What other methods can be used to value a trade name?

The noncompete employment agreement signed by Ben Owen provides value to the company by protecting future revenues from competition. The agreement is for a four-year period through December 8, 20X5. Arch Span estimates that direct competition by Ben Owen would cause a 20 percent loss in revenue declining to 8 percent by 20X5 and having no impact thereafter. The probability that Ben Owen would compete is considered to be remote and is assigned a 10 percent probability.

The noncompetition agreement is valued using a with/without method under the income approach in Exhibit 13.14.

---

28. Are there alternative methods that can be used to value a noncompetition agreement? What assumptions form the basis for this valuation?

Six months before selling Software^2 to Arch Span, Ben Owen registered a copyright on the revolutionary upgrades contained in the second generation release of Software^2's graphic design software. Software^2 was in the process of negotiating contracts with two international engineering firms

EXHIBIT 13.12 Software Squared: Design and Engineering Software Industry, as of December 8, 20X1

Licensor	Licensee	Date	Terms	Royalty	
				Low	High
Undisclosed	Payton Technologies, Inc.	NA	International	1.0%	1.0%
AAB Design Query Inc.	O.J.S Engineering Company, Shelby Industry Design Co. Ltd. & J.T. O.N.I Century Manfg.	Dec-X5	International, nonexclusive, and nontransferable	2.0%	5.0%
Bolinger Company Inc.	Coleman Design Inc.	Feb-X2	NA	8.0%	8.0%
DSC Holding Corp.	Central Engineering Corp.	May-X4	NA	3.0%	3.0%
Design Technology Corp.	Temic & Sons GMBH	Jan-X8	NA	0.0%	0.8%
Forrestner Winthrop Design Development Company Limited	Heilfield Yang Group Co., Ltd.	NA	Exclusive	1.0%	1.0%
Gideon Engineering	Seychelle Engineering Technologies, Inc.	Jun-X2	NA	1.0%	1.0%
Harrington Technologies, Inc.	Miller Material Handling Inc.	Mar-X8	International, sole, and exclusive	0.8%	0.8%
North Hamption Company	Jenkins Corp.	Dec-X9	NA, nonassignable, nontransferable, and exclusive	3.0%	3.0%
Safety International Inc.	National Safety Assoc. of North America	Apr-X6	NA, limited, nontransferable and exclusive	3.0%	3.0%
			High	8.0%	8.0%
			3rd Q	3.0%	3.0%
			Mean	2.3%	2.7%
			Median	1.5%	2.0%
			1st Q	1.0%	1.0%
			Low	0.0%	0.8%
			Mode	1.0%	1.0%
			Selected Royalty Rate:		1.0%

Source: Royalty rates are typically available from Royalty Source, www.royaltysource.com. However, the companies and royalty rates presented in this exhibit are not real.

347

EXHIBIT 13.13 Software Squared: Valuation of Trade Name, as of December 8, 20X1

	20X1		20X2		20X3		20X4		20X5		20X1 + 30 years	
Revenue	$26,042,000	100%	$27,344,000	100%	$29,258,000	100%	$31,306,000	100%	$33,185,000	100%	$55,532,380	100%
Growth			5%		7%		7%		6%		2%	
Pre-Tax Royalty Savings	260,420	1%	273,440	1%	292,580	1%	313,060	1%	331,850	1%	555,324	1%
Less: Taxes	(98,960)	0%	(103,907)	0%	(111,180)	0%	(118,963)	0%	(126,103)	0%	(211,023)	0%
After-Tax Royalty Savings	161,460	1%	169,533	1%	181,400	1%	194,097	1%	205,747	1%	344,301	1%
Partial Period	0.06		1.00		1.00		1.00		1.00		1.00	
Period	0.03		0.56		1.56		2.56		3.56		29.56	
Present Value Factor	0.995		0.907		0.762		0.640		0.538		0.006	
PV of After-Tax Royalty Savings	10,119		153,716		138,215		124,277		110,703		2,012	

Sum of PV of Savings		1,189,177
Amortization Benefit Multiplier	(1)	1.16
Preliminary Value		1,374,368
Concluded Value, Rounded		**$1,374,000**

Assumptions		Note
Discount Rate	19.0%	(2)
Long-Term Growth Rate	2.0%	(3)
Tax Rate	38.0%	(4)
Royalty Rate	1.0%	(5)
Remaining Useful Life	30 years	(6)

Notes:

(1) Represents the present value of the estimated tax benefit derived from the amortization of the intangible asset, over the tax life (15 years) of the asset, based on a 19% required rate of return.

(2) Weighted Average Cost of Capital plus 1%.

(3) Based on discussions with Management, growth prospects for the industry, and the overall economy.

(4) Estimated corporate tax rate.

(5) Royalty rate based on industry rates—Exhibit 13.12.

(6) Based on discussions with management.

EXHIBIT 13.14 Software Squared: Analysis of Noncompetition Agreement, as of December 8, 20X1

		20X1		20X2		20X3		20X4		20X5		Terminal	
Revenue		$26,042,000		$27,344,000		$29,258,000		$31,306,000		$33,185,000		$33,848,700	
Growth		*18%*		*5%*		*7%*		*7%*		*6%*		*2%*	
Revenue Lost to Competition	(1)	5,208,400	20%	5,468,800	20%	5,266,440	18%	4,695,900	15%	2,654,800	8%	—	
x Probability of Competition	(1)	10%		10%		10%		10%		10%			
Adjusted Revenue		25,521,160	100%	26,797,120	100%	28,731,356	100%	30,836,410	100%	32,919,520	100%	33,848,700	100%
Cost of Sales		15,312,500	60%	16,882,460	63%	18,101,206	63%	19,427,155	63%	20,738,752	63%	21,324,120	63%
Gross Profit		10,208,660	40%	9,914,660	37%	10,630,150	37%	11,409,255	37%	12,180,768	37%	12,524,580	37%
SG&A Expenses		5,393,920	21%	5,091,100	19%	5,458,938	19%	5,858,780	19%	6,255,552	19%	6,432,120	19%
EBITDA		4,814,740	19%	4,823,560	18%	5,171,212	18%	5,550,475	18%	5,925,216	18%	6,092,460	18%
Depreciation		346,865	1%	347,900	1%	373,160	1%	400,895	1%	427,552	1%	439,620	1%
EBIT		4,467,875	18%	4,475,660	17%	4,798,052	17%	5,149,580	17%	5,497,664	17%	5,652,840	17%
Less: Taxes		(1,697,792)	-7%	(1,700,751)	-6%	(1,823,260)	-6%	(1,956,840)	-6%	(2,089,112)	-6%	(2,148,079)	-6%
Debt-Free Net Income		2,770,082	11%	2,774,909	10%	2,974,792	10%	3,192,740	10%	3,408,552	10%	3,504,761	10%
Plus: Depreciation		346,865	1%	347,900	1%	373,160	1%	400,895	1%	427,552	1%	439,620	1%
Less: Capital Expenditures		(406,935)	-2%	(427,280)	-2%	(466,450)	-2%	(509,245)	-2%	(550,560)	-2%	(439,620)	-2%
Less: Incremental Working Capital		(623,980)	-2%	(232,216)	-1%	(352,018)	-1%	(383,106)	-1%	(379,112)	-1%	(120,789)	-1%

(Continued)

EXHIBIT 13.14 (*Continued*)

	20X1	20X2	20X3	20X4	20X5	Terminal
Cash Flows to Invested Capital	2,086,033	2,463,313	2,529,484	2,701,284	2,906,431	3,383,972
Terminal Value in 20X5						21,149,824
Partial Period	0.06	1.00	1.00	1.00	1.00	1.00
Period	0.03	0.56	1.56	2.56	3.56	3.56
Present Value Factor	0.995	0.911	0.772	0.654	0.554	0.554
Present Value of Cash Flows to Invested Capital	130,765	2,244,135	1,952,897	1,767,403	1,611,549	11,727,088
Fair Value without Noncompetition Agreement in Place	19,433,837					
Fair Value with Noncompetition Agreement in Place (3)	19,593,596					
Preliminary Value of Noncompetition Agreement	159,759					
Amortization Benefit Multiplier (2)	1.16					
Concluded Value of Noncompetition Agreement	**$186,000**					

Assumptions		
Discount Rate	(4)	18.0%
Tax Rate	(5)	38.0%
Long-Term Growth Rate	(6)	2.0%
Term of Benefit from Noncompete Agreement	(7)	5 years

Notes:

(1) Based on discussions with Management, direct competition would cause a 20% loss in revenue in 20X1, declining to 8% by 20X5, and having no impact thereafter. Management assumes a 10% probability of competition for all years.

(2) Represents the present value of the estimated tax benefit derived from the amortization of the intangible asset, over the tax life (15 years) of the asset, and an 18% required rate of return.

(3) Business enterprise value from Exhibit 13.3a.

(4) Weighted average cost of capital per Exhibit 13.4.

(5) Estimated corporate tax rate.

(6) Based on Management's projections, the growth prospects of the industry, and the overall economy.

(7) Per Noncompetition Agreement dated December 8, 20X1.

and several prominent architecture firms as of the date of the acquisition. In addition, the company had recently beefed up its sales force by hiring three seasoned salespeople and a new vice president of sales. Arch Span's CEO Bruce Tucker reviewed Software^2's sales projections as part of the acquisition's due diligence process and was favorably impressed.

Software^2's graphic design software is valued using the multiperiod excess earnings method in Exhibit 13.15.

---

29. The required rate of return on contributory assets is deducted from the cash flows of the company to arrive at excess earnings. What are contributory assets? Discuss how to estimate the required return on each of the contributory assets.
30. What is an appropriate discount rate to use for the cash flows attributable to the graphic design software? How does this rate compare to the company's weighted average cost of capital?
31. How would your analysis of the graphic design software using the multiperiod excess earnings method differ if the purpose of the valuation were to assist management in maximizing the benefit from the acquired graphic design software? Would projections include synergies with Arch Span? Would the discount rate differ?

In-process research and development is also valued using the multiperiod excess earnings method in Exhibit 13.16.

---

32. How is it possible to use the excess earnings method to estimate the value of two different assets?

Exhibit 13.17 shows the calculation of the required return on contributory assets for valuing Software^2's graphic design software and in-process research and development.

---

33. What is the difference between "return of capital" and "return on capital"?
34. Contributory charges under the multiperiod excess earnings method are one of the more controversial topics in valuation. What are some of the issues? How do you handle negative working capital as a contributory charge? Do you take a charge on goodwill, or not? How do you handle contributory charges on noncompete agreements when there is a mismatch between the contractual protection and the life of the expected benefit?

EXHIBIT 13.15 Software Squared: Valuation of Graphic Design Software, as of December 8, 20X1

	20X1	20X2	20X3	20X4	20X5	20X6
Projected Companywide Revenue	$26,042,000	$27,344,000	$29,258,000	$31,306,000	$33,185,000	$33,848,700
Growth	*18%*	*5%*	*7%*	*7%*	*6%*	*2%*
Projected Graphic Design Software Revenue	22,149,309	23,256,689	21,956,990	20,361,410	19,923,241	18,616,785
Graphic Design %	*85%*	*85%*	*75%*	*65%*	*60%*	*55%*
EBITDA	4,178,617	4,186,272	3,952,322	3,665,113	3,586,242	3,351,076
EBITDA Margin	*19%*	*18%*	*18%*	*18%*	*18%*	*18%*
Less: Depreciation (5)	(315,316)	(301,750)	(285,000)	(264,550)	(258,600)	(241,791)
EBIT	3,863,301	3,884,522	3,667,322	3,400,563	3,327,642	3,109,285
Less: Charge for Use of Tradename	221,493	232,567	219,570	203,614	199,232	186,168
Adjusted EBIT	3,641,808	3,651,955	3,447,753	3,196,949	3,128,409	2,923,117
Less: Taxes	(1,383,887)	(1,387,743)	(1,310,146)	(1,214,841)	(1,188,795)	(1,110,784)
Debt-Free Net Income before Contributory Charge	2,257,921	2,264,212	2,137,607	1,982,109	1,939,614	1,812,332
Less: Contributory Asset Charge (4)	(578,158)	(595,417)	(546,534)	(493,659)	(473,555)	(442,501)
Contributory Asset Charge as a % of Revenue	*2.6%*	*2.6%*	*2.5%*	*2.4%*	*2.4%*	*2.4%*
Debt-Free Cash Flow to Graphic Design Software	1,679,763	1,668,795	1,591,072	1,488,450	1,466,059	1,369,831
Partial Period	0.06	1.00	1.00	1.00	1.00	0.94
Period	0.03	0.56	1.56	2.56	3.56	4.56
Present Value Factor	0.995	0.907	0.762	0.640	0.538	0.452
Present Value of Debt-Free Cash Flows	105,270	1,513,105	1,212,297	953,029	788,818	580,335
Sum of PV of DFCF	5,152,853					
Amortization Benefit Multiplier (6)	1.16					
Preliminary Value	5,955,310					
Concluded Value Graphic Design Software	$5,955,000					

Assumptions		
Discount Rate	(1)	19.0%
Tax Rate	(2)	38.0%
Remaining Useful Life	(3)	5 years

Notes:

(1) Per Exhibit 13.20.

(2) Estimated corporate tax rate.

(3) Based on review of customer turnover in similar businesses.

(4) Charge for the use of the remaining assets that contribute to the cash flow forecast. See Contributory Asset Analysis 13.17.

(5) Tax depreciation may be forecasted based on MACRS.

(6) Represents the present value of the estimated tax benefit derived from the amortization of the intangible asset, over the tax life (15 years) of the asset, assuming a 19% required rate of return.

EXHIBIT 13.16 Software Squared: Valuation of IPR&D Project Planning Software, as of December 8, 20X1

		20X1	20X2	20X3	20X4	20X5	20X6	20X7
Projected Companywide Revenue		$26,042,000	$27,344,000	$29,258,000	$31,306,000	$33,185,000	$33,848,700	$34,525,674
Growth		*18%*	*5%*	*7%*	*7%*	*6%*	*2%*	*2%*
Projected Revenue Software[2] Project Software		—	—	4,391,398	7,831,312	9,961,620	11,847,045	12,083,986
Projected Revenue % Software[2] Project Software		*0%*	*0%*	*15%*	*25%*	*30%*	*35%*	*35%*
EBITDA		—	—	790,464	1,409,659	1,793,121	2,132,503	2,175,153
EBITDA Margin		*19%*	*18%*	*18%*	*18%*	*18%*	*18%*	*18%*
Less: Depreciation	(5)	—	—	(57,000)	(101,750)	(129,300)	(153,867)	(184,640)
EBIT		—	—	733,464	1,307,909	1,663,821	1,978,636	1,990,512
Less: Charge for Use of Trade Name		—	—	43,914	78,313	99,616	118,470	120,840
Adjusted EBIT		—	—	689,551	1,229,596	1,564,205	1,860,165	1,869,673
Less: Taxes		—	—	(262,029)	(467,246)	(594,398)	(706,863)	(710,476)
Debt-Free Net Income before Contributory Charge		—	—	427,521	762,349	969,807	1,153,302	1,159,197
Less: Contributory Assets Charge	(4)	—	—	(109,307)	(189,869)	(236,777)	(281,592)	(287,224)
Contributory Asset Charge as a % of Revenue		*2.6%*	*2.6%*	*2.5%*	*2.4%*	*2.4%*	*2.4%*	*2.4%*
Debt-Free Cash Flow to Software[2] Project Software		—	—	318,214	572,481	733,030	871,711	871,973
Partial Period		0.06	1.00	1.00	1.00	1.00	1.00	1.00
Period		0.03	0.56	1.56	2.56	3.56	4.56	5.56
Present Value Factor		0.993	0.878	0.697	0.553	0.439	0.348	0.276
Present Value of Debt-Free Cash Flows		—	—	221,738	316,599	321,736	303,655	241,069

Sum of PV of DFCF		1,404,796
Amortization Benefit Multiplier	(6)	1.12
Preliminary Value		1,571,285
Concluded Value Software[2] Project Software		**$1,571,000**

Assumptions		
Discount Rate	(1)	26.0%
Tax Rate	(2)	38.0%
Useful Life	(3)	5 years

Notes:

(1) Per Exhibit 13.20.

(2) Estimated corporate tax rate.

(3) Useful life is estimated to be 5 years beginning 1/1/20X3.

(4) Charge for the use of the remaining assets that contribute to the cash flow forecast. See Contributory Asset Anlysis Exhibit 13.17.

(5) Tax depreciation may be forecasted based on MACRS.

(6) Represents the present value of the estimated tax benefit derived from the amortization of the intangible asset, over the tax life (15 years) of the asset, assuming a 26% required rate of return.

EXHIBIT 13.17 **Software Squared: Required Return on Contributory Assets, as of December 8, 20X1**

('000s)		20X1	20X2	20X3	20X4	20X5
Total Revenue		$ 26,042,000	$ 27,344,000	$ 29,258,000	$ 31,306,000	$ 33,185,000
Growth		*18%*	*5%*	*7%*	*7%*	*6%*
Multiplied by: DFWC %		18.2%	18.2%	18.2%	18.2%	18.2%
Debt-Free Working Capital Balance		4,739,644	4,976,608	5,324,956	5,697,692	6,039,670
Required Working Capital Return	6.3% (1)	296,490	311,313	333,104	356,421	377,813
Capital Expenditures (2)		415,240	436,000	475,000	517,000	555,000
Less: Depreciation		353,944	355,000	380,000	407,000	431,000
Net Fixed Assets Balance	$ 1,833,487	1,894,783	1,975,783	2,070,783	2,180,783	2,304,783
Required Return on Capital Investment	6.8% (1)	127,927	133,396	139,810	147,236	155,608
Noncompetition Agreement Beginning Value	$ 186,000					
Noncompetition Agreement Required Return	18.0% (1)	33,480	33,480	33,480	33,480	33,480
Assembled Workforce Beginning Value	$ 489,000					
ASWF Required Return	18.0% (1)	88,020	88,020	88,020	88,020	88,020
Customer Relationships Beginning Value	$ 675,000					
Customer Relationships Required Return	20.0% (1)	135,000	135,000	135,000	135,000	135,000
Required Return on Contributory Assets (as a % of Revenue)		2.6%	2.6%	2.5%	2.4%	2.4%

Notes:

(1) Required return per Exhibit 13.20.

(2) Valuation specialists may make the simplifying assumption that capital expenditures are equal to depreciation expense, otherwise, based on management's forecasted capital expenditures and related depreciation.

The valuation of Software²'s graphic design software using the after-tax cost approach indicates a fair value of $5,576,000 and the valuation using the multiperiod excess earnings method indicates a $5,955,000 fair value.

---

35. Suppose the values calculated under the two valuation methods were significantly different. How would you decide which value to use? What guidance does FASB ASC 820, *Fair Value Measurements and Disclosures* (SFAS 157), provide when more than one valuation technique is appropriate?
36. Which of the intangible assets in this case study is subject to amortization? How do you estimate a remaining useful life?

Goodwill

---

37. How is the fair value of goodwill measured?
38. Once all the opening balance sheet adjustments are recorded, including those to intangible assets and goodwill, how is the total purchase price reflected on Arch Span's books, on Software²'s books, and on the consolidated company's books.

Exhibit 13.18 shows the final summary of intangible assets and goodwill under the acquisition method, and Exhibit 13.19 shows the remaining adjustments to the December 8, 20X1, balance sheet.

Reconciling the Required Rate of Return to the Weighted Average Cost of Capital

When valuing intangible assets under the acquisition method, an important final step is to calculate the Total Required Rate of Return (RRR) indicated by the respective asset's fair values, and to compare the RRR to the company's weighted average cost of capital (WACC). Exhibit 13.20 shows a calculation of the 18 percent Required Rate of Return for the acquired assets. Exhibit 13.21 provides the supporting calculation of debt free working capital.

---

39. Why would one calculate the total required rate of return (RRR) for the business combination? What is the difference between the RRR and the WACC? What is the difference between the RRR and the Internal Rate of Return (IRR) shown in Exhibits 13.3a and b?

EXHIBIT 13.18 Software Squared: Acquisition Summary, as of December 8, 20X1

			Dollar Amount
Cash	(1)		$ 18,200,000
Equity Consideration	(1)		1,000,000
Contingent Consideration	(1)		174,850
Note Payable to JAX Industrial Supply	(1)		2,037,363
Acquisition Costs	(2)		—
			$21,412,213

			Concluded Value Estimate
Tangible Assets			
Working Capital, Net	(3)		$ 3,888,073
Deferred Taxes, Net Asset	(3)		50,000
Fixed Assets	(4)		1,833,487
Intangible Assets			
Graphic Design Software, Cost Approach		5,576,000	
Graphic Design Software, Income Approach		5,955,000	
Concluded Value Graphic Design Software			5,800,000
Trade Name			1,374,000
Customer Relationships			675,000
Noncompetition Agreement			186,000
In-Process Research and Development, Cost Approach		1,267,000	
In-Process Research and Development, Income Approach		1,571,000	
Concluded Value In-Process Research and Development			1,450,000
Assembled Workforce	(5)		489,000
Goodwill	(6)		5,666,653
Total Assets Acquired			**$21,412,213**

Notes:
  (1) Stock Purchase Agreement dated December 8, 20X1.
  (2) Acquisition costs are expenses under ASC 805 (SFAS 141 (R)).
  (3) Per preliminary balance sheet in Exhibit 13.7.
  (4) Per Real Estate Appraisal Report prepared by Douglas Patterson Appraisers, LLC.
  (5) Assembled Workforce is not booked separate from goodwill per ASC 805 (SFAS 141(R)).
  (6) Residual amount based on estimated and calculated values in this schedule.

EXHIBIT 13.19 Software Squared: Final Balance Sheet—Acquisition Method, as of December 8, 20X1

Assets	Closing Unadjusted	Adjustments Debit	Adjustments Credit	Opening Adjusted
Current Assets				
Cash and Equivalents	296,526	8,582		305,108
Trade Receivables	2,975,097			2,975,097
Allowance—Doubtful Accounts	(50,000)		93,750	(143,750)
Inventories	3,832,377		1,040,000	2,792,377
Prepaid Expenses	291,136			291,136
Total Current Assets	7,345,136			6,219,968
Other Assets				
In-Process R&D	91,718	1,450,000	91,718	1,450,000
Software Development Costs, Net	3,256,000	5,800,000	3,256,000	5,800,000
Trade Name		1,374,000		1,374,000
Customer Relationships		675,000		675,000
Noncompete Agreement		186,000		186,000
Goodwill (Assembled Workforce)		6,155,653		6,155,653
Organization Costs, Net	59,390		59,390	—
Deferred Taxes	150,000			150,000
Total Other Assets	3,557,108			15,790,653
Property and Equipment				
Land	341,776		191,776	150,000
Building	1,534,502		1,284,502	250,000
Machinery and Equipment	2,525,687		1,725,687	800,000
Office Equipment	863,487		230,000	633,487
	5,265,452			1,833,487
Less-Accum Depreciation	3,839,052	3,839,052		—
Net Property and Equipment	1,426,400			1,833,487
Total Assets	12,328,644			23,844,108

(Continued)

EXHIBIT 13.19 (*Continued*)

Assets	Closing Unadjusted	Adjustments Debit	Adjustments Credit	Opening Adjusted
Liabilities and Stockholders' Equity				
Current Liabilities				
Accrued Interest—N/P			37,363	37,363
Accounts Payable	878,168			878,168
Accrued Liabilities	191,431			191,431
Deferred Income	450,000			450,000
Income Taxes Payable	77,296			77,296
Warranty Liability			735,000	735,000
Total Current Liabilities	1,596,895			2,369,258
Deferred Income Tax Liability	61,000		39,000	100,000
Long-Term Debt				
Notes Payable	2,000,000			2,000,000
Total Long-Term Debt	2,000,000			2,000,000
Stockholders' Equity				
Common Stock—$1 Par	22,000			22,000
Additional Paid-In Capital	1,638,000		17,714,850	19,352,850
Retained Earnings	4,388,644	4,388,644		—
Year to Date Earnings (Loss)	2,622,105	2,622,105		—
Total Equity	8,670,749			19, 374, 850
Total Liabilities & Equity	12,328,644	26,499,036	26,499,036	23,844,108

40. What is the purpose of reconciling the total RRR for acquired assets to the company's weighted average cost of capital?
41. How do you determine the risk premium over the weighted average cost of capital for each of the intangible assets and for goodwill?

Bargain Purchase

Now, suppose that all facts in the case study are the same except that cash consideration is $10.2 million instead of $18.2 million. Arch Span makes a bargain purchase when it acquires Software^2. Goodwill is now negative $1,844,347 (assembled workforce is not recognized separately).

EXHIBIT 13.20 Software Squared: Reconciliation of Required Rate of Return to WACC, as of December 8, 20X1

Assets Acquired	At 12/8/20X1	Estimated Required Return	Estimated Required Return ($000s)
Required Debt-Free Working Capital (DFWC) (1)	$ 4,739,473 (1)	6.26% (2)	$ 296,479
Fixed Assets	1,833,487	6.75% (3)	123,788
Software	5,800,000	19.00% (4)	1,102,000
Trade Name	1,374,000	19.00% (4)	261,060
Customer Relationships	675,000	20.00% (5)	135,000
Noncompete Agreement	186,000	18.00% (6)	33,480
Assembled Workforce	489,000	18.00% (6)	88,020
In-Process R&D	1,450,000	26.00% (7)	377,000
Goodwill	5,666,653	28.00% (8)	1,586,663
Total Operating Assets w/ Required DFWC	$22,213,613		$4,003,490
Total Required Rate of Return on Acquired Assets		18.0%	
WACC		18.0%	
Difference		0.0%	

Reconciliation to Fair Value of Acquisition Price

Total Operating Assets w/ Required DFWC	$22,213,613
Deficit Debt-Free Working Capital	(851,400) (9)
Deferred Taxes, Net Asset	50,000 (10)
Fair Value of Acquisition Price	$21,412,213

Notes:
(1) Required Debt-Free Working Capital is based on median industry requirements per computation in Exhibit 13.21.
(2) Assumes that DFWC would be financed with 20% equity and 80% debt at the prime rate of 4% as of the valuation date plus a 1% premium, tax affected.
(3) Assumes fixed assets would be funded with 20% equity and 80% debt at the prime rate of 4% plus a 2% premium, tax affected.
(4) Approximate cost of equity.
(5) WACC plus a 2% premium.
(6) WACC per Exhibit 13.4.
(7) Approximate cost of equity plus a 7% premium. The IPR&D premium reflects risks associated with entrance into new segments of the product planning software market.
(8) Approximate cost of equity plus a 9% premium.
(9) Acquired DFWC of $3,888,073 falls short of the normal level of working capital by $851,400.
(10) Reconciling item.

EXHIBIT 13.21 Software Squared: Debt-Free Working Capital Requirement

Industry Debt-Free Working Capital Requirements (1)

	SIC Code	
	7373 Computer Integrated System Design	**8711** Engineering Services
As a % of Total Assets		
Current Assets	58.4%	63.9%
Less: Current Liabilities	44.2%	36.7%
Working Capital	14.2%	27.2%
Working Capital	14.2%	27.2%
Plus: Notes Payable—Short-Term	10.7%	10.0%
Plus: Current Maturities—L.T.D.	2.8%	2.9%
Debt-Free Working Capital (DFWC)	27.7%	40.1%
Debt-Free Working Capital	27.7%	40.1%
Times: Total Assets—$000	$ 1,300,492	$ 1,150,180
Debt-Free Working Capital—$000	$ 360,236	$ 461,222
Debt-Free Working Capital—$000	$ 360,236	$ 461,222
Divided by: Total Sales—$000	$ 2,445,335	$ 2,128,674
DFWC as a % of Sales	14.7%	21.7%
Median Industry DFWC Requirements	(5)	**18.2%**
Software Squared Projected Full-Year Revenue, 20X1	(2)	26,042,000
Required DFWC	(3)	4,739,473
Actual DFWC	(4)	3,888,073
DFWC Excess (Deficit)		**($851,400)**

Notes:

  (1) Risk Management Association's 20X0–20X1 *Annual Statement Studies.*

  (2) Per Software Squared's historic financial statements through November 30, 20X1 and December 20X1 projection.

  (3) Software Squared revenues through November 30, 20X1, and December 20X1 projection multiplied by industry level DFWC requirement.

  (4) Per preliminary balance sheet.

  (5) Management believes a normal level of working capital is approximately 18%.

The summary of the acquisition method assuming the bargain purchase is shown in Exhibit 13.22.

---

42.   How is a bargain purchase treated under FASB ASC 805 (SFAS 141(R))?

Subsequent Testing for Impairment

Go back to the original facts with the cash consideration of $18.2 million. Assume that a year has passed and that Software^2 experienced a downturn in 20X2. The latest version of Software^2's graphic design software has not lived up to expectations. The product received less than favorable user reviews in trade publications. To make matters worse, a competitor introduced a superior product. A decline in sales that began in the first quarter became a free fall by the end of the year. Software^2 has also experienced an exodus of experienced design personnel due to poor morale and a culture clash with Arch Span. Software^2's marketing director recently announced her imminent departure, which was viewed by senior management as a serious blow to the company's prospects for future sales.

The value of Software^2 has dropped significantly. Management's latest estimate of business enterprise value based on discounted cash flows is $16.4 million, including the tax benefit from the amortization of intangible assets. This represents a decline in value of approximately 26 percent. Arch Span's stock price has also taken a beating, losing almost 18 percent in one year. It is currently trading at $25.75, down from the $31.25 price per share on the day it acquired Software^2. The decline in Arch Span's stock price is attributable to Software^2's poor performance. Arch Span's other operations and overall market conditions are unchanged from a year ago.

The calculation of company's latest estimate of enterprise value is presented in Exhibit 13.23.

Suspecting that a write-down of the graphic design software may be necessary and that goodwill may be impaired, Bruce Tucker, Arch Span's CEO, hired a valuation specialist to test the graphic design software individually and to perform the annual impairment test on the entire Software^2 reporting unit.

The reporting unit's 12/31/X2 balance sheet is presented in Exhibit 13.24.

The valuation specialist analyzes management's latest estimate of business enterprise value and concludes that the assumptions are reasonable and that it is properly calculated. However, he wants to use a market-based approach to confirm the value the company. After thoroughly researching the industry, he finds five companies that are roughly comparable in terms of size, market share, and financial characteristics.

EXHIBIT 13.22 Software Squared: Acquisition Summary—Bargain Purchase, as of December 8, 20X1

		Dollar Amount
Cash	(1)	$10,200,000
Equity Consideration	(1)	1,000,000
Contingent Consideration	(1)	174,850
Note Payable to JAX Industrial Supply	(1)	2,037,363
Acquisition Costs	(2)	—
		$13,412,213

		Concluded Value Estimate
Tangible Assets		
Working Capital, Net	(3)	$3,888,073
Deferred Tax Asset	(3)	50,000
Fixed Assets	(4)	1,833,487
Intangible Assets		
Graphic Design Software, Cost Approach	5,576,000	
Graphic Design Software, Income Approach	5,955,000	
Concluded Value Graphic Design Software		5,800,000
Trade Name		1,374,000
Customer Relationships		675,000
Noncompetition Agreement		186,000
In-Process Research and Development, Cost Approach	1,267,000	
In-Process Research and Development, Income Approach	1,571,000	
Concluded Value In-Process Research and Development		1,450,000
Assembled Workforce	(5)	489,000
Gain from Bargain Purchase	(6)	(2,333,347)
Total Assets Acquired		**$13,412,213**

Notes:

(1) Stock Purchase Agreement dated December 8, 20X1.

(2) Acquisition costs are expenses under SFAS 141 (R).

(3) Per preliminary adjusted balance sheet in Exhibit 7.

(4) Per Real Estate Appraisal Report prepared by Douglas Patterson Appraisers, LLC.

(5) Assembled Workforce is not booked separate from goodwill per SFAS 141(R).

(6) Residual amount based on estimated and calculated values in this schedule. A negative residual is recorded as a gain on the measurement date per SFAS 141(R), paragraph 36.

EXHIBIT 13.23 Software Squared: Discounted Cash Flow Analysis, Including Tax Benefit, as of December 31, 20X2

	20X3		20X4		20X5		20X6		20X7		Terminal Value	
Sales	$19,750,300	100%	$20,737,815	100%	$21,359,950	100%	$22,000,748	100%	$24,200,822	100%	$24,684,838	100%
Growth			*5%*		*3%*		*3%*		*10%*		*2%*	
Cost of Sales	11,850,180	60%	13,064,823	63%	13,456,769	63%	13,860,471	63%	15,246,518	63%	15,551,448	63%
Gross Profit	7,900,120	40%	7,672,992	37%	7,903,182	37%	8,140,277	37%	8,954,304	37%	9,133,390	37%
SG&A Expenses	4,147,563	21%	3,940,185	19%	4,058,391	19%	4,180,142	19%	4,598,156	19%	4,690,119	19%
EBITDA	3,752,557	19%	3,732,807	18%	3,844,791	18%	3,960,135	18%	4,356,148	18%	4,443,271	18%
Less: Depreciation	407,000	2%	427,350	2%	440,171	2%	453,376	2%	498,713	2%	508,687	2%
EBIT	3,345,557	17%	3,305,457	16%	3,404,620	16%	3,506,759	16%	3,857,435	16%	3,934,583	16%
Less: Taxes	(1,271,312)	–6%	(1,256,074)	–6%	(1,293,756)	–6%	(1,332,568)	–6%	(1,465,825)	–6%	(1,495,142)	–6%
Debt-Free Net Income	2,074,245	11%	2,049,383	10%	2,110,865	10%	2,174,191	10%	2,391,610	10%	2,439,442	10%
Plus: Depreciation	407,000	2%	427,350	2%	440,171	2%	453,376	2%	498,713	2%	508,687	2%
Less: Capital Expenditures	(311,400)	–2%	(337,800)	–2%	(359,800)	–2%	(469,700)	–2%	(490,300)	–2%	(508,687)	–2%
Less: Incremental Working Capital	223,800	1%	(179,721)	–1%	(113,224)	–1%	(116,621)	–1%	(400,399)	–2%	(88,088)	0%

(Continued)

EXHIBIT 13.23 (*Continued*)

	12%	9%	10%	9%	8%	10%
Cash Flows to Invested Capital	2,393,645	1,959,212	2,078,011	2,041,245	1,999,624	2,351,354
Terminal Value in 20X7						14,695,962
Period	0.50	1.50	2.50	3.50	4.50	4.50
Present Value Factor	0.921	0.780	0.661	0.560	0.475	0.475
Present Value of Cash Flows to Invested Capital	2,203,529	1,528,475	1,373,861	1,143,690	949,466	6,977,968
Sum of PV of CF	7,199,020					
PV of Terminal Value	6,977,968					
PV of Tax Benefit—Amortization of Intangibles	2,216,448					
Preliminary Value	16,393,437					
Enterprise Value, Rounded	**$16,393,000**					

Present Value of Tax Benefit—Amortization of Intangibles

Fair Value of Intangible Assets and Goodwill	15,640,653	(5)
15-Year Amortization Period	/15	
Tax Amortization Expense per Year	1,042,710	
Tax Rate	38.0%	
Annual Amortization Benefit	396,230	
Sum of PV Factors 20X3 to 20Y6	5.59	
Present Value of Amortization Benefit	2,216,448	

Assumptions		
Discount Rate	(1)	18.0%
Tax Rate	(2)	38.0%
Long-Term Growth Rate	(3)	2.0%
Debt-Free Working Capital %	(4)	18.2%

Notes:
(1) Weighted Average Cost of Capital per Exhibit 13.4.
(2) Estimated corporate tax rate.
(3) Based on Management's projections, the growth prospects of the industry, and the overall economy.
(4) Per Exhibit 13.21.
(5) Per Final Balance Sheet at Exhibit 13.19.

EXHIBIT 13.24 Software Squared: Balance Sheet, as of December 31, 20X2

Assets		Liabilities & Stockholders' Equity	
Current Assets		**Current Liabilities**	
Cash and Equivalents	998,426		
Trade Receivables	1,029,243	Accounts Payable	335,368
Allowance—Doubtful Accounts	(65,000)	Accrued Liabilities	128,000
Inventories	3,982,543	Warranty Liability	238,873
Prepaid Expenses	570,322	Income Taxes Payable	173,296
Total Current Assets	6,515,534	**Total Current Liabilities**	875,537
Other Assets		Deferred Income Tax Liability	25,000
In-Process R&D, Net	1,450,000		
Software Costs, Net	4,640,000		
Trade Name, Net	1,328,200		
Customer Relationships, Net	540,000		
Noncompetition Agreement, Net	148,800	**Long-Term Debt**	
Goodwill (Assembled Workforce)	6,155,653	Notes Payable—Jax Industrial Supply	2,000,000
Total Other Assets	14,262,653	**Total Long-Term Debt**	2,000,000

(Continued)

EXHIBIT 13.24 (*Continued*)

		Stockholders' Equity	
Property and Equipment			
Land	150,000	Common Stock—$1 Par	22,000
Building	878,408	Additional Paid-In Capital	19,352,850
Machinery and Equipment	1,514,753	Retained Earnings	158,722
Office Equipment	356,987	Year-to-Date Earnings	831,704
	2,900,148		
Less-Accum Depreciation	(412,522)	Total Equity	20,365,276
Net Property and Equipment	2,487,626		
Total Assets	23,265,813	Total Liabilities and Equity	23,265,813

Information on the comparable companies, including their price to earnings ratios (P/E) is presented in Exhibit 13.25.

---

43. What are some general indications that impairment has occurred? What are the indications in this case study?
44. Based on the selected P/E ratio of 8.5 and projected 20X3 earnings of $2 million, what is the implied value of Software²? How does the implied value compare to the $16.4 million value calculated using the discounted cash flows? What would be some possible reasons for the differences? How can the two values be reconciled?
45. What is the first step in impairment testing? Which two values are compared? Does impairment exist in this case study? Would your answer change if the carrying value of goodwill is negative?
46. How does EITF 02-13, *Deferred Income Tax Considerations in Applying the Goodwill Impairment Test in FASB Statement No. 142*, affect your analysis?
47. Discuss step two of the impairment test. Which group of assets do you examine first? Which intangible assets from this case study would be tested under FASB ASC 360-10-05, *Property, Plant, and Equipment—Impairment or Disposal of Long-Lived Assets* (SFAS 144)? Would you consider the fair value of the deferred tax assets and liabilities in step two?
48. Assume the carrying amount of the graphic design software is $4.6 million, its fair value is $3.5 million and the sum of the undiscounted cash flows expected to be generated by the software is $3.8 million. What is the test for impairment, and is the software impaired? What is the write-down?
49. Which intangible assets are subject to amortization and are tested for impairment under FASB ASC 360-10-35, *Property, Plant, and Equipment, Subsequent Measurement* (SFAS 144)? Which intangible assets are tested under FASB ASC 350-35, *Intangible—Goodwill and Other, Subsequent Measurements* (SFAS 142)? Is assembled workforce tested separately or as part of goodwill under SFAS 142?
50. What is the process for determining the implied value of goodwill?

The fair value of Software²'s intangible assets and the implied value of goodwill are presented in Exhibit 13.26.

---

51. Based on the fair value measurement of Software²'s intangible assets and the implied value of goodwill, calculate the impairment loss on goodwill.
52. When implied goodwill is negative, what does this indicate about the company?
53. Do you believe fair value measurements provide a more relevant presentation of financial statements than traditional, historical, cost-based accounting?

Solutions to the Case Study questions can be found in Appendix 13A.

EXHIBIT 13.25 Software Squared: Design and Engineering Software Industry, as of December 31, 20X2

Company Name	Ticker Symbol	Market Cap ($ millions)	Market	20X2 P/E	
				Low	High
Wacky Tacky Design	WTD	23.8	Northeastern U.S.	6.2	6.7
AAB Design Query Inc.	AABDZ	49.8	International	8.5	8.8
Gideon Engineering	EGID	18.7	U.S. and Canada	7.7	8.7
Forrestner Winthrop Design Development	FWDD	13.9	U.S.	9.7	9.9
Design Technology Corp.(1)	N/A—privately owned	56.2	International	8.8	8.8
			High	9.7	9.9
			3rd Q	8.8	8.8
			Mean	8.2	8.6
			Median	8.5	8.8
			1st Q	7.7	8.7
			Low	6.2	6.7
			Mode	8.8	8.8
			Selected P/E Ratio:	8.5	

(1) Based on June 30, 20X2, purchase of Design Technology Corp. by Hanover Corp. for $56.2 million.
Source: The *Wall Street Journal* is a source of P/E ratio information. However, the companies and data in this exhibit are not real.

EXHIBIT 13.26 Software Squared: Implied Value of Goodwill, as of December 31, 20X2

		Dollar Amount
Enterprise Value	(1)	$16,696,500
Tangible Assets		
Working Capital, Net	(2)	5,639,997
Fixed Assets	(3)	2,487,626
Liabilities		
Note Payable Jax Industrial Supply	(2)	(2,000,000)
Deferred Taxes	(2)	(25,000)
Intangible Assets		**Concluded Value Estimate**
Software	(4)	3,500,000
Trade Name	(4)	1,350,000
Customer Relationships	(4)	550,000
Noncompetition Agreement	(4)	150,000
In-Process Research and Development	(4)	1,500,000
Assembled Workforce	(4)	150,000
Goodwill		3,393,877
Total Assets		**$16,696,500**

Notes:

(1) Average of $16.4 million value from discounted cash flow analysis Exhibit 13.23 and P/E of 8.5 from Exhibit 13.25 times expected 20X3 earnings of $2.0 million.

(2) Per balance sheet at Exhibit 13.24.

(3) Per Real Estate Appraisal Report prepared by Douglas Patterson Appraisers, LLC.

(4) Per Valuation Specialist.

Suggested Case Study Solutions

The suggested solutions to Chapter 13's fair value measurement case study are presented in this appendix. The suggested solutions have been prepared using commonly accepted valuation techniques. Recognizing that other valuation specialists may choose different techniques and assumptions, alternative solutions are possible and may have merit. In order to provide clarification, many of the solutions contain references to applicable sections of this book.

---

1. You have been engaged by Arch Span Technology Inc. to perform an acquisition date intangible asset valuation under the acquisition method. Discuss the acquisition method. What are the steps in the acquisition method? What is the measurement date of the business combination? What would cause the measurement date to differ from the closing date?

Under the acquisition method, the fair values of acquired assets are no longer determined by an allocation of the purchase price. The fair value of those assets acquired in the business combination is independent of the price that was paid in the transaction. FASB ASC 805, *Business Combinations* (SFAS 141(R)), requires that the acquirer recognize the identifiable assets acquired in a business combination separately from goodwill. (Chapter 1)

The four steps in applying the acquisition method include:

1. Identify the acquirer.
2. Determine the acquisition date—the date control is obtained.
3. Recognize and measure the identifiable assets acquired, the liabilities assumed, and any noncontrolling interest in the acquiree as required by the recognition and measurement principles.
4. Recognize and measure goodwill or a gain from a bargain purchase. (Chapter 2)

One of the important changes introduced by FASB ASC 805 (SFAS 141(R)), *Business Combinations,* is the identification of the business combination's measurement date. Under the revised statement, the acquisition date is the date on which the acquirer obtains control of the acquired company. FASB ASC 805, *Business Combinations,* says that change of control typically is demonstrated when the acquirer transfers the consideration and obtains responsibility for the assets acquired and liabilities assumed. Often, the transfer of consideration and assumption of control occurs on the closing date of the transaction. However, this may not necessarily always be the case. There may be situations when the acquirer obtains effective control prior to the closing date. (Chapter 2)

---

2. **What information will you typically need to gather in order to perform an intangible asset valuation under the acquisition method? How does a valuation specialist obtain the requisite information?**

Information to be requested from the client may include:

- Any income or cash flow budgets or projections (three to five years preferable), including revenue, expenses, net income, depreciation, and capital expenditures
- Last three to five years of financial statements: income statement and balance sheet
- Detail of final purchase price accounting entry, if available
- The name and contact information (phone number and e-mail address) for your audit partner/manager
- A summary of all existing technology
- What date did the existing technology enter the market? Has it been significantly modified or enhanced?
- How much effort (in terms of work hours and dollar costs) would be required to reproduce or replace these assets?
- Is there a specific revenue stream associated with these assets? If so, please identify it, along with all the relevant costs.
- Complete list of customer relationships of the acquired company, including revenue and related expenses per customer for the last five years
- Are the customer relationships contractual in nature? If so, please provide sample contracts. Are the contracts for terms greater than one year? Are they typically renewed?
- What expenses are required to obtain a new customer? Please provide total sales and marketing costs for the last three years, including travel

and entertainment related to acquiring new customers. Is senior management involved in the sales effort? If so, which executives and what percentage of their time?

- What is the average revenue per customer?
- What is the average remaining useful life?
- List of trade names and trademarks held by the company
- Any revenue streams both historical and prospective that are closely associated with any of these assets
- Copies of noncompete agreements, if any
- Estimate the percentage of likely competition (from 0 percent to 100 percent) from the sellers or previous management in the absence of a noncompete agreement
- If any, an estimate of the likelihood of success of the seller's competitive efforts (from 0 percent to 100 percent) if they were to compete in absence of the noncompete agreement
- List of owners and top management of the company
  - Name
  - Position
  - Years with company
  - Years in the industry
  - Three-year compensation history by salary and bonus
  - Projected compensation
- Organization chart
- Employee listing by category, including average salary information
- How many total employees of the company?
- Provide the following information for each type of employee (executives, sales, engineers, manufacturing, administrative).
  - Number of employees
  - Average annual salary
  - Fringe benefits as a percentage of salary
  - Average advertising and recruitment costs
  - Average relocation costs
  - Number of months until full productivity
  - % effectivness of new hire
  - Amount of direct training costs
- Information from other resources may include:
  - Similar transactions involving the company itself
  - SEC filings often describe licensing arrangements
  - Commercial products often use SIC codes
  - Court cases decisions (tax court and civil cases)
  - Periodicals
  - Publications
  - Web sites

3. When using management forecasts as a basis for fair value measurement under income approaches, does a valuation specialist need to analyze management forecasts? Under what circumstances would it be appropriate to make adjustments to management projections? How are common-size statements used?

A valuation specialist should feel comfortable with the reasonableness of management's forecasts. Some of the more pertinent questions to ask when preparing or auditing a discounted cash flow analysis include:

- Can facts be obtained, and informed judgments made, about past and future events or circumstances in support of the underlying assumptions?
- Are any of the significant assumptions so subjective that no reasonably objective basis could exist to present a financial forecast?
- Would people knowledgeable in the entity's business and industry select materially similar assumptions?
- Is the length of the forecast period appropriate?
- Do forecasts include buyer-specific synergies, or are synergies available to all market participants?

The preparer or auditor should also be satisfied that there is a rational relationship between the assumptions used and the underlying facts and circumstances modeled in the discounted cash flow analysis, and be able to assert that:

- The assumptions are complete.
- It appears that the assumptions were developed without undue optimism or pessimism.
- The assumptions are consistent with the entity's plans and expectations.
- The assumptions are consistent with each other.
- The assumptions, in the aggregate, make sense in the context of the forecast taken as a whole.

(Chapter 2)

According to the AICPA's *Guide for Prospective Financial Information*, "Regardless of the extent of the accountant's participation, the assumptions remain the responsibility of the responsible party. The accountant may assist in the formulation of assumptions, but the responsible party must evaluate the assumptions, make key decisions, and adopt and present the assumptions as its own."

Common-size statements are used to gain a better understanding of the financial statements and allow a better comparison of forecasted data to historical data.

4. What does business enterprise value (BEV) mean, and why is it calculated? What are the common methods to calculate the BEV? When is it appropriate to include tax benefits in the calculation of BEV? How does the market participant assumption influence the BEV? Why would a valuation specialist calculate the BEV under the acquisition method?

One of the first steps in measuring the fair value of individual assets acquired in a business combination under FASB ASC 805, *Business Combinations* (SFAS 141(R)), is to measure the fair value of the entire acquired entity. This fair value is also known as the business enterprise value (BEV). The most common method to measure the fair value of the acquired entity is the discounted cash flow method under the income approach. The entity's fair value indicated by the discounted cash flow (DCF) can also be corroborated by other valuation techniques, such as the guideline company method under the market approach. The BEV or the fair value of invested capital is measured by discounting debt-free cash flows to the present at the weighted average cost of capital (WACC). The fair value of the entity's equity is then measured by subtracting the fair value of debt from the BEV. (Chapter 6)

Assuming the amortization of intangible assets and goodwill resulting from the business combination will be deductible for tax purposes, the valuation specialist should include the value of tax benefits in the calculation of the BEV.

In a business combination measurement of fair value, the prospective financial information should reflect those assumptions that a market participant would make rather than the assumptions that are specific to the acquiring entity. (Chapter 6)

5. How does the acquisition price compare to each of the business enterprise values in Exhibits 13.3a and b, and what does this generally indicate? How does the implied internal rate of return (IRR) compare to the discount rate? How does the inclusion of tax benefits impact the IRR?

One of the first steps in measuring the fair value of individual assets acquired in a business combination under FASB ASC 805, *Business Combinations* (SFAS 141(R)), is to measure the fair value of the entire acquired entity. This fair value is also known as the business enterprise value (BEV). Exhibit 13.3a shows the calculation of a $19,594,000 BEV, excluding any tax benefit from amortization. Exhibit 13.3b shows the calculation of a $22,216,000 BEV, including the tax benefit from amortization of the fair value of intangible assets and goodwill. The fair value of the acquisition price is calculated in Exhibit 13.5 as $21,412,213. This indicates that the IRR and the WACC may be very similar. The IRR is the discount rate that makes the present value of the acquired entity's expected future debt-free cash flows to be equal to the acquisition price. In financial theory, the IRR should approximate the WACC. However, in practice there is often a difference, sometimes a substantial difference. If the WACC is greater than the acquired entity's IRR, then the acquirer may have paid more than the sum of the fair values of the identifiable assets. This situation results in the recognition of goodwill at a higher value than would otherwise be expected if the WACC were equal to the IRR. If the WACC is lower than the IRR, it is probable that the acquirer made a bargain purchase and the resulting fair value of goodwill would be lower than would otherwise be expected if the WACC were equal to the IRR. Valuation specialists often compare the entity's IRR to the WACC to gain insight about the prospective fair value of goodwill in an acquisition. (Chapter 6)

The IRR is lower when tax benefits are excluded and higher when tax benefits are included. Tax benefits increase cash flows over the life of the depreciable tax life of the asset. The discounted present value of these increased cash flows will result in a higher IRR.

---

6. Discuss the following elements of the BEV in Exhibit 13.3a and 13.3b:
    Calculation of the terminal value
    What are the alternatives for calculating the terminal value?
    How is debt treated, and what are the alternatives to this treatment?

The terminal value, or perpetuity value, captures the value after the explicit forecast period. (Chapter 6) The terminal value is calculated by using the Gordon Growth Model, by dividing the debt-free cash flows by the capitalization rate (which is the discount rate less the long-term growth rate).

Alternatives to the Gordon Growth Model include the exit multiple model, the "H" model, and the value driver model.

In 13.3a, the enterprise value is calculated from the perspective of all investors in the entity, including equity and debt holders. Debt-free net income does not include any deduction for interest expense. The present value of debt-free cash flow is equal to the enterprise value.

The difference between 13.3a and 13.3b is that the enterprise value in 13.3a includes the tax benefit associated with the stepped up value of goodwill and intangible assets recognized in conjunction with the business combination.

An alternative calculation would be to calculate the value of the equity interest in the enterprise. The value of equity is calculated on cash flows after deducting interest expense and debt repayments and adding proceeds from debt financing.

The enterprise value to all capital investors less the fair value of debt is theoretically equal to the fair value of equity.

---

7. What is a weighted average cost of capital? How are the weights determined? Is the 18 percent weighted average cost of capital for Arch Span, Software[2], the combined entity, or some other hypothetical entity? What are the alternative methods for calculating the cost of equity? Why is the WACC appropriate in calculating the BEV for use in the acquisition method?

The weighted average cost of capital (WACC) is the rate of return required by all investors, both debt and equity, to compensate them for the risk associated with their investment. The WACC is typically used to discount an entity's debt-free cash flows and to measure the fair value of the entity's invested capital, or the BEV.

Theoretically, when measuring the fair value of an entity, a market participant's capital structure would be used to determine the relative weights of debt and equity in the calculation of the WACC. Estimating a hypothetical market participant's capital structure is often difficult because of limited information available for nonpublicly traded market participants. Consequently, valuation specialists typically rely on the capital structures of public companies as a proxy for the hypothetical market participant's capital structures. (Chapter 6)

The 18 percent WACC used in this case study is based on an average capital structure for guideline public companies.

A corollary to measuring the fair value of the equity using a DCF method at the WACC is to calculate the expected internal rate of return (IRR) on the investment. The IRR is the discount rate that makes the present value of the acquired entity's expected future debt-free cash flows to be equal to the acquisition price. In financial theory, the IRR should approximate the WACC. (Chapter 6)

The cost of equity is typically calculated using one of two models, the Capital Asset Pricing Model or a Build-Up Method. Another relatively new method is to estimate a required rate of return for equity by referring to studies on rates of return for venture capital investments. (Chapter 6)

---

8. Calculate the fair value of the acquisition price.

The fair value of the acquisition price is calculated in Exhibit 13.5.

---

9. How is the contingent consideration treated in the fair value acquisition price under FASB ASC 805 (SFAS 141(R))? How does this treatment differ from previous accounting for business combinations?

The fair value of the contingent consideration is recognized as of the acquisition date, as part of the purchase price per FASB ASC 805 (SFAS 141(R)). (Chapter 2) Previously, contingent consideration was recorded when the contingency was resolved.

Any change in the fair value of contingent consideration is recorded in earnings. Previously, any change in value associated with contingent consideration was treated as an adjustment to goodwill. (Chapter 2)

---

10. What is an alternative to calculating the fair value of the consideration paid under the acquisition method?

The acquisition price under FASB ASC 805, *Business Combinations* (SFAS 141(R)), is generally the fair value of the consideration paid for the acquirer's interest in the acquired company. Payments for the acquired entity may include cash and other assets, equity interests, and contingent consideration. All consideration is measured at the fair value on the acquisition date. An alternative is to measure the fair value of the interest acquired through a business combination using a method or methods under the income or market approaches. (Chapter 2)

---

11. Why is it necessary for the valuation specialist to analyze the company's preliminary acquisition balance sheet? What are the implications for fair value measurement if the balance sheet is misstated?

A valuation specialist will begin with the preliminary acquisition balance sheet when developing an economic balance sheet. Preparing an adjusted economic balance sheet can be a useful tool when analyzing a company's intangible assets. It will help determine the magnitude or aggregate value of all of the intangible assets owned by an entity. It will also provide a structure to analyze the company's cost of capital and estimate the required rates of return for intangible assets. (Chapter 3)

If the balance sheet is misstated, it could lead to misstatements of the fair values.

---

12. Why is the "highest and best" use assumption important in the fair value measurement of intangible assets?

A fair value measurement as described by FASB ASC 820, *Fair Value Measurements* (SFAS 157), assumes "the highest and best use" of the asset by market participants. Highest and best use considers the use of the asset that is physically possible, legally permissible, and financially feasible. The highest and best use is the use that maximizes the value of the asset, or the group of assets within which the asset would be used by a market participant rather than by the reporting entity. As such, assumptions in the fair value measurements as to the highest and best use of an asset or group of assets are determined by how the asset or group of assets would be used by market participants, even if the intended use of the asset by the reporting entity is different. (Chapter 1)

---

13. How does the analysis of deferred tax assets differ from deferred tax liabilities? What is the central issue for deferred tax assets?

FASB ASC 805 (SFAS 141(R)), *Business Combinations*, changes a number of items that create deferred tax assets and liabilities as a result of purchase accounting. In addition, remeasurement of tax accounts from previous acquisitions due to the settlement of tax contingencies will impact the income statement. As a result of these changes, the tax provision and effective tax rate will require additional consideration. (Chapter 2)

The FASB points out deferred tax issues relating to the impairment of goodwill should be considered when measuring fair value. Considerations include whether the fair value is determined based on a taxable transaction assumption or a nontaxable transaction assumption (should be based on judgment), whether deferred taxes should be included in the carrying amount of the reporting unit (deferred taxes should be included), and what tax bases should be used to measure deferred tax assets and liabilities (use the tax bases implicit in the tax structure). (EITF 02-13)

14. Why is revenue recognition an important consideration when performing an acquisition method valuation?

Deferred revenue is recorded when an entity receives cash for future services. The earnings process is not complete; therefore, the entity has an obligation to deliver additional services. Sometimes, deferred revenues are included as a component of working capital when calculating contributory charges, and sometimes they are not. The Working Group of the Appraisal Foundation has discussed whether deferred revenue should be included in the computation of working capital as a contributory asset. Their conclusion is that deferred revenue should be included as a current liability in working capital if the prospective financial information (PFI) is developed using an accrual basis because the deferred revenue is a part of ongoing operations. Deferred revenue that is not considered part of ongoing operations may or may not be included as a component of working capital depending on the circumstances. (Chapter 6)

15. How does a valuation specialist typically identify an acquired company's intangible assets? What are the likely acquired intangible assets in this case study?

In a business combination, intangible assets should be recognized in financial reporting if they meet either the separable or the contractual criteria. To help preparers identify intangible assets, the FASB introduced five broad categories for their classification. The categories are marketing, customer, artistic, contractual, and technology-related intangible assets. For financial accounting purposes, goodwill has a specific meaning. It is the excess purchase price paid in a business combination over and above the fair value of the company's other tangible and intangible assets. (Chapter 3)

An intangible asset is often found where a competitive advantage exists. Each intangible asset should benefit the business by saving costs or increasing revenue. In this case study, the likely intangible assets are graphic design software, in-process research and development, customer relationships, trade name, and noncompetition agreement.

16. What are the two criteria for recognizing intangible assets under FASB ASC 805 (SFAS 141(R))? Who is responsible for identifying the intangible assets? How does this occur in practice?

Economic benefits provide evidence as to the existence of intangible assets. The FASB provides specific criteria for recognizing an intangible asset in financial reporting. In a business combination, an intangible asset should be recorded on the balance sheet as of the acquisition date if it is considered identifiable. An intangible asset is considered identifiable (1) if it is separable; that is, capable of being separated or divided from the entity and sold, transferred, licensed, rented, or exchanged, either individually or together with a related contract, identifiable asset, or liability, regardless of whether the entity intends to do so; or (2) if it arises from contractual or other legal rights, regardless of whether those rights are transferable or separable from the entity or from other rights and obligations. (Chapter 3)

To help preparers identify intangible assets, the FASB introduced five broad categories for their classification. The five categories are (1) marketing-, (2) customer-, (3) artistic-, (4) contractual-, and (5) technology-related intangible assets. (Chapter 3)

In practice, the valuation specialist works with management to identify the intangible assets.

---

17. What are the three broad approaches to valuing intangible assets and specific methods within those approaches that you would use to value Software^2's intangible assets? What are the advantages and disadvantages of each of the approaches?

There are three general approaches to valuing any asset or interest in a business. The three are commonly referred to as (1) the cost approach, (2) the market approach, and (3) the income approach. (Chapter 3)

The cost approach is more successfully applied to intangible assets when they are newer, when substitutes exist, and when estimating the fair value from the perspective of the current owner under an "in-use" premise.

Three methods for applying the cost approach include (1) historical cost trending, (2) the unit cost method, and (3) the unit of production method. (Chapter 4) The cost approach has some limitations. First, the approach is not as comprehensive as the other two approaches. Second, the estimates used to develop reproduction and replacement costs are often subjective. A third limitation is that obsolescence is sometimes difficult to quantify. Finally, there is divergence in practice among valuation specialists with regard to the treatment of taxes and developer's profit and entrepreneurial incentive. (Chapter 4)

The methods under the market approach, including comparable transactions, the relief from royalty, industry rules of thumb, and actual transactions of the subject company itself, are appropriate methods to estimate the value of an intangible asset utilizing market information. The market approach attempts to value an asset based on what similar assets have sold for in the market. The disadvantage of this approach is in the difficulty of finding enough reliable information in the market.

The income approach methods include present value models, option-pricing models, and the multiperiod excess earnings method. (Chapter 6) The advantage of the income approach is that it clearly relates the expected economic income from the asset to its value.

---

18. Graphic design software is Software[2]'s most important asset, and it was the reason for Arch Span's acquisition of Software[2]. What additional consideration does this situation warrant? What alternate approaches can be used to value graphic design software?

The graphic design software can be valued using the cost and income approaches. For example, certain types of software can be developed within a specific range of cost per line of code. (Chapter 4)

The most important asset is generally the primary generator of cash flows for the entity and the best valuation method to use is the Multiperiod Excess Earning Method (MPEEM). The MPEEM is a variation of the discounted cash flow (DCF) analysis that is often used to measure the fair value of certain intangible assets. Unlike the DCF, which measures fair value by discounting cash flows for an entire entity, the MPEEM measures fair value by discounting expected future cash flows attributable to a single intangible asset. (Chapter 6)

---

19. When performing a valuation using the cost approach, which costs would you likely consider? What are the alternative treatments of taxes and the tax benefit from amortization? Why do some valuation specialists apply the cost approach on a before-tax basis and others apply it on an after-tax basis?

One of the shortcomings of the cost approach to measuring fair value is that traditionally entrepreneurial profit and opportunity costs have not often been included. There are two reasons for this. First, the historic costs on which the cost approach is based often tend not to measure entrepreneurial profit and incentive. This is particularly true for intangible assets as they are typically created or developed internally. Second, many valuation specialists do not adjust historic costs to include profit and incentive before using historic cost as the basis for the application of the cost approach to the measurement of fair value. There are inconsistencies in practice among valuation specialists and there is a lack of clear, authoritative guidance on the subject. (Chapter 4)

The cost approach can either be applied on a pre-tax or after-tax basis, and there is divergence in practice among valuation professionals with respect to this issue. The tax structure of the entity and the tax structure of the transaction will influence the treatment of taxes under the cost approach. Whether the fair value is being measured as the result of a business combination, litigation, for estate tax purposes, or for some other reason can potentially affect the tax treatment. Finally, the tax-related assumptions that the hypothetical market participant would make should be considered when measuring fair value.

When applying the cost approach on an after-tax basis, there are two components to calculate: the tax provision and the tax benefit from depreciation or amortization. The tax provision includes the impact of federal and state taxes. The amortization benefit reflects the additional value resulting from the ability to deduct amortization to the intangible asset over its tax life. (Chapter 4)

---

20. What is the difference between reproduction cost and replacement cost? Obsolescence is deducted from the reproduction cost to arrive at the replacement cost. What types of obsolescence would the valuation specialist consider? Based on the facts in this case study, does a 25 percent obsolescence factor seem appropriate?

Reproduction cost is the cost of creating an exact replica in today's dollars, and it is commonly referred to as "cost of reproduction new." The cost of replacement is the cost of purchasing or constructing an asset with equal utility in today's dollars. (Chapter 4)

All forms of obsolescence should be considered including physical deterioration, functional (technological) obsolescence, and economic obsolescence. (Chapter 4)

The facts of this case study included 16 obsolete copies of software currently held in inventory. The value of these copies combined is $1,040,000 (16 × $65,000). Inventory has a total value of $3,832,377. Therefore, 25 percent obsolescence seems appropriate.

---

21. Why would an opportunity cost of development and entrepreneurial profit be included as part of the costs? How are these percentages determined?

The difference between the price to purchase an asset and the cost to create a similar asset can often be attributed to entrepreneurial profit and opportunity cost. One of the shortcomings of the cost approach to measuring fair value is that traditionally entrepreneurial profit and opportunity costs have not often been included. There are two reasons for this. First, the historic costs on which the cost approach is based often tend not to measure entrepreneurial profit and incentive. This is particularly true for intangible assets because they are typically created or developed internally. Second, many valuation specialists do not adjust historic costs to include profit and incentive before using historic cost as the basis for the application of the cost approach to the measurement of fair value. A potential solution to this problem is to adjust replacement costs by adding an entrepreneur's profit and opportunity cost. If the entrepreneur's profit and incentive are included in the cost to create an asset, then the fully burdened historic cost would more closely resemble a historic market price and would serve as a better base from which to measure fair value under the cost approach. (Chapter 4)

The opportunity cost is equal to WACC.

---

22. The fair value measurement of customer relationships includes opportunity costs and entrepreneur's profit. Why is there a time frame included in this calculation?

Management estimates it would take 2.5 years to rebuild customer relationships. Opportunity costs and entrepreneur's profit percentages are annual costs that are multiplied by the 2.5-year time frame.

---

23. Exhibit 13.10a includes an amortization benefit factor of 1.15. What is an amortization benefit factor? What is the purpose of this adjustment? How is it calculated?

When applying the cost approach on an after-tax basis, an amortization benefit is added to the before-tax fair value. The amortization benefit reflects the additional value resulting from the ability to deduct amortization to the intangible asset over its tax life. The amortization benefit applies only to intangible assets that are deductible for tax purposes. If the subject asset were a tangible asset, a depreciation benefit would apply. The formula for the amortization benefit follows:

$$AB = PVCF \times [n/(n-\{[PV(r,n, -1) \times (1+r)\hat{\ }0.5] \times T\})-1], \text{ where:}$$
$AB = $ Amortization benefit

$PVCF$ = Present value of cash flows from the subject asset

n = Amortization period

r = Asset specific discount rate

$PV(r,n, -1) \times (1+r)^{0.5}$ = Present value of an annuity of $1 over n years, at the discount rate r

T = Tax rate

(Chapter 4)

---

24. What are the alternatives to using the replacement cost method to estimate the fair value of customer relationships?

Customer relationships may also be valued using an income approach, such as the multiperiod excess earning method. (Chapter 6)

---

25. Is assembled workforce an identifiable intangible asset under the acquisition method? Why would the fair value of an assembled workforce be determined under the acquisition method? Why are opportunity costs and entrepreneur's profit excluded? Can other methods be used to value the assembled workforce?

An assembled workforce is not specifically recognized as an identifiable intangible asset under FASB ASC 805, *Business Combinations* (SFAS 141(R)). The assembled workforce is included in goodwill. (Chapter 6)

The fair value of the assembled workforce is calculated to determine an appropriate contributory charge.

Opportunity costs are included as part of the cost to hire and train the workforce and are not added as an adjustment. Entrepreneurial profit is the expected profit when sold. Since a workforce cannot be sold, it is not increased for this amount.

Only the cost approach is typically used to value an assembled workforce.

---

26. The fair value of the trade name is determined using a royalty savings rate of 1 percent based on comparable industry rates. What factors should the valuation specialist consider when selecting an appropriate industry royalty rate? What are some of the challenges in applying the relief from royalty method?

The terms of the license agreements should be analyzed, which includes considering the royalty rate, the economic measure to which the royalty rate is applied, the geographic region to which the agreement applies, whether the agreement is exclusive or nonexclusive, and the length of time the agreement is in effect. Other aspects of the intangible license agreement require analysis to determine whether the agreement reflects similar risk and required rates of returns as the intangible asset under consideration. If not, then any differences in risk should be considered by adjusting the selected royalty rate.

The second step is to analyze the industry in which these license agreements fall. An understanding of the industry is important to provide a framework in determining a royalty rate derived from market transactions that are appropriate to apply to the intangible asset being valued. This process is similar to determining what the market would support if the intangible asset under consideration was licensed to a third party. (Chapter 5)

---

27.   Is the relief from royalty method a market or an income valuation approach? What assumptions are incorporated into this valuation? The valuation of the trade name is presented after taxes and includes the tax benefit of amortization. Why is the after-tax application preferred in the relief from royalty method? What other methods can be used to value a trade name?

The relief from royalty method contains assumptions from both the market and the income approaches. The theory behind the relief from royalty method is that an entity that owns an intangible asset has a valuable right since the entity does not have to pay a third party a license fee for the right to use that intangible asset. The fair value of that right can be measured through an analysis of royalty rates charged by third parties for the use of similar intangible assets. Since the entity already owns the intangible asset, the entity is "relieved" from having to pay a third party a royalty for the use of the intangible asset. The fair value of the intangible asset is measured as the present value of hypothetical royalty payments that the entity is relieved from paying by not having to license the use of the intangible asset from a third party. (Chapter 5)

The trade name can also be valued using the profit split method. (Chapter 6)

---

28.   Are there alternative methods that can be used to value a noncompetition agreement? What assumptions form the basis for this valuation?

The incremental income/cost decrement method is most often used to measure the fair value of noncompetition agreements and is sometimes referred to as the "with versus without" method. Incremental cash flows resulting from the use of the asset are estimated over the asset's remaining useful life and discounted to arrive at a present value. The incremental cash flow can be in the form of additional revenues or can be related to cost saving from the use of the assets. This method is sometimes referred to as the scenario method because it compares the operating results under two scenarios to measure the incremental cash flow benefit attributable to the use of the subject asset. The first scenario incorporates the assumption that the subject intangible asset is being used by the entity to generate incremental cash flows. The second scenario projects cash flows assuming the subject intangible asset is not available for use by the entity. The difference in the present value of cash flows from the two scenarios is the fair value of the subject intangible asset. (Chapter 6)

---

29. The required rate of return on contributory assets is deducted from the cash flows of the company to arrive at excess earnings. What are contributory assets? Discuss how to estimate the required return on each of the contributory assets.

To isolate cash flows attributable to a specific intangible asset, the portion of cash flows attributed to all other assets is deducted from total entity cash flows. The deduction of cash flows attributable to all other assets is accomplished through a contributory asset charge (CAC). The CAC is a form of economic rent for the use of all other assets in generating total cash flows. (Chapter 6)

The required rates of return for individual assets should reflect the relative risk of that asset. The required return for individual assets can often be determined based on market-derived rates of return and based on the way the asset is typically financed. (Chapter 6)

---

30. What is an appropriate discount rate to use for the cash flows attributable to the graphic design software? How does this rate compare to the company's weighted average cost of capital?

In Exhibit 13.20, the required return on software is estimated to be 18 percent, which is equal to the 18 percent weighted average cost of capital.

Asset	Basis of Contributory Charge
Debt-Free Working Capital	After-tax short-term rates that would be available to market participants. Examples include bank prime rates, commercial paper rates, and 30- to 90-day U.S. Treasuries. Each should be adjusted for entity specific risk. Consideration should also be given to the mix of debt and equity financing required to fund working capital.
Fixed Assets	Rates of "return on" would include financing rates for similar assets for market participants. Examples include observed vendor financing and bank debt available to fund a specific fixed asset. Consideration should be given to a blended mix of debt and equity financing if market participants typically fund these assets with a mixture of debt and equity.
Workforce, Customer Lists Trademark's, and Trade Names Intangible Assets	Weighted average cost of capital for market participants, particularly entities with single-product assets, adjusted for the relevant mix of debt and equity and adjusted for relative risks. Many intangible assets are 100 percent funded with equity; therefore, an equity rate of return should be considered for those assets.
Technology-based Intangible Assets	Since most technology-based assets are funded with equity, the cost of equity is considered the base. It is adjusted upward for the increased relative risk of the technology-based asset compared to other company assets.
Other Intangibles, Including IPR&D Assets	Rates should be consistent with the relative risk of the subject intangible asset. When market participant inputs are available, that information should be used in calculating a required rate of return. Riskier assets such as IPR&D should require higher rates of return.

31. How would your analysis of the graphic design software using the multiperiod excess earnings method differ if the purpose of the valuation were to assist management in maximizing the benefit from the acquired graphic design software? Would projections include synergies with Arch Span? Would the discount rate differ?

If management were interested in maximizing the benefit from the acquired graphic design software, projections could be prepared that include synergies with Arch Span. The applicable discount rate could differ from the previous rate used because different risks would be inherent in the investment with synergies.

---

32. How is it possible to use the excess earnings method to estimate the value of two different assets?

A simple way to avoid the difficulties associated with using the excess earnings method to simultaneously measure the fair value of two identified intangible assets is to split the entity's revenue and cash flows. (Chapter 6) The Working Group of the Appraisal Foundation strongly believes that the use of simultaneous application of the excess earnings method to two intangible assets should be avoided when possible. (*Best Practices for Valuations in Financial Reporting: Intangible Asset Working Group*, The Appraisal Foundation, 19.)

---

33. What is the difference between "return of capital" and "return on capital"?

The "return on" contributory assets are based on the assumption that the entity pays a hypothetical economic rent or royalty for the use of the asset. It is a required rate of return on the fair value of all the contributory assets to compensate for the entity's use of those assets to produce economic benefits. A "return of" contributory assets is analogous to the return of principal that is part of each mortgage payment. However, the "return of" portion of the contributory charge is not appropriate for all contributory assets. It is only applicable when the cost to replenish the asset is not already part of the cash flow analysis. (Chapter 6)

---

34. Contributory charges under the multiperiod excess earnings method are one of the more controversial topics in valuation. What are some of the issues? How do you handle negative working capital as a contributory charge? Do you take a charge on goodwill, or not? How do you handle contributory charges on noncompete agreements when there is a mismatch between the contractual protection and the life of the expected benefit?

When using the excess earnings method to measure the fair value of the subject asset, a contributory charge is not typically taken for goodwill as a contributory asset. However, there are some exceptions. Some elements of goodwill are considered contributory assets and a contributory charge is appropriate. One common example is an assembled workforce. An assembled workforce is not specifically recognized as an identifiable intangible asset under FASB ASC 805, *Business Combinations* (SFAS 141(R)). The assembled workforce is included in goodwill. However, from an economic perspective, the workforce obviously contributes to the generation of cash flows. So, the contribution of the assembled workforce should be considered when calculating contributory charges under the excess earnings method. (Chapter 6)

The assumptions used in arriving at the fair value of the subject intangible asset should reflect those assumptions that a market participant would use in pricing the asset. Therefore, the prospective financial information should reflect the market participant assumptions and levels of required contributory assets. To the extent the prospective financial information reflects excess or deficient levels of the contributory assets, it should be adjusted to reflect normalized levels. The appropriate level of working capital to use as a contributory asset should be a normalized level of working capital. (*Best Practices for Valuations in Financial Reporting: Intangible Asset Working Group*, The Appraisal Foundation, 10.)

Contributory asset charges for the contributory intangible assets should be applied throughout the life of the subject intangible asset. If a contributory intangible asset would not be maintained or replaced upon expiration, for example, in the case of a non-compete agreement arising from a transaction between a buyer and seller, the contributory asset charge would only be applied through the economic life of the contributory asset. (*Best Practices for Valuations in Financial Reporting: Intangible Asset Working Group*, The Appraisal Foundation, 12.)

---

35. Suppose the values calculated under the two valuation methods were significantly different. How would you decide which value to use? What guidance does FASB ASC 820, *Fair Value Measurements and Disclosures* (SFAS 157), provide when more than one valuation technique is appropriate?

FASB ASC 820 (SFAS 157) states "Valuation techniques that are appropriate in the circumstances and for which sufficient data are available shall be used to measure fair value. In some cases, a single valuation technique will be appropriate ... In other cases, multiple valuation techniques will be appropriate ... If multiple valuation techniques are used to measure fair value, the results shall be evaluated and weighted, as appropriate, considering the reasonableness of the range indicated by those results. A fair value measurement is the point within that range that is most representative of fair value in the circumstances." (Chapter 3)

---

36. Which of the intangible assets in this case study is subject to amortization? How do you estimate a remaining useful life?

In this case study, software, trade name, customer relationships, and the noncompetition agreement are amortizable. In-process research and development is not subject to amortization in the case study because the underdeveloped software is not yet commercially available. Once the project is complete, it would be appropriate to amortize the research and development intangible asset.

FASB ASC 350 (SFAS 142) describes several important factors that should be considered when estimating the useful life of an intangible asset for financial reporting purposes:

- Expected use of the asset
- Expected use of similar assets
- Legal, regulatory, and contractual provisions that may limit the useful life or enable renewal or extension
- The effects of obsolescence, demand, competition, and other economic factors
- Required future maintenance expenditures

In the absence of experience, the company's management should consider the assumption that market participants would use about useful life.

---

37. How is the fair value of goodwill measured?

Goodwill is the excess purchase price paid in a business combination over and above the fair value of the company's other tangible and intangible assets. (Chapter 3)

38. Once all the opening balance sheet adjustments are recorded, including those to intangible assets and goodwill, how is the total purchase price reflected on Arch Span's books, on Software^2's books, and on the consolidated company's books.

Identifiable intangible assets acquired as part of a business combination are recorded at their respective fair value as of the measurement date. (Chapter 2). See Exhibit 13.19.

39. Why would one calculate the total required rate of return (RRR) for the business combination? What is the difference between the RRR and the WACC? What is the difference between the RRR and the Internal Rate of Return (IRR) shown in Exhibits 13.3a and b?

The required rates of return (RRR) for individual assets should reflect the relative risk of that asset. (Chapter 6) The total RRR should be similar to the overall WACC since the total investment is made up of the individual assets.

The WACC is initially calculated as the return on the investment in the subject entity required by market participants, including both debt and equity investors. The IRR for an acquisition should be compared to the derived market-based WACC. An IRR in an acquisition may be greater or lesser than the WACC depending on the relationship of the acquisition price to expected future cash flows of the acquired entity. An IRR that is significantly different from the WACC may warrant a reassessment of both the prospective financial information and the WACC calculation to determine if market participant assumptions are being consistently applied or if adjustments need to be made in either the prospective financial information or the WACC. (*Best Practices for Valuations in Financial Reporting: Intangible Asset Working Group*, The Appraisal Foundation, 23–24.)

In the case study, the RRR is calculated to be 18.0 percent, and the two IRRs are 18.6 percent, including tax benefits, and 16.6 percent, excluding tax benefits.

40. What is the purpose of reconciling the total RRR for acquired assets to the company's weighted average cost of capital?

See the preceding answer.

---

41. How do you determine the risk premium over the weighted average cost of capital for each of the intangible assets and for goodwill?

See the chart provided in the solution to question 29.

---

42. How is a bargain purchase price treated under FASB ASC 805 (SFAS 141(R))?

Under FASB ASC 805 (SFAS 141(R)), when there is a bargain purchase price and the fair values of the assets acquired are greater than the consideration given up, then the acquirer recognizes a gain equal to the excess fair value. Negative goodwill is no longer recognized under *Business Combinations.*

---

43. What are some general indications that impairment has occurred? What are the indications in this case study?

When there is indication that an intangible asset or goodwill is impaired, testing should be immediate. When no impairment is indicated, then such assets are to be tested annually at a minimum. Under FASB ASC 350 (SFAS No. 144), a long-lived asset that is currently being depreciated or amortized should be tested for impairment if there is a "triggering event" such as:

- A significant decrease in the market value of the asset
- A significant change in the extent or manner in which the asset is used or significant physical change to the asset
- A significant adverse change in legal factors or in the business climate that could affect the value of an asset, or an adverse action or assessment by a regulator
- An accumulation of costs significantly in excess of the amount originally expected to acquire or construct an asset
- A current period operating or cash flow loss combined with a history of operating or cash flow losses or a projection or forecast that demonstrates continuing losses associated with an asset used for the purpose of producing revenue

A long-lived asset, which is not being amortized because its remaining life is unknown, is also tested for impairment but under the "triggering events" described in FASB ASC 350 (SFAS No. 142). The triggering events under FASB ASC 350 are similar to those mentioned earlier; however, there are some differences to note in the following list:

- A significant adverse change in legal factors or in the business climate
- Adverse action or assessment by a regulator
- Unanticipated competition
- Loss of key personnel
- Expectation of sale or disposal of a reporting unit or a significant portion of the reporting unit
- Testing under FASB ASC 350 (SFAS No. 144) of a significant asset group in a reporting unit
- Recognition of a goodwill impairment loss in the financial statements of a subsidiary that is a component of a reporting unit

(Chapter 2)

Specific to this case, the severe decline in sales of the software indicates a decrease in the value of the software and a need for an impairment test.

---

44. Based on the selected P/E ratio of 8.5 and projected 20X3 earnings of $2 million, what is the implied value of Software^2? How does the implied value compare to the $16.4 million value calculated using the discounted cash flows? What would be some possible reasons for the differences? How can the two values be reconciled?

Using the market approach, the implied value of Software^2 is $17 million, which is slightly more than the value determined by the discounted cash flow method. If applicable, a control premium may be applied to the market approach if the value was determined using a guideline company approach. (Chapter 2) The different approaches create a range of possible values. In this case study, the analyst selected the $16,696,500 midpoint of the range.

---

45. What is the first step in impairment testing? Which two values are compared? Does impairment exist in this case study? Would your answer change if the carrying value of goodwill is negative?

Under the first step, the fair value of the reporting unit is measured through a discounted cash flow analysis, or other appropriate method. The fair value is compared to the reporting unit's carrying amount, or book value. If the reporting unit's fair value is greater than its carrying amount, the reporting unit's goodwill is not considered to be impaired. If the unit's fair value is less than its carrying amount, then goodwill impairment is a possibility, and the second step is required. (Chapter 2)

In this case study, an impairment is indicated. The enterprise fair value of $16,696,500 is less than the carrying value of $20,365,276. It is necessary to perform step two of the impairment test.

---

46. How does EITF 02-13, Deferred Income Tax Considerations in Applying the Goodwill Impairment Test in FASB Statement No. 142, affect your analysis?

EITF 02-13 states that "the determination of whether to estimate the fair value of a reporting unit by assuming that the unit could be bought or sold in a nontaxable transaction versus a taxable transaction is a matter of judgment that depends on the relevant facts and circumstances and must be evaluated carefully on a case-by-case basis. In making that determination, an entity should consider (a) whether the assumption is consistent with those that marketplace participants would incorporate into their estimates of fair value, (b) the feasibility of the assumed structure, and (c) whether the assumed structure results in the highest economic value to the seller for the reporting unit, including consideration of related tax implications."

---

47. Discuss step two of the impairment test. Which group of assets do you examine first? Which intangible assets from this case study would be tested under FASB ASC 360-10-05, *Property, Plant and Equipment—Impairment or Disposal of Long-Lived Assets* (SFAS 144)? Would you consider the fair value of the deferred tax assets and liabilities in step two?

Under the second step, goodwill's implied value is calculated by subtracting the sum of the fair values of all of the tangible and other intangible assets less liabilities existing on the measurement date from the fair value of the reporting unit. The calculation of implied goodwill includes all assets and liabilities existing on the test date, whether they were previously recorded. If the implied, fair value of goodwill exceeds the carrying amount of goodwill, there is no impairment. If goodwill's carrying amount exceeds its implied value, goodwill is impaired and the difference must be written off. (Chapter 2)

In addition to testing goodwill for impairment, FASB ASC 350 (SFAS No. 142) provides guidance on testing intangible assets that are not being amortized (indefinite-lived assets) for impairment. Intangible assets that are not currently being amortized, because their remaining useful life is not known, are tested for impairment at least annually. The test for impairment is rather simple. If the fair value as of the test date is less than their carrying value, the difference is the amount of impairment. If the fair value is greater than the carrying value, the asset is not considered impaired. The carrying value remains on the financial statements. According to FASB ASC 350 (SFAS No. 142), if goodwill and another asset, or goodwill and a group of assets in a reporting unit (defined as an operating unit per FASB ASC 280, *Segment Reporting* [SFAS No. 131]) are tested for impairment at the same time, the other asset, or asset group, is to be tested for impairment before goodwill. In other words, the long-lived assets that are being amortized or depreciated as of the test date under FASB ASC 360 (SFAS 144) are tested first, then indefinite-lived assets other than goodwill are tested under FASB ASC 350 (SFAS 142). After all other assets have been tested (assuming triggering events), then goodwill is tested for impairment under the two-step test described in FASB ASC 350 (SFAS 142). (Chapter 2)

In this case study, the software and the goodwill (including assembled workforce) are subject to impairment.

Taxable temporary differences will arise in the future as goodwill is amortized for tax purposes but not for book purposes. In those circumstances, an excess of the book basis over the tax basis of goodwill is a taxable temporary difference for which a deferred tax liability must be recognized under SFAS 109. Like goodwill, absent amortization, the deferred tax liability will remain on the balance sheet until such time as the intangible asset is impaired, sold, or otherwise disposed of FASB ASC 350. (SFAS 142)

---

48. Assume the carrying amount of the graphic design software is $4.6 million, its fair value is $3.5 million, and the sum of the undiscounted cash flows expected to be generated by the software is $3.8 million. What is the test for impairment, and is the software impaired? What is the write-down?

The test for impairment for intangible assets subject to amortization is based on a comparison of the carrying amount to the fair value. In this case the software is impaired because its fair value is $1.1 million less than its book value. An impairment is recognized if the carrying amount is not recoverable and if the carrying amount exceeds fair value. The carrying amount is not considered recoverable if it exceeds the sum of undiscounted cash flows expected to result from the use and ultimate disposal of the asset. In this case, an impairment should be recognized, as both conditions are met. The amount of impairment loss recognized is the difference between the carrying value and the fair value, or $1.1 million.

---

49. Which intangible assets are subject to amortization and are tested for impairment under FASB ASC 360-10-35, *Property, Plant, and Equipment, Subsequent Measurement* (SFAS 144)? Which intangible assets are tested under FASB ASC 350-35, *Intangible—Goodwill and Other, Subsequent Measurements* (SFAS 142)? Is assembled workforce tested separately or as part of goodwill under SFAS 142?

FASB ASC 350-35 (SFAS 142) provides guidance on testing intangible assets that are not amortized. In this case study, goodwill is tested under FASB ASC 350-35 (SFAS 142). Assembled workforce is tested as part of goodwill under FASB ASC 350-35 (SFAS 142).

---

50. What is the process for determining the implied value of goodwill?

The implied fair value of goodwill is determined in the same manner that goodwill is measured in a business combination. The fair value of an entity or reporting unit is allocated to all the assets and liabilities, including any unrecognized intangible assets. The excess fair value over the amounts assigned to assets and liabilities is the implied value of goodwill. It is important to note that the allocation process is only performed for purposes of testing goodwill for impairment. The entity should not write up or write down the value of any asset nor recognize any previously unrecognized intangible asset. (See Exhibit 13.26.)

---

51. Based on the fair value measurement of Software[2]'s intangible assets and the implied value of goodwill, calculate the impairment loss on goodwill.

Goodwill was recorded at $6.155 million (including assembled workforce). The implied value is $3.544 million; therefore, the impairment charge is $2.611 million.

---

52. When implied goodwill is negative, what does this indicate about the company?

Which intangible assets are subject to amortization and tested for impairment under FASB ASC 360-10-35, *Property, Plant and Equipment, Subsequent Measurement* (SFAS 144)? Which intangible assets are tested under FASB ASC 350-35, *Intangibles—Goodwill and Other-Subsequent Measurements* (SFAS 142)?

Negative implied goodwill indicates that the value of the reporting unit has decreased significantly and that it may no longer be a viable entity. The assets may be worth more in a liquidation scenario than they are worth as part of the ongoing entity. When recognizing an impairment charge for goodwill with a negative implied value, the loss can not exceed the carrying amount of goodwill. It would be reduced to $0.

---

53.   Do you believe fair value measurements provide a more relevant presentation of financial statements than traditional, historical, cost-based accounting?

Advocates of fair value accounting believe that this presentation more fairly represents the financial position of the entity and provides more relevant information to the users of the financial information. Detractors of fair value accounting point to is complexity and inherent use of judgment. Either way, fair value accounting is becoming more and more prominent in financial information presentation and will continue to be the fundamental basis for accounting in the future.

Information Request—SFAS 142

Depending on the available information, or the answers to the questions, additional information may be required.

Financial Information

1. What is the impairment test date for the reporting units? With regard to the timing of the impairment test, please note that the annual impairment test can be performed at any time during the year, as long as that measurement date is used consistently going forward.
2. Five years of financial statements including balance sheets, income statements and statements of cash flow.
3. For each reporting unit, please provide latest balance sheet for the impairment test date.
4. For each reporting unit, please provide latest statement of cash flow for the impairment test date.
5. For each reporting unit, please provide latest income statement for the impairment test date.
6. For the reporting units, please provide any income or cash flow budgets or projections (3 to 5 years preferable), including revenue, expenses, net income, depreciation, and capital expenditures.
7. For the reporting units, please provide information on any idle or non-operating assets, if applicable.
8. Please provide copies of any appraisals, performed within the last year, of any tangible or intangible assets that you still report on your financial statements of the salient reporting units.
9. Copies of any business plans, bank submissions, investment bankers' reports, fairness opinions, or other estimates of value, developed within the previous year for any of the reporting units.

Information Request for Business Combinations— SFAS 141R

Currently, we have identified the following five intangible assets as potentially having value.

1. Customer list
2. Existing technology
3. Assembled workforce
4. Trade name
5. Noncompetition agreements

Financial Information

1. Any income or cash flow budgets or projections (3 to 5 years preferable), including revenue, expenses, net income, depreciation, and capital expenditures.
2. Last two years of financial statements: Income Statement and Balance Sheet.
3. Detail of final purchase price accounting entry.

Additional Information

4. Please provide the name and contact information (phone number and e-mail address) for your audit partner/manager.

Existing Technology

5. Please provide a summary of all existing technology.
6. What date did the existing technology enter the market? Has it been significantly modified or enhanced?

7. How much effort (in terms of work hours and dollar costs) would be required to reproduce or replace these assets?
8. Is there a specific revenue stream associated with these assets? If so, please identify it, along with all the relevant costs.

Customer Relationships

9. Complete list of customer relationships of the acquired company, including revenue and related expenses per customer for the last three years.
10. Are the customer relationships contractual in nature? If so, please provide sample contracts. Are the contracts for terms greater than one year? Are they typically renewed?
11. What expenses are required to obtain a new customer? Please provide total sales and marketing costs for the last three years, including travel and entertainment. Is senior management involved in the sales effort? If so, which executives and what percentage of their time?
12. What is the average revenue per customer?
13. What is the average remaining useful life?

Trade Name

14. List of trade names and trademarks held by the company.
15. Please identify any revenue streams that are closely associated with any of these assets.

Noncompetition Agreements, if Applicable

16. Copies of noncompete agreements, if any.
17. If any, an estimate of the likelihood of competition (from 0 percent to 100 percent) from the sellers in the absence of a noncompete agreement.
18. If any, an estimate of the likelihood of success of the seller's competitive efforts (from 0 percent to 100 percent) if they were to compete in absence of the noncompete agreement.

Workforce

19. List of owners and top management of the company.
    a) Name
    b) Position
    c) Years with company
    d) Years in the industry
    e) Three-year compensation history by salary and bonus

20. Organization chart
21. Employee listing by category, including average salary information
22. How many total employees of the company?
23. Please complete the table on the next page for the company regarding the workforce. (Please note that the employee classifications are examples only, so use whatever categories are appropriate to your business.)

Class	# of Employees	Average Annual Salary	Fringe Benefits as % of Salary	Average Cost of Advertising or Search Fee/ Employee	Average Relocation Costs/ Employee	# of Interviews Required to Hire/ Employees	% Effective- ness of New Hire	# of Months Until Full Productivity	$ Amount of Direct Training Costs/Emp.
Executive									
Sales									
Engineers									
Admin.									
Manuf.									

Glossary of International Business Valuation Terms

To enhance and sustain the quality of business valuations for the benefit of the profession and its clientele, the following identified societies and organizations have adopted the definitions for the terms included in this glossary.

The performance of business valuation services requires a high degree of skill and imposes on the valuation professional a duty to communicate the valuation process and conclusion in a manner that is clear and not misleading. This duty is advanced through the use of terms with meanings that are clearly established and consistently applied throughout the profession.

If, in the opinion of the business valuation professional, one or more of these terms needs to be used in a manner that materially departs from the enclosed definitions, it is recommended that the term be defined as used within that valuation engagement.

This glossary has been developed to provide guidance to business valuation practitioners by further memorializing the body of knowledge that constitutes the competent and careful determination of value and, more particularly, the communication of how that value was determined.

Departure from this glossary is not intended to provide a basis for civil liability and should not be presumed to create evidence that any duty has been breached.

American Institute of Certified Public Accountants
American Society of Appraisers
Canadian Institute of Chartered Business Valuators
National Association of Certified Valuation Analysts
The Institute of Business Appraisers

Adjusted Book Value Method. A method within the asset approach whereby all assets and liabilities (including off-balance sheet, intangible, and contingent) are adjusted to their fair market values. (*Note:* In Canada on a going concern basis.)

Adjusted Net Asset Method. *See* Adjusted Book Value Method

Appraisal. *See* Valuation

Appraisal Approach. *See* Valuation Approach

Appraisal Date. *See* Valuation Date

Appraisal Method. *See* Valuation Method

Appraisal Procedure. *See* Valuation Procedure

Arbitrage Pricing Theory. A multivariate model for estimating the cost of equity capital, which incorporates several systematic risk factors.

Asset (Asset-Based) Approach. A general way of determining a value indication of a business, business ownership interest, or security using one or more methods based on the value of the assets net of liabilities.

Beta. A measure of systematic risk of a stock; the tendency of a stock's price to correlate with changes in a specific index.

Blockage Discount. An amount or percentage deducted from the current market price of a publicly traded stock to reflect the decrease in the per share value of a block of stock that is of a size that could not be sold in a reasonable period of time given normal trading volume.

Book Value. *See* Net Book Value

Business. *See* Business Enterprise

Business Enterprise. A commercial, industrial, service, or investment entity (or a combination thereof) pursuing an economic activity.

Business Risk. The degree of uncertainty of realizing expected future returns of the business resulting from factors other than financial leverage. *See* Financial Risk

Business Valuation. The act or process of determining the value of a business enterprise or ownership interest therein.

Capital Asset Pricing Model (CAPM). A model in which the cost of capital for any stock or portfolio of stocks equals a risk-free rate plus a risk premium that is proportionate to the systematic risk of the stock or portfolio.

Capitalization. A conversion of a single period of economic benefits into value.

Capitalization Factor.   Any multiple or divisor used to convert anticipated economic benefits of a single period into value.

Capitalization of Earnings Method.   A method within the income approach whereby economic benefits for a representative single period are converted to value through division by a capitalization rate.

Capitalization Rate.   Any divisor (usually expressed as a percentage) used to convert anticipated economic benefits of a single period into value.

Capital Structure.   The composition of the invested capital of a business enterprise, the mix of debt and equity financing.

Cash Flow.   Cash that is generated over a period of time by an asset, group of assets, or business enterprise. It may be used in a general sense to encompass various levels of specifically defined cash flows. When the term is used, it should be supplemented by a qualifier (for example, "discretionary" or "operating") and a specific definition in the given valuation context.

Common Size Statements.   Financial statements in which each line is expressed as a percentage of the total. On the balance sheet, each line item is shown as a percentage of total assets, and on the income statement, each item is expressed as a percentage of sales.

Control.   The power to direct the management and policies of a business enterprise.

Control Premium.   An amount or a percentage by which the pro rata value of a controlling interest exceeds the pro rata value of a noncontrolling interest in a business enterprise, to reflect the power of control.

Cost Approach.   A general way of determining a value indication of an individual asset by quantifying the amount of money required to replace the future service capability of that asset.

Cost of Capital.   The expected rate of return that the market requires in order to attract funds to a particular investment.

Debt-Free.   We discourage the use of this term. *See* Invested Capital

Discount for Lack of Control.   An amount or percentage deducted from the pro rata share of value of 100 percent of an equity interest in a business to reflect the absence of some or all of the powers of control.

Discount for Lack of Marketability.   An amount or percentage deducted from the value of an ownership interest to reflect the relative absence of marketability.

Discount for Lack of Voting Rights.   An amount or percentage deducted from the per share value of a minority interest voting share to reflect the absence of voting rights.

Discount Rate.   A rate of return used to convert a future monetary sum into present value.

Discounted Cash Flow Method.   A method within the income approach whereby the present value of future expected net cash flows is calculated using a discount rate.

Discounted Future Earnings Method.   A method within the income approach whereby the present value of future expected economic benefits is calculated using a discount rate.

Economic Benefits.   Inflows such as revenues, net income, net cash flows.

Economic Life.   The period of time over which property may generate economic benefits.

Effective Date.   *See* Valuation Date

Enterprise.   *See* Business Enterprise

Equity.   The owner's interest in property after deduction of all liabilities.

Equity Net Cash Flows.   Those cash flows available to pay out to equity holders (in the form of dividends) after funding operations of the business enterprise, making necessary capital investments, and increasing or decreasing debt financing.

Equity Risk Premium.   A rate of return added to a risk-free rate to reflect the additional risk of equity instruments over risk free instruments (a component of the cost of equity capital or equity discount rate).

Excess Earnings.   That amount of anticipated economic benefits that exceeds an appropriate rate of return on the value of a selected asset base (often net tangible assets) used to generate those anticipated economic benefits.

Excess Earnings Method.   A specific way of determining a value indication of a business, business ownership interest, or security determined as the sum of (1) the value of the assets derived by capitalizing excess earnings and (2) the value of the selected asset base. Also frequently used to value intangible assets. *See* Excess Earnings.

Fair Market Value.   The price, expressed in terms of cash equivalents, at which property would change hands between a hypothetical willing and able buyer and a hypothetical willing and able seller, acting at arms length in an open and unrestricted market, when neither is under compulsion to buy or sell and when both have reasonable knowledge of the relevant facts. (*Note:* In Canada, the term "price" should be replaced with the term "highest price.")

Fairness Opinion.   An opinion as to whether or not the consideration in a transaction is fair from a financial point of view.

Financial Risk.   The degree of uncertainty of realizing expected future returns of the business resulting from financial leverage. *See* Business Risk

Forced Liquidation Value.   Liquidation value, at which the asset or assets are sold as quickly as possible, such as at an auction.

Free Cash Flow.   We discourage the use of this term. *See* Net Cash Flows

Going Concern.   An ongoing operating business enterprise.

Going Concern Value.   The value of a business enterprise that is expected to continue to operate into the future. The intangible elements of Going Concern Value result from factors such as having a trained work force, an operational plant, and the necessary licenses, systems, and procedures in place.

Goodwill.   That intangible asset arising as a result of name, reputation, customer loyalty, location, products, and similar factors not separately identified.

Goodwill Value.   The value attributable to goodwill.

Guideline Public Company Method.   A method within the market approach whereby market multiples are derived from market prices of stocks of companies that are engaged in the same or similar lines of business, and that are actively traded on a free and open market.

Income (Income-Based) Approach.   A general way of determining a value indication of a business, business ownership interest, security, or intangible asset using one or more methods that convert anticipated economic benefits into a present single amount.

Intangible Assets.   Nonphysical assets such as franchises, trademarks, patents, copyrights, goodwill, equities, mineral rights, securities and contracts (as distinguished from physical assets) that grant rights and privileges, and have value for the owner.

Internal Rate of Return.   A discount rate at which the present value of the future cash flows of the investment equals the cost of the investment.

Intrinsic Value.   The value that an investor considers, on the basis of an evaluation or available facts, to be the "true" or "real" value that will become the market value when other investors reach the same conclusion. When the term applies to options, it is the difference between the exercise price or strike price of an option and the market value of the underlying security.

Invested Capital.   The sum of equity and debt in a business enterprise. Debt is typically (1) all interest bearing debt or (2) long-term interest-bearing debt. When the term is used, it should be supplemented by a specific definition in the given valuation context.

Invested Capital Net Cash Flows.   Those cash flows available to pay out to equity holders (in the form of dividends) and debt investors (in the form of principal and interest) after funding operations of the business enterprise and making necessary capital investments.

Investment Risk.   The degree of uncertainty as to the realization of expected returns.

Investment Value.   The value to a particular investor based on individual investment requirements and expectations. (*Note:* In Canada, the term used is "Value to the Owner.")

Key Person Discount.   An amount or percentage deducted from the value of an ownership interest to reflect the reduction in value resulting from the actual or potential loss of a key person in a business enterprise.

Levered Beta.   The beta reflecting a capital structure that includes debt.

Limited Appraisal.   The act or process of determining the value of a business, business ownership interest, security, or intangible asset with limitations in analyses, procedures, or scope.

Liquidity.   The ability to quickly convert property to cash or pay a liability.

Liquidation Value.   The net amount that would be realized if the business is terminated and the assets are sold piecemeal. Liquidation can be either "orderly" or "forced."

Majority Control.   The degree of control provided by a majority position.

Majority Interest.   An ownership interest greater than 50 percent of the voting interest in a business enterprise.

Market (Market-Based) Approach.   A general way of determining a value indication of a business, business ownership interest, security, or intangible asset by using one or more methods that compare the subject to similar businesses, business ownership interests, securities, or intangible assets that have been sold.

Market Capitalization of Equity. The share price of a publicly traded stock multiplied by the number of shares outstanding.

Market Capitalization of Invested Capital. The market capitalization of equity plus the market value of the debt component of invested capital.

Market Multiple. The market value of a company's stock or invested capital divided by a company measure (such as economic benefits, number of customers).

Marketability. The ability to quickly convert property to cash at minimal cost.

Marketability Discount. *See* Discount for Lack of Marketability

Merger and Acquisition Method. A method within the market approach whereby pricing multiples are derived from transactions of significant interests in companies engaged in the same or similar lines of business.

Mid-Year Discounting. A convention used in the Discounted Future Earnings Method that reflects economic benefits being generated at midyear, approximating the effect of economic benefits being generated evenly throughout the year.

Minority Discount. A discount for lack of control applicable to a minority interest.

Minority Interest. An ownership interest less than 50 percent of the voting interest in a business enterprise.

Multiple. The inverse of the capitalization rate.

Net Book Value. With respect to a business enterprise, the difference between total assets (net of accumulated depreciation, depletion, and amortization) and total liabilities as they appear on the balance sheet (synonymous with Shareholder's Equity). With respect to a specific asset, the capitalized cost less accumulated amortization or depreciation as it appears on the books of account of the business enterprise.

Net Cash Flows. When the term is used, it should be supplemented by a qualifier. *See* Equity Net Cash Flows and Invested Capital Net Cash Flows

Net Present Value. The value, as of a specified date, of future cash inflows less all cash outflows (including the cost of investment) calculated using an appropriate discount rate.

Net Tangible Asset Value. The value of the business enterprise's tangible assets (excluding excess assets and nonoperating assets) minus the value of its liabilities.

Nonoperating Assets.   Assets not necessary to ongoing operations of the business enterprise. (*Note:* In Canada, the term used is "Redundant Assets.")

Normalized Earnings.   Economic benefits adjusted for nonrecurring, noneconomic, or other unusual items to eliminate anomalies and/or facilitate comparisons.

Normalized Financial Statements.   Financial statements adjusted for nonoperating assets and liabilities and/or for nonrecurring, noneconomic, or other unusual items to eliminate anomalies and/or facilitate comparisons.

Orderly Liquidation Value.   Liquidation value at which the asset or assets are sold over a reasonable period of time to maximize proceeds received.

Premise of Value.   An assumption regarding the most likely set of transactional circumstances that may be applicable to the subject valuation; for example, going concern, liquidation.

Present Value.   The value, as of a specified date, of future economic benefits and/or proceeds from sale, calculated using an appropriate discount rate.

Portfolio Discount.   An amount or percentage deducted from the value of a business enterprise to reflect the fact that it owns dissimilar operations or assets that do not fit well together.

Price/Earnings Multiple.   The price of a share of stock divided by its earnings per share.

Rate of Return.   An amount of income (loss) and/or change in value realized or anticipated on an investment, expressed as a percentage of that investment.

Redundant Assets.   *See* Nonoperating Assets

Report Date.   The date conclusions are transmitted to the client.

Replacement Cost New.   The current cost of a similar new property having the nearest equivalent utility to the property being valued.

Reproduction Cost New.   The current cost of an identical new property.

Required Rate of Return.   The minimum rate of return acceptable by investors before they will commit money to an investment at a given level of risk.

Residual Value.   The value as of the end of the discrete projection period in a discounted future earnings model.

Return on Equity. The amount, expressed as a percentage, earned on a company's common equity for a given period.

Return on Investment. *See* Return on Invested Capital and Return on Equity.

Return on Invested Capital. The amount, expressed as a percentage, earned on a company's total capital for a given period.

Risk-Free Rate. The rate of return available in the market on an investment free of default risk.

Risk Premium. A rate of return added to a risk-free rate to reflect risk.

Rule of Thumb. A mathematical formula developed from the relationship between price and certain variables based on experience, observation, hearsay, or a combination of these; usually industry specific.

Special Interest Purchasers. Acquirers who believe they can enjoy postacquisition economies of scale, synergies, or strategic advantages by combining the acquired business interest with their own.

Standard of Value. The identification of the type of value being utilized in a specific engagement; for example, fair market value, fair value, investment value.

Sustaining Capital Reinvestment. The periodic capital outlay required to maintain operations at existing levels, net of the tax shield available from such outlays.

Systematic Risk. The risk that is common to all risky securities and cannot be eliminated through diversification. The measure of systematic risk in stocks is the beta coefficient.

Tangible Assets. Physical assets (such as cash, accounts receivable, inventory, property, plant and equipment.

Terminal Value. *See* Residual Value

Transaction Method. *See* Merger and Acquisition Method

Unlevered Beta. The beta reflecting a capital structure without debt.

Unsystematic Risk. The portion of total risk specific to an individual security that can be avoided through diversification.

Valuation. The act or process of determining the value of a business, business ownership interest, security, or intangible asset.

Valuation Approach.   A general way of determining a value indication of a business, business ownership interest, security, or intangible asset using one or more valuation methods.

Valuation Date.   The specific point in time as of which the valuator's conclusion of value applies (also referred to as "Effective Date" or "Appraisal Date").

Valuation Method.   Within approaches, a specific way to determine value.

Valuation Procedure.   The act, manner, and technique of performing the steps of an appraisal method.

Valuation Ratio.   A fraction in which a value or price serves as the numerator and financial, operating, or physical data serve as the denominator.

Value to the Owner.   *Note:* In Canada, *see* Investment Value

Voting Control.   *de jure* control of a business enterprise.

Weighted Average Cost of Capital (WACC).   The cost of capital (discount rate) determined by the weighted average, at market value, of the cost of all financing sources in the business enterprise's capital structure.

Bibliography

Adobe. "Adobe Systems Incorporated Corporate Overview," available at www.adobe.com (accessed April 21, 2009).

Agiato, Joseph A., Jr., and Michael J. Mard. *Valuing Intellectual Property and Calculating Infringement Damages,* American Institute of Certified Public Accountants Consulting Services Practice Aid 99-2, 1999.

American Institute of Certified Public Accountants (AICPA). *Audit and Accounting Guide: Guide for Prospective Financial Information,* sections AAG-PRO 7.01–7.07.

AICPA. *Audit and Accounting Guide, Guide for Prospective Financial Information.*

AICPA. *Audit and Accounting Guide: Investment Companies.*

AICPA. "Assets Acquired in a Business Combination to Be Used in Research and Development Activities: A Focus on Software, Electronic Devises, and Pharmaceutical Industries." AICPA Practice Aid, 2001: paragraph 5.3.88.

AICPA Auditing Fair Value Measurements and Disclosures. "A Toolkit for Auditors," available at www.aicpa.org.

AICPA. Draft Issues Paper "FASB Statement No. 157 Valuation of Considerations for Interests in Alternative Investments" (January 2009), available at www.aicpa.org.

AICPA. "Measurement of Fair Value in Illiquid (or Less Liquid) Markets, CAQ Alert #2007-51, Center for Audit Quality" (October 3, 2007), available at www.aicpa.org.

AICPA. "Practice Aid to Be Released on Business Combinations," *The CPA Letter* (December 2001), available at www.aicpa.org (accessed May 17, 2009).

AICPA Professional Standards. Statement of Auditing Standards 57, "Auditing Accounting Estimates AU Section 342," available at www.aicpa.org.

AICPA Professional Standards. "Auditing Fair Value Measurements and Disclosures AU Section 328," available at www.aicpa.org.

AICPA. Statement on Standards for Valuation Services, Number 1, AICPA, 2007.

Amazon. "Wireless Access with Whispernet," available at www.amazon.com (accessed April 16, 2009).

American Accounting Association. "The Report of the Committee on Basic Auditing Concepts," *Accounting Review*, vol. 47.

American Society of Appraisers. Business Valuation Standards BVS-I IV A, BVS-VI II B, III A & B, 2008.

American Society of Appraisers. "Valuation of Intangible Assets for Financial Reporting Purposes," Business Valuation 301 Course Materials.

Appraisal Foundation. "Our Mission & Vision," available at www.appraisalfoundation.org.

Appraisal Foundation, Appraisal Issues Task Force. "Illustrated Valuation Issues" (February 6, 2006), available at www.appraisalfoundation.org.

Appraisal Foundation. Business Valuation Best Practices Working Group, "The Identification of Contributory Assets and the Calculation of Economic Rents," Exposure Draft, available at www.appraisalfoundation.org.

Appraisal Institute. *The Appraisal of Real Estate, Twelfth Edition*. Appraisal Institute, 2001.

AT&T. "2008 Annual Report," available at www.att.com/Common/about_us/annual_report/pdfs/2008ATT_FullReport.pdf (accessed July 29, 2009).

Bay Area Radio. Schneider, John, "The NBC Chimes Machine," available at www.bayarearadio.org/schneider/chimes.shtml.

Bishop, Jody C. " The Challenge of Valuing Intellectual Property Assets," *Northwestern Journal of Technology and Intellectual Property*, Volume 1, Issue 1 (Spring 2003).

Board of Governors of the Federal Reserve System. Chairman Ben S. Bernanke's Testimony before the Committee on Banking, Housing and Urban Affairs of the U.S. Senate, September 23, 2008, available at www.federalreserve.gov.

Beneda, Nancy L. "Estimating Cost of Capital Using Bottom-up Betas," *The CPA Journal*, available at www.nysscpa.org.

Business Valuation Resources. "International Glossary of Business Valuation Terms, 2001," available at www.bvresources.com/FreeDownloads/IntGlossaryBVTerms2001.pdf.

Business Valuation Resources. "International Glossary of Business Valuation Terms," AICPA SSVS No.1 Appendix B, available at www.aicpa.org (accessed April 16, 2009).

Business Valuation Resources. "International Glossary of Business Valuation Terms," available at www.bvresources.com/freedownloads/BVGlossary09.pdf (accessed July 10, 2009).

"CAQ Issues White Papers on Illiquidity in the Markets," CAQ Alert # 2007-51, Center for Audit Quality (October 3, 2007).

Chartered Financial Analyst Institute Center for Financial Market Integrity. "A Comprehensive Business Reporting Model: Financial Reporting for Investors" (July 2007), available at www.cfapubs.org (accessed June 22, 2009).

Chartered Financial Analyst Institute Center for Financial Market Integrity. "Comment Letter on FSP 157-e: Determining Whether a Market Is Not Active and a Transaction Is Not Distressed, Addressed to Robert Herz, Chair of the FASB," dated March 30, 2009, available at www.cfainstitiute.org/center/topics/comment/2009/pdf/090330.pdf.

Chartered Financial Analyst Institute Center for Financial Market Integrity. Letter on "The Progress Report of the SEC Advisory Committee on Improvement to Financial Reporting," March 31, 2008.

Chance, Don M. *Analysis of Derivatives for the CFA Program*, Charlottesville, VA: Association for Investment Management and Research, 2003.

Chance, Don M., and Pamela P. Peterson. *Real Options and Investment Valuation*. The Research Foundation of the AIMR, CFA Institute: Charlottesville VA, 2002.

Chiovari, Cory R., and Robert F. Reilly. "The Financial Adviser and the AICPA Statement on Standards for Valuation Services," *Insights* (Winter 2008).

CNN Money.com. "Fortune 500 Database: 50 Years of Fortune's List of America's Largest Corporations," available at www.money.cnn.com/magazines/fortune/fortune500_archive/snapshots/1980/3547.html (accessed July 30, 2009).

Coca-Cola Company, The. "The Coca-Cola Company Form 10-K December 31, 2008," available at www.thecoca-colacompany.com.

Cohen, Jeffery A. *Intangible Assets: Valuation and Economic Benefit*. Hoboken, NJ: John Wiley & Sons, 2005.

"Council of Institutional Investors and the CFA Institute Opposing Suspension of Mark-to-Market Accounting," Joint Statement of the Center for Audit Quality (October 1, 2008).

Cox, John C., Stephen Ross, and Mark Rubinstein. "Option Pricing: A Simplified Approach," *Journal of Financial Economics*, September 1979, p. 2.

Current Partnering. Rowell, Simon. "Strategic Tips for Adding Value to Licensing Transactions," available at www.currentpartnering.com/articles/1488 (accessed June 15, 2009).

Damodaran, Anaswarth. "An Excellent Source of Valuation Models." Damodaran Online, available at http://pages.stern.nyu.edu/~adamodar/.

Delta Airlines, Inc. "Delta Air Lines, Northwest Airlines Combining to Create America's Premier Global Airline," Delta Newsroom April 14, 2008, available at www.delta.com.

Delta Airlines, Inc. "Form 10-K," December 31, 2008. F-18.

Downes, John, and Jordan Elliot Goodman. *Dictionary of Finance and Investment Terms, Sixth Edition*. New York: Barron Educational Series, Inc. 2003.

Ellsworth, Richard K. "Retirement Behavior and Customer Life Expectancy," *Business Valuation Review*, Spring 2009, Volume 28, No. 1.

Financial Accounting Standards Board. Board Activities-International, FASB-IASB, Memorandum of Understanding, "The Norwalk Agreement," available at www.fasb.org.

Financial Accounting Standards Board. "Completing the February 2006 Memorandum of Understanding: A Progress Report and Timetable for Completion," September 2008, available at www.fasb.org.

Financial Accounting Standards Board. Emerging Issues Task Force, "EITF 02-13: Deferred Income Tax Considerations in Applying the Goodwill Impairment Test in FASB Statement 142."

Financial Accounting Standards Board. Financial Crisis Advisory Group (FCAG), available at www.fasb.org/fcag/index.shtml.

Financial Accounting Standards Board. Financial Crisis Advisory Group (FCAG) press release dated 7/28/09, "FCAG Publishes Wide-Ranging Review of Standard Setting Activities Following the Global Financial Crisis," available at www.fasb.org/fcag/index.shtml.

Financial Accounting Standards Board. "Financial Accounting Series, Statement of Financial Accounting Standard No. 141 (revised 2007), Business Combinations" (ASC805), available at www.fasb.org.

Financial Accounting Standards Board. "Master Glossary," available at www.fasb.org.

Financial Accounting Standards Board. News release 10/29/02, "FASB and IASB Agree to Work Together toward Convergence of Global Accounting Standards," available at www.fasb.org.

Financial Accounting Standards Board. News release 12/04/07, "FASB Issues FASB Statements No. 141(R), Business Combinations, and No. 160, Non-controllilng Interests in Consolidated Financial Statements," available at www.fasb.org.

Financial Accounting Standards Board. News release 2/18/09, "FASB Initiates Projects to Improve Measurement and Disclosure of Fair Value Estimates," available at www.fasb.org.

Financial Accounting Standards Board. "Original Pronouncements (as amended), Statement of Financial Accounting Standard No. 142: Goodwill and Other Intangible Assets" (ASC 350), available at www.fasb.org.

Financial Accounting Standards Board. "Original Pronouncements (as amended), Statement of Financial Accounting Standard No. 141: Accounting for the Impairment or Disposal of Long-Lived Assets" (ASC 360), available at www.fasb.org.

Financial Accounting Standards Board. "Original Pronouncements (as amended), Statement of Financial Accounting Standard No. 157: Fair Value Measurements" (ASC 820), available at www.fasb.org.

Financial Accounting Standards Board. "Original Pronouncements (as amended), Statement of Financial Accounting Standard No. 159: The Fair Value Option for Financial Assets and Financial Liabilities Including an Amendment of FASB Statement No. 115," available at www.fasb.org.

Financial Accounting Standards Board. "Projects—Technical Plans and Project Updates," available at www.fasb.org/jsp/FASB/Page/Secction Page&cid=1176156240004, accessed 8/11/2009.

Financial Accounting Standards Board. "Project Update FAS 157—Improving Disclosures about Fair Value Measurements," available at www.fasb. org/fas157_improving_disclosures_about_fvm.shtml (accessed July 19, 2009).

Financial Accounting Standards Board. "Statement of Financial Accounting Concepts No. 7. Using Cash Flow Information and Present Value in Accounting Measurements," available at www.fasb.org.

Financial Accounting Standards Board. "Summary of Statement No. 142," available at www.fasb.org.

Financial Accounting Standards Board. "Use of Residual Method to Value Acquired Assets Other Than Goodwill, Topic No. D-108, EITF Discussion September 29030 2004," available at www.fasb.org.

Financial Accounting Standards Board. Projects. "Technical Plans and Project Updates," available at www.fasb.org/jsp/FASB/Page/Section Page&cid=1176156240004 (accessed 8/11/09).

Financial Accounting Standards Board Staff Position. "FAS Nos. 107-2 and APB 28-1, Interim Disclosures about Fair Value of Financial Instruments," available at www.fasb.org.

Financial Accounting Standards Board Staff Position. "FAS Nos. 115-2 and 124-2, Recognition and Presentation of Other-Than-Temporary Impairments," available at www.fasb.org.

Financial Accounting Standards Board Staff Position. "FAS No. 141(R)-1, Accounting for Assets Acquired and Liabilities Assumed in a Business Combination That Arise from Contingencies," available at wwww.fasb.org.

Financial Accounting Standards Board Staff Position. "FAS No. 142-3, Determination of the Useful Life of Intangible Assets," available at www.fasb.org.

Financial Accounting Standards Board Staff Position. "FAS No. 157-2, Effective Date of FASB Statement No. 157," available at www.fasb.org.

Financial Accounting Standards Board Staff Position. "FAS No. 157-3, Determining the Fair Value of a Financial Asset When the Market for That Asset Is Not Active," available at www.fasb.org.

Financial Accounting Standards Board Staff Position. "FAS No. 157-4, Determining Fair Value When the Volume and Level of Activity for the Asset or Liability Have Significantly Decreased and Identifying Transactions That Are Not Orderly," available at www.fasb.org.

Financial Accounting Standards Board Staff Position. "Proposed FAS No.157-f, Measuring Liabilities under FASB Statement No. 157," available at www.fasb.org.

Financial Accounting Standards Board Staff Position. "Proposed FAS No.157-g, Estimating the Fair Value of Investments in Investment Companies That Have Calculated Net Asset Value per Share in Accordance with the AICPA Auditing and Accounting Guide," available at www.fasb.org.

Financial Crisis Advisory Group. Press Release dated 28 July 2009, "FCAG Publishes Wide-Ranging Review of Standard-Setting Activities Following the Global Financial Crisis," available at www.fasb.org/fcag.org.

Financial Executives International's Committee on Corporate Reporting and Small Public Company Task Force, October 1, 2007, Letter to the FASB, available at www.financialexecutives.org/eweb/upload/FEI/FAS%20157%20101107.pdf.

Fitch Ratings. Accounting Research Special Report, "Fair Value Accounting: Is It Helpful in Illiquid Markets?" April 2008, available at www.fitchratings.com.

Fratto, Mike. "Broadcom Raises All-Cash Tender Offer for Emulex to $11.00 per Share," press release dated June 29, 2009, available at www.byteanswitch.com (accessed July 23, 2009).

Fried, Haim D., Ashwinpaul C. Sodhi, and Gerald I. White. *The Analysis and Use of Financial Statements, Second Edition*. Hoboken, NJ: John Wiley & Sons, 1994.

Garuto, Loren, and Oliver Loud. "Taking the Temperature of Health Care Valuations," *Journal of Accountancy* (October 2001): 4.

Gersen, James S., Henry R. Jaenicke, Patrick J. McDonnell, Vincent M. O'Reilly, and Barry N. Winograd. *Montgomery's Auditing*, Twelfth Edition. Hoboken: Wiley, 1998.

Global Public Policy Symposium. "Global Capital Markets and the Global Economy: A Vision from the CEOs of the International Audit Networks," (November 2006), available at www.globalpublicpolicysymposium.com.

Global Public Policy Symposium. "Global Dialogue with Capital Markets Stakeholders: A Report from the CEOs of the International Audit Networks" (January 2008), available at www.globalpublicpolicysymposium.com.

Goldscheider, Robert, John Jarosz, and Carla Mulhern. "Use of the 25 Per Cent Rule in Valuing IP," *les Nouvelles* (December 2002).

Gooch, Lawrence B. "Capital Shares and the Valuation of Intangibles," *Business Valuation Review* (March 1992): 5–21.

Grabowksi, Roger, and Lawrence B. Gooch. "Advanced Valuation Methods in Mergers & Acquisitions," *Mergers & Acquisitions* (Summer 1976): 15–29.

Grabowski, Roger J., and Shannon P. Pratt. *Cost of Capital: Applications and Examples, Third Edition*. Hoboken, NJ: John Wiley & Sons, 2008.

Hitchner, James R. *Financial Valuation Application and Models*, Second Edition. Hoboken, New Jersey: John Wiley & Sons, 2006.

Hitchner, James R., Steven D. Hyden, Michael J. Mard, and Mark L. Zyla. *Valuation for Financial Reporting: Intangible Assets, Goodwill and Impairment Analysis, SFAS 141 and 142*. Hoboken, NJ: John Wiley & Sons, 2002.

Hyden, Steven D., Michael J. Mard, and Edward W. Trott. *Business Combinations with SFAS 141R, 157 and 160*. Hoboken, NJ: John Wiley & Sons, 2009.

Ibbotson Stock, Bonds, Bills and Inflation, 2008 Valuation Yearbook. Chicago: Morningstar Inc.

Inside Counsel. "On the Block" (July 2006), available at www.insidecounsel.com.

International Accounting Standards Board. "Business Combinations Phase II Project Summary and Feedback Statement" (January 2008), available at www.iasb.com (accessed April 20, 2009).

International Accounting Standards Board. "Completing the February 2006 Memorandum of Understanding: A Progress Report and Timetable for Completion, September 2008," available at www.iasb.org (accessed April 21, 2009).

International Accounting Standards Board. Discussion Paper "Fair Value Measurements," available at www.iasb.org (accessed April 24, 2009).

International Accounting Standards Board. Discussion Paper "Fair Value Measurements Part 1: Invitation to Comment and Relevant IFRS Guidance" (November 2006).

International Accounting Standards Board. "Fair Value Measurement: Where Are We in the Project," available at www.iasb.org (accessed April 21, 2009).

International Accounting Standard Board. "International Accounting Standard No. 36—Impairment of Assets." paragraph 6.

International Accounting Standard Board. "International Accounting Standard No. 38—Intangible Assets."

International Accounting Standards Board. "Who We Are and What We Do," available at www.iasb.org (accessed April 22, 2009).

International Auditing and Assurance Standards Board. "Challenges in Auditing Fair Value Accounting Estimates in the Current Market Environment" (October 2008).

International Valuation Standards Council, "About the International Standards Valuation Council (IVSC)," available at www.ivsc.org (accessed May 1, 2009).

International Valuation Standards Council. "Global Standards for Valuation Process Reach New Phase, press release 3 March 2009," available at www.ivsc.org (accessed May 1, 2009).

Kemmerer, Jonathan E., and Jiaqing Lu. "2008 Profitability and Royalty Rates across Industries: Some Preliminary Evidence," *The Free Library* (March 1), available at www.thefreelibrary.com (accessed June 15, 2009).

Kennedy, G. William. "Using Statistical Measures in BVFLS Engagements." Unpublished presentation to CPAAI, July 20–21, 2009.

Kodukla, P., and C. Papudesu. *Valuation Using Real Options: A Practitioner's Guide*. Ft. Lauderdale, FL: J. Ross Publishing, 2006.

KPMG Defining Issues. "The Accounting Implications of Illiquid Markets, No. 07-30," *KPMG Defining Issues* (October 2007).

ktMINE. "About ktMINE," available at www.ktmine.com.

Lev, Baruch. *Intangibles: Management, Measurement, and Reporting*. Washington, DC: Brookings Institution Press, 2001.

Mard, Michael J. "Financial Factors: Cost Approach to Valuing Intellectual Property," *Licensing Journal* (August 2000): 27.

Mard, Michael J. Steven D. Hyden, and Edward W. Trott, *Business Combinations with SFAS 141R, 157 and 160*. Hoboken, NJ: New Jersey: John Wiley & Sons, 2009.

Mard, Michael, et al. *Valuation for Financial Reporting: Intangible Assets, Goodwill and Impairment Analysis, SFAS 141 and 142*. Hoboken, NJ: John Wiley & Sons, 2002.

McGregor, Scott A. President and CEO of Broadcom. "Letter to the Board of Directors of Emulex Corporation, dated June 29, 2009," posted by Mike Fratto, available at www.byteanswitch.com.

Mears, Chris. Principal in Charge of Rothstein Kass. "SFAS 157 Fair Value Measurements: Implementation Challenges for the Alternative Investment Industry," September 2008, available at www.rko.com/pdfilb/SFAS_157_Fair_Value.pdf.

Menelaides, Susan L., Lynford E. Graham, and Gretchen Fischbach. "Auditor's Approach to Fair Value," *Journal of Accountancy* (June 2003), available at www.aicpa.org.

Merrill Lynch & Company. "Form 10-Q, for the quarterly period ended June 27, 2008."

Microsoft Encarta Online Encyclopedia, 2009. "Intellectual Property," available at encarta.msn.com (accessed April 19, 2009).

Modern Metrix. "Modern Metrix Measurement and Analytics in Marketing, Media and Political Research in XXI Century," available at www.mmx.typepad.com/mmx/.

Myer, Lisa M. "The Life of a Patent." *eHow*, available at www.ehow.com/about_5194971_life-patent.html.

Nakamura, Leonard I. "What Is the U.S. Gross Investment in Intangibles? (At Least) One Trillion Dollars a Year!" Working Paper No. 1-15, Federal Reserve Bank of Philadelphia (October 2001).

Nath, Eric. "Control Premiums and Minority Interest Discounts in Private Companies." *Business Valuation Review*, Volume 9, No. 2 (June 1990), American Society of Appraisers.

Ocean Tomo Intellectual Capital Equity. "IP Markets2009 Featuring Ocean Tomo Live IP Auctions," available at www.oceantomo.com/ipmarkets2009.com.

Oracle Corporation. "Crystal Ball," available at www.crystalball/index.html.

O'Reilly, Vincent M. et al. *Montgomery's Auditing*, Twelfth Edition. New York: John Wiley & Sons, 1998.

Orrick, Harrington and Sutcliffe, LLP. "Sarbanes-Oxley Executive Summary." Orrick Securities Law Update, Corporate Department of Orrick, Herrington & Sutcliffe LLP (August 2002), available at www.orrick.com/fileupload/144.pdf (accessed June 23, 2009).

Palisade Corporation. @Risk 5.5: A New Standard in Risk Analysis, available at www.palisade.com/risk.

Parr, Russell L., and Gordon V. Smith. *Intellectual Property, Valuation, Exploitation and Infringement Damages*. Hoboken, NJ: John Wiley & Sons, 2005.

Plummer, James L. "QED Report on Venture Capital Financial Analysis," QED Research, Inc., 1987.

Pratt, Shannon P. *The Market Approach to Valuing Businesses*. Hoboken, NJ: John Wiley & Sons, 2001.

Public Company Accounting Oversight Board. "Staff Audit Practice Alert No. 2 Matters Related to Auditing Fair Value Measurements of Financial Instruments and the Use of Specialists" (December 10, 2007), pages 4–5.

Pratt, Shannon P., and Roger J. Grabowski. *Cost of Capital: Applications and Examples*, Third Edition. Hoboken, NJ: John Wiley & Sons, 2008.

Private Equity Industry Guidelines Group. "Updated U.S. Private Equity Valuation Guidelines," available at www.PEIGG.org.

Public Company Accounting Oversight Board. Staff Audit Practice Alert No. 2, "Matters Related to Auditing Fair Value Measurements of Financial Instruments and the Use of Specialists" (December 10, 2007).

QED Research, Inc. "QED Report on Venture Capital Financial Analysis," 1987.

Razgaitis, Richard. *Valuation and Pricing of Technology-Based Intellectual Property*. Hoboken, NJ: John Wiley and Sons, 2003.

Reilly, Robert F., and Robert S. Schweihs. *The Handbook of Business Valuation and Intellectual Property Analysis*. New York: McGraw-Hill, 2004.

Reilly, Robert F., and Robert S. Schweihs. *Valuing Intangible Assets*. New York: McGraw-Hill, 1999.

Rowell, Simon. "Strategic Tips for Adding Value to Licensing Transactions," Current Partnering, available at www.currentpartnering.com/articles/1488.

Rothstein, Kass. "Statement of Financial Accounting Standards 157 Fair Value Measurements: Implementation Challenges for the Alternative Investment Industry, September 2008," Rothstein Kass, available at www.rkco.com/pdflib/SFAS_157_Fair_Value.pdf.

Sahlman, William, and Daniel R. Scherlis. *A Method for Valuing High-Risk, Long Term, Investments: The Venture Capital Method*. Boston: Harvard Business School Publishing, 1987.

Scherlis, Daniel R., and William Sahlman. *A Method for Valuing High-Risk, Long Term, Investments: The Venture Capital Method*. Boston: Harvard Business School Publishing, 1987.

Schlosser, Pamela R. "Statement by SEC Staff: Remarks before the 2005 AICPA National Conference on Current SEC and PCAOB Developments, December 5, 2005," available at http://www.sec.gov/news/speech/spch120505ps.htm, (accessed May 26, 2009).

Stout, William M. "A Comparison of Component and Group Depreciation for Large Homogeneous Groups of Network Assets," A Presentation to the Accounting Standards Executive Committee of the American Institute of Certified Public Accountants (August 28, 2002), available at http://www.aicpa.org/download/members/div/acctstd/general/PPE.pdf (accessed July29, 2009).

Tiffany & Co. "Tiffany Blue: A Color of Distinction," available at press.tiffany.com/About/Tiffany/TiffanyBlue.aspx.

Trugman, Gary R. "Evolution of Business Valuation Services—A CPA's Guide to Valuing a Closely Held Business," available at www.fvs.aicpa.org (accessed May 17, 2009).

UK Statute Law Database, The. "Statute of Monopolies 1623," Office of Public Sector Information, available at www.statutelaw.gov (accessed April 21, 2009).

United States Court of Appeals for the Federal Circuit (03-1615).

United States District Court for the Eastern District of Virginia, Richmond Division. *Civil Action Number 3:01CV767*. Memorandum of Opinion (filed May 23, 2003).

United States Patent and Trademark Office. "Glossary," available at www.uspto.gov (accessed April 18, 2009).

United States Securities and Exchange Commission. "Congressionally-Mandated Study Says Improve, Do Not Suspend, Fair Value Accounting," available at www.sec.gov/news/press/2008/2008-307.htm.

United States Securities and Exchange Commission. "Delta Airlines, Inc. Form 10-K for Fiscal Year Ended December 31, 2008," available at www.sec.gov/Archives/edgar/data/27904/000119312509042726/d10k.htm, accessed 6/22/09.

United States Securities and Exchange Commission. "Meritage Hospitality Group, Inc. Form 10-K," available at www.sec.gov.

United States Securities and Exchange Commission. "Office of the Chief Accountant and FASB Staff Clarifications on Fair Value Accounting, 2008-234," available at www.sec.gov/news/studies/2008/marktomarket123008.pdf.

United States Securities and Exchange Commission. "Regulatory Actions Proposed Rules 2009 First Quarter 33-9905" (February 3, 2009), available at www.sec.gov.

United States Securities and Exchange Commission. "Release No. 33-8879 Acceptance from Foreign Private Issuers of Financial Statements Prepared in Accordance with International Financial Reporting Standards without Reconciliation to U.S. GAAP," available at www.sec.gov/rules/final/2008/33-8879fr.pdf.

United States Securities and Exchange Commission. "Report and Recommendations Pursuant to Section 133 of the Emergency Economic Stabilization Act of 2008: Study on Mark-to-Market Accounting," Office of the Chief Accountant, Division of Corporate Finance (December 30, 2008).

United States Securities and Exchange Commission. "Roadmap for the Potential Use of Financial Statements Prepared in Accordance with International Financial Reporting Stands." Release No. 33-8982, available at www.sec.gov (accessed April 21, 2009).

United States Securities and Exchange Commission. "Spotlight On: Fair Value Accounting Standards," available at www.sec.gov/spotlilght/fairvalue/htm.

United States Securities and Exchange Commission—Senior Assistant Chief Accountant. "Sample Letter Sent to Public Companies on MD&A Disclosure Regarding the Application of SFAS 157 (Fair Value Measurements), March 2008," available at www.sec.gov/divisions/corpfin/guidance/fairvalueltr0308.htm (accessed June 22, 2009).

United States Securities and Exchange Commission—Senior Assistant Chief Accountant. "Sample Letter Sent to Public Companies on MD&A Disclosure Regarding the Application of SFAS 157 (Fair Value Measurements), September 2008," available at www.sec.gov/divisions/corpfin/guidance/fairvalueltr0908.htm (accessed July 16, 2009).

Valuation Resource Group (July 2008), available at www.fasb.org.

Webster's II New College Dictionary. Boston: Houghton Mifflin Company, 1995.

White, Gerald I. Ashwinpaul C. Sodhi, and Dov Fried, *The Analysis and Use of Financial Statements, Second Edition.* Hoboken, NJ: John Wiley & Sons, 1997.

Willamette Management Associates. "Property Tax Valuation White Papers: Economic Obsolescence Is an Essential Procedure of a Cost Approach to Valuation of Industrial or Commercial Properties," available at www.propertytaxvaluation.com/economic_obsolescence_essential_procedure.html (accessed April 16, 2009).

World Intellectual Property Organization. "Intangible Asset & Intellectual Property Valuation: A Multidisciplinary Perspective," available at www.wipo.int.

World Intellectual Property Organization. "What Is Intellectual Property?" available at www.wipo.int (accessed April 16, 2009).

Zyla, Mark L. "Assessing the Impact of Synergy on Value." *CPA Expert* (Fall 1999).

Index